Queer TV China

Queer Asia

The Queer Asia series opens a space for monographs and anthologies in all disciplines focusing on nonnormative sexuality and gender cultures, identities, and practices across all regions of Asia. Queer studies, queer theory, and transgender studies originated in, and remain dominated by, North American and European academic circles. Yet the separation between sexual orientation and gender identity, while relevant in the West, does not neatly apply to all Asian contexts, which are themselves complex and diverse. A growing number of scholars inside and beyond Asia are producing exciting and challenging work that studies Asian histories and cultures of trans and queer phenomena. The Queer Asia series—the first of its kind in publishing—provides a valuable opportunity to develop and sustain these initiatives.

Editorial Collective

Chris Berry (King's College London, UK), John Nguyet Erni (Hong Kong Baptist University, Hong Kong), Peter Jackson (Australian National University, Australia), Helen Hok-Sze Leung (Simon Fraser University, Canada), and Shawna Tang (University of Sydney, Australia).

Selected titles in the series:

Boys' Love, Cosplay, and Androgynous Idols: Queer Fan Cultures in Mainland China, Hong Kong, and Taiwan
Edited by Maud Lavin, Ling Yang, and Jing Jamie Zhao

Contact Moments: The Politics of Intercultural Desire in Japanese Male-Queer Cultures
Katsuhiko Suganuma

Falling into the Lesbi World: Desire and Difference in Indonesia
Evelyn Blackwood

First Queer Voices from Thailand: Uncle Go's Advice Columns for Gays, Lesbians and Kathoeys
Peter A. Jackson

Gender on the Edge: Transgender, Gay, and Other Pacific Islanders
Edited by Niko Besnier and Kalissa Alexeyeff

Maid to Queer: Asian Labor Migration and Female Same-Sex Desires
Francisca Yuenki Lai

Obsession: Male Same-Sex Relations in China, 1900–1950
Wenqing Kang

Oral Histories of Older Gay Men in Hong Kong: Unspoken but Unforgotten
Travis S. K. Kong

Queer Chinese Cultures and Mobilities: Kinship, Migration, and Middle Classes
John Wei

Queering Chinese Kinship: Queer Public Culture in Globalizing China
Lin Song

Queer Politics and Sexual Modernity in Taiwan
Hans Tao-Ming Huang

Queer Singapore: Illiberal Citizenship and Mediated Cultures
Edited by Audrey Yue and Jun Zubillaga-Pow

Shanghai Lalas: Female Tongzhi *Communities and Politics in Urban China*
Lucetta Yip Lo Kam

Undercurrents: Queer Culture and Postcolonial Hong Kong
Helen Hok-Sze Leung

Queer TV China

Televisual and Fannish Imaginaries of Gender, Sexuality, and Chineseness

Edited by Jamie J. Zhao

Hong Kong University Press
The University of Hong Kong
Pok Fu Lam Road
Hong Kong
https://hkupress.hku.hk

© 2023 Hong Kong University Press

ISBN 978-988-8805-61-7 (*Hardback*)

All rights reserved. No portion of this publication may be reproduced or transmitted in any form or by any means, electronic or mechanical, including photocopying, recording, or any information storage or retrieval system, without prior permission in writing from the publisher.

British Library Cataloguing-in-Publication Data
A catalogue record for this book is available from the British Library.

Digitally printed

Contents

List of Figures vii
Acknowledgments viii
Notes on Romanization and Chinese Characters x
Introduction: Making "TV China" Perfectly Queer 1
   Jamie J. Zhao

I. Queer/ing Genders and Sexualities through Reality Competition Shows

1. Growing Up with "Tomboy Power": Starring Liu Yuxin on Post-2010 Chinese Reality TV 29
   Jamie J. Zhao

2. When *"Jiquan"* Fandom Meets "Big Sisters": The Ambivalence between Female Queer (In)Visibility and Popular Feminist Rhetoric in *Sisters Who Make Waves* 52
   Jia Guo and Shaojun Kong

3. A Dildonic Assemblage: The Paradoxes of Queer Masculinities and Desire on the Chinese Sports Variety Show *Let's Exercise, Boys* 67
   Wangtaolue Guo and Jennifer Quist

II. Queer/ing TV Dramas through Media Regulations

4. *Addicted* to Melancholia: Negotiating Queerness and Homoeroticism in a Banned Chinese BL Drama 87
   Aobo Dong

5. Taming *The Untamed*: Politics and Gender in BL-Adapted Web Dramas 105
   Jun Lei

6. Disjunctive Temporalities: Queer Sinophone Visuality across Mainland China, Hong Kong, and Taiwan 124
   Alvin K. Wong

III. Queer/ing Celebrities across Geocultural Boundaries

7. Queer Vocals and Stardom on Chinese TV: Case Studies of Wu Tsing-Fong and Zhou Shen 145
   Linshan Jiang
8. Gay Men in/and *Kangsi Coming* 161
   Oscar Tianyang Zhou
9. Queer Motherly Fantasy: The Sinophone Mom Fandom of Saint Suppapong Udomkaewkanjana 177
   Pang Ka Wei

References 201
About the Contributors 230
Index 233

Figures

Figure 2.1: In a *Jiquan* Gossip Group discussion thread about *SWMW*, the show was described as "Sappho's lesbian island" — 62

Figure 3.1: A screenshot of one of Qiu Yiwei's Weibo videos, showing that he is taking off his shirt — 79

Figure 3.2: A screenshot of one of Zhang Xindong's Weibo photos — 81

Figure 3.3: A screenshot of the show's logo — 83

Figure 5.1: Rotten and pan-rotten culture — 110

Figure 6.1: Lan Wangji (left) and Wei Wuxian (right) fighting under the moon — 129

Figure 6.2: Tin (left) kissing Muk (right) in a queer presentist mode — 136

Acknowledgments

Producing an edited volume in an emerging academic field during a global pandemic has been a much harder task than I could have ever imagined. I conceptualized the idea of *Queer TV China* in December 2019. In 2022, I finalized its manuscript after experiencing the most depressing time of my life, with endless worldwide COVID-related lockdowns and quarantines. I wish to thank all the individual authors who have given me their unwavering trust and contributed their highly astute writings to this volume. During this tortuous yet always inspiring journey with unexpected ups and downs in my academic, professional, and personal lives, I have been indebted to a number of scholars and academic friends who have encouraged and sustained me along the way.

I feel deeply grateful for the priceless time, patience, advice, and dialogue provided by Chris Berry and Hongwei Bao, especially their emotional, intellectual, and moral support during the early stages of preparing this book. Meanwhile, I would like to express my gratitude to Shi-yan Chao, Adam Chen-Dedman, Victor Fan, Jie Guo, Li Guo, Heidi Huang, Kelvin Ke, Maud Lavin, Liang Luo, Gina Marchetti, Fran Martin, Hui Miao, Rachel Moseley, Eve Ng, Ziquan Ni, Karl Schoonover, Geng Song, Qingning Wang, Shuaishuai Wang, Yiman Wang, Alvin K. Wong, Jim Wren, Hui Faye Xiao, Yanrui Xu, Ling Yang, Ting-Fai Yu, Charlie Yi Zhang, Kaixuan Zhang, Xiaoling Zhang, and many others who are not included in this short, incomplete list for their generous time and companionship through a difficult period. I also thank the two anonymous reviewers, as well as the editorial board of Hong Kong University Press's Queer Asia series, for their insightful, constructive feedback.

Some parts of the introductory chapter were published in the following two online entries:

Zhao, Jamie J. "Queer TV China as an Area of Critical Scholarly Inquiry in the 2010s." *criticalasianstudies.org* Commentary 26, December 25, 2019. https://criticalasianstudies.org/commentary/2019/12/25/201926-jamie-zhao-queer-tv-china-as-an-area-of-critical-scholarly-inquiry-in-the-2010s.

Zhao, Jamie J., and Hongwei Bao. "'Queer/ing China': Theorizing Chinese Genders and Sexualities through a Transnational Lens." *criticalasianstudies.org* Commentary Board, April 5, 2022. https://doi.org/10.52698/KLCE9376.

Substantial revisions and updates have been made to the previously published portions. I extend my gratitude to *Critical Asian Studies*'s editors, Robert J. Shepherd and Tristan R. Grunow, for their professionalism and academic support. They encouraged me to publish on the topics of "Queer TV China" and "queer/ing China" with their journal, and later allowed me to revise and reprint the online entries in this current anthology project.

Last but not least, I am thankful for the generous grants from the Center for Gender and Media Studies in the Department of Journalism and Communication in the School of Media and Law at NingboTech University for my academic and publishing activities, without which the publication of this project and sharing its ideas globally would have been impossible.

Notes on Romanization and Chinese Characters

This book uses *hanyu pinyin* to denote certain Chinese-language terms (such as *qinglang*, *ku'er*, and *tongxing ai*). Chapters 6 and 9 are written by authors located in Hong Kong and focus on Sinophone issues. Both chapters, based on the authors' own preferences, use traditional Chinese characters. All of the other chapters use simplified Chinese characters. Place names and personal names in mainland China, Hong Kong, Taiwan, and other non-English-speaking regions are romanized by following local conventions.

Introduction

Making "TV China" Perfectly Queer

Jamie J. Zhao

As noted in *TV China*, one of the first and most comprehensive academic books dedicated to Chinese-language TV studies, television has become "a global phenomenon" in the People's Republic of China (PRC) and has been "fully established as the dominant medium among all Chinese populations" since the new millennium (Zhu and Berry 2009, 3). At the same time, at the beginning of the third decade of the twenty-first century, the mainstream society of mainland China remains largely authoritarian, patriarchal, and heteronormative. Against this backdrop, in a beguiling yet highly ambivalent way, the Chinese-language televisual world, with its related celebrity-fan economy, has become increasingly accessible and relevant to gender, sexual, and sociocultural minorities. Alongside an escalation in official media censorship of what is considered "vulgar," "immoral," "irrational," and "negative" content (Bai and Song 2015; Jia and Zhou 2015; Shaw and Zhang 2018; L. Yang 2022) and the party-state's misogynistic and homophobic policies (Bao 2021; Xiao 2014, 2020), an unexpectedly burgeoning queer media and cultural landscape—what I call "queer TV China" in this edited volume—has been discursively produced and filled with nonnormatively gendered, sexualized, or eroticized narratives, personas, affects, and sentiments (Song 2022a; Yang and Bao 2012; J. Zhao 2016, 2018b).

Particularly during the past decade (2010–2020), the TV screens of the PRC have presented more and more norm-transgressive images and subjectivities, made available to audiences through online and digital media platforms. These queer televisual scenes include, but are not limited to, masculine female and effeminate male celebrities, who have proliferated and been promoted on various provincial station-produced reality TV shows; homosociality and homoeroticism (especially between cis males) in many TV dramas; transgender personalities, same-sex intimacies, participants who identify as lesbian, gay, bisexual, transgender, and queer (LGBTQ) featured on Chinese-language talk shows; and even explicitly gay-themed stories and topics in online TV programs (see, for example, Kam 2014; Ng and Li 2020; Song 2022a; A. Wong 2020; Zhao,

Yang, and Lavin 2017; J. Zhao 2016, 2018b, 2020a). This boom in post-2010 queer TV China has been appealing to a broad range of local and international audiences and fans with diverse gender, sexual, and cultural interests, linguistic preferences, and geopolitical identities.

The simultaneous mainstreaming, capitalization, and globalization of queer TV China, along with the wide use of the internet and digital media in the twenty-first century, has been further complemented by numerous cross-geolinguistically connected cyber queer fan communities and an increasing number of mainland China-based queer fan sites and practices dedicated to Euro-American, East Asian, and Southeast Asian TV programs and stars (Hu 2016; Zhao 2017b). Yet these seemingly progressive TV productions and fan cultures have been constantly contested by, and even subjected to, multilayered capitalist, sociocultural, and political-ideological forces and interests on local, transnational, and global levels. A recent sensational case is the large-scale global queer fandom, as well as the local government's endorsement, of *The Untamed* (陈情令; Tencent, 2019), the story of which is set in a fantasy immortal world (also known as the *xianxia*/仙侠 genre). *The Untamed* is a mainland China-produced TV drama in the genre of boys' love (BL; a kind of East Asian popular genre featuring male same-sex romance, which originated in Japan and is also known in China as *danmei*/耽美). As Jun Lei opines in Chapter 5 of this edited volume, the drama's unanticipated success "in domestic and overseas markets exemplifies it as a model that aligns with the official ideology to establish cultural confidence, spread positive values, and erect Chinese heroic characters" to both local and international audiences. Using a different approach, Alvin K. Wong, the author of Chapter 6, reads its global popularity as a result of the "unhistorical queerness" of many mainland Chinese BL dramas, which eventually renders "gay male homoeroticism . . . easily consumable as commodity."

This prosperous queer TV culture within, originating from, or associated with a (hetero-) normative-structured nation-state (the PRC, which this edited volume is directed toward) raises some pertinent questions that call for urgent academic consideration. For instance, what are the relationships between this queer TV scene, mainland media regulatory policies and national projects, and the reality of Chinese-speaking gender and sexual minorities in the off-screen world? What dynamics play out between these queer televisual representations and their related star personas and fan practices inside and outside the PRC? What roles have local and transnational Chinese feminist movements and queer identity politics played in the emergence and development of this queer TV culture in the past decade? How do explorations of queer TV in the Chinese-speaking context depart from the already flourishing Euro-American queer TV studies (see, for example, Davis and Needham 2009; Hart 2016; Straayer and Waugh 2005; Villarejo 2014)? Finally, how do queer Chinese TV cultures and studies open up new empirical and analytical possibilities for post-2020 inter-Asian, transnational, and global TV studies, as well as for global queer studies, in a world that may be undergoing a difficult restructuring of the old global order during and after the COVID-19 pandemic, if not a simultaneous process of deglobalization, transnationalization, and "deterritorialization" (Iwabuchi 2002, 2004; Iwabuchi, Tsai, and Berry 2017; Martin et al. 2020; Zhao 2021c)?

Queer TV China: Televisual and Fannish Imaginaries of Gender, Sexuality, and Chineseness (QTC hereafter) recognizes the intricacy of these questions and their implications for TV studies, queer media studies, global gender and sexuality studies, and China and Sinophone studies. To advance the scholarly treatment of the above-described queer pop cultural phenomenon in a highly normative, strictly surveilled social setting as an interdisciplinary field of critical inquiry, this anthology proposes an analytical framework of "queer/ing TV China." Employing the term "queer" as a verb, an adjective, and/or a noun in various case studies, QTC's contributors work together to highlight the nonnormative potential, nature, and denotations and connotations of TV and its celebrity and fan cultures in the PRC and the Chinese-speaking world at large.

As I will elaborate on in other sections of this introduction, LGBTQ images, narratives, and celebrities in the televisual landscape of the PRC—mainly produced, circulated, and consumed in a heterosexual-dominated society and a heteronormative-structured nation-state—have been assumed by many media scholars and critics around the world to be made invisible, marginal, or stereotypical. This subsequently led to a relative scarcity of research about queer TV culture within the context of mainland China until the recent rise of local BL TV and related fan cultures (see, for example, Lavin, Yang, and Zhao 2017; Ng and Li 2020; A. Wong 2020; Yang and Xu 2017; Zhao 2020a; Zhao and Wong 2020). Even when mainland Chinese queer TV and fan cultures are discussed in most of the existing queer TV and fan scholarship, scholars often consider media regulatory and censorial practices a major repressive force that closes rather than proliferates the possibilities of nonnormative embodiment and imaginary on and through TV screens. To challenge the widespread "repressive hypothesis" (Foucault 1978) rooted in existing queer Chinese TV studies, QTC takes as its primary focus emerging queer televisual and fannish discourses that have been contested and reworked within the PRC.

Meanwhile, the approach of "queer/ing TV China" acknowledges the interconnection and mutual implications of the two overly essentialized and forcibly disassociated notions, *Chineseness* and *queerness*, in the televisual and fannish imaginaries examined throughout this book. Previous scholarship has powerfully showcased the importance of decolonializing and denationalizing both terms, the imaginations of which cannot be based on a monolithic categorization of identities and subjectivities (Ang 2001; Chun 1996; Leung 2008; Liu and Rofel 2010; Martin 2014). For example, some global queer studies scholars have noted that "neither 'Chineseness' nor 'queerness' can or should be understood within national boundaries" (Leung 2008, 129) because both formulations "are 'always already' transnational" in nature (Martin 2014, 35; see also Liu and Rofel 2010). As Fran Martin brilliantly states,

> Chineseness is conceptualized as multiple, contradictory and fragmented: not the expression of a timeless national essence but instead the produce of disjunctive regimes of cultural regulation across the multiple transnational contexts where claims to various forms of Chineseness are made. (Martin 2014, 35)

Although concurring with the call to juxtapose and examine "the margins of gender and sexuality with the margins of China and Chineseness" that have been made by many queer Sinophone scholars (Heinrich 2014; see also Chiang and Heinrich 2014; Chiang and Wong 2020a), Martin also emphasizes the necessity of including queer cultures and subjects "located inside the territorial borders of the PRC" in queer Sinophone and queer Asian studies as well as part of global queer flows in general (2014, 43). As she further elaborates,

> Mainland China is more and more interlinked into the transnational networks of Sinophone cultural flows, both of broader popular culture and specifically of queer texts, practices and identities. Hence, in a practical sense, it becomes harder than ever to conceive of mainland Chinese queer cultural life as sealed off from that of Sinophone queer communities outside China. Analysis of material exchanges between queer peripheral Sinophone sites and queer mainland Chinese sites can surely be made while continuing to avoid the uncritical China-centrism of which the Sinophone studies project is so suspicious. (Martin 2014, 43)

QTC takes Martin's cue and further pushes the limits of existing queer China and queer Sinophone studies by inspecting queer Chinese TV and fan cultures on local, transcultural, and global scales. Some of the contributors explore Chinese-language TV phenomena which have been (re)configured across the borders of various Chinese-speaking societies and communities (as seen in Chapters 6, 7, and 8), while others explore issues concerning the transnational fandom of mainland Chinese BL-adapted TV (Chapters 4 and 5); the Chinese queer fandom of Thai BL TV stars (Chapter 9); gender- and sexually nonnormative foreign stars in mainland reality programs and Chinese cyberspace (Chapters 1 and 2); and the domestication of cosmopolitanism in queer representations of and self-performances by male reality sport TV stars (Chapter 3). By so doing, *QTC* reveals some prominent, yet severely underexamined, means through which queer TV in and beyond the geocultural borders of the PRC *not only* participates in and links to *but also* directs and reshapes global queer-centered flows, knowledge production, and subject formation and remaking.

In the remainder of this introduction, I first situate the studies of queer TV China within existing scholarship and conceptualize the notion of "queer/ing" in this field of inquiry. I then discuss the sociopolitical contexts and transformations that have contributed to the rise of nonnormative representations on Chinese TV in the twenty-first century. My discussion also challenges the assumption that queer TV culture did not come into existence in the PRC until the late 2000s by unpacking the queer nature and contours of Chinese TV. This queer deconstruction highlights the theoretical and methodological contributions of this edited volume. By drawing multiple connections among the chapters included in this project, I emphasize the importance of unsettling the dichotomous, categorical logics often employed to understand meanings associated with various TV genres and formats and televisual imaginings of gender, sexuality, class, ethnicity/race, nationality, and age. I conclude this introduction by suggesting promising directions and areas for future research through the critical lens of "queer/ing TV China."

Situating "Queer/ing TV China" in the Twenty-First Century

Queer TV studies, especially in the Anglophone context, is no longer a nascent scholarly field. Research on the "queering" or queer readings of Euro-American public TV images and narratives can be traced back to the 1980s (Bacon-Smith 1992; Jenkins 1992; Penley 1997; Russ 1985). The years since the 1990s have seen the "mainstreaming" of LGBTQ characters in Euro-American commercial media, especially through the makeover TV and advertising industries (Sender 2004; see also Campbell 2005; Chasin 2000; Gross 2001). Following from this, a body of scholarship on Western queer TV studies has been flourishing since the early 2000s (Davis and Needham 2009; Day and Christian 2017; Hart 2016; Joyrich 2014; Kohnen 2016; Lewis 2007; Lovelock 2019; Malici 2014; McCarthy 2001; McIntyre 2016; Miller 2014, 2019; Ng 2008, 2013; Peele 2007; Straayer and Waugh 2005; Villarejo 2014). Scholarly interest in racial, class-based, and cross-geocultural representations and interpretations of Anglophone queer TV has also grown (Bradley 2012; Christian 2016; Day and Christian 2017; Horvat 2020; Martin 2021; Ng 2021; Peters 2011).

This body of research often draws on classic scholarly definitions of "queer" in Anglophone queer theory and queer cinema studies, such as that offered by Eve Kosofsky Sedgwick in her 1993 monograph *Tendencies*. According to Sedgwick, queer is "the open mesh of possibilities, gaps, overlaps, dissonances and resonances, lapses and excesses of meaning when the constituent elements of gender, of anyone's sexuality aren't made (or *can't* be made) to signify monolithically" (1993, 8). In another influential and widely cited work published in 1993, *Making Things Perfectly Queer*, queer media scholar Alexander Doty also extended the uses of "queer" and "queer theory" in his study of nontraditional "positions, pleasures, and readings of" the media audience (xviii). Adopting a poststructuralist perspective, Ki Namaste (1994) summarized Doty's theoretical remaking of queerness as the powerful proposition that *queer* can be a practice, a spectatorial position, a temporary desiring moment, a media device, or a nonheterosexual connotation without explicit self-identification or representational denotation, all of which are "different strategies for interpreting mass culture" produced and consumed in "supposedly 'straight' settings" (225). Nevertheless, with more and more LGBTQ images, narratives, and celebrities represented and commodified on Western TV, queer TV scholar Lynne Joyrich also reminds us that

> some televisual forms may be becoming, in a sense, more queered doesn't necessarily mean that more queers appear in them—that *queering* as a verb (the process of playing, transforming, and making strange) lines up with *queer* as a noun (identifying people who are "recognizably" LGBT). (Joyrich 2014, 135)

Moreover, the past two decades have seen the publication of a number of scholarly books dedicated to Asian and Chinese TV cultures, mostly by media and cultural studies scholars based in Hong Kong, North America, the United Kingdom, and Australia (Bai 2015b; Bai and Song 2015; Cai 2016; French and Richards 2000; Gorfinkel 2018; Iwabuchi 2004; Keane 2015; Keane, Fung, and Moran 2007; Lewis, Martin, and Sun 2016; Moran and Keane 2004; Song 2022b; Tay and Turner 2015; Wen 2014; Zhong 2010; Zhu 2008, 2012; Zhu and Berry 2009; Zhu, Keane, and Bai 2008). Some studies have addressed gendered aspects of Chinese TV, such as its representations of women's familial, romantic, and marital lives and various forms of racialized and class-based masculinities portrayed in Chinese TV series (for example, Gong and Yang 2018; Hird and Song 2018; Louie 2016; Song 2022b; Xiao 2014). However, research on the ethnic, industrial, sociopolitical, and geolinguistic intricacies of the increasing number of queer TV phenomena emerging from predominantly authoritarian, heteropatriarchal Chinese-speaking societies and communities, especially with regard to queer theory and LGBTQ cultures in the Chinese and Sinophone contexts, remains rare.

In contrast, in recent years, scholarly surveys of Asian queer TV and its fan cultures, especially those of Japan, South Korea, Thailand, and Singapore, have proliferated and succeeded in directing attention to the diversities of gender, sexuality, identity, and subjectivity mediated through televisual representations and imaginaries (Baudinette 2019; Chao 2021; Jung 2011; Lavin 2015; Liew and Ismail 2018; Liew, Manokara, and T'a'at 2016; Martin 2010a; Miller 2000; Yuen 2011; Zhang and Dedman 2021). While some of these explorations have focused on the queer-enacting characteristics of televisual narratives, styles, genres, formats, and industries in diverse Asian contexts, the discussions have predominantly focused on either inter-Asian media and information flows or local media productions about gender and sexual minorities in cosmopolitan, queer-friendly contexts.

In the post-2010 years, an exciting surge of scholarly publications in the fields of queer Chinese and queer Sinophone media and cultural studies has occurred (Bao 2018, 2020, 2021; Chiang and Heinrich 2014; Chiang and Wong 2020b; Engebretsen and Schroeder 2015; Liu 2015; Zhao 2020a; Zhao and Wong 2020). These works indicate the growing academic interest in the mutually implicative relationship between *queerness* and *Chineseness* in queer media cultures in the Chinese and Sinophone worlds. Among the most prolific endeavors of this scholarship is the underscoring of the cross-geocultural traveling and local appropriation of the Anglophone term *queer* "as a powerful, generative tool in the political, cultural and scholarly dimensions of diverse Chinese-speaking contexts" (Zhao and Wong 2020, 477).

In particular, the queer Asian scholar Petrus Liu famously stated,

> The possibility of practicing queer theory in Chinese contexts demonstrates that critical attention to local knowledges and concerns does not immediately constitute a categorical rejection of "the queer;" rather it shows that what is "queer" is constantly expanded, supplemented, and revised by what is "Chinese." (Liu 2015, 297)

Furthermore, following Chinese-language film scholar Song Hwee Lim's (2006) recording of local renderings of "queer" as *ku'er* (酷儿; literally meaning "cool kid" or "a generation of being cool") or *guaitai* (怪胎; literally meaning "strange fetus") in mid-1990s Taiwan, Hongwei Bao (2018) has also emphasized the elitism- and cosmopolitanism-charged adoption of "queer" and "queer theory" in mainland Chinese scholarly publications, media spaces, and political activism since the early 2000s. Bao (2018) underlines the significant political and activist potential of the word *ku'er* in mainland China in evading the government's censorship of homosexuality and in working as a practical strategy for subjects who live on the social margins to negotiate with the mainstream, normative social policing of behaviors, desire, and identities.

This has been paralleled by queer Sinophone research that has relied heavily on and developed Shu-mei Shih's problematization of China-centrism rooted in area and Chinese diasporic studies, which encourages "the study of Sinitic-language cultures on the margins of geopolitical nation-states and their hegemonic productions" (2011, 710). Queer Sinophone scholars have strived to "deconstruct what the category of China itself might mean in a nonnormative sense—that is, to queer China from the outside in" (Chiang 2014b, 365). More recent queer Chinese-language media studies have also addressed this theoretical advancement of, and the implicative linkage between, the queer essence of Chineseness and the indispensable inclusion of queerness as a key, constitutive element in mainstream Chinese (especially mainland Chinese) culture and society. Some research has specifically examined "the world-making potential and struggles of the media praxis of subjects who have been constantly cast out of mainstream media and public spaces" (Zhao and Wong 2020, 478).

In addition, since 2009, the amount of English-language scholarship on cross-cultural, transnational queer fandoms in the Chinese and Sinophone worlds or devoted to Chinese-speaking celebrities has noticeably increased (Bai 2022; Chiang 2016; Chin and Morimoto 2013; Feng 2013; Gong 2017; Li 2009; Li 2017; Liu 2009; Morimoto 2013; Yang and Xu 2013, 2016a, 2016b, 2017; Zhang 2017; Zhao 2017a, 2017b). Many early studies in this body of research focused on BL culture in Taiwan and Hong Kong—two relatively liberal, sexually open, and feminist- and queer-supportive Chinese-speaking societies. Since the early 2010s, a parallel body of literature has emerged that sheds light on the production and interpretation of homoerotic imaginaries and gender-ambiguous performing spaces on mainland Chinese TV, as well as their negotiation with and contesting of local gender and sexual systems and histories (He 2013; Hu and Wang 2020; Lavin, Yang, and Zhao 2017; Ng and Li 2020; Wang 2015; A. Wong 2020; Yang and Bao 2012; J. Zhao 2016, 2018c, 2020b; Zheng 2019; Z. Zhou 2020).

QTC responds to this growing interest in queer Chinese TV, celebrities, and fandoms in English-language academia. In line with previous global queering theory, queer Asia, queer Sinophone, and queer China studies (see, for example, Bao 2020, 2021; Berry, Martin, and Yue 2003; Chao 2020; Chiang 2012; Chiang and Heinrich 2014; Chiang and Wong 2020b; Liu 2015; Liu and Rofel 2010; Martin et al. 2008), *QTC* cautions against equating contemporary queer Chinese TV culture with a straightforward capitalist exploitation and stereotyping of LGBTQ identities, lives, and politics. The contributors to this volume present a variety of persuasive case studies to demonstrate that the nuances, contextual specificities, global influences, and theoretical significance of queer TV China diverge from, yet might also parallel or interconnect with, the prevalent queer marketing strategies conceptualized in the Euro-American and East Asian entertainment industries as "gaystreaming," "post-queer," "queerbaiting," or "fanservice" (Boyd 2016; Brennan 2018b; Green 2002; Gross 2001; Maris 2016; Ng 2013; Sender 2004, 2007; Wood 2013). This anthology also contests the universalization of a Western conception of homosexuality (as well as a Western conception of queerness) as the only way to represent and understand nonnormative identities, relationships, and forms of desire in the Chinese-speaking world. Instead, by proposing the framework of "queer/ing TV China," we consider *queer* as a contingent and flexible assemblage of nouns, verbs, or adjectives that can be used to unveil "whatever is at odds with the normal, the legitimate, the dominant" (Halperin 2003, 62) and to interrogate unconventional ways of being, doing, desiring, and imagining in and through televisual spaces.

In her pioneering work *Backward Glances*, Martin (2010a, 16) identified two ways of representing (and conceptualizing) nonnormative gender and sexual subjects in contemporary Chinese-language media. One is the "minoritizing" approach, which involves self-conscious, identitarian-based LGBTQ subjects who have emerged out of and are recognizable in location-specific contexts of feminist and queer politics. The other is the "universalizing" approach, which captures nonidentitarian, "ephemeral yet powerfully—often troublingly—memorable" moments of nonnormative embodiment, performances, and intimacies. While concurring with Martin's (2010a, 16) observation that the majority of mainstream Chinese-language media representations of homoeroticism, especially those set within a largely heteronormative society, are visualized through the "universalizing rather than minoritizing" approach, the framework of "queer/ing TV China" encompasses both forms of televisual representations and fannish imaginations. More importantly, *QTC* includes critical analyses from both perspectives. Some chapters examine progressive, self-identified LGBTQ TV images, stardom, and fandom (as seen in Chapters 2 and 8), while others move beyond the binary categories of masculinity versus femininity, heterosexuality versus homosexuality, past versus presence, positivity versus negativity, and reality versus fictionality to demystify "the contradictory, ambiguous, playful, anti-essentialist, transgressive" characteristics of televisual and fannish spaces "made by, for, about and/or associated with sociocultural groups, identities and stances positioned as peripheral in mainstream Chinese-speaking societies," which do not necessarily self-identify or may not be publicly recognized as LGBTQ (Zhao and Wong 2020, 478).

Through this innovative lens of "queer/ing TV China," *QTC* highlights the multivalent queer potential of both China/Chineseness and TV/televisuality (which is, in fact, made possible through their mutual shaping and constitution) in not only representing and signifying but also concocting and refashioning nonnormative subjects. To achieve this goal, *QTC* recognizes the inherently intertwined queer and normative dimensions of TV as an effective sociocultural platform within and beyond mainstream Chinese-speaking spaces. For instance, Chapters 1 and 3 uncover the performativity of a particular TV genre—reality TV—in representing real-life gender-nonnormative groups while actively negotiating the nation-state's gendered policies and ideological projects. Addressing TV drama, Chapter 6 focuses on the queer-enabling power of televisual narrativity and temporality in mainland China, Hong Kong, and Taiwan. Chapter 7 explores the vocal queerness realized through Chinese-language talk and singing programs, while Chapter 8 explores the gendered performance and negotiation of gayness on queer-friendly Mandarin talk shows hosted by publicly out Chinese-speaking gay celebrities. *QTC* also captures research on the cross-cultural circulation, translation, and remaking of ethnic-Chinese-related queer TV cultures in multiple trans-geolinguistic contexts. Chapter 9, in particular, uncovers how ethnic Chineseness, rather than simply being imagined as an arbitrary geopolitical identity, serves as a key element in mobilizing transnational queer readings and encouraging disruption of the conventional Sinophone form of mother-son kinship. Furthermore, QTC unveils the paradoxical, yet queer-essenced, aspects of Chinese televisual-industrial-cultural discourses in the contemporary era. Chapters 4 and 5, for example, demonstrate the diverse discourses through which the media censorship of homosexuality in the PRC has generated innovative strategies for homoerotic content production, adaptation, and viewing in an increasingly digitized and globalizing Chinese TV landscape complicated by cross-cultural communication, transnational access to online sites, and local concessions to political-national ideologies. These "queer-inviting" nature and contours of TV China are discussed in depth in the next section.

Queer/ing the Contours of TV China

In a departure from research that aims to recognize and capture self-identified Chinese LGBTQ groups' underground cultural productions and sociopolitical movements, QTC is especially attentive to a queer televisual spectacle crystalized in contemporary mainstream Chinese culture's censoring, appropriation, shaping, mobilization, and commercialization of local, transnational, and global gender and sexual knowledge. Queer TV China, in this sense, is neither necessarily subversive of, nor submissive to, hegemonic sociocultural and political-economic systems characterized by heteronormativity, patriarchy, nationalism, globalism, and capitalism in the twenty-first century. Rather, it has been shaped by premodern Chinese gendered paradigms and local performing arts (for example, the *wen/wu* 文武 male masculinity praxis and the cross-gender roles in regional operatic, theatrical aesthetics mentioned in a number of chapters in this volume; see also He 2013, 2014; Hird and Song 2018; Louie 2015, 2016; Song 2022a, 2022b; Tan 2000, 2007) and the local same-sex erotic modalities, such as the famous cases of "passions of the cut sleeve" (断袖之癖; denoting male homoeroticism) and "mirror rubbing" (磨镜; denoting female homoeroticism), which were widespread in premodern classical literature and historical records (Chiang 2012; Hinsch 1990; Kang 2009; Rocha 2010; Sang 2003; Shi 2014). In the premodern and early modern era of China, these local forms and media representations of same-sex desire and intimacies were not necessarily unequivocally forbidden or ostracized, but tacitly endured as part of hetero-marital harmony and/or elitist heterosexual fantasies (Sang 2003).

Certainly, the modern history of Chinese gender and sexuality has not been a static perpetuation of a traditional past, nor has it taken the form of a subversive, anti-hegemonic lineal process. Instead, since the beginning of China's self-modernizing process and the birth of Chinese feminist movements in the first decade of the twentieth century, gender and sexual neologisms, shaped by modern Western and Japanese sexological, medical, and scientific knowledge imported through Chinese male intellectuals' translations, have been constantly invented and manipulated in Chinese public discourses to propel local ideological-political movements (Barlow 2004; Liu, Karl, and Ko 2013; Rocha 2010). For instance, following Chinese intellectuals' deployment of the modern concept of "love" during the May Fourth New Culture period (1915–1937) as "a symbol of freedom, autonomy, and equality" (Lee 2007, 5), the Chinese term for homosexuality, *tongxing ai* (同性爱; literally "same-sex love"), emerged as part of local modern sexology in the 1920s (Rocha 2010). Moreover, both republican and socialist China tactically used these imported ideas of modern (homo)sexuality to imagine a modern China and distinguish it from what was perceived as either backward and primitive from a discriminative, Western-centric, Orientalist viewpoint or as obsequious to the Western capitalist modernity or local feudal residues (Sang 2003; see also Q. Zhang 2014, 2015). Admittedly, the political-ideological manipulations of Chinese gender and sexuality during the Maoist years, especially the socialist feminism and women's "androgynous" public images as discussed in Chapter 1, enhanced Chinese women's social status to some extent and diversified their nonnormatively gendered (as well as potentially nonheterosexual) positionalities (see Jiao 2021; Lei 2015; Zhu and Xiao 2021). This historical trajectory of queer genders and sexualities in premodern and modern times has inevitably silhouetted today's queer TV China.

Post-2000 queer TV China has certainly been rendered more visible by a series of cultural-political events, digital technological transformations, and neoliberal economic reforms that occurred after the PRC's participation in the global economy starting from the late 1970s. The PRC entered a post-Mao age after the Cultural Revolution era (1966–1976), which was characterized by a radical break from previous Maoist politics and a "resurging discourse of liberal individualism [in] the intersections of society, family, and state" (Xiao 2014, 16). Meanwhile, the economic experiments and restructuring in the post-Mao time, such as the "reform and opening up" (改革开放) and "marketization" (市场化) of various sectors of Chinese society, led to significant growth in the number of local TV stations and TV sets owned by individuals (Huang 1994). Together with the development of transmission technologies during the 1980s, these reforms eventually resulted in the rapid commercialization, internationalization, and decentralization of the Chinese TV industry in the early 1990s (Sun and Gorfinkel 2015; Webber, Wang, and Zhu 2002; Yu 2011). TV as a key mass communicative platform in the PRC has thus been transformed from the party-state's tool for political mobilization to a "financially self-reliant" industry that relies "strongly on market forces and commercial interests to operate," while still constantly bargaining and complying with the government's ideological supervision and its national and political projects (Sun and Gorfinkel 2015, 21–25). At the same time, competitions for ratings and broadcasting reach between the national TV station China Central TV (CCTV), the provincial stations, and other "privately owned and operated media systems" also intensified (Keane 2004, 93; Yu 2009, 7; Zhao 2008, 96). In addition, the popularity of "television entertainment"

(电视娱乐), especially in the forms of TV serials, reality TV, and variety shows, has increased among both TV producers and audiences since the late 1980s (Bai and Song 2015, 2).

Starting in the late 1990s, a series of cultural-political events and neoliberal transformations occurred, which expedited the PRC's integration into global capitalism (Keane and Liu 2009, 246). For instance, national and global media and political events, such as the British handover of sovereignty over Hong Kong to China in 1997, China's entry into the World Trade Organization (WTO) in 2001, and significant increases in information exchange and human mobilization (most often in the forms of entertainment media and migratory flows) within China and internationally, captured the world's attention (Keane 2004, 90–95). Coupled with the emergence of multimedia broadcasting and participatory platforms (mobile TV and video-streaming and livestreaming sites, for example) for TV distribution and consumption in mainland China in the early 2000s, these signs of progress and change combined to facilitate transcultural traffic, drastically diversifying the Chinese TV industry and related cultures (Bai and Song 2015). In the meantime, the decriminalization of homosexuality in the PRC's Criminal Law in 1997 and the subsequent "partial removal of homosexuality as a mental disorder from" the third edition of *Chinese Classification of Mental Disorders* in 2001, as well as the rapid rise of urban China-based, transnational-connected feminist, LGBTQ, and HIV/AIDS-concerned non-governmental organizations (NGOs) and activists in the 2000s, have all contributed to "an increasing LGBTQ rights consciousness, [an expansion] of queer-friendly spaces and a burgeoning 'pink economy'" in mainland China (Bao 2021, 2–3, 32–33).

As further evidenced in Chapters 1, 2, and 3 in this volume, gender- and sexually nonnormative people in the PRC who can embody forms of Chinese-specific cosmopolitanism, neoliberalism, and neo-Confucianism are often treated as constructive elements rather than "the most politically sensitive and subversive social groups" (Bao 2021, 34) in the party-state's economic and political projects of creating and sustaining fantasies of "great China" and "strong nation" at the center of the global stage (Hird and Song 2018; Rofel 2007; Song 2022a; J. Zhao 2016, 2018a, 2020b). This ideological subjectivization and capitalist manipulation of LGBTQ groups in media and public spaces, though fundamentally problematic and perpetuating sociocultural hierarchies, has also perpetuated the government's somewhat ambiguous, performative, and even generative attitude toward queer media images (in both minoritizing and universalizing senses).

Notably, the government has practiced a hidden "Three No's" rule concerning LGBTQ issues in contemporary Chinese society: namely, "no approval, no disapproval, and no promotion" (Chen and Wang 2019). As recorded by Bao,

> Since the 1990s, LGBTQ issues have started to emerge in China's mainstream media and public discourses, although they have often been framed in limited ways and often associated with pathology, criminality, and abnormality.... In December 2000, Li Yinhe, Cui Zi'en, and Shi Tou participated in the talk show *Approaching Homosexuality* (*Zoujin Tongxinglian*) on Hunan Satellite Television, openly discussing queer issues in China's mainstream media for the first time. In December 2004, China Central Television broadcast a news feature *Tongxinglian: Huibi Buru Zhengshi* (*Homosexuality: Better Face It Than Avoid It*), discussing homosexuality in relation to HIV/AIDS prevention. (Bao 2021, 36)

Indeed, these early TV representations of LGBTQ subjects, especially the minoritized ones, often reproduced the "sad young men" (Berry 2000) imaginary of homosexuality in which gay men were persistently othered and repressed, if not portrayed as being ghettoized, hopeless, "deviant, abnormal, and anonymous" (Bao 2018, 113; Martin 2010a; Yu 2009). Although in the 2010s transgender and openly gay Chinese-speaking celebrities, such as the Mainland-born, male-to-female transgender TV personality Jin Xing (金星) and the Taiwanese gay-identifying talk show host Kevin Tsai (蔡康永), can be seen in seemingly "positive" representations on Chinese TV, their images have been largely refashioned in discourses of Chinese-specific elitism, cultural pride, cosmopolitanism, and neoliberalism. As our authors Linshan Jiang (in Chapter 7) and Oscar Tianyang Zhou (in Chapter 8) point out, even in the late 2010s, male effeminacy, which has been closely associated with the gender identities and aesthetics of gay men, is often negatively framed on Chinese TV or stereotypically interpreted through Chinese-speaking stars' on-TV performances. These stereotypes may have incurred the widespread "sissyphobia"—"the fear or hatred of effeminate men" who might undermine the heterosexualized and masculinist ideologies of the PRC nationalism and global power—in the post-2010 mainstream Chinese society (Song 2022a, 68–70).

In sharp contrast, as revealed in the discussions in Chapters 1 and 3 concerning images of real people and celebrities with norm-defying genders or same-sex intimacies in reality competition shows, universalized queer images and star personas have been not only increasingly visible but also blatantly commercialized, celebrated, and "normalized" by the media market, the government, and audience and fan groups (J. Zhao 2016, 2018b). More often than not, these defiant genders, connotated nonheterosexualities, and unconventional desires (which belong to the universalized queer representations, identities, and subjectivities on entertainment TV) have been fictionalized, detached from real-life LGBTQ identities and relationships (which are denoted, identity politics-based, minoritized nonheterosexuality), or fetishized and "straightened" as precious human qualities or characters (J. Zhao 2016, 2018b). On the one hand, since 2020, this omnipresent "queering" of TV narratives, media characters, and celebrity personas, widely practiced by both the media producers and the fan communities (as explicated in Chapters 2 and 5), incurred a sudden official top-down curtailment of BL media cultures and the formerly exponentially burgeoning celebrity-fan economy.[1] On the other hand, this ubiquitous queerness on TV and in Chinese cyberspace frequently led to unexpected online anti-pornography, anti-misogyny, and anti-homophobia/transphobia protests in digital spaces, initiated by different kinds of Chinese-speaking fan and activist groups (which is explored in depth in Chapters 1, 2, and 5; see also Bai 2022). These intricacies and conflicts within this post-2010 Chinese queer pop scene involving queer TV and fan cultures demonstrate the complex, inconsistent, vague ways media and online censorship systems in the PRC have worked (which can also be contemplated as "queer" in some sense).

Research has found that the Chinese TV and cyber censorship systems have been characterized by performativity and "generative"-ness within a "panoptic" social structure (Ng 2015; see also Bai 2022; Tsui 2003; Zhao 2020a). The party-state considers "a healthy moral order for Chinese society" as the fundamental key to its national progress and social-political stability and reinstates "itself as the moral center of Chinese society with ideological innovations" (Bai 2015a, 69–73). Meanwhile, the post-Mao government sees TV "as the guardian of a coherent, dominant morality system" and has strived to restrain TV entertainment from "promoting inappropriate morals and dubious values, catering to vulgar tastes, and staging the ugly, the dark, and abnormal" (Bai 2015a, 71–73). In addition, the often contradictory attitudes of the official censors at the various levels of TV production and broadcasting, as well as the self-censorship of media practitioners who "tend to produce materials . . . [that are] commercially successful," morally permissive, and less politically offensive to "the conversative morals of mainstream Chinese consumers" (Gorfinkel 2018, 75; see also Amar

---

1. The most recent practice of official crackdowns on the celebrity-fan economy happened in cyberspace in June 2021, targeting illegal, irrational, immoral, and even chaotic activities and communication in fan circles (饭圈; meaning "fannish social networks") and celebrity-related rumors and disputes on social media (see dramapotatoe 2021; L. Yang 2022). Known as the "Qinglang Rectification on the 'Fan-Circle' Chaos" (清朗·'饭圈'乱象整治) initiated by the Central Cyberspace Affairs Commission, this crackdown is part of the state-endorsed movement to create and sustain a "clean and bright" cyberspace (清朗网络空间), which was encouraged by President Xi Jinping in a speech in October 2017 at the nineteenth National Congress of the Chinese Communist Party (Wang and Liu 2020, 699; G. Yang 2022, 36; L. Yang 2022). Aiming to tame unruly fan activities and discipline the celebrities active in local entertainment industries, the government's *qinglang* (清朗) campaign indeed helped to cease some long-lasting issues and abuses in online Chinese fandoms and celebrity cultures, such as some idols' "manipulation of their fame for personal gain" and sexual harassment and certain fan groups' illegal economic activities and personal attacks (Tao and Liu 2021). Nevertheless, with a nature of censoring dissident opinions and public speech, this movement has largely impinged on freedom of speech and civil activities, especially those from feminist and LGBTQ groups, in cyberspace (Wang and Liu 2020; G. Yang 2022).

2018), often lead to the censoring of information that is incompatible with the political-ideological projects of the party-state and to unreasonable (self-)crackdowns on "politically innocuous" content in public spaces (Balding 2017; see also Zhao 2018a). Yet, in response to this official "morality" regulation, the Chinese TV industry often "embraces resilience" and pragmatically tailors ways of content production and distribution (Guo 2017, 488).

In terms of regulating homosexual media content, official policies have deemed homosexual topics in mass media and cyberspace "abnormal" and "perverted" since 2008. Some official guidelines directly associated homosexuality with "pornography, sex, and vulgarisms" and claimed it should be excluded from Chinese mass media (Jia and Zhou 2015). In 2016, the official media supervision and regulation executive agency, the State Administration of Press, Publication, Radio, Film, and Television (国家广播电影电视总局; SAPPRFT),[2] issued a set of new stipulations expressing unequivocal disapproval of media materials that "express or display abnormal sexual relations or sexual behavior, such as incest, homosexuality, perversion, sexual assault, sexual abuse, and sexual violence" or "promote unhealthy views of marriage and relationships, including extramarital affairs, one-night stands, and sexual freedom" (Shaw and Zhang 2018, 273). As thoroughly investigated in Chapter 4, one of the mainland Chinese TV productions severely affected by this policy is the 2016 popular online drama *Addicted* (上瘾; iQIYI). The show, also known as *Heroin*, involves a high school male same-sex romance. It was pulled off the air before the online distribution of its final three episodes in mainland China for its portrayals of male homosexuality and was accused of promoting "vulgar, immoral, and unhealthy content" and "the dark side of society" (Ellis-Petersen 2016). Yet, unexpectedly, this censoring of the show before the airing of its finale, as pointed out by Aobo Dong in Chapter 4, drove its fans to resume their consumption of the drama on English-language video-streaming websites based outside of the Mainland. In this sense, the censorship unexpectedly generated a resistive practice of queer Chinese TV fans based in the PRC that bypassed both the government's censorship of homosexuality and its digital geo-blocking of political-ideologically sensitive media information.

The online censoring of *Addicted* and the fan resistance provoked by the government's regulation both showcase the censorial logic that was reinforced in an official media regulatory memo circulated internally in June 2018. The memo states that in order to create an ideologically positive, politically correct media environment, the "self-censorship" of media producers is encouraged and "homosexuality is respected, but gay-themed content or gay characters are not allowed" in mass media (Feng 2018). Moreover, official media outlets, such as the

---

2. SAPPRFT existed between 2013 and 2018. Since March 2018, it has been restructured as the National Radio and Television Administration (国家广播电视总局; NRTA).

newspaper of the Chinese Communist Party, *People's Daily*, sometimes self-contradictorily criticized the disrespect and depathologization suffered by gender and sexual minorities in cyberspace and on TV that caused public anxiety and transnational protest against the PRC's heteronormative ideology, while also in the same statement advising Chinese LGBTQ people to be self-disciplined and behave like socially responsible, "normal" Chinese citizens (Zhao 2018a; see also Bao 2021, 35).[3] This official attitude is often more concerned with maintaining the nation's social-political stability in a neoliberal discourse and its global image as a culturally diverse, liberal, open-minded, modern, strong nation than with gender and sexual equality within mainland China.

What has further complicated this queer TV culture in the PRC is the queer nature and history of Chinese televisual and fannish discourses. As Jamie J. Zhao expounds in Chapter 1, "Reality talent shows [especially those adapting foreign formats and produced in the 2000s] have been credited with the emergence and popularity" of young Chinese idols with gender-nonnormative personas and performances. Nonetheless, it would be a mistake to assume that queer TV is a recent local phenomenon or limited to reality TV. As Joyrich noted, "*queer* is defined precisely as the subversion of the ordinary, as the strange, the irregular, which would seem to necessitate some sort of disruption to 'our regularly scheduled [TV] programming'" (2014, 134). Accordingly, contemporary TV is increasingly

> intriguing in its concepts and politics, complex in its story structure and visuals, multiple in its address and mediations. Thus, . . . television itself is being remade, some might say, as more queer: more eccentric and playful, more connective and transformative, with more stand-out strangeness than just stand-up straightness. (Joyrich 2014, 135)

This is particularly true for mainland Chinese TV and its stardom and fandom, which have been shaped by and actively transforming both local and global queer cultures, though often in subtle and negotiative ways.

Some notable cases of queerness on mainland Chinese TV prior to the "ubiquitous queerness" (Zhao 2018b, 2020a) on contemporary reality TV can be identified. Take, for example, the annually televised Chinese Lunar New Year special *Spring Festival Gala* (春晚; CCTV, 1983–present), which has continually featured cross-gender and cross-dressing performances or nonconforming gender personas (often legitimized through the theatricality of Peking opera/京剧 or other local Chinese folk art forms such as *er'ren zhuan*/二人转); the delicate homoeroticism between Prince Hong (太子弘) and his catamite Hehuan (合欢) in

---

3. Take, for example, the official media responses to the online communicative platform Weibo's ban on homosexual content in April 2018 and to Mango TV's self-censoring of LGBTQ images during its broadcasting of the European reality singing competition *Eurovision* (EBU, EU) in May 2018.

Palace of Desire (大明宫词, CCTV-8, 2000), the mega-hit historical TV drama of the Tang Dynasty; the male-to-female cross-dressing servant girl Da Meizi (大梅子) in *Xuese Canyang* (血色残阳; BTV, 2005), the suspense drama portraying a story of pre-1949's modern China; and the surprisingly large number of "handsome" single young women on the heterosexual match-making show *If You Are the One* (非诚勿扰; Jiangsu TV, 2010–present) who were rumored to be lesbians and have long-term same-sex partners in their offscreen lives.

Along with the rise of online audience and fan groups dedicated to non-Mainland TV in the early 2000s, both the East Asian pop culture of androgynous beautiful males (also known as 花美男/flower-like men) and images of androgynous girls and young women (also known as 中性女孩儿/少男系少女/neutrosexual or tomboyish girls) in variety shows and TV dramas produced in Taiwan, Hong Kong, Thailand, and the United States have largely facilitated the development and intricacy of local mainland Chinese LGBTQ cultures and subject positions (Zhao, Yang, and Lavin 2017; see also Lu and Hu 2021). After the Mainland entered the era of digital TV production, distribution, and consumption in the years since 2010,[4] both Chinese-language and foreign TV programs featuring homoerotic and homosocial scenes, connotations, and storylines have proliferated in Chinese cyberspace. In addition to the TV shows discussed in *QTC*'s essays, other noteworthy cases in recent years include the comedy *Go Princess Go* (太子妃升职记; LeTV, 2015), which was released online and presents a time-traveling, gender-reversal story; the 2016 *Super Voice Girl* (超级女声; Mango TV), a reality singing competition that featured numerous high-profile masculine girl stars; and the Thai BL TV series *I Told Sunset About You* (Line TV, 2020) and *I Promised You the Moon* (Line TV, 2021), the online subtitled release of which drew a large Chinese-speaking queer fan base in the Chinese and Sinophone worlds.

Despite this flourishing queer TV culture within and beyond the geolinguistic, political-ideological confines of mainland China, what has yet to emerge in existing queer Chinese TV and fan studies is a comprehensive text that recognizes the usefulness of universalizing and minoritizing approaches and highlights the interdigitated root and route of the discursive formations of queerness, Chineseness, and TV in the field. Through the framework of "queer/ing TV China," *QTC* addresses this urgent need to explore the subtleties, anxieties, and confrontations within and surrounding the collisions of global TV flows, international politics, cross-racial issues, ethnic-cultural connections, historical divergence within various Sinophone communities, transcultural traveling and mutations of feminist and queer politics, and the local adaptation and reinvention of televisuality. The contributors collaborate to provide powerful proof of the omnipresence of queer subjects and cultures in forming and transforming

---

4. The first online mainland Chinese TV drama was released in 2007. Yet, online TV shows were rare in the pre-2010 years.

Chinese commercial and entertainment media industries, televisual aesthetics and digital communication, sociocultural developments, and political-ideological regulations.

Chapter Breakdowns

This volume is divided into three sections, each of which includes three original studies dedicated to the most attention-grabbing "queer/ing" issues in the field. The first section is titled "Queer/ing Genders and Sexualities through Reality Competition Shows." As mentioned above, reality TV is one of the queerest TV genres, often characterized by easily adaptive formats and performativity in representing "reality," gender, sexuality, and race/ethnicity (Zhao 2018b; see also Gater and MacDonald 2015; Hill 2005; Skeggs and Wood 2012). Set in heteronormative societies, these features of reality competitions can offer and intensify ambiguous, yet ubiquitous, homosocial settings and same-sex erotic tensions (Zhao 2018b). Meanwhile, research has attributed the state-backed popularity of reality TV in the twenty-first-century PRC to the genre's ideological-propagandistic function in promoting "positive" and "happy" voices to the audience (Yang 2014) and articulating the government's ethno-nationalistic projects, such as "China Dream" and "root-seeking," in sonic or visual representations (Jiang and Gonzalez 2021; Song 2022b; Xiao 2020; Zhao 2020b). These also partly explain why reality TV is intrinsically both queer and hegemonic, as well as both ideologically orthodoxic and commercially successfully, in the PRC.

Chapter 1, "Growing up with 'Tomboy Power': Starring Liu Yuxin on Post-2010 Chinese Reality TV," captures this self-contradictoriness of reality TV and elaborates on the nuances of how gender-norm-defying girls and young women have been framed by and are actively navigating through reality TV's dual function. Jamie J. Zhao explores this queerly gendered televisual phenomenon by examining a particular form of female masculinity, "tomboyism," which is embodied by one of the most successful girl pop stars in the post-2010 era: Liu Yuxin, who rose to stardom in the most recent girl band-manufacturing reality program, *Youth With You 2* (青春有你2; iQIYI, 2020). Zhao presents a critical televisual analysis of Liu's tomboyism as presented on mainland Chinese reality TV between 2012 and 2020. Her analysis unpacks the intricate relationship between televised Chinese tomboyism and the local Chinese term signifying a young, butch lesbian, "T." She demonstrates how, along with the drastic changes in local queer and feminist cultures over the past decade, the constantly self-fashioning format and televisuality of reality TV subjectivize tomboyish stars who cite local, transnational, and global pop cultural discourses on youth, androgynous beauty, girl power, and neoliberalism to validate their gender and potentially sexual non-normativities while, either voluntarily or unwillingly, being fabricated into the official imaginary of China as a globalized, modernized nation-state that appreciates female gender diversity, feminist expressions, and self-cultivation.

Chapter 2, "When '*Jiquan*' Fandom Meets 'Big Sisters': The Ambivalence between Female Queer (In)Visibility and Popular Feminist Rhetoric in *Sisters Who Make Waves*," looks at queer female images and same-sex intimacies in, as well as the queer fandom of, another extremely successful girl group-manufacturing reality show in the Mainland in 2020, *Sisters Who Make Waves* (乘风破浪的姐姐; Mango TV). Diverging from the first chapter's focus on norm-defying girls and young women, Jia Guo and Shaojun Kong examine how a show featuring female celebrity participants over the age of thirty successfully devises a "big sister" persona by incorporating popular feminism. These images of mature, independent, and brave "big sisters" coincide with the preference of *jiquan* (姬圈; literally meaning "lesbian circle") fandom, a queer female fan culture that has been emerging in post-2010 Chinese cyberspace. The authors explore the ambivalent relations between queer female visibility and popular feminist rhetoric on TV through *jiquan* fans' queer readings of the show. They find that, on the one hand, the popular feminist rhetoric of the show creates a viable space for *jiquan* fans to project their queer desires onto female celebrities and foster their understanding of female homoeroticism. On the other hand, *jiquan* fandom marginalizes masculine queer women and promotes elitism and lookism in lesbian culture.

While the preceding two chapters are dedicated to queer female images on reality TV, Chapter 3, "A Dildonic Assemblage: The Paradoxes of Queer Masculinities and Desire on the Chinese Sports Variety Show *Let's Exercise, Boys*," turns to norm-negotiating male gender and sexual representations on the 2020 sports reality show *Let's Exercise, Boys* (运动吧少年; Hunan TV). Wangtaolue Guo and Jennifer Quist present textual and paratextual analyses and explore the dynamics between contestants on the show, male bodies in the mediascape, and the making of spornosexuals under Chinese censorship and in a postsocialist society. Guo and Quist also add to this analytical approach the concept of the "dildonic assemblage," applying it to the show's spornosexuality as it is read through the female gaze and through latent queer erotics. By doing so, they uncover the show's representations of male masculinity, desire, and queerness through a polysystematic lens. The authors argue that, despite the ambivalent attitudes toward homoeroticism, commodification, and the ironic queering of male bodies in Chinese media, *Let's Exercise, Boys* subverts and complicates the discourses that would suppress this new spornosexual iteration of Chinese male masculinity.

The second section, "Queer/ing TV Dramas through Media Regulations," focuses on the transnational, cross-linguistic circulation and consumption of queer TV dramas in and beyond the Chinese-speaking world that have always been under the government's cultural surveillance, economic exploitation, and political manipulation. This section contains three chapters that, from different perspectives, emphasize the queer-enabling power of the seemingly repressive official media policies and the negotiative potential of contemporary queer Chinese televisual production, distribution, and consumption.

Chapter 4, "*Addicted* to Melancholia: Negotiating Queerness and Homoeroticism in a Banned Chinese BL Drama," spotlights the transgressive potential of queer Chinese TV under erasure. Aobo Dong examines the affect and plot in *Addicted*, an immensely popular BL web series that was abruptly banned by state censors in 2017. Focusing on the dynamics between two same-sex lovers, he explores the critical themes of performativity, melancholia, and identification underlying the plot and reception of the series. Drawing on Judith Butler's (1995, 1997) theory of gender melancholia and José Esteban Muñoz's (2009) vision for a queer utopia, Dong illustrates the role of grief in enabling their same-sex love and argues that overcoming their shared grief and precariousness threatens the heterosexual symbolic in the Chinese and Confucian social orders. Dong's analysis also shows that *Addicted* is an attempt to construct a utopian parallel reality in which same-sex love trumps same-sex rivalry, class difference, and compulsory filial piety. Because the narrative of *Addicted* never attaches a gay identity to the characters, the series frees same-sex love from the constraints of LGBTQ identity politics and disguises it as other forms of same-sex intimacy—making it both ubiquitous and dangerous to the hegemonic gendered matrix in contemporary Chinese society.

Chapter 5, "Taming *The Untamed*: Politics and Gender in BL-Adapted Web Dramas," by Jun Lei, looks at one of the most widely discussed and debated Chinese BL dramas of the digital TV era. The author proposes "BL-adapted" (耽改) as a genre related to, but differentiated from, BL, because media industry infiltration and state regulations have depleted the BL-adapted sexual and homoerotic content and converted it into "bromance." As Lei shows, the two queer media genres differ in narrative modes, fan objects, fan participation patterns, cultural function, and ideological positioning to dominant political and commercial forces. Lei reassesses optimistic scholarly claims about fans' digital dexterity, initiative, and capacity to be a subversive force of heteronormativity and state ideology. Her analysis also reveals contention and compliance between audience, industry, and state censors in "taming" BL-adapted dramas. She unravels controversies revolving around the lead actors of *The Untamed* to situate the BL-adapted genre as part of the Chinese entertainment industry's "pan-rotten" strategy of clickbaiting for profitmaking. Her examination extrapolates how the ideological expressions of BL-adapted dramas are shaped by state regulatory strategies. As Lei finds, while gesturing toward new possibilities of queer representations and fantasies and public agencies for female fans and viewers, the current form of BL-adapted dramas actually bespeaks a heteronormative conservatism and can distract attention from politically sensitive and often severely censored LGBTQ media in China.

The hypermasculinist and heteronormative geopolitics of the PRC in the Xi Jinping era are often framed as less progressive in the domains of gay marriage, anti-discrimination laws, and LGBTQ public cultures in comparison to post-Martial Law Taiwan, as well as less friendly than the queer-supportive environment of postcolonial Hong Kong. In response, Alvin K. Wong, in Chapter 6, "Disjunctive Temporalities: Queer Sinophone Visuality across Mainland China, Hong Kong, and Taiwan," examines the textual and contextual disjunctions of BL cultural productions in the three major Chinese-speaking societies. The author finds that while *The Untamed*, produced in the PRC, captures a form of "unhistorical queerness" whose queer appeal lies precisely in its portrayals of bromance and queer desire in a non-historical world of *jianghu* (rivers and lakes of the heroic world), recent queer dramas and films in postcolonial Hong Kong are by contrast more concerned with social issues such as aging, HIV prevention, and familial conflicts. The HIV-related online film *For Love, We Can* (愛，不難; dir. Chi-Lung Lam, 2014) and the recent hit TV drama *Ossan's Love* (大叔的愛; ViuTV, HK, 2021) visualize queer Hong Kong through what Wong describes as "queer presentism." Finally, the legalization of gay marriage in Taiwan in 2019 has significantly impacted the queer imaginary of BL in films and media. In lighthearted films and TV dramas such as *Formula 17* (2004) and *Because of You* (因為愛你; LINE TV, TW, 2020), a world in which gay men no longer need to come out and can simply be as ordinary as any other Taiwanese citizen is highlighted. Wong conceptualizes this as a certain "postliberal temporality" that emerges in post-2019 Taiwan. By delineating the three modalities of "unhistorical queerness" in mainland BL dramas, "queer presentism" in postcolonial Hong Kong BL media, and "postliberal temporality" in contemporary Taiwanese BL productions, he theorizes the overall disjunctive temporalities across queer Sinophone visuality and mediascapes.

The last section, "Queer/ing Celebrities across Geocultural Boundaries," shifts the focus to issues concerning post-2010 queer Chinese-language TV star and fan cultures with a transcultural dimension. As noted earlier, queer Chinese TV stardom and fandom in the first decade of the twenty-first century were largely shaped by inter-Asian and global queer media, such as Japanese BL media and Western LGBTQ pop cultures (Lavin, Yang, and Zhao 2017; Li 2015; Zhao 2017a). Post-2010 global TV market and transnational TV flows have allowed further queer dynamics and possibilities, which have been mobilized by Chinese-speaking queer stars and fans. Therefore, the last three chapters of *QTC* examine these queer/ing phenomena in the Chinese glocalization of and participation in transnational and global TV, celebrity, and fan cultures. They provide cross-cultural, comparative perspectives for studying the intricacies of queer TV stardom and fandom in different Chinese-speaking societies as well as across geopolitical borders and linguistic boundaries.

Linshan Jiang's essay, "Queer Vocals and Stardom on Chinese TV: Case Studies of Wu Tsing-Fong and Zhou Shen," offers a critical reading of gendered representations of and self-performances by Wu Tsing-Fong (吳青峰) from Taiwan and Zhou Shen (周深) from mainland China—two Chinese-speaking pop singers—on TV. Both Wu and Zhou possess "androgynous" voices as male singers. Although their appearances and personalities correspond to popular inter-Asian imageries of "soft masculinity," Jiang argues that their vocal queerness further destabilizes the mainstream's assumed univocal masculinity and adds to the diversity of male gender subject positions. Her examination focuses on the two singers' negotiations with the state and the market based on their queer masculinities within the dissimilar social-political environments and gendered histories of mainland China and Taiwan. She argues that Wu and Zhou continue to seek room for existence between sissyphobia, homophobia, transphobia, and voyeurism on Chinese-language TV. As they gain popularity and find a broad audience in the Chinese-language mainstream media and public spaces, Wu and Zhou not only maintain queer voices and personae but also form affective bonds with audiences to elicit queer sociocultural transformation.

While Jiang's study unpacks how vocal queerness works in Chinese-language media industries, Oscar Tianyang Zhou's research in Chapter 8, "Gay Men in/ and *Kangsi Coming*," analyzes the ways in which gay men are (mis)represented on Chinese-language entertainment TV. Zhou interrogates two dominant gay types represented in two top-rated Mandarin talk shows—*Kangsi Coming* (康熙来了; CTi Variety, Taiwan, 2004–2016) and *U Can U Bibi* (奇葩说; iQIYI, China, 2014–present)—namely, the "sissy" and the "macho," which both signify a gay male subject and object of desire. He suggests that media representations play a crucial role in establishing cultural understanding of what it means to be gay in Taiwan and mainland China today. Zhou points out that the televised gay representations in question promise to enhance the visibility of gay men in the Chinese-speaking world. Yet, when gay visibility and cultural practices become good business prospects in a digital age, they also create and sustain disappointing stereotypes and hierarchies in TV representations.

The last chapter of *QTC*, "Queer Motherly Fantasy: The Sinophone Mom Fandom of Saint Suppapong Udomkaewkanjana" by Pang Ka Wei, presents a sophisticated investigation of an emerging yet understudied topic—"mom fans" (妈妈粉)—in transnational Chinese queer fandom of Thai BL TV. As Pang opines, when the Thai BL TV series boom meets the burgeoning mom fandom, the two synergize transnational queer motherly fantasies of fans that go beyond parasociality and heteronormativity. Focusing on the Sinophone mom fandom of Saint Suppapong Udomkaewkanjana (Saintsup hereafter), a Sino-Thai BL actor, Pang looks into how the family metaphor is at work among mom fans. She observes that in viewing BL TV series along with Saintsup's words and deeds, fans acquire a motherly position framed in the heteropatriarchal envisioning of the family. As Pang finds, Saintsup's *ke'ai* (being cute and lovable) fosters fans' infantilization of the idol, the star's diverse masculinities defy the toxic patriarchal masculinity, and his Chinese descent nurtures kindred feelings among the mainland Chinese fans. Pang argues that Saintsup's Sinophone mom fandom illustrates how "Chineseness" is homogenized and essentialized, as well as how the fan-as-mother/idol-as-child positioning complicates and transforms the inelastic kinship in the Sinophone setting. As desiring subjects, these mom fans form an affective alliance that opens up possibilities for multifarious queer fantasies to be played out.

Taken together, through a "queer/ing TV China" lens, the essays in *QTC* explore the various TV narratives, temporalities, genres, formats, censorial practices and policies, celebrity images, and fan practices over the past decade. The authors highlight the ubiquitous existence and negotiative power of queerness in identity formation and desire voicing within a largely authoritarian, heteropatriarchal society. They also shed light on the intricate ways in which official political-ideological manipulations inside and outside of the PRC, mainstream commercial forces, digital technological affordances, and defiant desires intersect, compete, and collaborate through transnational, cross-media TV adaptation, production, and consumption. Overall, *QTC* presents a rich, fecund inspection of how these intersections manifest in and complicate the queer manufacturing and queering potential of TV images and stars and contribute to the interests of and conflicts among their fan communities.

The Future of Queer TV China

Delving into the deeply interwoven queer and normative dimensions of Chinese-language televisual screens, stardom, and fandom, *QTC* details how queer TV China, as a vital part of global TV and queer studies, carefully positions itself in relation to other more politically sensitive, less commercially profitable, and thus often censored LGBTQ cultural productions in Chinese media and digital spaces. Analytically, *QTC* radically redefines "queer" as a televisual-cultural-industrial-fannish position that is diacritically opposed to the normative ideals and expectations in the public and popular discourses surrounding gender, sexual, geocultural, and sociopolitical identities in the highly authoritarian, heteropatriarchal, and predominantly Chinese-speaking world. Through the idea of "queer/ing," the contributors have worked together to highlight the interdigitated meanings and implications of queer/*ku'er* in Chinese and Sinophone studies as a self-identification point for gender and sexual minorities, a media practice to push forward social-political changes, a response to different queer politics and censorship systems in diverse Chinese-speaking communities, a media industry's production and marketing strategy for profit making and gimmick creating, and/or an alternative representation or interpretation of nonnormative genders and sexualities that are not necessarily self-identified as nonheterosexual.

The studies included in the volume exemplify the usefulness of the lens of "queer/ing TV China" in spotlighting queerness as an indispensable, constitutive element to the media-cultural discourses surrounding TV—the seemingly "most ordinary, everyday, and commonplace of our media forms" (Joyrich 2014, 134)—and Chineseness, especially the too-often assumed most heteronormative mainstream Chinese spaces and identities in the PRC. Rather than reiterating that the political edge of queer Chinese TV and fan cultures is simply erased or de-radicalized by the converging forces of economic neoliberalization and state surveillance, *QTC* takes a step further to offer a complex understanding of today's mainstream, commercial Chinese-language media and cultural landscapes. It conceives contemporary cultures, industries, creativities, and policies concerning queer TV China as being constituted and continually remade by multiple forces and factors (including historical and contemporary values, as well as local, transcultural, and global information flows, cultural hybridization, and social-political contestations), while persistently negotiating with both queer and normative elements to sustain the official imaginaries of both a neoliberal-heteropatriarchal China and a geopolitically essentialized and self-centered Chineseness, domestically, transnationally, and globally.

Through critical reflections on various emerging queer TV and fannish phenomena and deconstructive analyses of specific sensational cases, *QTC* also challenges the dichotomy of "positive" and "negative" representations of gender and sexual minorities and cautions against the simplistic, generalizing view of Chinese media regulatory and censorial practices as straightforward "repressive" regimes. In doing so, the volume's essays suggest new and exciting approaches and perspectives to the multilayered constructedness and performativity of identity and desire, such as those of tomboyism, adult womanhood, male homosociality and homoeroticism, mother-son relationships, and Chineseness and Sinophonicity, in the televisual-cultural productions of gender, sexual, ethnic, and geolinguistic identities and subjectivities. The contributors not only demonstrate that TV is queer in essence and has enormous queering potential, but also expose the queer problems and nuances that have mushroomed through contemporary Chinese-language media and creative productions. More importantly, the empirical discussions offered in the book showcase the cultural agency of insubordinate genders, sexualities, bodies, relationalities, and subjectivities mediated through the transnational, cross-racial, digital dimensions of contemporary Chinese-language screens and fan practices. By emphasizing the queer characteristics and promises of certain trans-local and transnational TV phenomena, *QTC* expands the existing Western-centered and Japanese- and South Korean-focused scholarship on queer media, celebrity, and fan studies to include up-to-date investigations of queer TV production, distribution, circulation, and consumption in and beyond the PRC.

QTC aims to inspire sophisticated scholarly endeavors to inspect queer TV China and related subjects. As noted earlier in this Introduction, a growing number of academic works devoted to examinations of queer Chinese fan cultures (especially centering around BL TV) have been published in recent years in both English and Chinese languages. Yet most of the works tend to cluster around ethnographical approaches to specific fan sites (Zhao, Yang, and Lavin 2017, xiii). Even today, critical analyses that can meaningfully fuse Euro-American queer TV theories with Chinese media studies to inspect queer-natured Chinese TV formats, adaptations, and cross-media and cross-cultural flows and to produce a "more global synthesis" (Chiang 2014b, 355) remain sporadic. Further, the research methods and topics of some *QTC* chapters, such as the non-participant observation used in Chapter 2 to explore online queer gossip surrounding female TV stars, have often been marginalized in existing media scholarship, if not negatively feminized and trivialized in both social-scientific-centric communication studies and heteropatriarchal societies. The diversity and novelty of the methodologies employed by the contributors, therefore, can be seen as a particular strength of this volume.

Acknowledging the importance and fruitfulness of scholarly publications on LGBTQ lives in contemporary China (see, for example, Engebretsen 2014; Kam 2013; Bao 2018, 2021), *QTC* is one of the first English-language scholarly projects that strives to establish queer Chinese-language TV studies as a critical field of inquiry and look at queer lives, politics, voices, and struggles through entertainment media and pop cultural imaginaries. Far from narrowly focusing on a dashing, cosmopolitan, middle-class-oriented urban scene and a Euro-American-centric celebrity-fan economy, *QTC* has an emphasis on queer cultural-televisual landscapes and takes pains to join more social scientific, political-economic analysis-endorsed, and ethnographic approach-based queer research. This book showcases that boundary-transgressing, norm-contesting subjects, knowledge, and voices have been made and remade omnipresent in mainstream media and cyber spaces, despite the plural, unpredictable censorial practices from both commercial and political sectors. It ultimately problematizes and deconstructs the cosmopolitan, neoliberal bubble of queer Chinese media cultures from the inside out.

In addition, the past decade has witnessed both an enhanced visibility of ethnic-Chinese or foreign lesbian celebrities, leftover women, divorced women, women with immense political-economic power, or female sex workers (who are often positioned in highly homosocial scenarios in women-centered Chinese dramas) on TV and a growing number of cyber-TV programs that are produced by and for Chinese lesbians, such as online talk shows and sitcoms. Nevertheless, research dedicated to such topics remains particularly rare. To fill the gap in studies of queer women's TV images and fandom in the existing scholarship, *QTC* contains a number of chapters scrutinizing queer TV representations of and queer fannish imaginations about women. Some other promising directions for future research that can be generated from the discussions in the book include Anglophone, especially English-speaking, fandom of Chinese BL and other queer TV productions; the queer-initiating potential of TV genres and formats, such as sports TV and factual TV, that have previously been assumed to be hypermasculine, nationalistic, hegemonic, heterosexual-oriented, or under strict official surveillance; the norm-defying power of too-often femininized TV genres and means of communications, such as talk shows and gossip; and the nonnormative imaginaries of ethnic-minority Chinese nationals on mainstream TV that often frame Han-centered, Confucian gender and sexual norms as the ultimate ideals in the Chinese-specific heterosexual matrix. Of course, along with the drastic transformation in sociocultural contexts, global flows, and transnational relations with regard to Chinese feminist and LGBTQ rights and queer media productions in the post-2020 years, these will become only a few among numerous emerging queer Chinese pop scenes, for which *QTC* hopes to stir up scholarly attention and critical conversations.

I. Queer/ing Genders and Sexualities through Reality Competition Shows

1
Growing Up with "Tomboy Power"
Starring Liu Yuxin on Post-2010 Chinese Reality TV

Jamie J. Zhao

Introduction

On May 30, 2020, a twenty-three-year-old boyish girl, Liu Yuxin (刘雨昕), from Guizhou province in Southwest China, won first place in the hit girl-group cultivation reality show *Youth With You 2* (青春有你2; iQIYI; *YWY2* hereafter) with over seventeen million audience votes. Taking the "center position" (C 位; meaning the most important all-around member) in the group, Liu formed the new Chinese girl band THE9 with the eight other girls who received the most votes in the competition. Over the past fifteen years, mainland China has seen several waves of reality singing competitions (Keane and Zhang 2017; Yang 2014), starting with the female-only *Idol*-style singing contest *Super Voice Girl* (超级女声; Hunan TV, 2004–2006, 2009, 2011, 2016; *SVG* hereafter) and followed by *The Voice of China* (中国好声音; Zhejiang TV, 2012–2021), which was adapted from a format originating in the Netherlands, the celebrity singing competition show *I Am a Singer* (我是歌手; Hunan TV, 2013–2020), the rap competition *The Rap of China* (中国有嘻哈; iQIYI, 2017–2020), and the music-group manufacturing show *Produce 101* (创造101; Tencent Video, 2018–2021).

Reality talent shows have been credited with the emergence and popularity of young Chinese female idols with masculine personas or cross-dressing looks (Huang 2013; Xiao 2012; Yang and Bao 2012; Yue and Yu 2008; J. Zhao 2016, 2018b, 2019b; Zhao, Yang, and Lavin 2017). A classic example that has been frequently discussed in existing scholarship is Li Yuchun (李宇春; also known as Chris Lee), who rose to fame after unexpectedly winning the 2005 season of *SVG* with her androgynous onstage persona and unconventional singing style (Meng 2009; Xiao 2012, 2020; Yang 2009; Yue and Yu 2008). Following Li's sudden success, there was a boom of gender-nonnormative female reality TV stars, especially in singing and dancing competition shows produced between 2005 and 2016 (Zhao 2018b, 2019b). This androgynous TV hype was often interpreted as part and parcel of a new wave of contemporary Chinese feminism and the democratic potential of the post-2000 Chinese pop cultural landscape (Meng 2009; Yue and Yu 2008).

In the late 2010s, the local Chinese entertainment industry witnessed the rise of feminine girl pop, which was marked by East Asian hyperfeminine beauty norms featuring "white, skinny, young, and innocent" women (白、瘦、幼; Ma 2018; see also Jung 2018; Xiao 2020, 146). For instance, the girl group Rocket Girls (火箭女孩), formed during the 2018 season of *Produce 101*, was emblematic of this rejuvenated sexualization and commodification of young women's bodies in the Mainland. This girl group culture has been naturalized through a neoliberal discourse of "girl power" (Hains 2012), which has been commonly deployed in the mainstream commercialization of young women's sexual empowerment in the Euro-American and South Korean music and idol industries. Within the East Asian context, this discourse projects a desirable girlhood "within the entangling discourses of feminism, neoliberalism and conventional femininity" (Jackson and Westrupp 2010, 348) and thus perpetuates "the neo-cultural imperialist convergence between patriarchal nationalism, nationalistic ambition for global competition, and corporate interests in the maximization of economic profits from the governance of young femininity" (Kim 2011, 336). Although some "feminist" voices and "unconventional" personas of young women are identified in the recent wave of Chinese girl pop (Xiao 2020, 148),[1] this form of women's agency replicates a "pseudo-feminist" rhetoric in a neoliberal, consumerist China that emphasizes "self-expression and self-actualization" (Peng 2020, 67). Marshaled by the "neoliberal globalization" of Chinese entertainment and digital media (Xiao 2020, 130), the retrieving and marketing of traditional female gender and sexual ideals through the televisual manufacturing of young Chinese girl idols have been simultaneously encouraged by East Asian *kawaii* (cuteness), girl-group cultures, and the state's gender policies, as well as the multivalent feminist and queer thoughts glocalized and proliferating in mainstream Chinese society in more recent years.

Since the late 2000s, in response to the increasing gender imbalance of the Chinese population and the growing number of "leftover women" (referring to groups of educated, single, urban women who are over twenty-seven years old), the government has employed its mass media and cyberspace "to concertedly push young women to marry at all costs, including foregoing their careers and entitlement to marital property" (Wu and Dong 2019, 478; see also Hong Fincher 2014). Furthermore, on January 1, 2016, the government ended its one-child rule,

---

1. For instance, one of the most popular participants of the show *Produce 101* in 2018, Wang Ju (王菊), was said to be "China's Beyoncé" for her tanned skin tone and curvy figure, as well as for "her candid personality, independence and ambition" (RADII China 2018; Zhang 2018). Wang also received massive support from Chinese feminist and queer groups during the competition (Xiao 2020, 148). Yet, she was eventually eliminated and did not make it to the top eleven finalists who formed the Rocket Girls band.

which had been in effect since 1979 (Coonan 2016). Instead, a two-child policy, which encouraged married couples to have two children, was enacted.[2] These changes to the local family-planning system aimed to "ease demographic pressures," remedy the "labor shortage," and "boost the birth rate," especially in urban areas of mainland China (BBC 2021; Coonan 2016). Since 2018, the growing popularity of Chinese effeminate male stars in the past decade, which was influenced by the inter-Asian androgynous beauty cultures circulated to mainland China in the late 1990s, has generated further nationalistic-masculinist anxieties over the "national virility" and led to an official "sissyphobic discourse" that denigrates and even censors gender-nonnormative male representations on TV (Song 2022a, 70). In the meantime, socioeconomic situations, the government's political agenda, and the "rekindled patriarchal values" of mainland China in the late 2010s have all aligned to produce public and official backlashes against the hitherto-booming Chinese feminist cultures and practices (Wu and Dong 2019, 478). These intertwining social-political, cultural, and economic factors and forces have, in turn, reinvigorated certain heteropatriarchal-endorsed gender norms and expectations, especially manifesting through China's TV representations of young women.

It is also worth noting that the highly gender-norm-deviating televisual phenomenon mentioned at the beginning of this chapter is emblematic of an intriguing "youth"-focused political rhetoric revived by the contemporary government. Rather than serving as "a category of biological age or a transitional stage of human development," the word *youth* (青年) was used in modern Chinese culture to signify the dual projects of "self-reformation" and "national rejuvenation" (Xiao 2020, 2; see also Song 2015, 3). Nevertheless, in postsocialist, neoliberal China, its political edge has mostly evaporated. Instead, social-political imaginaries and aspirations associated with the idea of youth or of being youthful have often been revamped in gendered narratives and spaces to perpetuate a market-oriented, consumerist economy (Xiao 2020, 20). For instance, the youthful and nonnormatively gendered discourses surrounding Li Yuchun's TV stardom and fandom have largely contributed to a "marketable diversity" pursued and favored by the Chinese entertainment industry (Xiao 2020). Li's queer persona, in this sense, becomes part of "an all-inclusive . . . post-Fordist cultural industry" that can "attest to the mainstream neoliberal discourse of self-sufficiency and individual fulfillment, and attac[h] a more liberal and more individualized humane face to the grand discourse of China Dream" (Xiao 2020, 156).

Against this background, this chapter explores the (nonnormatively) gendered televisual phenomenon exemplified through Liu Yuxin's rise to fame during the

---

2. Later, in May 2021, the government announced that married couples are allowed to have up to three children (BBC 2021).

first half of 2020. Liu's career as a girl pop idol started with her participation in the reality show *Up Young!* (向上吧！少年; Hunan TV, 2012). After that, she participated in several high-profile reality singing and dancing shows. This study looks at Liu's nonconforming persona as it was performed, revised, and eventually mainstreamed and celebrated on reality TV between 2012 and 2020. Methodologically, I employ a queer televisual discourse analysis. TV itself is "an, if not *the*, agent of forms of queer life" (Villarejo 2014, 55). Nonnormatively defined forms of life and televisual temporalities have been in symbiotic relationships and have mutually contributed to one another's development (Villarejo 2014, 15). As Richard Dyer eloquently stated, "How social groups are treated in cultural representations is part and parcel of how they are treated in life" (1993, 1). This is particularly true for gender-norm-defying young women featured on contemporary Chinese reality TV.

Michael Lovelock (2019) once elaborated on the complexities of queer images on Western reality TV in this way:

> *reality television itself*—its generic conventions, thematic norms and network contexts—functions as the discursive matter which brings LGBTQ (short for "lesbian, gay, bisexual, transgender, and queer") identities into being through representations. These televisual factors form the conditions of possibility for these very identities. (Lovelock 2019, 23)

In this vein, a critical reading of Liu's reality TV appearances between 2012 and 2020 reveals how her embodiment of "tomboyism" (denoting a Chinese-specific form of a young, masculine female persona) was manufactured, rejected, evaluated, modified, and commercialized alongside the development of reality TV formats in post-2010 China. This televisual queer-feminist analysis also captures the ways in which contemporary Chinese gender/sexual minority identities and cultures have been actively negotiating with, yet also inevitably subjugated by, local gender traditions, market forces, official policies, and transnational pop-cultural flows.

In the rest of this chapter, I first explain my use of the term "tomboyism" and its connotative (dis)association with lesbianism in the Chinese-speaking context. I also briefly trace a social-political trajectory of female gender and sexuality in mainland China that has heavily shaped today's Chinese tomboyish subjectivities. Then, I explore Liu's reality TV performances and career development. My analysis pays special attention to Liu's gendered, youthful persona in *YWY2* to understand how the show produced "tomboy" stars and legitimized the prescribed sociocultural non-normativities associated with tomboyism. I reveal that with constantly revised formats, reality talent shows afford a queer platform for subject making in contemporary China.

My discussion is situated within the post-2010 postsocialist Chinese feminist context in which "a market-individual discourse" is appropriated in the official and public patriarchal backlash against "the socialist feminist legacy" (Zhu and Xiao 2021, 12), while glocalized postfeminist thoughts emphasizing "the formation of an expressive personal lifestyle and the ability to select the right commodities to attain it" are promoted (Negra 2008, 4). To some extent, *YWY2* neutralized tomboyism to an innocuous and ubiquitous gendering process for girls and young women in a heterosexual-dominated, Chinese-specific, party-state-endorsed feminist context that does not necessarily threaten heteronormative expectations for adult women. This manufacturing of young adult "tomboy" idols contributes to the imagining of China as an open-minded, globalized, inclusive society that appreciates the form of "tomboy power," selling the seemingly progressive ideas of female gender diversity and fluidity, female empowerment, and self-cultivation. Ultimately, I argue that the televisual representation (and documenting) of Liu's growing-up as a "tomboy" onscreen over the years demonstrates how Chinese entertainment media crops and regulates desiring queer female subjects in intertwined discourses of neoliberal reform, "feminisms with Chinese characteristics" (Zhu and Xiao 2021), and gender and sexual globalization. Diverging from the scholarship concerning the "crisis" of authenticity on reality TV (Banet-Weiser 2012; van Leeuwen 2001), my critical analysis demystifies this televisual discourse as an "authentic" elegy of younger generations of queer women in mainland China. The historicization of gendered local Chinese reality TV culture in this chapter poignantly and vividly records the social pressure, traumas, compromises, and sacrifices adolescent girls and young women of nonnormative gender and/or sexual identities are forced to face, experience, and cope with in real life.

Embracing Tomboyism in Mainland China

To unpack the unique subject-making and -negotiating processes revolving around tomboyism (rather than exclusively on identitarian lesbianism) in this study,[3] I use the terms "androgynous," "tomboyish," and "masculine" to describe norm-disruptive gendered personas and performances of young female stars on post-2010 Chinese reality TV and in mainland Chinese public and popcultural discourses generally. While the notion of androgyny usually describes people who "combine masculine and feminine or male or female traits or a person whose gender or sex is difficult to determine" (Califia 2004, 58), the word "tomboy" is used in this chapter to denote masculine or androgynous women who are widely believed by the public to be nonheterosexual, yet who may not be explicitly self-identified as such. Additionally, it is worth noting that most

---

3. The striving of nonnormatively gendered groups for sociocultural recognition and identity categorization can sometimes "resolve into new and counter-productive forms of identitarianism" (Halberstam 2012, 337).

of the well-known stars manufactured in the talent shows are adolescent girls or young women (under thirty years old), though there are some middle-aged Chinese female celebrities who exhibit visibly masculine personas, such as the fifty-year-old Tibetan musician Han Hong (as well as some "big sister" celebrities discussed in Chapter 2 in this book). Rather than being interpreted as a sign of adult lesbianism, their female masculinity is often reduced by mass media or by the celebrities themselves to "a gendered imitation of a preadolescent, asexual girl," thereby offering an imitated form of tomboyism (Zhao 2021b, 3).

The word "tomboyism" is a Western-originated notion that describes a form of female masculinity embodied by young (often prepubescent or adolescent) girls (Halberstam 1998). Unlike the adult lesbian identity of "butchness," tomboyism has been commonly considered as a transient gendered phase for women (Halberstam 1998; Martin 2010a), a "fashion statement" (Skerski 2011), a "protective identity" (Craig and LaCroix 2011), or girls' positive expressions of "self-assertion" and "independence" that are usually appreciated and rewarded in a (Western) masculinist society (Burn, O'Neil, and Nederend 1996). Frequently, because of social and psycho-physical changes (such as peer and social pressure, and "menstruation and the development of secondary sex characteristics"), masculine girls either are expected to "grow out of" this form of "childhood tomboyism" or will "self-regulat[e]" to conform to conventional adult femininity in a later stage of life (Burn, O'Neil, and Nederend 1996, 420; see also Hyde 1991; Martin 1990). In other words, tomboyism is a fluid, subjective gender display closely associated with girlhood in Western societies, the embodiment of which does not necessarily signal adult lesbianism (Carr 2005).

Nevertheless, shaped by cross-linguistic and trans-geocultural flows of queer politics and information, the meanings of tomboyism in the Chinese context, especially its relationship to lesbianism, have been rendered more intricate and multidimensional. As an imported term from modern Western sexology, the neologism "lesbianism" was only adopted after the modernization of China in the early twentieth century (Sang 2003). Nonetheless, Chinese female same-sex eroticism has had a long history that can be traced back to premodern times, the various paradigms and patterns of which were often made invisible (in the form of Confucian-charged heterosexual polygamous marriage or through female same-sex relationship's emphasis on "sentiment" rather than sexual encounters) to a Euro-American-centric or a contemporary heteropatriarchal position (Sang 2003; see also Martin 2010a). Meanwhile, the English word "tomboy" has been glocalized and rendered into "T" in the Chinese-speaking world, denoting a butch or masculine lesbian who presumably prefers the dominant, active role during same-sex sexual activities (Zhao 2021b). The term T/tomboy has been specifically widely known and used within post-2000 Chinese and Sinophone lesbian communities (Chao 2000; Engebretsen 2014; Kam 2013). Thus, unlike its loose linkage with adult lesbianism in the Western context, contemporary

Chinese tomboyism has a double edge that "potentially subverts both traditional feminine ideals and heteronormative expectations for women" (Zhao 2021b, 2). In turn, it can be used to refer to the female masculinity of girls or adult women who might or might not be nonheterosexual.

Admittedly, the Chinese and Sinophone worlds have a long history of female masculinity in both public and pop cultural spaces (Ho, Li, and Kam 2021, 130), which allocated women's androgynous or masculine behaviors and looks to forms of bravery, self-reliance, self-protection, ambition, moral power, or national-political adherence (Louie 2016). Nevertheless, modern knowledge and politics about T, as well as other queer female genders and sexualities, were circulated from Taiwan to mainland China in the late 1990s (Engebretsen 2014; see also Y. Hu 2019; Li 2015; Zhao, Yang, and Lavin 2017). In addition, there has been a sharp disparity in the public voicing and visibility of female homoeroticism in Taiwan and mainland China, especially after the Cultural Revolution years (Martin 2010a; Sang 2003). As Tze-lan D. Sang (2003) notes, since the 1990s, "the Taiwanese lesbian feminist persona is not just a new lesbian identity. It is an unprecedented public female identity" (245). This can also be seen from the rich and overt lesbian representations in post-2000 Taiwan's variety shows and reality singing competitions, where many masculine lesbian stars are (self-)identified or openly out and high-profiled on TV (Y. Hu 2019; Lu and Hu 2021; Zhao 2018b).

Conversely, mainland China has a more complicated historical trajectory concerning female masculinity, as well as lesbianism. The subjectivities of Chinese women have always been simultaneously enabled by and constrained within the country's self-modernizing and globalizing processes (Zhu and Xiao 2021, 24). In particular, since the founding of the People's Republic of China (PRC) in 1949, the state has engaged in the retooling of the gender, body, and sexuality of women to serve its "socialist modernization" (Barlow 2004, 38). The socialist subjectivization of woman as a national subject indeed greatly improved Chinese women's "social status, literacy rate, educational level, and workforce participation" (Zhu and Xiao 2021, 10). This socialist feminism became more salient during the years of the Cultural Revolution, which began in the mid-1960s. The government further emphasized gender equality during the Maoist years (even through some radical manners), some parts of which, according to many researchers, replaced gender issues with class struggles and silenced both women's individual gendered identity and "public discourses on sex" (Yang 1999, 40–42).

The best-known example of this is "socialist androgyny," which resulted from the state-backed gender-erasing and desexualizing of women in public spaces (Yang 1999; Yue and Yu 2008). For instance, some research shows that it encouraged a distorted sociocultural atmosphere that forced women to wear loose-fitting, plain-colored clothes, similar to men's attire (Honig 2002, 257). In addition to women's sartorial changes, aggressive behaviors among women and "female militancy (meant literally), if not ferocity, w[ere] valorized" during the revolutionary years (Honig 2002, 261–62). Consequently, this socialist androgyny criticized "women who tried to look 'feminine' . . . for their improper attitude" and eventually propagandized a "masculinization" of Chinese women during the Cultural Revolution (Brownell and Wasserstrom 2002, 251). Nonetheless, some other studies understand this critique of socialist feminism to be a self-legitimization of "postsocialist market Chinese feminism," the ultimate goal of which is to capitalize and marketize post-Mao Chinese society (Barlow 2004; Zhu and Xiao 2021, 15). For instance, as Jieyu Liu opines, within such a market-driven, individualist-masculinist society, "the Maoist image of strong, heroic women was ridiculed as a symbol of backward obstacles to China's modernization" (2007, 143–44).

Indeed, the socialist feminism in Maoist years achieved some progress in liberating young women and girls from Confucian gender ideals prevalent in feudal China (Honig 2002). Nonetheless, gender-based discrimination and exploitation of women in both the work and domestic spaces remained prevalent in Maoist and post-Mao China (Xiao 2014; Yang 1999). Further, the historically specific female masculinity, "sexual sameness," and "defeminization of female appearance" significantly shaped the representations of gender-nonnormative women in postsocialist public and pop cultures (Evans 1997, 2). As Ping Zhu and Hui Faye Xiao elaborate, a postmodern landscape has emerged in contemporary China, "where new Confucianism exists side by side with neoliberalism, where socialist aspirations merge with capitalist expansion, and where politics and culture join hands to cement the traditional gender hierarchy" (2021, 16). Taking one step further, my queer/ing examination of Liu's TV stardom does not conceive of Maoist and post-Mao gendered cultures as part of an essentialist binary structure. Rather, I uncover the ambivalent dimension of today's Chinese TV culture and industry in which the discourse of female masculinity—especially the youthful imaginaries and the specters of heteronormativity, male dominance, misogyny, and homophobia historically associated with it—has been reinvigorated as a useful, marketable element of China's nationalist-masculinist processes of neoliberalization, marketization, and globalization.

Entering the twenty-first century, along with the further globalization and industrialization of Chinese media and pop culture and the wide personal use of the Internet, "unprecedented intellectual exchanges . . . of information of gender, sexuality, feminism, and LGBTQ activism," along with cinematic and televisual representations of queer women from East Asia, Hong Kong, Taiwan, Australia, and Euro-America flowing through legal and underground venues, have together "enabled mainland China to become part of global and regional circulations of vocabularies, images, and knowledge about [female gender and] sexual minorities" (Wang 2021, 2; see also Engebretsen 2014; Ho et al. 2018; Kam

2014; Martin 2008; Rofel 2007; Kong 2020; Zhao, Yang, and Lavin 2017). As Lisa Rofel (2007) found, gender and sexual minorities have been actively making and negotiating their identities in a neoliberal China as "desiring" subjects under the national project of "cosmopolitanism with Chinese characteristics" (5, 116). This Chinese-specific, cosmopolitan-cum-neoliberal discourse emphasizes citizens' capabilities of "domesticating" and embodying cosmopolitanism and "individual responsibility and self-reliance," which can contribute to the official fantasy of a global, powerful China (Rofel 2007; Yan 2010). This discourse has been unpacked to account for the boom in the number of young, masculine female stars on mainland Chinese TV (J. Zhao 2016, 2018b). Meanwhile, some research draws upon the context-specific gendered history of female masculinity to explain the public tolerance and celebration of tomboyish celebrities, especially those manufactured during the second half of the 2000s in China, a still largely heteropatriarchal society (Huang 2013; Yue and Yue 2008). Furthermore, some Sinophone pop cultural studies have also conceptualized this phenomenon as part of a trans-Asian *zhongxing* (中性; neutral gender or sex) culture originating from the entertainment industries of Taiwan and Hong Kong in the 1980s (Y. Hu 2019; Li 2015; Lu and Hu 2021).

Indeed, *zhongxing* has been commonly employed in the promotional materials, official media accounts, and pop media reports of many post-2000 mainland Chinese reality talent shows featuring androgynous stars. The term has also been used by participants, viewers, and fans to refer to the queer images, styles, and personas on and off the stage (Zhao 2018b, 2019b). Nevertheless, unlike the relatively liberal, queer-friendly sociocultural environment in Hong Kong and Taiwan, contemporary mainland China remains an authoritarian-governed, heteronormative-structured society. Accordingly, while *zhongxing* is often closely associated with lesbianism in other Sinophone societies, it works as a mainstream, market-driven label in mainland China that emphasizes a contradictory "disassociation" of tomboyish stars and representations from politically charged lesbian identification and realities (Zhao 2018b, 2019b). In a more disturbing way, colluding with a normative, if not homophobic, rhetoric that interprets female gender non-normativities as "new" or "post-" feminist expressions, this *zhongxing* discourse in mainland China has contributed to the "depoliticizing" and erasing of the existence of female sexual non-normativities (such as the visibility of lesbians and bisexual or trans women) in public and pop cultural domains (Zhao 2018b, 2019b).

Against this complex backdrop, my employment of tomboyism underlines the ways in which young, masculine Chinese female stars (either voluntarily or forcibly) draw on the Chinese history of female masculinity and contemporary plural, Chinese-specific feminist thoughts to negotiate and (dis)identify with lesbianism on TV. More importantly, it puts an emphasis on tomboyish pop culture's conflicting relationships with emerging feminist and LGBTQ awareness in the mainstream society and entertainment industry of mainland China. Elsewhere, I have suggested that the growing knowledge of the general public about queer identity politics in post-2010 China, such as the identity of "iron T" (铁T; a Chinese-specific hypermasculine lesbian gender subjectivity, similar to the Western notion of "stone butch"—"a non-feminine, sexually untouchable" lesbian; see Halberstam 1998, 21), might have incurred the public condemnation directed at some androgynous celebrities (Zhao 2018b, 2021b). As discussed in more detail in Chapter 2 of this volume, this hostility toward certain tomboys' gender subjectivities sometimes originates from local self-identified feminist and queer groups (Zhao 2021b), who consider being "iron T" as a women-hating, male-imitating practice and misogynistic way to gain or sustain "access to male privileged spaces, activities, and conversations" (Abate 2011, 409; see also Craig and LaCroix 2011). In the following sections, my analysis explores the gendered dimension of Liu's tomboyish persona and its evolution over the years on TV. I show that her tomboyism has been carefully tailored from a visible hypermasculine image (connoting a T identity) to a desirable figure of a cosmopolitan, hard-working, self-motivated, attractive, androgynous woman—a form of "tomboy power." Her later tomboy persona, therefore, becomes a new figuration of a physically and mentally strong young woman whose gender display reflects a continuum of female masculinity and femininity. Her stardom produced through reality TV captures the process of her transformation into a representative of tomboy power sanctioned within contemporary Chinese socioeconomic and political-ideological discourses on female gender and sexuality.

Growing Up on Reality TV as a Tomboy

On February 16, 2012, Hunan TV initiated a new "talent teenager" (才艺少年) show, *Up Young! (Xiangshang ba! Shaonian)*. The term *shaonian* (少年) in the Chinese-language context is a "signifier for teenagers" (Song 2015, 29), which "primarily refers to a boy or a young man, but can also be used as an adjective that denotes youthfulness" (27). Using the term in its title not only delimited the show's preferred age range of participants, but also implied that it welcomed both teenage girl and boy participants. *Up Young!* featured a "conventional" talent show format that centered on grassroots participants and relied on judges' decisions. It included a preliminary selection, rounds of national competition, and player killing (PK) eliminations. In the preliminary selection, the show had more than 200,000 young Chinese-speaking participants from all over the world who were born in or after 1990 (China Daily 2012).

Besides presenting onstage competitions and offstage training, the show entailed many documentary-style sequences of the participants' monologues, media interviews, background stories, and personal impressions narrated by their friends, relatives, and competitors. Liu participated in the show as a fifteen-year-old teenage girl with a visibly masculine look and remarkable hip-hop dancing skills. She impressed both the judges and the audience by always wearing shorts, boyish hair, and androgynous outfits in yuppie or hip-hop styles. When dancing in a group with other young male participants, she sometimes dressed in an urban-style men's suit with a necktie, vest, dress shirt, or trilby hat. These masculine sartorial features and looks often led people to mistake her for a preadolescent boy and thus triggered heated discussions surrounding her gender both onstage and backstage.

For instance, after her onstage performances, the show's host and judges often asked other invited guests who did not know her well whether they could tell Liu's gender. Most of the received responses claimed that they could not tell whether Liu was a girl, but that Liu always looked very debonair and dashing. In a teaser of the show featuring Liu, her *jia xiaozi* (假小子; tomboyish; literally meaning "fake boy") look was put under the spotlight in interviews and monologues. At the beginning of this five-minute video clip with a gloomy undertone, Liu's mother, who was a professional local opera performer, expressed her worries about Liu's tomboyism by saying that "girls should have a girly look" (女孩应该有女孩的样子). Other participants also described Liu as a very quiet person who seemed to be ungregarious and asocial. In response to the doubts and worries, Liu explained several times in her monologue that she was not a "fake boy" but was just "being herself" (做自己). As she said, she had quite short hair because she disliked that many mischievous boys would tease and pull girly girls' long hair. Liu also considered her muscular body and men's outfits indispensable requirements for practicing the popping dance, which is masculine in nature and demands muscle strength. Although admitting in her monologue that she felt very lonely and misunderstood most of the time, Liu still received many compliments from the show's judges. After the show's six months of training and competition, with her outstanding performances and charisma, Liu won the title of "the most motivated youth" (最向上少年) and eventually formed the "Team of the Chinese Dream" (中国梦之队) with the six other best participants. This "dream" team represented mainland China to battle with youth teams from Taiwan, South Korea, and the United States in the last stage of the competition.[4]

As a reality show, *Up Young!* inadvertently revealed a Chinese tomboy's thorny path to survival and success. As Halberstam (1998) observed, "while childhood in general may qualify as a period of 'unbelonging', for the boyish girl arriving on the doorstep of womanhood, her status as 'unjoined' marks her out for all manner of social violence and opprobrium" (7). This program intensely depicts such a painful "reality": rather than considered a natural, legitimate gender display in female adolescence, Liu's embodiment of tomboyism was constantly

---

4. For the detailed competition course, see https://baike.baidu.com/item/%E5%90%91%E4%B8%8A%E5%90%A7%EF%BC%81%E5%B0%91%E5%B9%B4/3137271.

rejected, questioned, and disrespected by not only her peers but also by senior adults in her life as "deviant" and "unbecoming." As a teenager, during puberty, Liu wore a breast binder to flatten her chest. This is a common practice among some T-identified Chinese lesbians, who attempt to hide the development of breasts in order to pass as male in public or to decrease "the saliency of [their own] femaleness to [themselves] and others" (Burn, O'Neil, and Nederend 1996, 420; see also Halberstam 1998, 21). However, women's breast-binding and even passing as men in public, such as in military, athletic, or other male-dominated spaces, as ways to avoid sexist violence and the surveillance of women's bodies, were not rare in premodern and modern Chinese histories (Lei 2015; Jiao 2021). Following a similar logic, Liu's scrupulous explanation credited her breast-binding on and off the screen, as well as her tomboyism in general, to a combination of her professional needs, individual characteristics, fashion aesthetics, and sociocultural resistance to harassment from men or boys.

Unfortunately, this rendering of gender-norm insubordination as a manifestation of feminist subjectivity and personal choice awkwardly coerced her to "claim" her girlhood in a gender-binarist, male-gazing mainstream society, rather than leaving it self-evident (as either a rebellious tomboyish girl or a T lesbian). Her eventual triumph in the competition was enwrapped in a Chinese-specific, neoliberal-feminist environment that emphasized "self-fashioning," "self-motivation," and "self-empowerment," and was ultimately epitomized in the show's appropriation of the ideological discourse of the China Dream—"the unification of both domestic and periphery into a Confucian normative order" (Liu 2018, 109).

Although no one openly questioned her breast-binding at the time, the show's hosts always underscored her identity as "a girl" (一位女孩) and strived to negate the possibility of interpreting Liu's flat-chested body, as well as her tomboyish behaviors and attitudes, as that of a boy. Similarly, in her later participation in a dancing talent show, the Chinese version of *So You Think You Can Dance* (舞林争霸; Dragon TV, 2013), Liu wore a men's tank top and loose-fitting jeans, which further foregrounded her flat chest and muscular body.[5] Right before she started to perform in the open audition for the show, one of the male judges asked Liu with an almost affirming tone that "You are a boy, right?" Liu answered that she was a "girl." In the next shot, while the questioning judge exclaimed "You are a girl!?" with an incredulous gasp through the voiceover, the other male judge gaped in astonishment.

This dancing competition largely followed the original format of the American TV franchise of the same title, yet the Chinese version's unique highlight was its featuring of Jin Xing (金星)—the first male-to-female transgender

---

5. For example, see her images on the show at https://www.youtube.com/watch?v=6Hh KeK-4IJU.

TV personality in China—as one of the four judges overseeing the auditions and performance competitions. Jin is known as a public figure in mainland China and previously as a famous dancer who combined an intersected gender, sexual, and ethnic minority identity with a cosmopolitan, elitist background (Davies and Davies 2010). Self-presenting in mass media as a successful Chinese mother (with adopted ethnic-Chinese children) and wife in a transnational marriage with a German Caucasian businessman, Jin reconciled being transgender with a Chinese heteropatriarchal, neoliberal society, which she survived with a self-imagined desirable womanhood and a cosmopolitan citizenship. Jin's serving as a judge for the show to evaluate the competitions set up a relatively queer- and feminist-friendly, neoliberal ambience for the gender-nonnormative participants and performances.

This was made apparent when Jin delightfully commented on Liu's popping performance at the open audition while waving the pass ticket in her hand:

> Thanks to *SVG* and thanks to Li Yuchun, China has been brought into an era of *zhongxing* in a natural way. These kinds of girls with strong personalities had a hard time being accepted as "natural" (自然) by our society before. . . . The most invaluable thing is to respect nature, return to nature, and revert to nature, especially to restore the nature rooted in the innermost being of individuals. . . . What excited me the most today is that you (referring to Liu) are only fifteen years old. You have already mastered the dance and outperformed all the other popping boys. For this reason, you presented the best popping!

In this commentary, Jin deliberately linked Liu's tomboyism to her dancing skills and interpreted them together as a mixed exhibition of the *zhongxing* style (commodified and popularized eight years earlier through Li Yuchun's championship in the 2005 *SVG*) and a feminist practice that effectively challenges a male-dominated, masculine dance style. Jin's recounting of the recent hype of tomboyish stars in contemporary China not only normalized Liu's excessive masculinity as her individualism and inner self, but also tactfully disparaged the male judge's mistaking of Liu as a boy and his implied heteronormative model of gender conformity by emphasizing a self-imagined, open-minded Chinese society celebrating female gender diversity. While this strategy helped to resolve the awkwardness encountered by Liu, it also persistently pulled Liu's tomboyism back to a rhetoric on Chinese-specific neoliberal compliance with popular feminism.

This reconfiguration of tomboyism to a masculine manifestation of "girl power" can also be found in the 2016 girl group cultivation show *LadyBees* (蜜蜂少女队; Zhejiang TV; *LB* hereafter). Although Liu's performances received waves of applause and screams from both the audience and the judges in previous singing and dancing competitions, her career did not make significant progress until 2016. The show *LB* had a different "idol cultivation" (偶像养成)

format, appropriated from the South Korean idol-manufacturing and reality TV industries. The cultivation format captured the performers' hard work, personal growth, everyday life, and work struggles, along with the cruel processes of training, competition, and elimination in producing pop idols—a transformation that can last for months or even years. Before the show started in March 2016, it recruited 100 young female trainees to receive three months of basic training. As a competition aiming to select qualified trainees to form a girl band, the show chose two established male celebrities—Nicky Wu (吴奇隆) from Taiwan and Nicholas Tse (谢霆锋) from Hong Kong—as mentors to the contestants. This setup betrayed the intrinsic male gaze it spotlighted when cultivating the girl trainees.

Wu was particularly famous for being one of the three members of the well-known Taiwanese boy band the Little Tigers (小虎队), who made a sensation in Asia in the late 1980s and early 1990s. Liu was picked to be a member of Wu's team in the very first round of selection. Although largely sustaining a masculine look on the show, Liu demonstrated exceptional talents in not only singing and dancing but also in playing instruments and in musical composition, skills that Wu complimented as "versatile" (多才多艺).[6] On the show, Liu also proved her ability to be "versatile" in performing both masculine and feminine dancing styles. For instance, in the seventh episode of the show, Liu performed the piece "Magic Aladdin" (魔幻阿拉丁) with several other girls (China Entertainment Network 2016). In this dance performance adapted from the Middle Eastern folk tale in *One Thousand and One Nights*, Liu first dressed up as the male protagonist Aladdin and performed a Bollywood group dance mixed with hip-hop dance movements. During this cross-dressing part, she interacted with other female dancers who wore belly dance skirts in intimate, sexually alluring ways. In the middle of the performance, Liu disappeared from the stage. After the genie of the magic lamp was released, Liu returned to the stage in an Arabian women's dress to dance in a feminine style as the female protagonist, Princess Jasmine.[7] This was the first time that Liu had worn women's attire and performed a feminine belly dance on TV, and it was well-received and largely contributed to her later winning the competition.

In the late 2010s, mainland Chinese reality talent shows trended toward a "queer sensationalism," which produced queer images as attention-grabbing, profitable entertainment while strategically downplaying or negating the implied sexual nonnormativity of these queer-natured performances, personas, and celebrities (Zhao 2018b, 472). *LB*'s generic convention in "sensationalizing" Liu's "original" tomboyism and her gendered difference from, and same-sex tensions with, other feminine participants showcased this marketing strategy

---

6. See https://www.bilibili.com/s/video/BV1xQ4y1N7Mh.
7. See https://www.youtube.com/watch?v=AKPQh4wflJE.

well. Meanwhile, the show's centering of Liu's ability to switch between female masculinity and femininity on the stage also legitimized her tomboyism as a young woman's gendered expression and created some limited spaces for her to survive the heterosexual male gaze.

This remaking of Liu's tomboyism as "tomboy power," which embodied female gender fluidity and empowerment in a heterosexual male-dominated society and commercialized not only young women's feminine bodies but also tomboys' "flexibility" in pleasing both queer and normative gazes, became more salient after Liu's winning of the show. Her championship led to her debut in May 2016 as one of the seven members in the girl band LadyBees. In particular, the group's 2018 mini-album, "Queen Bee," was explicitly promoted as a record that aimed to escape the clichés of previous generations of girl bands, such as being "cute," "sexy," and "young." Instead, it highlighted the group members' real characters, charming talents, and journeys of the heart, and was produced based on the core concept of "a new age of girl power" (新女力时代; Sohu 2018). With the slogan "Be Yourself! Be Your Queen!", this album was said to demonstrate that "no matter whether your biological sex is male or female, your personality is outgoing or reserved, LadyBees is willing to bring you heart-inspiring strength. Being your own queen. Let's witness each other's growth. Let's get stronger together!" (Sohu 2018). Liu, as the center of the group, also starred in an online minifilm entitled *A New Age of Girl Power*.[8] In the film, Liu played the role of a masculine young woman who had dreamed of becoming a policewoman ever since she was a little girl. Although all the people around her kept denying this possibility, she worked hard to fight for gender equality and against sexism and eventually became an accomplished policewoman with her perseverance, courage, and bravery. While this framing unsurprisingly reconfigured Liu's tomboyism as a "positive" characteristic and as the power of young women who can contribute to social stability and equity, it also forcibly and overtly weaved it into the rhetoric of (tomboyish) girl power to market the girl band and its associated girl pop culture.

Youth with Tomboy Power on *YWY2*

LadyBees disbanded in May 2019, during a time when there was not only a growing knowledge of feminist and queer cultures in mainstream Chinese society but also a resurgence of hyperfemininity in Chinese girl pop. In late 2019, Liu's plan to participate in the new 2020 girl band cultivation show *YWY2* was revealed in cyberspace. The news led to the formation and protest of a large-scale online anti-fandom on Chinese social media platforms, such as Douban

---

8. See the minifilm here at https://www.bilibili.com/video/BV18A411E7d8/?spm_id_from=333.788.

and Weibo, even before the show was officially started. The anti-fan group mainly targeted tomboys, especially Liu, who was considered by many anti-fans as a potentially-T (or even an iron-T) pop star.[9] Since there were many tomboyish participants with similar styles in *YWY2*, the show was even jokingly renamed as "Youth with T" (青春有T) by some fans and audiences.

Both *LB* and *YWY2* were idol cultivation reality formats that only allowed female participants. Therefore, the female homosocial environment in the shows further encouraged a queer ambiance and same-sex tensions between the participants (Zhao 2018b). Yet, unlike the blatant commercial exploitation of queer images on previous reality shows and in response to the backlash against the mainstreaming of androgynous Chinese celebrities, *YWY2*, as one of the most popular idol reality programs in recent years, adopted a more subtle, carefully managed mentor-trainee format. In the pilot episode, the show introduced 109 girl trainees and a team of four mentors—Cai Xukun (蔡徐坤), Chen Chia-hwa (陈嘉桦; also known as Ella), Jony J, and Lalisa Manoban (also known as Lisa)—who oversaw the rating, training, and elimination of the trainees. To select the top nine trainees to form a girl group, the show was produced on the basis of "concept X" (X概念), which promoted the ideas of "non-defining and all infinite possibilities" (不定义，无限可能).[10] The core concept was a crafty hint at the show's meticulous marketization of young women's gender diversity, fluidity, and empowerment that, to a certain degree, transgressed scripted gender ideals and expectations in mainstream media and society.

For example, the mentorship system was not uncommon in many recent Chinese reality competitions borrowing their format from South Korea. However, the mentorship of *YWY2* was nonnormatively gendered. Three of the four mentors were at least once considered gender-nonnormative in their professional lives. Cai was a typical cosmopolitan young Chinese male idol (namely, "little fresh meat" or 小鲜肉) who studied in the United States and trained in South Korea as a teenage boy. His star persona had been heavily influenced by transnational queer images and inter-Asian androgynous beauty standards (Song 2022a). Cai was the champion of the 2018 boy band cultivation show *Idol Producer* (iQIYI) and has since been mocked by many netizens for his effeminacy and softness. In *YWY2*, Cai served as the "youth producer" (青春制作人) of the show, as well as a representative winner of a similar competition, to help manufacture the girl idols. The music mentor Ella was also known as the

---

9. Many of the anti-fan sites and posts online were either removed by the authors or deleted by the site administrators. Some information and discussions about the anti-fan discourse and practices can be found at https://www.zhihu.com/question/392507532/answer/1248291748.
10. See discussions of the show's concept at http://fun.youth.cn/gnzx/202003/t20200320_12249302.htm, and https://www.163.com/ent/article/F1KVCSCM00037VVV.html.

tomboyish (and once constantly labeled as *zhongxing* or *jia xiaozi*) member of the popular Taiwanese girl group S.H.E, which debuted in 2001 (Lu and Hu 2021, 184). While Ella had been rumored to be a T in the Sinophone music industry for years, her tomboyish persona gradually transformed into normative adult femininity as she began wearing womanly long hair, feminine dresses, and high heels in public, especially after she got married and gave birth in the early 2010s. In addition, the dance mentor Lisa was a Thai K-pop star in the globally influential South Korean girl group Blackpink. She had been famous for her boyish personality and has had a global-scale queer fanbase since her debut in 2016. Lisa's tomboyism, which is closely associated with her "immature, naughty, hip-hop style," non-East Asian exotic look, and Thai identity, has been fetishized and commodified in global K-pop queerbaiting discourse (Zhao 2021a, 1034).

Interestingly, both the groups S.H.E and Blackpink are excellent examples of "the local reworking of globalizing discourses of popular feminism and 'girl power'" (Lee and Yi 2020; Martin 2010b, 90). Presenting these three mentors together on the show fashioned an ultimate transnationally queer-feminist stage, where not only were various forms of gender-nonnormativity from different parts of Asia naturalized, commercialized, and centered, but also the linkage between gender-nonconforming personae and nonheterosexuality was powerfully denied (especially through the presence of Ella, who was tomboyish and rumored to be a T lesbian, but has become a successful wife and mother). In sharp contrast, the rap mentor and the only gender-conforming man on the stage, Jony J, was always very quiet and rarely provided feedback to the trainees after their performances. As he explained, this was because the music style of the trainees was not his specialty and thus beyond his knowledge. Nonetheless, representing a heterosexual male gaze, he frequently complimented Liu's rap skills and dancing as very charming.

In the first round of rating all the trainees, when Liu showed up on the stage, Cai said that he knew Liu well and had watched a lot of Liu's online training videos. Then he suddenly asked Liu, "Do you think you are making progress [over the years]?" In the next shot, the camera caught the reaction to this bold question, which made many trainees who were sitting under the stage gasp in shock. The question contained a twist because Cai and Liu had crossed paths eight years earlier. In 2012, when Liu won the *Up Young!* competition, Cai only finished as one of the top 200 contestants in the same show. Yet even though they were both young androgynous idols, Cai had risen to pop star status in 2018 and was qualified to serve in 2020 as the mentor for Liu, who once outperformed him but remained a trainee in *YWY2*. In response to this strident question, Liu hesitated for a short moment and confirmed that she had made progress in her performance and music. After hearing this response, Cai asked Liu to start her performance to prove it to the others.[11]

This episode seemed to be abrupt or even hostile. Nevertheless, throughout the course of the show's training and battling, Cai was simultaneously caring and strict with the gender-norm-defying girls. For example, after several rounds of rating and elimination, the show presented a short episode of an offstage, talk show-style, experience-sharing conversation between Cai and the trainees.[12] In this conversation, Liu said that she would like to ask Cai a "private question" about his advice on how to deal with the doubts about the idols' nonnormative personal characteristics, which were repetitively questioned and criticized in mainstream society. In his frank response, Cai admitted that he had faced this "issue" (referring to the questions and attacks on his own nonconforming persona) for years. After narrating his awkward experiences and struggles with his androgyny on the stage, he told Liu that "when your [gender] style is different from others, there would definitely be different voices [complimenting and criticizing you]. But, when you are different from others, there would definitely be people who appreciate you because you are different." Through this conversational, self-narrating style, Cai not only provided encouragement and advice to Liu but also to the tomboyish girls on the show and in the audience.

In a later recorded conversation, entitled "Liu is brave enough to refuse to be defined," between Yang Tianzhen (杨天真), a famous celebrity agent in mainland China, and the trainees, Liu narrated her own painful experience of being a tomboyish girl in the Chinese entertainment industry.[13] As Liu revealed, she felt that she had outstanding competition records and capabilities, yet had experienced a lack of popularity in the entertainment industry even after years of rigid training. Liu was frustrated that even though she believed that everyone should be free-spirited and refuse to be defined by norms, her look was always defined by others and even blamed as the main reason for the lack of success and disbanding of her former girl band, LadyBees. After hearing this, Yang rhetorically asked Liu, "Is there another possibility that you are not good enough yet to let others ignore your nontraditional look and pay full attention to your potential in becoming an idol?" Yang also suggested Liu work harder to make people see her potential instead of only focusing on her look.

Research finds that "the act of talking" on TV is "the very technology of re-subjectification" (Yu 2009, 68). This is especially evident through TV talk shows, which are "a new form of confession that testifies to state strategies about

---

11. iQIYI, "*Youth With You 2* Clip: All the Trainees Screamed for Xin Liu's Performance," video, 3:15, March 21, 2020, https://www.youtube.com/watch?v=Eip_FYZUj_Q.
12. PPTV, "Liu Yuxin Wanted to Ask Cai Xukun a Personal Question, but Cai Xukun Panicked," video, 1:36, accessed July 1, 2021, http://v.pptv.com/show/4SCIA2vRQXiciaYMg.html.
13. iQIYI, "XIN Liu Bravely Shows Her Real Undefined Self | *Youth With You 2* | iQIYI," video, 4:30, May 16, 2020, https://www.youtube.com/watch?v=M3w1h8iUbfw.

'human improvement' and social control to achieve . . . the 'exemplary society' in China" (Yu 2009, 69). Also, as Helen Wood notes, "telling the self, working on the self, and potentially transforming the self are common traits" of reality TV and makeover programs that became popular during the neoliberalization of Western culture and politics (2009, 27). Following a similar logic, the hybrid formats of *YWY2* verified a Chinese-specific, neoliberal-feminist discourse, in which tomboys were persuaded to work on and transform themselves into desirable, marketable female subjects to "make up" for their tomboyism (and its associated nonheterosexuality), which remains a disagreeable element in a heteronormative society. Cai's advice for Liu aimed to offer support while retaining her more tomboy-friendly or queer-supportive fans. In contrast, Yang's response inspired Liu to strategically cater to the still-dominant male gaze and her anti-fans who despised tomboyism or were homophobic. Both conversations positioned Liu as a tomboy idol in a Chinese-specific neoliberal context and advocated practices of self-assurance and self-improvement, instead of challenging the deeply rooted capitalist-masculinist manipulation and deprecation of young gender and potentially sexual minorities.

In the next cooperative stage, with mentors following the conversations, Liu chose to work with the dance mentor Lisa for the famous song "I'm Not Yours," originally performed by Taiwanese female pop star Jolin Tsai (蔡依林) and Japanese female pop star Namie Amuro. The song promotes girls' resolution, determination, and freedom to be themselves in love relationships and is appreciated as a work of "girl power" (McCarthy 2015). For this stage, Liu was convinced to wear a wig, women's shorts, and a pair of feminine calf-length boots to perform this flirty yet sassy girly hip-hop group dance led by Lisa.[14] Intriguingly, the other visibly tomboyish trainee, Lu Keran (陆柯燃), who also was harshly attacked by the online anti-fans for being an "iron-T," joined the same performance with a similar feminine costume. As the dance leader and mentor for the collaborative stage, Lisa was surprised to see Liu (as well as Lu) choosing her team, which would perform a feminine yet powerful dance. Despite the doubts and frustration during practice, the cooperative stage with Lisa was successful. In addition to other strategies, such as "emphasizing their exquisite, heavy makeup, luxurious jewelry, and soft and nurturing personalities" throughout the competition (Zhao 2021b, 5), this "girl power" stage, as part of the tomboyish trainees' audiovisual responses to their anti-fandom, further contributed to the recuperation of their assumed iron-T identity onstage as "brave, defiant, progressive [de-lesbianized] young women who can learn to perform both feminine and masculine traits" (Zhao 2021b, 6; see also Zhao 2019b).

---

14. iQIYI, "Collab stage: 'I'M NOT YOURS' of Lisa Group | Youth With You 2 |iQIYI," video, 5:09, May 24, 2020, https://www.youtube.com/watch?v=oNMz3GOH_L0.

This "girl power" reinvention of tomboyism was further deployed in the final episode of *YWY2* on May 30, 2020. In April 2020, Liu was voted to be the center position in the group performance of the show's theme song "Yes! OK!" in the final episode. Afterward, her tomboyism was further criticized by many audience members and anti-fans for not being properly feminine in a girl group cultivation show.[15] During the backstage interview, Liu responded:

> I feel topics like whether girls like us can perform girl group dances should be discussed only in the last century. I want to be myself. Girls rated as A-class (the best rating in the show) like us can pull off any style. Bravery is our only response.[16]

In the episode showing the trainees' practicing the performance for the last time, Cai saw Liu as the only one in the dance group who was wearing boyish shorts instead of girly skirts. He asked Liu if she was under a lot of pressure. Liu said yes and admitted that she was thinking about whether she should change back to a skirt. But because this show was about infinite possibilities, she decided to wear shorts. While the other trainees applauded her response, Cai comforted her by saying that it was okay to feel stressed, and he would stand with Liu to face the pressure together.

The last performance in the show's final episode, before the eventual ranking of the trainees was revealed, was singing the song "For Every Girl" (给女孩). It was performed by the most famous tomboyish idol in contemporary Chinese TV history, Li Yuchun, together with all the trainees who had participated in the competition of *YWY2*.[17] The lyrics of the song, which were written by Li in 2019, convey ideas of young women's vitality, self-recognition, and empowerment:

> Please believe that you are a very beautiful being
> No need to doubt that
> This is a unique color in the universe
> May you be treated tenderly by the world
> Love fills your heart
> Let go of all defenses and be free
> Look up to the sky, broaden your mind
> Hold tight to the beloved
> Black hair into white, never stop dreaming
> Do what you gonna do

---

15. See, for example, Elfish, "Liu Yuxin Becomes the Center Position of the Theme Song of *Youth With You 2!*" Goody25 (blog), April 6, 2020, https://www.goody25.com/mind7483993.
16. See, Sina Video, "Liu Yuxin Responded about Wearing Pants to Record the Theme Song," video, 0:32, April 5, 2020, https://k.sina.cn/article_5522810625_m1492f670103300ps2g.html?from=ent&subch=oent.
17. See, iQIYI TW, "Pure Share of *Youth With You 2*: 'For Every Girl' Chris Lee's Best Wishes to the Trainees | iQIYI TW," video, 4:33, May 30, 2020, https://www.youtube.com/watch?v=Tc87rVc1UPc.

All the girls
People do what you gonna do
May you see the scenery through the seasons
Still keep the original intention
Brave, healthy, independent
Reflect on life
Do what you gonna do
May your dream come true
No matter how far you travel
Sparks in your heart[18]

Recognized as a positive, encouraging song by and for women, "For Every Girl" was highly reputed and made into a music video for the celebration of International Women's Day by the official media outlet, *People's Daily*, on March 8, 2020.[19] The song and its music video were also widely promoted and circulated on several state-authorized official women's organization sites, such as womenvoice.cn.[20]

When performing this state-sanctioned "girl power" song on *YWY2*, all the eliminated girls, standing in two lines on the stage, started singing the chorus part. Then the camera switched to Li, who sang alone with a guitar at the center of the stage. When she was singing the line "all the girls" repeatedly, she turned around to face the back of the stage. And then, the background screens opened, and the top twenty trainees walked onto the stage. Li waved her hands to the finalists and walked toward them. The finalists bowed to Li and joined her to sing the song together. In the climax of the performance, Li and Liu stood side by side at the center of the stage as all the other trainees sang in chorus with them. In the last scene of the performance, the camera revolved around Li, who finished the last part alone with all the trainees dancing and waving in the background.

In this way, this sensational performance staged an epic and particularly queer-essenced moment, though conditioned within an entangled Chinese-specific neoliberal-feminist discourse. On the one hand, it centered Chinese tomboyish reality TV stars of different generations, who strategically positioned themselves as representatives of female gender freedom and as symbols of Chinese feminist progress in recent years, with the help of the increasingly globalized, capitalized TV and music industries in mainland China. On the other hand, the dazzling scene in this reality TV program visualized the loneliness, frustration, sacrifice,

---

18. The English version of the song's lyrics is adapted from this site: https://www.echinesesong.com/gei-nv-hai-%E7%BB%99%E5%A5%B3%E5%AD%A9-to-the-girl-lyrics-%E6%AD%8C%E8%A9%9E-with-pinyin-by-li-yu-chun-%E6%9D%8E%E5%AE%87%E6%98%A5-chris-lee/.
19. See, Sohu, "Chris Lee's 'For Every Girl' Dominates the Internet! *People's Daily:* May You Be Treated Tenderly by the World . . . ," March 9, 2020, https://www.sohu.com/a/378823410_627450.
20. See https://www.womenvoice.cn/html1/report/2003/2198-1.htm.

camaraderie, proliferation, and situational freedom that defiant young women in mainland China had pulled and pushed through in the past fifteen years.

Conclusion

The show *YWY2* was held during the most distressing period of the global pandemic, during a time when mainland China was unambiguously criticized for its widespread sexism and misogyny during the early stages of the outbreak (Y. Yang 2022). This might partly explain why the official media appropriated the song "For Every Girl" for its celebration of women's beauty on International Women's Day. This official feminist appropriation of tomboyish girls on reality talent shows might also encourage the emergence of "tomboy power" under the camouflage of popular feminist rhetoric. The notion of "girl power" as part of the popular feminism in contemporary female idol and girl group industries has been understood as a capitalist way to commodify and market "female sexual empowerment" in a "context of neoliberal compliance with post-feminism and . . . the increasing commercialization of young femininities" (Kim 2011, 335; see also Gill 2007; Kim 2019; McRobbie 2009). Similarly, as demonstrated in this chapter, this "tomboy power" can be seen as a hybrid result of a commercial appropriation of female gender defiance and local feminist history, interdigitated with both the revival of Confucian traditions and an enhanced awareness of global and transcultural feminist and queer knowledge and politics among the general public.

Undeniably, this queer televisual history signals new and promising visual-cultural narratives of Chinese tomboys in mass media in the post-2010 years. But it often limits, and even eliminates, the imagining of gender and sexual diversities within lesbian communities in a market-driven media space that paradoxically imagines itself as feminist-awakening, women-centered, and cosmopolitan, just as it is highly heteronormative. Ironically, this history, exemplified by Liu's tomboyism on TV,

> offers a unique vantage point for assessing why certain models of queer life [have] been conferred a degree of relative acceptance in contemporary popular culture, whilst others, those which might challenge particular normative logics of sexuality, gender and the self, remain beyond the peripheries of mainstream public discourse. These less normative subject positions are not screened out of mainstream media, mainstream media does not produce them. (Lovelock 2019, 24)

As a result, this discourse on how reality TV manufactures queer female stars in mainland China illustrates the ways in which a desirable queer female subject is produced and reconfigured. Regarding popular and public cultural imaginings of tomboyism, Fran Martin (2010a) once identified two popular modes of tomboy representation in contemporary Chinese-language media: one is the "memorial mode," in which young tomboys vanish from their feminine lesbian partners' adult life; the other is "tomboy melodrama," which tends to ghettoize tomboys (13–14, 132–35). What this chapter has unveiled is a different, yet no less melancholy, tomboy tale in post-2010 mainland Chinese entertainment. It delimits a somber popular cultural scenario where only certain tomboys with "feminist" potential and market value can be imagined in adult life, while many undesirable queer women growing up without such "tomboy power" still face brutal real-life stigmatization, marginalization, silencing, and erasure.

2
When *"Jiquan"* Fandom Meets "Big Sisters"

The Ambivalence between Female Queer (In)Visibility and Popular Feminist Rhetoric in Sisters Who Make Waves

Jia Guo and Shaojun Kong

Introduction

In the summer of 2020, a unique girl group cultivation reality show[1] (女团养成真人秀) entitled *Sisters Who Make Waves* (乘风破浪的姐姐) gained enormous attention and success in China. On the night of its debut on Mango TV,[2] *Sisters Who Make Waves* (hereafter *SWMW*) drew over 307 million views; a hashtag tied to the Chinese name of this show attracted 18 billion views on Weibo, a Chinese social media platform equivalent to Twitter.[3] Different from other music band cultivation shows, whose participants are usually younger unknown trainees, the first season of *SWMW* invited thirty female singers, actresses, and media personalities aged 30 to 52 who were highly accomplished in their respective fields.[4] The mature, independent, and brave personas of "big sisters" that these women represent in the show coincide with the preference of *jiquan* (姬圈; lesbian circle) fandom, a kind of queer female fandom that has emerged in recent Chinese subculture. This chapter explores the ambivalent relations between queer female visibility and popular feminist rhetoric on mainland Chinese TV through *jiquan* fans' queer readings of *SWMW*.

---

1. Idol group cultivation reality shows originated with the South Korean reality TV show *Produce 101* in 2016. Typically, idol group cultivation reality shows place large numbers of same-sex trainees from different agencies in competition by singing and dancing individually and in groups. The most popular competitors are identified by the audience, usually through online voting. After the show, the winners debut as a new idol group, but for a limited time. In the next one or two years, the new groups release new songs or albums and perform in public. After the contract period, the group will be disbanded.
2. Mango TV is the online broadcaster of Hunan TV.
3. The statistics can be viewed at https://pandaily.com/how-female-empowerment-advanced-mango-tvs-video-streaming-business/.
4. The celebrities cast in the show are mostly self-presenting as heterosexual women. Although several single celebrities are rumored to be queer women, they have never verified their nonheterosexuality in public.

The *jiquan* fans' reading of *SWMW* enriches queer TV culture in mainland China. In this chapter, we use queer/queerness to refer to the expressions, performances, representations, and celebration of nonnormative gender and sexual identities and desires (Griffin 2017). Retrospectively, mainland Chinese TV culture has witnessed a range of queer spectacles in the new millennium. Singing competition reality TV shows have featured androgynous performers and negotiated with traditional gender and sexual ideals (Bassi 2016; Kam 2014; Zhao 2018c). TV dramas adapted from boys' love (BL) online fictions have highlighted the tension of government censorship amidst the highly commercialized industry and increasingly diversified fan practices (Ng and Li 2020; Wong 2020). Narratives of transgender and gender-bending experiences have emerged in TV programs under the guise of historical, time-traveling, and "immortal hero" genres (Zhao 2019a). Fan communities have produced various forms of queer fantasy, from same-sex love fan fictions based on either fictional characters or reality TV celebrities (C. Zhang 2016; Zhao 2017c) to fan-made videos which subvert the gender and sexual canons of original televisual materials (Wang 2020b). *SWMW*, as a new hit, provides its female fans with a playground in which to project their queer desires and understandings of nonnormative female genders and sexualities, which encourages the formation of a *jiquan* fandom.

Jiquan fandom thrives along with local and global flows of LGBTQ information and flourishing youth culture in contemporary China (Xiao 2020). According to our observations of online *jiquan* communities on Douban Groups (豆瓣小组) from December 2019 to November 2020,[5] many *jiquan* fans identify themselves as lesbian or bisexual women. Although the claimed identities online do not necessarily evidence their real-life identities, *jiquan* fans often accept and celebrate lesbianism. While cis-male homoerotic/homosocial imaginaries dominate mainland Chinese queer TV as well as its fandoms, *jiquan* fandom provides women with a fannish space to express their queer interests and desires. With *jiquan* fandom, lesbian culture and images become more visible in Chinese cyberspace.

Interestingly, *jiquan* fandom offers an alternative to the dominant aesthetics of previous queer female star and fan cultures prevalent in the Chinese and

---

5. Douban Groups, an attached function of the popular Chinese communicative platform Douban, provides forums for fans of movies, TV shows, music, and broad topics of youth culture. We joined the *jiquan* fan community *Jiquan* Gossip Group (姬圈八卦小组, found at https://www.douban.com/group/jiquan/) in December 2019. As of December 2020, the group has more than 17,000 members. We also conducted online observations of other similar communities as non-members, such as the Non-Straight Goose Group (弯弯的鹅小组, found at https://www.douban.com/group/617624/) and *Jiquan* Friends who Love Idol Groups, Cultivation Shows and CPs Group (喜欢搞团搞秀磕cp的姬友小组, found at https://www.douban.com/group/688326/). These fannish spaces are open to the general public; any unregistered visitor can browse the forums' content, but they cannot leave comments.

Sinophone worlds. In the past, discussions in queer Sinophone female fandoms mainly focused on *zhongxing* (中性, which translates to "neutrosexual" or "gender-neutral") celebrities or media characters (Bassi 2016; Kam 2014; Zhao 2018b). However, in *jiquan* fandom, female celebrities and characters with a more feminine appearance and mature persona are more welcomed, and are often labeled as "big sisters" by the fans. For instance, Australian actress Cate Blanchett, who played a middle-aged lesbian in the romantic film *Carol* (dir. Todd Haynes, 2015), and American actress Amy Acker, who played the main character Root in the TV show *Person of Interest* (CBS, USA, 2014), are queerly iconized in Chinese *jiquan* fan communities. Such independent, strong-minded, and capable female characters are often recognized as "feminist" by the general public. However, while *jiquan* fans hold a celebratory attitude toward both nonheterosexuality and feminism, many take a normative stance on female femininity. A "big sister" recognized in *jiquan* fandom is a capable, mature woman and often also a "feminist," but she is expected to look traditionally feminine, attractive, and gentle. On the contrary, female masculinity is often marginalized in *jiquan* fandom, and biases such as elitism and lookism are very commonly seen in *jiquan* fans' queer imaginaries.

One important reason that *SWMW* has attracted *jiquan* fans is the show's successful presentation of the "big sister" persona. By inviting female celebrities over the age of thirty to train and compete together, *SWMW* showcases a (quasi-)feminist discourse that emphasizes female competitiveness, power, maturity, and elitism. In this sense, *jiquan* fans' gossip about *SWMW* and its celebrity contestants becomes valuable to analyze how queer female fans watch, discuss, and fantasize about such "big sister" personas on Chinese TV. Drawing on Sarah Banet-Weiser's (2018) notion of "popular feminism"—a new visibility for commercialized feminism in consumer societies—this chapter proposes that the *jiquan* fandom of *SWMW* is complicated by the show's popular feminist rhetoric.

In this research, we employ non-participant online observation to collect *jiquan* fans' queer gossip in the *Jiquan* Gossip Group and the *Sisters Who Make Waves* Group (hereafter *SWMW* Group).[6] The former is one of the main *jiquan* fan communities in Douban Groups, and the latter is a popular fan forum of *SWMW*. In *SWMW* Group, there are both *jiquan* fans who enjoy the show and mainstream (non-queer) fans who are not interested in or even repel queer readings of the show. The non-participant online observation method allows researchers to look for patterns in "posted but not personally identifiable information" on social

---

6. See the *Sisters Who Make Waves* Group (乘风破浪的姐姐小组) at https://www.douban.com/group/689431/. We use two ways to identify *jiquan* fans in the *SWMW* Group: first, some fans self-identify themselves as *jiquan* fans; second, a user's individual profile on Douban shows the groups that this user often visits. Fans that we identify as *jiquan* fans often visit *jiquan* fandom groups such as the *Jiquan* Gossip Group, *Jiquan* Friends who Love Idol Groups, and Cultivation Shows and CPs Group, and so forth.

media sites or in online discussion groups, yet not involve themselves in interactions with the online communities (Salmons 2015, 152). The method enables us to analyze *jiquan* fans' "self-making" and highlight their agency in online queer gossip (Leung 2008, 91).

In the following study, we first explore the emergence of popular feminist rhetoric in Chinese TV culture along with neoliberal rationality, and explain how the popular feminist rhetoric of *SWMW* has nourished its *jiquan* fandom. Then, we discuss the complex (re)imaginations surrounding female gender identity and lesbianism in *jiquan* fandom. With increased flows of LGBTQ knowledge and culture in mainland China, *jiquan* fandom not only exhibits a more explicit connection to lesbianism compared to previous Chinese queer fandoms devoted to female TV stars and characters, but also creates a new gender hierarchy in the reimagined female gender ideals. Through a discourse analysis of *jiquan* fans' readings of Zhu Jingxi (朱婧汐) and Wan Qian (万茜), two "big sister" competitors in *SWMW*, the chapter demonstrates how *jiquan* fans manufacture an ideal queer female image. These fannish imaginaries reveal an enhanced, though problematic, queer female visibility enabled by contemporary Chinese TV's popular feminist context. Finally, the chapter concludes with findings on the entanglement between *jiquan* fandom and popular feminist rhetoric. We argue that, while both challenging and being complicit in the discourses of heteropatriarchy and commercialization, *jiquan* fandom marginalizes masculine queer women and promotes elitism and lookism in lesbian culture. Ultimately, this study shows the ambivalent relations between the visibility of female queerness and neoliberal popular feminist discourses in the context of contemporary Chinese TV.

SWMW, Popular Feminism, and Elitist "Big Sisters"

Originating from South Korea's idol industry, girl group cultivation reality shows have achieved constant success after being adapted in China since 2018. Popular Chinese video-streaming platforms have produced their own idol group cultivation reality shows with subsequent seasons. Unlike the idol girl groups in Japan, whose targeted audiences are mainly heterosexual men (Galbraith and Karlin 2012), Chinese idol girl group cultivation reality shows are produced for audiences predominantly consisting of urban, educated young women. To attract this group of audience, (quasi-)feminist cultures have been (re)produced in these shows. *SWMW* is one of the most well-received examples in manufacturing "big sister" images (C. Wu 2020), which are also a major focus of *jiquan* fans' fantasies.

The rhetoric in *SWMW*, no matter whether it is feminist or quasi-feminist, can be conceptualized as a form of popular feminism. Banet-Weiser (2018) defines popular feminism as the accessible practices and conditions circulating in media culture that expose some types of feminism to a broad public, such as celebrity feminism and corporate feminism. She argues that the high, spectacular visibility of a safely affirmative feminism eclipses a feminist critique of structure, "as if *seeing* or purchasing feminism is the same thing as changing patriarchal structures" (Banet-Weiser 2018, 4). What stands behind popular feminism is a gendered neoliberal rationality (Banet-Weiser, Gill, and Rottenberg 2019). Although *SWMW* attempts to express feminist beliefs by highlighting the empowerment of mature women, it often fails to challenge the policing of women's bodies, rooted in the capitalism-consumerism matrix. With the slogan "Life begins at thirty; Youth returns from now on" (三十而骊, 青春归位), *SWMW* claims to smash ageism faced by Chinese women through manufacturing the "big sister" persona characterized by female maturity, bravery, and confidence. Seemingly, the show is more "feminist" than many other Chinese TV programs that feature marital and mother-child relationships, yet its celebrity participants are still appraised, consumed, and favored for their attractive appearances, svelte figures, dewy skin, unrealistic pep, and extreme self-discipline, which do not challenge the "fashion-beauty complex" of the heteropatriarchal matrix (McRobbie 2009). Moreover, the "big sister" persona in *SWMW* is no doubt elitist. As famous actresses, singers, or TV personalities, the privileged "big sisters" in the show have the capital to maintain their youthful looks, accept challenges in their careers, and assert that they are not afraid of getting old.

SWMW's "big sister" image is also successfully embedded into the *jiquan* fans' queer readings. Rosalind Gill (2017, 614) argues that "queer spaces are increasingly shaped by neoliberal values," such as the proliferation of LGBTQ corporate and celebrity successes in Western countries. While girls and young women are targeted as the ideal neoliberal subjects (Banet-Weiser 2012; Gill and Scharff 2011; McRobbie 2009), queer women are no exception (McNicholas-Smith and Tyler 2017). In postsocialist Chinese society, LGBTQ groups are also disciplined by neoliberal ideologies as other social groups (Ong and Zhang 2011; Yang 2007; Y. Zhang 2014). For instance, an online Chinese podcast, distributed by *Bie Girls* (BIE的女孩, a Chinese we-media channel focusing on broad topics concerning gender, feminism and LGBTQ), uses "sunshine middle-class good gay" (阳光中产好gay) to criticize the homonormativity of gay males represented in Chinese popular cultures.[7] Similarly, "big sister" images that *jiquan* fans favor have produced a new (though not yet as prevalent as the "sunshine middle-class good gay") homonormativity (with Chinese characteristics) for lesbians. "Big sisters" are mature-minded, capable, independent, educated, feminine, and beautiful women. They are the ideal lesbian images in *jiquan* fandom. Such an ideal not only incorporates heteropatriarchal norms of female bodies and appearances, but also connotes social hierarchies. To some extent, *jiquan* fandom popularizes a new, Chinese-specific kind of female homonormativity through its queer idealization of "big sisters."

---

7. See https://shows.acast.com/bierenxing/episodes/073.

A Burgeoning *Jiquan* Fandom

In recent years, the character "*ji*" (姬) has been widely used by Chinese netizens to denote lesbian identity, and is particularly prevalent in online young lesbian communities and queer female fan spaces. In Chinese, "姬" is a homophonous character of "基,"[8] a Cantonese transliteration of the English word "gay" widely used in Chinese-speaking regions to refer to (mainly male-engaged) homosexuality. The use of "姬," instead, emphasizes both queer female gender and sexuality. One noteworthy feature of *jiquan* fandom is its strong link to lesbian culture. Although China remains a heteropatriarchal-structured society, urban youth have shown increasingly open, friendly attitudes toward homosexuality in recent years (Ho 2009; Lin et al. 2016; Rofel 2007). Meanwhile, online Chinese queer fan communities provide a way for younger generations to reconfigure normative genders and sexualities (Yang and Bao 2012; C. Zhang 2016; Zhao, Yang, and Lavin 2017). Nevertheless, in the past decade, Chinese fans in queer female fandoms have often separated their queer imaginations from real-life lesbianism and LGBTQ politics (Zhao 2014; 2018c). In a study of the queer fandom of the 2006 season of *Super Voice Girls* (Hunan TV), Jamie J. Zhao (2014, 2) demonstrates that fans usually projected "normative cultural positions" drawn from heteronormative ideologies onto their virtual queer imaginations. Zhao argues that queer female fandom acted as "a middle ground" between "queer fantasies about media characters" and "normative notions of deviant lesbianism" (2014, 3). However, with reference to the subcultural meaning of "*ji*," *jiquan* fans in more recent years often embrace lesbian identities of both themselves and their fannish objects.

Most participants in *jiquan* fandom self-identify as lesbian or bisexual women. For example, on the main page of the *Jiquan* Gossip Group on Douban Groups, the administrator of the group states, "Discussing [celebrity] gossip in the Les Sky Group (天空组) doesn't feel right,[9] and discussing *baihe* (百合) in those gossip groups is even less regarded. So . . . we combined these two and created this group."[10] *Baihe* is a local Chinese term appropriated from a Japanese ACG (Animation, Comics, and Games) concept—*yuri*, a media genre of female intimacies. In *jiquan* fandom, the usage of *baihe* tends to refer to both "girls' love" and lesbianism. This description indicates that the participants of the *Jiquan* Gossip

---

8. The pronunciation of 基 is also *ji*. In this chapter, *ji* is only used to refer to 姬—that is to say, female homosexuality, homoeroticism, and homosociality.
9. The Les Sky Group (天空组, located at https://www.douban.com/group/lala/) is the most popular online lesbian community on Douban Groups. Most discussions in this Group focus on real-life scenarios such as dating life, how to come out to family or friends, and so forth.
10. This description was posted by Qianshuiting (潜水艇) on March 26, 2016. It can be viewed at https://www.douban.com/group/jiquan/.

Group, at least its early members, also participate in the Les Sky Group, a famous online Chinese lesbian community. Some *jiquan* fans share anecdotes about their personal life as lesbians as well and discuss questions about lesbian relationships in the *Jiquan* Gossip Group.[11] Numerous fan discussions in the *Jiquan* Gossip Group focus on non-Chinese female celebrities, such as Kristen Stewart, who have come out to the public as lesbian or bisexual women.[12] Queer female identities—especially lesbian identities—and female homoerotic relations are displayed, discussed, and explicitly celebrated in *jiquan* fandom.

In the Chinese TV industry, where queer female identities and relations remain underrepresented, *jiquan* fandom provides a viable space to voice female homoerotic desires. Jamie J. Zhao (2020a, 473) points out that "cis-male-centered homoerotic or homosocial cultural scenarios" dominate post-2010 mainstream Chinese entertainment market and queer fan cultures. Even under strict censorship of homosexual content, BL-adapted TV dramas (耽改剧) have had the chance to air on satellite TV channels (as discussed in other chapters in this anthology), and a group of young male celebrities have gained fame by starring in these kinds of dramas or through displaying homosocial sentiments in public. However, Chinese TV dramas and reality programs often encourage a misogynistic attitude toward female homosociality by representing gossip, drama, and envy among female characters or participants (Ji 2020). In the *Jiquan* Gossip Group, fans have discussed why *baihe* movies and TV shows are relatively rare in mainland China, while BL-adapted TV dramas are extremely popular.[13] In a largely misogynistic TV environment, the popular feminist rhetoric which has

---

11. These kinds of posts can be evidenced by the following examples: "I came out to my colleague," posted by yisuda, at 12:42:54 on June 2, 2019, can be viewed at https://www.douban.com/group/topic/142215467/; "How you and your girlfriend/ex-girlfriends met," posted by Yuanshanchongying (远山重影) at 21:39:41 on April 10, 2020, can be viewed at https://www.douban.com/group/topic/170935975/; "I did not tell a senior that I liked her, and then she is with my classmate," posted by Yinhenaiyoudangaoga (银河奶油蛋糕糕) at 22:57:36 on November 14, 2020, can be viewed at https://www.douban.com/group/topic/201129802/.
12. Stewart, who came out in 2017, is one of the most widely discussed international celebrities in the *Jiquan* Gossip Group. As an example, "How the Twilight girl shakes the whole lesbian world," posted by Xiye (西野) at 20:07:48 on April 20, 2018, can be viewed at https://www.douban.com/group/topic/115868792/, and "Kristen and Mackenzie's new movie will be aired online," posted by Xixilimeiyoulan (西西里没有蓝) at 18:49:16 on October 21, 2020, can be viewed at https://www.douban.com/group/topic/198139330/. Other Western queer female celebrities include King Princess, Rianne Van Rompaey, Freja Beha Erichsen, Taylor Schilling, and so on (an example post is "Talk about European-American *jiquan*," posted by dumbass at 19:11:35 on February 20, 2021, available at https://www.douban.com/group/topic/212101256/).
13. This kind of discussions can be seen in several posts. For instance, "If there are popular 'gay' shows like *Addicted*, why there are no good *baihe* TV shows?", posted by wolforget at 23:33:09 on December 2, 2019, can be viewed at https://www.douban.com/group/topic/159707413/.

emerged in girl group cultivation reality shows, exemplified by the "big sister" persona, has manufactured more local cultural texts and contexts for *jiquan* fans' queer reading.

The Controversial "T" in *Jiquan* Fandom

Close associations with lesbian identity and an explicit demand for queer female-centered content do not mean that *jiquan* fandom is unproblematic. Rather, it has produced new stereotypes and hierarchies surrounding female queerness by reproducing essentialist understandings of queer female gender identity. One long-lasting controversy among *jiquan* fans is the attitude toward female masculinity and "iron-T" (*tie-T*/铁T) lesbians.

"T/P," similar to "butch/femme," is a generic lesbian identification system widely accepted in mainland China, Hong Kong, and Taiwan. T denotes a lesbian woman with masculine gender traits; while P denotes a feminine lesbian gender identification (Fung 2021; Kam 2012, 2014). Iron-T is a subdivision of T identification associated with a strong sense of masculinity (Engebretsen 2014).[14] Lucetta Y. L. Kam asserts that T-style is one among "certain kinds of gender transgression" in contemporary China, which becomes a female gender style recognizable in both popular culture and local lesbian communities (2014, 263). Intriguingly, in Chinese *jiquan* fandom, fans have shown a more complicated attitude toward T-style celebrities and iron-T culture.

In the *Jiquan* Gossip Group, celebrities with more feminine styles are widely welcomed.[15] Existing scholarship shows that female homoerotic fantasies are often mediated by the coupling of tomboyish and feminine celebrities, such as the queer fandom of the female participants in *Super Voice Girls* (Zhao 2018c), However, many *jiquan* fans instead tend to exclude celebrities with a strong T-style—"short hair, a casual dress style, loosely fitting clothes, and a culturally identifiable masculine way of body presentation" (Kam 2014, 253)—from their queer fantasies. As discussed in Chapter 1, this became evident in the (anti-)fandom of another girl group cultivation show in 2020—*Youth With You 2* (hereafter *YWY2*). Such disdain also happens in *jiquan* fan communities. In a discussion about two popular tomboyish contestants of *YWY2*, Liu Yuxin

---

14. Engebretsen found that "iron-T" was often used interchangeably with "pure-T" (纯T) and "*ye*-T" (爷T; meaning "hypermasculine *T*") in mainland China (2014, 173). In *jiquan* fans' communities, *ye*-T is sometimes used as well. Compared with *tie-T*, *ye-T* is a more stigmatized term. As Engebretsen suggests, *ye-T* is considered a controlling, superior, and "patriarchy-imitating" role in a lesbian relationship.
15. This preference may be more accurate when it is applied to mainland Chinese celebrities. For celebrities from Western countries, Taiwan, and Hong Kong, *jiquan* fans tend to focus on those who have come out as queer women, though there are exceptions, such as Taylor Swift.

(刘雨昕) and Lu Keran (陆柯燃), some *jiquan* fans showed their dislike for T-style celebrities.[16] Some *jiquan* fans distance themselves from some T-style celebrities simply because these celebrities do not display feminine straits. One fan said, "A *ji* likes women. If she does not like men at all, how could she like copies of men?"[17] In contrast, some other *jiquan* fans believe that such aversion to T-style idols like Liu and Lu is very problematic, as queer female fans should not create further discriminative cultures and gender hierarchies within the group.[18] While celebrities with feminine appearances are widely welcomed among the fans, iron-T-associated female celebrities are rather controversial in the fan group. *Jiquan* fans' preference for female celebrities with more feminine aesthetic styles is entangled with negative attitudes toward iron-T lesbian identification. The problematic association between normative femininity and lesbian sexuality exhibited by some *jiquan* fans leads to discrimination against female masculinity and creates a hierarchy within female queerness.

While celebrities with feminine appearances are widely admired as empowered "big sisters" in *jiquan* communities, T-style celebrities are kept at a distance from such a popular feminist persona by some *jiquan* fans. In *SWMW* season 1, Li Sidanni is a contestant with a distinct T-style, and it has been rumored that she is a lesbian since she first rose to stardom in 2011. Li has a large *jiquan* fanbase, but her fans do not classify her as an iron-T. Instead, she is described as a *nai*-T (奶T; *nai* is used to describe young and gentle) or a *niang*-T (娘T; feminine T),[19] in which her young, gentle, and more feminine traits are addressed. Even though the show highlights Li's perseverance and diligence onstage, she is rarely considered a "big sister" by *jiquan* fans. On the contrary, in *jiquan* fans' reading, Li admires some "big sister" contestants just like *jiquan* fans do.[20] For some *jiquan* fans, a T-style celebrity usually cannot be considered a "big sister" because of her embodiment of a typical masculine aesthetic. In this way, an essentialist female gender identity is established in the queering of "big-sister" images. To further

---

16. The post "The disdain for *iron-T* after the show" was posted by Zhesheruwang (折射入网) at 01:21:50 on May 31, 2020. It can be viewed at https://www.douban.com/group/topic/178078563/.
17. This discussion was posted by Chenwujiang (澄雾酱) at 01:34:50 on May 31, 2020. It can be viewed at https://www.douban.com/group/topic/178078563/.
18. The thread starter Zhesheruwang (折射入网) of the post "The disdain for iron-T after the show" holds such a view, and many participants of this thread agree with them. For example, the thread starter posts: "The hate on them (Liu and Lu) is the hate on LGBT groups." It can be viewed at https://www.douban.com/group/topic/178078563/.
19. For example, in the post "Lisi and Feiei have CP feeling" in the *Jiquan* Gossip Group, Xinghai (星海) uses *nai* (奶) to describe Li, posted at 00:45:24 on August 30, 2020, available at https://www.douban.com/group/topic/191586652/.
20. Such a reading is exemplified by "Lisi and Feiei have CP feeling," posted by *Xinghai* (星海) at 00:45:24 on August 30, 2020 and available at https://www.douban.com/group/topic/191586652/, as well as "Lisi and Yuqi at Xi'an," posted by Xinghai (星海) at 15:07:56 on January 10, 2021 and available at https://www.douban.com/group/topic/207799640/.

address this point, the next section will focus on *jiquan* fans' queer readings of two feminine-style *SMMW* contestants: Zhu Jingxi and Wan Qian, who are more frequently discussed as "big sisters" in *jiquan* fan communities.

Queering "Big Sisters": When *Jiquan* Fandom Meets *SWMW*

The first season of *SWMW* was a nationwide TV phenomenon in 2020. The moment Mango TV announced the program schedule of *SWMW*, some members of the *Jiquan* Gossip Group immediately expressed their interest in the show. On May 7, one month before the first episode aired, a discussion thread about *SWMW* had already started in the *Jiquan* Gossip Group.[21] In this post, *jiquan* fans expressed their expectations that the show would appreciate female maturity and smash the discrimination directed toward female ageing in the Chinese entertainment industry. In the thread, the starter posted, "A 30-year-old has the beauty of a 30-year-old! Big sisters have the beauty of big sisters! Girls at every age are all the most beautiful!"[22] Simultaneously, the *jiquan* fans believed the show could provide ways to express their preferences and project queer fantasies onto the "big sisters." A *jiquan* fan posted that the show would be "Sappho's lesbian island" in her dreams, and other fans agreed (as seen in Figure 2.1).[23]

Meanwhile, in the *SWMW* Group, *jiquan* fans often showed their queer desires for certain competitors and discussed the rumors about several competitors' sexuality, which provoked the anger of "mainstream fans" in the *SWMW* Group, who enjoyed the show but did not interpret it in a queer way, especially those who were worried such discussions related to lesbianism would affect their idols' reputation and career. Facing homophobic criticism in the *SWMW* Group, many *jiquan* fans struck back and stressed their support of LGBTQ rights. In a discussion thread posted on June 12, 2020, the thread starter used the tag "pride month" to show the direct connection between *jiquan* fandom and lesbian culture.[24] This thread starter also posted,

---

21. "SWMW Group got more than 80 thousand members!" was posted by Yinhechaoteji (银河超特急) at 11:43:26 on May 7, 2020 and can be viewed at https://www.douban.com/group/topic/174571851/.
22. This comment was posted by Yinhechaoteji (银河超特急) at the start of this discussion thread at 11:43:26 on May 7, 2020, which can be viewed at https://www.douban.com/group/topic/174571851/.
23. The comment was posted by Yuerguan (鱼儿观) at 21:01:17 on May 7, 2020 and can be viewed at https://www.douban.com/group/topic/174571851/. Sappho was a lesbian Archaic Greek poet from the island of Lesbos.
24. The post "How come that lesbian or not, bisexual or not cannot be discussed?" was posted at 17:59:30 on June 15, 2020, and can be viewed at https://www.douban.com/group/topic/180326419/. The thread starter, however, canceled their account in July 2020. After their account was canceled, the posts and comments posted by this account can still be seen, but there is no name shown.

Figure 2.1: In a *Jiquan* Gossip Group discussion thread about *SWMW*, the show was described as "Sappho's lesbian island"

> Is it because there are too many men in this group? I am just a lesbian who wants to watch big sisters . . . No matter whether you are a fan or a long-time fan, I can always use my *ji*-dar[25] on everyone and I do not care how straight people think.[26]

This fan then listed several *SWMW* competitors and said, "I want to have sex with them or see them having sex with each other." This bold post shows that *jiquan* fandom voices female queer desire in a straightforward way. It is also noticeable that the thread starter used "too many men" instead of "too many straight people" to criticize the homophobia of the fan group. Emphasizing gender identity rather than sexual orientation to criticize the homophobia implies the clear conflation of queer and feminist sentiments in *jiquan* fandom. Such conflation is clearer when celebrities with "big sister" personas are queerly read by *jiquan* fans.

SWMW manufactured "big sister" celebrities who embody powerful femininities. Such characters, to some extent, subvert the traditional aesthetics and cultural disciplines concerning women in contemporary Chinese society. The competitors framed their participation in *SWMW* as a chance to challenge gender rules and the social stereotypes surrounding aging women. As the show

---

25. "*Ji*-dar," a popular term in *jiquan* fandom, is similar to "gay-dar."
26. This is cited from the thread starter, whose account is canceled. It was posted at 17:59:30 on June 15, 2020, and can be viewed at https://www.douban.com/group/topic/180326419/.

went on, *jiquan* fans' discussions gradually focused on several popular celebrity participants and their interactions in the show and on their social media.

Zhu Jingxi, a 32-year-old low-profile electronica musician with fashionable feminine looks, has gained fame in *jiquan* fandom. As the least well-known competitor in *SWMW*, Zhu was eliminated in the first-round public performance. However, in her limited time on the show, Zhu successfully demonstrated the "big sister" persona, featuring independence and self-empowerment, that *SWMW* intended to manufacture. In the third episode of *SWMW*, when Zhu and her teammates discussed the meaning of the song *Beautiful Love*, which they would perform in the first-round public performance, Zhu said her understanding of beautiful love is "I love you, but I do not rely on you," and "the deepest love is to love oneself." The framing of independence as women's empowerment is prevalent in Chinese popular culture. However, it tends to obscure structural and institutional gender inequalities, and passes the buck to individual women. Independence is seen as a fundamental modernizing form of progress for Chinese women; meanwhile, it is also a globally circulated symbol of LGBTQ popular culture and social activism (Engbretsen 2014). In this vein, independence has a dual significance for Chinese queer women. Zhu's artistic temperament, musical talent, and independent spirit are widely welcomed in *jiquan* fandom.[27]

Zhu's caring character, as presented in the show, also drew *jiquan* fans' attention. For example, in the second episode, when all of the competitors were choosing songs that they would perform, Zhu and another competitor, Xu Fei (许飞), wanted to choose the same song, but Zhu generously gave the chance to Xu. In a thread on the *SWMW* Group entitled "straight people please click the close button," a *jiquan* fan said that Zhu gave the chance to Xu because "The big sister (Zhu) could not bear that she (Xu) was struggling. When Xu Fei was nervous and biting her lip, every *ji* would be moved with compassion."[28] During the rehearsal of the song *Beautiful Love* in the third episode, Zhu constantly helped her team members practice the song and played piano accompaniment for them. The same fan commented that "I feel pity for the big sister [because Zhu was eliminated in the third episode]. She is only giving but never taking. She quietly takes care of others. This is exactly the big sister that a *ji* loves." In this post, *jiquan* fans read Zhu's generosity to other celebrity participants as evidence of her queer sexuality, which should be appreciated by other queer women. In Zhu's case, her

---

27. In a poll named "the top 20 most welcomed Chinese female celebrities" in the *Jiquan* Gossip Group, Zhu was the fourth most welcomed celebrity in the first-round vote. The poll was posted by Qianshuiting (潜水艇) at 21:47:01 on November 30, 2020, and can be viewed at https://www.douban.com/group/topic/203014897/. The poll remains ongoing without a final result at the time of writing this chapter.
28. The post "I do not believe only my legs are trembling" was posted by Jianghupianzi (江湖骗子) at 19:30:19 on June 22, 2020 and can be viewed at https://www.douban.com/group/topic/181362567/.

stylish looks, independent spirit, and generosity are the elements that make her a model of a self-empowered "big sister" in a popular feminist sense (as *SWMW* showed), as well as in a queer sense (as *jiquan* fans read). The conflation becomes more obvious when *jiquan* fans read the interactions between Zhu and another popular *SWMW* competitor in *jiquan* fandom—Wan Qian.

Wan, a 38-year-old actress who starred in several small-budget independent movies, has gained fame by being called an "ideal idol in *jiquan*" (姬圈天菜) and a "*jiquan* master" (姬圈扛把子).[29] Wan presents herself to the public as a mature-minded woman who prioritizes her career and is supported by her husband, who takes care of their child when Wan is working. This popular feminist rhetoric, focusing on individual success stories, underpinned the narratives about Wan in *SMWM*. Before the show, Wan was already discussed by fans in the *Jiquan* Fandom Group as a "big sister" figure. A *jiquan* fan posted in a thread discussing Wan's movies, "I think she is very beautiful!!! Her beauty is not the beauty that complies with male hormones. Hers is purely feminine."[30] On the show, Wan Qian had intimate interactions with several competitors, including Zhu.[31] In the third episode, Wan was also a team member for the group performing *Beautiful Love*. In the rehearsal scene, Wan commented on Zhu's generosity by saying that "We are all women, and we stand together. Women should help women, and it is a kind of female empowerment." When Zhu learned of her elimination, Wan said to Zhu, "Please come back. For me." To which Zhu answered, "I will try to come back, for you." From the perspective of mainstream fans, the friendship between Wan and Zhu, which continued after the show, is a model of feminist alliance or sisterhood. However, according to *jiquan* fans' queer interpretation, Zhu had a crush on Wan, but Zhu had to repress her love because Wan is married.

The climax of the discussion about the relations between Zhu and Wan took place when Zhu released her new song, *Performance Tool* (表演工具), and dedicated it to Wan after Zhu left the *SWMW* stage. In the *Jiquan* Gossip Group, *jiquan* fans looked at the details of the lyrics and speculated about whether the two's intimate relationship was more than just a friendship. A *jiquan* fan, Xiaohei, related Zhu's lyrics to specific scenes showed in *SWMW*.[32] For example, with the lyric "I stand under a Joshua tree in a desert, look up at the pink moon,"

---

29. In the "the top 20 most welcomed Chinese female celebrities" vote in the *Jiquan* Gossip Group, Wan was the fifth most welcomed celebrity in the first-round vote.
30. It was posted by Yizhongjishu (一种技术) at 22:37:05 on January 28, 2020 in the post "I love Wan Qian in *The New World*," which can be viewed at https://www.douban.com/group/topic/163997757/.
31. However, with *SWMW* going on, Wan was accused of exploiting the label of "ideal idol in *jiquan*" to draw public attention, especially due to the fact that she is married with a child. Wan's case can be an example of the employment of queerbaiting in Chinese celebrity culture.
32. The post "Zhu Jingxi wrote a song to Wan Qian" was posted by Xiaohei (小黑) at 03:58:22 on June 29, 2020 and can be viewed at https://www.douban.com/group/topic/182214720/.

Xiaohei pointed out that Joshua trees belong to the lily family.³³ In Chinese, *baihe* literally means "lily flowers." According to Xiaohei, "a Joshua tree in a desert" implies that "*baihe* can grow in infertile fields like the desert, just like Zhu Jingxi always pursues the 'beautiful love' bravely." Meanwhile, "the pink moon" was read by the fan as symbolizing Wan, because Wan wore a pink suit the first time she appeared on the *SWMW* stage. *Jiquan* fans interpreted the song in such complicated and trivialized ways to seek the validation of Zhu's queer sexuality and her sentiments for Wan. However, Xiaohei also posted,

> Zhu really appreciates, even really likes Wan. But I do not support [imagining] them as lovers . . . Either romantic love or friendship are oversimple expressions . . . What I see from this song is two mature and clever souls attracted to each other.³⁴

This contradictory comment shows the blurry boundary between female same-sex romance and female friendship in the *jiquan* fans' imagination.

In the process of reading the public personas of Zhu and Wan and the friendship between them, *jiquan* fans achieve their queer interpretations of the show in relation to a popular feminist rhetoric. After all, in the case of Zhu and Wan, their feminist sensibilities, such as female independence, female maturity, and mutual appreciation between self-empowered women, are the preconditions of *jiquan* fans' queering of the "big sister" personas and their friendships. For *jiquan* fans, understanding popular feminist rhetoric through a queer lens is their strategy for constructing queer meanings in a situation where LGBTQ content is censored and self-censored in mainland Chinese mainstream media (Zhao 2019a). In *SWMW*, for instance, in the seventh episode, competitors' affectionate stage gestures, such as kissing and touching each other, were all removed from the official broadcast version.³⁵ What is noteworthy is that, even with such strict (self-)censorship, popular feminist rhetoric provides a space for *jiquan* fans to project their queer fantasies onto female celebrities in one of the most influential Chinese reality shows in 2020.

Examining *jiquan* fandom unravels the emerging entanglement of neoliberal feminist values and female queerness in Chinese popular culture. The popular feminist rhetoric of *SWMW* does not challenge idealized feminine norms and gender inequality. The show, although projecting an inspiring manifesto, remains embedded in the patriarchal fashion-beauty complex and narrates elitist individual success, sustaining normative femininity and neoliberalism. By constructing

---

33. In fact, the Joshua tree (*Yucca brevifolia*) belongs to the asparagus family, not the lily family. This is an original error in Xiaohei's post.
34. The post "Zhu Jingxi wrote a song to Wan Qian" was posted by Xiaohei (小黑) at 03:58:22 on June 29, 2020 and can be viewed at https://www.douban.com/group/topic/182214720/.
35. The deleted parts can be viewed at https://new.qq.com/omn/20200726/20200726A0DONY00.html.

the "big sister" figure as the ideal queer female image, *jiquan* fandom perpetuates particular lookist and elitist understandings of female gender and sexuality.

Conclusion

By analyzing the *jiquan* fandom of *SWMW*, this chapter has unpacked the relations between queer female visibility and popular feminist rhetoric in contemporary Chinese TV culture. The current *jiquan* fandom, intertwining with a popular feminist rhetoric, provides mediated spaces for female queer readings, and shows a more direct connection with real-life lesbian identity and politics. However, *jiquan* fandom also often caters to heterosexual aesthetics, commercialized gender norms, and elitist biases in this popular feminist rhetoric. *Jiquan* fans' queer reading of the big sister personas in *SWMW* displays the interference of popular feminism in queer female fandoms of Chinese reality TV shows. The impact of neoliberal rationality on queer cultural spaces certainly warrants further scholarly examinations, and such examinations should be carefully situated in specific social and cultural contexts.

3
A Dildonic Assemblage

The Paradoxes of Queer Masculinities and Desire on the Chinese Sports Variety Show Let's Exercise, Boys

Wangtaolue Guo and Jennifer Quist

Introduction

In the summer of 2020, Hunan TV launched the competitive sports variety show *Let's Exercise, Boys* (运动吧少年; *LEB* hereafter). The program was a departure from reality TV competitions based on conventional show business talents such as singing and dancing. At the heart of this departure was a deliberate move to create distance between young Chinese men and the delicate, effeminate aesthetics referred to on *LEB* as the "flower boy" (花美男) image, a term that springs from South Korean popular culture. The Chinese counterpart of "flower boy" is "little fresh meat" (小鲜肉), which likewise refers to a soft masculinity popular among younger generations (Song 2022a, 70).

The show's format was one where attractive, fit young men were locked in sweating, straining, head-to-head competitions of speed, power, and agility. The show's sports competition format aimed to achieve two chief objectives. As explained by its director and producer, Li Chao, in an interview with *The Paper* tellingly subtitled "Everyone Competes on Actual Strength, Not on Appearances" (Huang 2020), the first goal of the show was to cater to underserved emerging markets arising from new trends toward personal fitness and health in contemporary China. Not only have an increasing number of gyms and fitness studios been opened in urban and coastal areas of China, but customer demands have been expanding and diversifying, creating a ready market for sports-oriented TV entertainment. The second goal was to establish the personal and aesthetic characteristics of *LEB*'s contestant-athletes as reimagined models of youthful male masculinity that were meant to attract the admiration and the emulation of viewers accustomed to effeminate flower-boy media idols. With this second objective, *LEB* enters the cultural space of sports and fitness poised to influence not only aesthetic preferences, but the ethics and ideals developing around these trends.

Over the course of the interview, producer Li extols the show's foregrounding of sportsmanship, discipline, and personal empowerment. Of the cast, Li says, "We need this group of young, sunny athletes to show audiences another type of youthful disposition, to launch a new image of a new generation of Chinese youth." Li's mission echoes with "an imagined Chinese harmony" laden with Western, neoliberal desires (J. Zhao 2016, 167) and in tune with "the nation-state's image building on the global stage" (Zhao 2020a, 463–64). Indeed, state-owned media outlets have praised *LEB* for its entertainment value, positive energy, and for its reconfiguration of rugged, youthful male masculinity (X. Wu 2020).

However, the official, heteronormative, nationalistic promotional and critical rhetoric surrounding *LEB* forms only one facet of the show's reception. Another facet is visible in promotional spots and posters which are marked not by fresh, sunny faces but by depersonalized, chiseled, bare torsos and smoldering sexual glares. Along with the show, and with the fitness trends from which it arose, comes a spectacle characterized by British pop culture journalist Mark Simpson in 2014 as "spornosexuality." Highly conscious of his image, a spornosexual subject is distinguished and celebrated for his fitness and his dedication to the conditioning of his body. Along with doing actual body-work, a spornosexual dresses, undresses, poses, and photographs himself to attract and to gratify a social media following. In the case of *LEB*, social media converges with mass media presentations of spornosexuality. Wherever they appear, spornosexual images tend to be hypersexualized, read as homoprovocative images of male masculinity appealing to masculine queer desire. Glamorous and enticing as spornosexuality appears on the small screen, the repetitive, mechanical reproduction of such an image in the context of a transnational entertainment complex confounds the diversification of masculine ideals and flattens local queer polyvalence, just as Walter Benjamin warned it would (2010, 1053–55). Furthermore, as *LEB* reworks politicized aesthetics, it maintains old hierarchies along the matrices of age, location, class, and attitudes. Through a critical televisual-cultural discourse analysis of the spornosexuality of *LEB*, we argue that the show operates with a *de facto* transformative queer core. *LEB* constitutes what we will call hereafter a "dildonic assemblage" (Deleuze and Guattari 1987, 7–11, 380–87; Preciado 2018, 64–73), eliciting a multiplicity of pleasures—male, female, genderqueer; sensual and sexual. In spite of existing within the largely heteronormative regime of contemporary China, *LEB* penetrates ultra-fit "powdered" masculinity. Ultimately and ironically, *LEB* subverts and complicates the discourses that would suppress this new spornosexual iteration of Chinese male masculinity.

Hereafter, we pose the following questions: What changes in Chinese ideals of male masculinity does *LEB* promote? How do viewers rework the show's paratexts and subtexts to provoke gay/*tongzhi*[1] discourses about queer fantasy and desire in spite of increasingly stifling censorship? How does the polyphony of audience responses correspond to the contestation of spornosexual masculine heartthrobs and androgynous idols? Our analyses of *LEB* explore these questions by examining the show's "poetico-literary performativity" (Derrida 1992, 55) and representations of male masculinity, desire, and queerness. We add to this analytical approach the concept of the "dildonic assemblage," applying it to *LEB*'s spornosexuality as it is read through the female gaze, and through latent queer/*tongzhi* erotics. Through these readings, ambivalent attitudes toward homoeroticism as well as toward the commodification and the ironic queering of male bodies in Chinese media are revealed.

Overview: Oscillating Masculinities in Contemporary China

In January 2021, the Ministry of Education of the People's Republic of China proposed measures to tackle what top officials claimed was a masculinity crisis, in which "the feminization of Chinese boys threatens China's survival and development" (Wang, Chen, and Radnofsky 2021). The initiative increased the number of physical education (PE) teachers and revamped school gym classes to boost traits deemed traditionally masculine among male students. Fierce debate on social media followed, with some commenters expressing support for the initiative and others criticizing the move as a form of sexual and gender discrimination. Feminist journalist and activist Li Jun said, "The proposal has represented some stereotypes in China on male masculinity, which is against gender equality and diversity" (quoted in Qian and Woo 2021). Li's remarks object to the reduction of masculinity to a monolithic, heteropatriarchal construct. Male masculinity, in fact, would best be viewed as a set of flickering signifiers representing "transnationally circulating images and practices, and locally situated identities, practices, and locales" (Song and Hird 2013, 6).

This transnational turn in Chinese male masculinity studies has been widely discussed by some scholars (as well as in some chapters in this volume, such as Chapter 7). Kam Louie's (2014) foundational critical framework of the *wen/wu* dyad of masculine traits (*wen* being cultural attainments while *wu* is physical prowess) has been traced beyond China into larger East Asian "contact nebulae" (Thornber 2014, 463). Louie (2014, 23–27) argues that, due to influences from Japanese and South Korean pop cultures, the *wen/wu* dyad has been challenged by new hybrid ideals such as metrosexuality and androgyny. Similarly, by analyzing the protagonist in Chinese-born American writer Ha Jin's 2007 novel *A Free Life*, Lezhou Su (2018) notes that during the mass migration of the 1990s,

---

1. *Tongzhi* is a Chinese translation of the English term "homosexuality," and carries context-specific political and queer connotations (see Bao 2018).

at a time when Chinese society was fixated on market reforms and economic growth, the *wen* ideal was on the verge of irrelevance. In the novel, while socioeconomic changes problematized traditional *wen/wu* reasoning, the protagonist's sojourn in the United States shows that increasing movements across borders play a critical role in developing an Americanized neo-*wen* masculinity of free-spiritedness and mobility.

Moreover, addressing diverse representations of Chinese male masculinity in TV dramas, films, and in reality, Geng Song and Derek Hird (2013, 11–12) direct attention to popular masculine representations where mediated images and texts offer new sites of heterogeneity and provide a vital heuristic for producing and circulating transnational masculinities. Song (2013 with Derek Hird; 2016, 2018) explores the multifaceted-ness of mediated Chinese masculinity, unraveling the too-often entangled concepts of cosmopolitanism, nationalism, and consumerism. His analysis of TV dramas reveals how diverse masculinities (the self-made businessman, emotional family man, athletic rebel, and so on) are reimagined, and how they are negotiated by audiences. In a similar vein, Sheldon Lu (2016, 2018) examines nuances in portrayals of working-class and white-collar men in Chinese-language films. Lu not only addresses the struggles of constructing "suitable new subjectivities" (2016, 174) for Chinese men, but also engages with ideological forces, thereby challenging essentialist bases of Chinese male masculinity. Adding to the complexity of Chinese masculinities in an age of globalization, media scholars are investigating nonnormative, queer masculine ideals represented on TV. Jamie J. Zhao (2016), for instance, discusses the onscreen persona of Li Daimo (李代沫), a popular contestant on the competitive variety singing show *The Voice of China* (中国好声音; Zhejiang TV, 2016–2020). Zhao uncovers the interplay between the orthodoxy of the show's wholesome formula for creating contestant personas which reflect the party-state's ideal of hetero-masculinity, and viewers' queer readings of the show which amplify and celebrate Li's potential gayness. The disjuncture between China's official attitude toward nonnormative masculinities and these masculinities' reception among young people is further explored through the conceptualization of "little fresh meat" (小鲜肉). For instance, Song (2022a) examines the politics of shifting masculinity in postsocialist China through a critical analysis of two recent web TV dramas featuring actors deemed "little fresh meat" by fans. While the proliferation and the public reception of effeminate male images evinces an "increasing diversity of gender representations" in Chinese media, it also exposes a "deep-seated anxiety over what an effeminate younger generation will mean for China" (Song 2022a, 69).

The transnational turn, along with the media and popular culture turn in gender and sexuality studies, challenges the facile notion of a singular Chinese masculinity and further opens spaces for scrutinizing masculine ideals at the intersections of gender, class, and socioeconomics. Inspired by these previous discussions, we consider a new "figure of personhood" (Agha 2011a, 164; 2011b, 173), the spornosexual as depicted on *LEB*. According to Asif Agha (2011a, 2011b), figures of personhood are part of mediatization wherein media images provoke negotiations of their meanings. Once tacitly agreed upon, the images' constructed meanings are socially recognizable without much depth or nuance. Actors and characters become typed as personas to be performed. As an ideal of male masculinity, spornosexuality was imported from outside the popular culture of East Asia contact nebulae. A study of spornosexuality includes a consideration of the transnational dynamics triggered when spornosexuality meets the Chinese masculinities. These may be the "little fresh meat"/"flower boy," the traditional *wu*, or the overarching official national initiative to reclaim a generation of boys the Chinese Education Ministry fears are in danger of emasculation.

LEB as a Dildonic Assemblage

In spite of ambiguous signals from China's complex censorship system, queer-related entertainment survives and thrives in Chinese society where, paradoxically, LGBTQ expressions remain officially suppressed. Not only have recent entertainment media productions adapted to suit the current regulations of the official executive censorial agency, the National Radio and Television Administration (NRTA), but they have had a subtle reciprocal effect on censorship. In the case of *LEB*, the production risked experimenting with a new variety show format, and also with molding attractive young idols closer to traditional masculinity than is typically showcased on Chinese reality competition shows. More than a gimmick, this was a renegotiation of sensual and sexual capital under censorship and within a state which maintains a tense and invasive relationship between nationalism and male masculinity. Nationhood and manhood in postsocialist China, as Song (2022a, 81–82) observes, are intricately interconnected, with both concepts being expressed and regulated by a discourse of heteronormativity and virile hegemony.

In light of these complexities and contradictions, we argue that *LEB* interacts with the censorship and with the culture under official surveillance as a "dildonic assemblage." As a portmanteau, the term dildonic assemblage has a twofold meaning. First, it suggests a version of the theoretical term "assemblage" based on the concept presented in the work of Giles Deleuze and Félix Guattari (1987). The metaphor of the assemblage as a curving, forking active movement mirrors queer discourses which must likewise find and make their ways through the complex, often unpredictable terrain of state-regulated Chinese media. Second, the theoretical dildo is an apt metaphor for the phallicity of the imagery of *LEB*, which centers its promotional material and opening monologue around calls for *cipo* (刺破). Literally, this term means a puncturing, an insertion. Figuratively, it is the penetration of the normative gaze of contemporary Chinese TV audiences with something unconventional, both in terms of the competitive sports variety show format and the show's reimagining of male masculinity. Talk of *cipo* draws *LEB* even closer to the metaphor of the dildo, a concept established in Paul B. Preciado's *Countersexual Manifesto* (2018) as a theoretical device particularly well-suited for questions of gender, sexuality, and power. Preciado (2018) introduces possible etymologies of the English word *dildo* and concludes that there are two recurring connotations: delight/pleasure and male effeminacy. From there, he unveils the epistemological possibilities of the dildo, arguing that it can operate as more than a technology of sexual pleasure, becoming a commanding analogy for exploration and development. Preciado's concept of the dildo functions as "a reference of power and sexual arousal . . . moving into other signifying spaces . . . that are resexualized by dint of their semantic proximity" (2018, 66). For us, Preciado's argument excavates new directions, and reveals the paradoxical dynamics between the power of pleasure derived from queer content in media and the suppressive forces regulating China's mainstream sociocultural space. We link the work of Deleuze and Guattari with Preciado's argument to produce the concept of "the dildonic assemblage," which is at once multiplicious, constructive, and contradictory.

Like other Deleuzian assemblages, the dildonic assemblage entails heterogeneous composition and constructive mechanisms. The dildonic assemblage, however, consistently contradicts itself, contributing to the search for queer pleasure-knowledge while consolidating a heteronormative sexual regime. This contradiction is precisely what makes a dildonic assemblage a fitting analytical metaphor for *LEB*. The show simultaneously suppresses and rehabilitates queer media representations and interpretations. Preciado's conceptualization of the dildo reveals the supplemental constructedness of gender and sexuality, which is made possible through repetition and imitation. All of this accentuates the plasticity of the body, of gender identity, and of sexuality. As RL Goldberg (2019) points out, the dildo expands the way the subject experiences bodies, desires, and fantasies. Such metaphorics align with Michel Foucault's (1978) four *dispositifs* and Judith Butler's (1990) idea of gender performativity. Thereby, a dildonic assemblage provides a tool for analyzing how creative industries explore and capitalize on queerness. As an illustration, consider the niche market of physique magazines which appeared in the United States in the 1950s and 1960s. These magazines effectively externalized a kind of homosexual pleasure. David K. Johnson observes that, in a departure from existing fitness and bodybuilding publications, physique magazines attracted gay men by "depict[ing] men gazing at other men . . . [and] offer[ing] coded references to the Grecian way of life, a chance to be part of 'the limited aesthetic group who appreciate the glorification of the male body'" (2019, 8). The photographs and images featured in physique magazines abandoned the anatomical organ as the provenance of carnality and constituted "spaces of slippages and resignification" (Spurlin 2014, 300; 2017, 174) where consumers could visualize their queer sexual pleasure.

Decades after American physique magazines, new niches where queer desire may be performed and visualized are likewise forming around China's TV industry, among them the spornosexuality of *LEB*. As new niches form, those who inhabit them engage in delicate maneuvers of skirting political confrontation and preserving these shows' availability within the mainstream. Qian Wang (2015, 171–72) notes that the moral standards and political projects of the Chinese state have intensified the politicization of gender and sexuality. However, the TV industry crafts what Wang calls "media queerness" (2015, 167) to work around official censorship and to meet the demands of China's growing fashion market, which sells queerness as a cosmopolitan lifestyle (166–67; see also J. Zhao 2016, 165). Young men from China's millennial and Generation Z cohorts are now investing in grooming and cosmetics more than ever, embracing effeminacy as social capital (Song 2022a, 70). Beyond fashion, this shift has expanded critical discursive spaces where viewer-consumers can participate, consciously or not, in challenging and perhaps dismantling gender and sexual binaries. Meanwhile, official critics have sent mixed messages on these androgynous images. For instance, while an op-ed article from the official news outlet Xinhua.net denounced "little fresh meat" images in the media as endorsements of a "sick culture" (Xin 2018), commentary in another party-state newspaper, *People's Daily*, argued the time had come for greater diversity in lifestyle, aesthetics, and male roles (Gui 2018).

Ongoing debates around performances of male gender reflect mounting frustration with the contradictions between ideals of male masculinity propagated by some official media, and state movements toward "mediatizing" (Agha 2011a, 163; Jaffe 2011, 565) queerness. *LEB* debuted at a time when traditional *wu* masculinity, characterized by physical prowess, emotional stoicism, and old-fashioned social sensibilities, had come to be seen by Chinese youth as backward (Hird and Song 2018, 6–7; Louie 2014, 22). In this moment, *LEB* emerged with a compromise between *wu* masculinity and the well-groomed effeminacy already seen on TV. Nodding in the direction of "little fresh meat," personal appearance remains central on *LEB*, but the index of desirability is shifted toward *wu*-like displays of physical strength, bulk, and power. This is manifest on *LEB* not only through the results of the competitions, but in the aesthetics of well-built, sometimes scantily clad, rigorously conditioned male physiques. The scene on *LEB* is set for the athletic male body to assume dildonic value as both a supplement and a contradiction to male effeminacy. The spornosexual thus becomes a new TV token of male eroticization within neoliberal China.

On the Scene: Watching *LEB*

In the 2020 debut season of *LEB*, 33 contestants competed in challenges which amounted to indoor parkour and the manipulation of heavy apparatuses. Beyond contestants' will and strength, electronic voting by a studio audience of conventionally attractive young Chinese women was used to determine eliminations.

At first glance, the show's formula may seem familiar. *LEB* is unapologetically derivative of reality shows like *The Titan Games* or *Beat the Champions* (来吧冠军; Zhejiang TV, 2016–2017). What makes it semiotically different from its predecessors is *LEB*'s accentuation of the high-performing, fit male body as a sign of an ideal expression of male masculinity. Like the early spornosexuals Simpson originally wrote about, the men who set the pattern for cultivating fit images and enthusiastic social media followings, *LEB* is involved in crafting figures of personhood. However, unlike independent Internet celebrity spornosexual subjects, *LEB* contestants condition their bodies while the show's production team styles them, selects and refines images of them, and circulates those images within the mediascape. The presentation of these engineered images unfolds according to predetermined statements on male masculine ideals.

For example, Episode 5 begins with a training session in a pool. Close-ups and split-screen shots highlight contestants' bare chests and thighs, showing evidence of the extensive labor they have put into body-work. While the episode was airing, video clips featuring contestants Qiu Haiyang (求海洋) and Qiu Yiwei (仇奕炜) displaying their bodies during the training session were posted to the show's Weibo page, garnering admiration from commenters of all genders and sexualities. Such images become a deferred center of sexual and political signification, thus gaining a dildonic quality. Preciado claims that in a countersexual society, "anything can become a dildo" (2018, 66). In this sense, the show effectively made its contestants' bared, chiseled bodies into nodes of sexual pleasure. Through mediatization, images of these bodies become media commodities, which are simultaneously a "diffusion and defusion" (Hebdige [1979] 2002, 93) of the carnality and the aesthetics of spornosexuality. As this process proceeds, ideal images of male masculinity shift away from rugged *wu* ideals to those of spornosexual showmanship. This not only allows for, but also depends upon, queer representations, interpretations, and the consumption of contestants' bodies as commodities.

With forms of media queerness controlled and regulated in China, the promotion of *LEB* contestants as antitheses to "little fresh meat" idols may have helped the show to out-maneuver censorial interference. According to the pilot episode's opening monologue, young male TV idols with delicate features, meticulous skincare, and high fashion are what audiences are most accustomed to seeing. "However," the voiceover narrator insists, "we have to ask ourselves:

Is that the only way to define the entire younger generation?" From the show's beginning, this rhetorical question distinguishes *LEB* from other reality TV shows reproached by Chinese authorities for propagating "sissy" (娘炮) images (Xin 2018). The monologue goes on to celebrate male masculine characteristics endorsed by the show, including toned bodies, tanned skin, strong will, and virtues of bravery and perseverance. At first glance, many of the qualities *LEB* aspires to are values promoted by the government in initiatives such as its 2021 physical education reforms.

LEB's approach to gender performance attempts to uphold a model where iterations of male masculinity are discrete, clearly defined, and locked in place. To help make the opposition between "flower boy" images and the show's revitalized, modernized version of *wu* masculinity intelligible, the concepts are juxtaposed with the femininity (and a deliberate feminization) of the studio audience. Throughout filming, the studio audience of young, telegenic women stands corralled behind a bar, cheering, chanting, and waiting to be called on to vote for their favorite contestants to advance in the competition. Audience members are more than viewers and voters. They are part of *LEB*'s message, presented as model consumers of the show, enjoying the spectacle with virtuous enthusiasm, clear boundaries, and from a respectful but critical distance. They demonstrate the state's preferred partners for the young men of the cast. By inviting the audience to interact with contestants through voting, the show's narrative hints at young women's potential to happily fulfill traditional gender roles with ideal partners and as ideal partners. However, this well-plotted narrative is simultaneously supported and disrupted, confirmed and contradicted as the competition unfolds onscreen.

In the first episode, a contest of strength is held between tall, muscular, aggressive bodybuilder Qiao Wenyi (乔文一) and the lean, easy-going, so-called "flower boy" Xu Zhibin (徐志滨). The simple, preconceived narrative is complicated when Qiao appears annoyed that his speech cannot be heard over the audience cheering for his opponent. Instead of calling for quiet on the set, the production team isolates and amplifies the women's voices and waits for Qiao himself to confront the audience. The scene can be read as if the women are intruding upon and frustrating Qiao's connection to Xu, who is the true object of Qiao's attention. In the unscripted moment, Qiao breaches the intended narrative by not showing adequate concern for performing a desirable masculine image for the gaze of the female audience. The three-sided drama is elaborated on by fans who have reedited official show footage to reimagine Qiao and Xu as a queer character pair. Fan-edited videos were posted on the video-sharing website Bilibili.com, labeled with queer pairing hashtags and widely circulated. For instance, in a video titled "My Macho Opponent Has a Crush on Me" (霸

道对手爱上我),[2] Xu is cast as overwhelmed and fascinated by Qiao's forceful confessions of romantic interest. Though the dynamics between the men are not even subtextually romantic on the show itself, and though they are not presented as a queer character pair, fan-made videos portray homosexual physical and emotional intimacy between the men.

The configuration of relationships between Qiao, Xu, and their live studio audience can be understood through Eve Sedgwick's (1985) reconceptualization of René Girard's erotic male-male-female triangles. Girard's original work in *Deceit, Desire, and the Novel* (1961) speaks of conventional love triangles in literature where the active members of a triangle, usually men, form intense connections to one another through rivalry for women. This is the narrative *LEB* offers, heightening onscreen drama by depicting Qiao and Xu in a confrontation intensified by the obligatory heterosexuality implied in a rivalry for the favor of the women in the audience. When it is Qiao and the audience who are vying for Xu's attention, and he becomes the triangle's beloved object, the conventional triangle breaks down. Upon inspection, as Sedgwick says, the erotic triangle is revealed to be not "an ahistorical, Platonic form . . . but a sensitive register precisely for delineating relationships of power and meaning and for making graphically intelligible the play of desire and identification" (1985, 27). In light of the images captured by the camera, *LEB*'s intended, censor-approved narrative of fixed gender identities is exposed as faulty. As natural interactions are documented on the show, planned and scripted heteronormativity is visibly upended. Qiao and Xu do not need to be a genuine queer pair in order for their onscreen connections to launch a robust online queer discourse on contestants' masculinities and on their relationships. Asymmetry within the Qiao-Xu-audience triangle confirms Sedgwick's observation that the drawing of boundaries between genders and sexualities "*is* variable, but *not* arbitrary" (1985, 22). Xu and Qiao's relationship can move in the minds of viewers from a homosociality not marked with sexual desire to a homosexuality of intense desire. This perceived movement from friendly rivals to frustrated lovers within online fan discourse is closely connected to Xu and Qiao's positions on a spectrum of masculinities, from "flower boy" to the spornosexual. Chinese male masculinities are not the fixed alternatives put forward in the show's script. This exposure of continuity and plasticity is another dildonic function of *LEB*'s spornosexuality, excavating and connecting male masculinities and sexualities rather than dividing and denouncing them.

As the competition progresses, *LEB*'s filming moves to training grounds at a seaside resort. In Episode 6, montages of close-ups and overhead shots draw a fetishizing, (homo)erotic gaze to cast members dressed down for the beach.

---

2. The video, made by Chuchushe, was uploaded to Bilibili.com on July 16, 2020. The video had gained more than 17,000 views by March 2022. See https://www.bilibili.com/video/BV1DZ4y1u7Vr?from=search&seid=5713221601729206672.

By contrast, as these visuals appear onscreen, the show's dialogue spotlights the celebrity team leaders/trainers. Among them is Zhang Jike (张继科), a well-known Olympic medalist, who makes a stern call for total commitment to training, ending with a warning that "[a]nyone who can't stand mess and the hot sun can go right back home." Here, the show reveals its two simultaneous narratives: the visual spectacle of contestants' bodies, and their team leaders' rhetoric of stoic discipline and fortitude. The dual narrative acts as a mediatizational strategy operating as a form of self-censorship as found in Hebdige's ([1979] 2002, 96) transactional model of deviant behavior. The duality creates an inlet for contradiction between the implicitly heteronormative ethos of the sports celebrity team leaders and the subversion of that ethos offered in the (homo) erotic visual spectacle.

To resolve similar tensions, relationships between male characters in fictional, non-reality Chinese TV have been read as depicting a "socialist brotherhood" (Ng and Li 2020, 486). This term emerged organically from fan commentary and has come to mean having superficial conformity to government insistence that male relationships be non-romantic even as they cultivate a subtext of homoeroticism (Ng and Li 2020, 486). While Eve Ng and Xiaomeng Li's (2020) analysis highlights the ways the socialist brotherhood preserves homoerotic stories and readings, our analysis emphasizes not only the preservative but the ironically transformative power of this duality as it functions through a dildonic assemblage. The *LEB* cast are real people who have been spornosexualized, presented as male masculine ideals, and made into TV idols of a different sort than their "little fresh meat" counterparts. As real people, *LEB*'s spornosexual subjects resist transformation into meaningless exotica, as opposed to how the media often handles LGBTQ characters in fictional TV. The reality of *LEB*'s spornosexual subjects adds gravity to their representations of male gender performance, easing these representations' passage into mainstream ideals of male masculinity. This is not to say that real people are immune to being dismissed or lampooned in TV productions, as has been the case with certain queer contestants on reality singing competitions. Rather, *LEB*'s dual narrative of traditional and spornosexual masculinities, combined with the reality of the cast members as people, does enough to satisfy expectations that the show will consolidate the heteronormative Chinese gender/sexual regime in a credible, relatable way. After meeting these expectations, the show's disruption of male gender and sexual ideals, either in reality or in fans' imaginations, is tolerated by the state.

Male Bodies in the Mediascape

LEB's celebration of the spornosexualized athletic male body perpetuates and amplifies consumerist discourse about body-work and the social and erotic capital associated with it. The project of advancing the spornosexual as an ideal figure of personhood in China is perhaps best achieved by showing it to the audience rather than telling them about it. Accordingly, among *LEB*'s 33 contestants, those with bulkier athletic physiques receive more screen time than the lithe, trim bodies of flower-boy contestants.

One such contestant is Qiu Yiwei, who immediately garnered popularity in the pilot episode for his well-built body, full beard, and dry, quick wit. Close-ups of Qiu glut the show's footage and render his physique into a media commodity which functions as a semiotic symbol to index gender transgression and showmanship in postsocialist China. An instant in Episode 1 when Qiu is briefly shirtless, preparing for competition while the rest of the cast is fully dressed, is illustrated in Figure 3.1. The image is fleeting, but captured and drawn out in the show's final edit. It is a moment of mediatizational objectification which frames and sexualizes his body. Qiu is lit to highlight his chest and deltoid muscles, transforming them into embodiments of phallic potency (Dyer 1997, 300–301). This image supplants his personality with a constructed persona, a sporno-sexualized body presented as a vector of sensual/sexual pleasure.

This reification of the bodies of *LEB* contestants is further established with a comment captured on a contestant's hot mic. The commenter was Xu Zhibin, the "flower boy" mentioned above, who witnesses the moment of Qiu's undress and observes that this exposure of Qiu's body will attract lots of fans. Aware of the camera, Qiu averts his eyes, offering the floating gaze which, according to sociologist Erving Goffman, is a gender display traditionally associated with women modeling in advertisements ([1976] 1979, 2–3, 57). Turning the gaze from the camera is known as "licensed withdrawal" (Goffman [1976] 1979, 57) and it creates an impression that a model is disoriented in a social situation and responding by withdrawing from viewers. The precise moment when Qiu looks away, leaving the image of his body exposed to inspection and consumption by viewers, is captured in Figure 3.1. The "to-be-looked-at-ness" (Mulvey 1975, 11) of the display is attributed to the male body, catering to the sensual/sexual desires of contemporary Chinese women and of gay men. Each of these groups is growing both in their purchasing power and in their power to articulate and advocate for their own needs and desires. They are a market to be served. In this sense, Qiu and the rest of the spornosexualized subjects of *LEB* become a *leitmotif* of a sexual and a queer spectacle.

In addition to the mediatizational strategies used in the televised episodes of *LEB*, contestants themselves were active on social media during production. By curating their own images, comments, and fan interactions, the contestants visualized and expanded the spornosexual ideal in nuanced, humanized ways. They engaged in rescaling their own figures of personhood in the post-rugged-masculinity era. *LEB* contestants opened Weibo accounts to post selfies, behind-the-scenes photos, and personal updates. Aside from being a means of interacting with fans, these public profiles are in keeping with the personal

Figure 3.1: A screenshot of one of Qiu Yiwei's Weibo videos, showing that he is taking off his shirt

sharing Simpson (2014) identified in his original concept of spornosexuality. Social media images have always formed a part of how spornosexual subjects generate erotic and social capital. Beyond amassing this capital, however, *LEB* contestants' social media posts may be considered a semiotic practice that creates "potential anarchy" (Hebdige [1979] 2002, 79) in mainstream gender and sexual representations.

Figure 3.2, for instance, features contestant Zhang Xindong (张鑫栋) complicating his straightforward, heroic onscreen TV persona. In Episodes 1, 4, and 11, Zhang, a former special forces soldier, is praised by the celebrity team leaders as well as his teammates and competitors for his physical prowess and strong will. He is established as a role model, a leader, an inspiration to his fellow contestants and, by extension, to their viewers. On his social media, however, Zhang tampered with this scripted figure of his personhood through self-mediatization. The photo shown in Figure 3.2 might not be as sexually explicit as photos uploaded by fitness influencers outside China, where Weibo's bans on erotic and homosexual content do not apply. That is not to say, however, that this photo cannot be read through the homoerotic lens fans may bring with them to the site. Zhang not only turns his gaze away from the camera, but also lowers himself, kneeling, onto the floor. This posture illustrates a gendered display of "ritualization of subordination" (Goffman [1976] 1979, 40), which can be understood as another stereotypically feminine gesture of deference (Goffman [1976] 1979, 46). The knee bend, which can be interpreted as an expression of submissiveness and appeasement, is in stark contrast to Zhang's macho image on screen: tough, competitive, posture always held erect. The combination of two gender displays typically associated with figures of submissive women in advertisements enhances the self-objectification and the suggestion of femininity in Zhang's photo. Moreover, centered in the frame as the focus of the photo are Zhang's white socks, an object of fetishistic scopophilia within Chinese gay culture. Whether or not Zhang was baiting his LGBTQ fans is unclear. Regardless, within this image, his figure of personhood undergoes (homo)sexual objectification. One gay follower commented that he "would like to lick those socks forever,"[3] while another announced he would allow Zhang "to do anything to my bussy" with those socks on.[4]

For some female audiences, the white socks are disarming, suggesting the purity, the trustworthiness of a hard-working provider and protector on the verge of a well-deserved rest. Zhang plays up this domestic connection with the caption: "Work's done. Now to relax." Overall, Zhang's social media presence seems to largely uphold the hegemonic Chinese gender and sexual ideology, foregrounding virility, competitiveness, stoicism, domesticity, and compulsory heterosexuality. Yet, through a queer reading, the body conscious, media-enthusiastic, heteroflexible spornosexuality of his media image can simultaneously support and disrupt conservative gender ideals.

The homoerotic potential of visuals such as these was apparent in online discourse on *LEB* even before the show's 2020 premiere. In a widely circulated note on one of the most popular online Chinese communicative venues for media and celebrity fans, Douban, a fan observed that *LEB*'s promotional images promised a visual feast for gay viewers. As evidence, the user offered a list of homoerotic elements beyond muscular bodies, including sneakers, white socks, the Arabic

---

3. The comment was made by ChunRyaoyoutaiyang on August 11, 2020 under Zhang's post. See https://weibo.com/6325666375/Jfk6plAlB?filter=hot&root_comment_id=0&ssl_rnd =1611098261.182&type=comment#_rnd1611098262913. Disclaimer: The link worked at the time of writing. However, due to China's ongoing crackdown on LGBTQ digital content and space, the comment appears to have been removed either by the user or a censor.
4. The comment was made by YdangsangwangboC on August 10, 2020 under Zhang's post. See https://weibo.com/6325666375/Jfk6plAlB?filter=hot&root_comment_id=0&ssl_rnd= 1611098261.182&type=comment#_rnd1611098262913. Disclaimer: The link worked at the time of writing. However, due to China's ongoing crackdown on LGBTQ digital content and space, the comment appears to have been removed either by the user or a censor.

Figure 3.2: A screenshot of one of Zhang Xindong's Weibo photos

number "1," and the letter "S."[5] In another note published on the widely used Chinese social networking app, WeChat, an author reported that the repeated use of the Arabic number 1 "made me giggle uncontrollably. You know what I mean."[6]

What the authors of these comments do not need to explain to their queer-informed readers is that within Chinese gay subculture, the Arabic number "1" is a euphemism for the sexual disposition of *top*, while the letter "S" stands for *shou* (受), which is an equivalent of the English gay jargon for the sexual disposition of *bottom*. For these commenters, *LEB*'s promotional materials beckon to an unprecedented demand for "explicit and erotic body fetishization" (Z. Zhou 2020, 576) in Chinese gay communities. Rightly or wrongly, both of these

---

5. It was posted on July 5, 2020. See https://www.douban.com/group/topic/183132955/.
6. It was posted on July 13, 2020. See https://mp.weixin.qq.com/s/Bj0HTufJSFP-6jE_6fIxxw.

commenters believed *LEB* was engaged in "queerbaiting" (Ng 2017). This is a strategy used within media productions aware of LGBTQ engagement with their stories and characters, who then tacitly encourage queer readings but ultimately resist including definitively queer relationships and stories within the productions proper. During the pre-premiere days, when these comments on *LEB*'s promotions were posted, the burgeoning *LEB* gay fandom appears to have been in the early stages of a queerbaiting process, somewhere between having their attention engaged by the show and having their enthusiasm for queer readings of the show encouraged, led along by ambiguously queer references in the promotional imagery. These fans had not yet reached the point in queerbaiting when fans come to understand their expectations of LGBTQ characters and narratives will not be realized and react with betrayal. Based on a June 2020 press release on hunantv.com, it seems that such a deception was never intended. The network explained that, in the context of *LEB*, the Arabic number "1" symbolizes the spirit of achieving the best results, and the letter "S" stands for the qualities of sunshine, solidity, speed, strength, sensitivity, stamina, and supremacy ("Hunan weishi" 2020). Taking this press release at face value, the promotional images were not meant as markers and signs directed at the diacritical frontiers between genders and sexualities.

LEB fans probably did not earnestly expect to see unambiguous gay love and desire on a Hunan TV sports variety show. Like these fans, we are not naïve as we view *LEB*. There is no revolution written into the show. *LEB* producers were not fomenting a shift within state-censored Chinese media powerful enough to allow queer stories to be told hereafter in frank, straightforward ways. There is no call to set aside the idea of a single, discrete, preferred Chinese male masculinity among a range of competing masculinities. We are left with the same ambivalence, the same paradoxes Chinese TV had to offer before the spornosexuals were deployed to penetrate audiences' expectations. The time for a shift in the way gender is understood and performed in Chinese media has not yet arrived. What we do find exemplified in *LEB* is a theory for identifying and conceptualizing these familiar paradoxes. Within an ambiguous censorship system, it is possible to achieve tacit tolerance for diversity in male masculinity. Herein, a dildonic assemblage begins to operate, creating a space for *cipo*, for penetration. In that space, a slow, careful, queerly pleasurable reshaping of culture can commence its work. Online queer discourses on *LEB* question dominant gender and sexual systems. These discourses effectively queer the spornosexualized subjects through readings of the show as coded with queer character pairings and gay cultural references (as seen in Figure 3.3). As a dildonic supplement, an "*étranger*" (Preciado 2018, 68), queer discourses on *LEB*'s spornosexuality are, paradoxically, both reflections and refractions of a mass-produced text.

Figure 3.3: A screenshot of the show's logo

Conclusion

LEB may have succeeded in its stated mission of reconfiguring the *wu* masculinity largely rejected by younger generations of Chinese men. It may also have succeeded in challenging effeminate versions of onscreen male masculinity with its vision of well-groomed, fit, but strong and athletic male masculinity, more along party-state approved lines. Whether this image, with the large investments of time and money required to craft and maintain it, will ever be affordable for average viewers and fans is another matter, and perhaps a serious miscalculation.

Another miscalculation is the assumption that queer readings of the show would be somehow excluded. Queer readings have not only appeared, they have sprung from unpaid fan labor. They deviate from Hunan TV's official narrative, and they test the limits of queering the mainstream Chinese mediascape. *LEB* fans have become prosumers, producers, and trailblazers, embracing a global queer media culture. As this dildonic assemblage works, it exposes and expands, finding its way through regulated media channels. The firm lines drawn between different kinds of Chinese male masculinities—the traditional *wu*, the "little fresh meat," the spornosexual—are revealed as being not as discrete, not as fixed in place as authorities would prefer to have them. A large part of Chinese TV's potential for change, for moving toward depicting something less like the masculine beauty contests of idol showcases or *LEB* and more like the reality of lived gender and sexual identities, may depend upon the ongoing creative labor of fans.

II. Queer/ing TV Dramas through Media Regulations

4
Addicted to Melancholia

Negotiating Queerness and Homoeroticism in a Banned Chinese BL Drama

Aobo Dong

Introduction

In 2017, official media censors in mainland China abruptly took down *Addicted* (上瘾; iQIYI, China, 2016), a highly popular gay web series, from its Chinese streaming platforms before it could air the remaining episodes of its first (and only) season (Lin and Chen 2016). But despite the web series' ephemeral legal life span, it had received more than 100 million views in less than a month of streaming (BBC 2016), attracted millions of loyal fans, and enjoyed its afterlife abroad. The abrupt nature of the ban, coupled with harsher censorship guidelines targeting homosexual content released in the following year, indicate the government's anxiety and paranoia over the growing influence of queer-themed TV like *Addicted*.[1] Having passed the initial censors, *Addicted*, with its own self-sanitizing efforts that preemptively cut down the graphic sex scenes that were ubiquitous in its original literary version, carried an insidious threat to the social order that only manifested itself to state officials after it had reached millions.

In the age of a partitioned internet and omnipresent state censors, it is an impressive feat for any homosexual content to be broadcasted to millions of viewers in China, even for just a brief period. To stand a chance, queer TV must deploy a series of strategies for negotiating a form of TV aesthetics tolerable to the normative state standards and the public's moral palate. Under this power relation between queer TV and the heteronormatively structured state, queerness escapes total erasure if it appears in its abject, tragic form, deprived of a viable, threatening futurity. A generic coming-out story that fractures a previously

---

1. In this chapter, I use the terms gay and homosexual to denote explicitly homosexual or homoerotic referents. My use of "queer" as an adjective is inclusive of all LGBTQ concepts and beyond (including certain forms of homosociality). I also occasionally use "queer" as a verb to refer to the act of rendering the familiar strange in the general sense, and "queerness" as an ambiguous, abjected positionality outside of normative social meanings.

harmonious Chinese family may be more tolerable, for its narrative further coheres straight time—affirming the impossibility of gay life under a hegemonic symbolic order.[2] In the case of *Addicted*, the exact reasons for the ban may never be fully known, but the particular queer threat that prompted an expansion of heteronormative state censorship policy can be analyzed and theorized from the TV drama itself. Focusing on the desires of the two main characters, this chapter demonstrates how *Addicted* offers a radical queer utopianism that escapes the normative trappings of Chinese filial obsessions and prohibitions. Instead of replicating a more familiar narrative of the clash between homosexuality and Chinese kinship, the banned drama succeeded in circumventing and deferring this queer fatalism—an achievement that was ironically made possible by the very abrupt ban at the hands of state censors. Building on Judith Butler's (1995, 1997) notion of gender melancholia and José Esteban Muñoz's (2009) work on queer utopia, this chapter argues that the state ban has inadvertently created a form of public mourning that performatively reenacts the melancholic structure of desire that is both at the heart of the *Addicted* world and at the margins of straight temporality.

For Muñoz, "Utopia is an idealist mode of critique that reminds us that there is something missing, that the present and presence (and its opposite number, absence) is not enough" (2009, 100). This utopian mode of critique conforms neither to the homophobic violence of the present nor to the pragmatic goals of queer politics. Rather than obsessing over the problems and solutions in the here and now, Muñoz looks forward to what the future might bring by means of queer performances that challenge straight time. As a TV series without any explicit references to queer political goals or even homophobia in China, *Addicted* is playfully oblivious to the serious tensions between queer Chinese children, their families, and the homophobic state, at least in its aired episodes. This strategic innocence/ignorance can be thought of as a rejection of the homophobic present and an invitation to alternative queer imaginations in the future. However, to move beyond the present requires a foreclosure of what is familiar, including ideas such as homosexual orientation and queer abjection, which I will argue are both disavowed and censored by the plot and the state censors alike.

Building on the tropes of melancholia and utopian futurity, my theorization of a queer utopianism in *Addicted* consists of three key elements. First, a refusal to name the forbidden homosexual desires explicitly, thereby bypassing a sexual

---

2. I use the "symbolic order" to refer to various hegemonic systems of language, law, and norms that govern conscious day-to-day life under a heteronormative society. This Lacanian psychoanalytic concept is commonly used by queer theorists like Judith Butler (1995, 1997) and Lee Edelman (2004) to theorize gender and queerness. Without subscribing to a universal theory of the symbolic, I aim to illustrate how multiple hegemonic systems (including norms of filial piety) work in tandem in the fictional world of *Addicted* and the larger Chinese society.

binarism underlying the structure of conflict between the queer community in China and the normative Chinese society. Second, a rejection of the abject status quo that most LGBTQ people in China must live with in everyday life through a phantasmatic reimagining of kinship and queer romance in the fictive world. Third, a deferral of catharsis, a satisfying ending/resolution, or victory in conventional queer politics, thanks to the state ban, that ironically keeps queer alternatives and desires alive through a structure of mourning. In reaching these theorizations, I rely primarily on plot analysis that critically juxtaposes its fantasy structures with the lived reality outside the *Addicted* world, and speculates on what symbolic terms the plot resignifies and why the series was so "addictive" to viewers. To substantiate the third element pertaining to public mourning, I turn to a discourse analysis of viewers' online discussions of the series (and its ban) in major social media platforms, including Zhihu (知乎), Baidu Forums (百度论坛), and YouTube. This analysis of hundreds of viewer reactions took place multiple times between 2017 to 2021, as the popular series continued to attract new viewers during the pandemic. This prolonged melancholic public attachment to the series years after its ban further strengthens my hypothesis that state censorship unintentionally helped make the series even more addictive and powerful as a blueprint for queer desires on the horizon.

Following the termination of the *Addicted* web series, the Chinese government rolled out new media regulations in June 2017, targeting several issues of high sensitivity, including religious and sexual expressions. In the official statement, homosexuality is listed among a range of "abnormal sexual relations and behaviors," ranging from incest to sexual violence (CNSA 2017). This hardline position from the party-state and the ban of *Addicted* spurred a public outcry that reverberated across social media sites in China and beyond (Sonmez 2016). From a mainstream LGBTQ activist perspective, the omnibus regulation unfairly groups homosexuality with incest, rape, and unauthorized religious content—a backward step that fails to recognize members of the Chinese LGBTQ community as good citizens of the state, deserving of respect and normalization. Alternatively, however, the comprehensive ban can be interpreted as an effect of state panic and paranoia: how can homosexuality or homoeroticism be effectively banned if it never appears under the sign of LGBTQ, but disguises itself under an umbrella of unspeakable desires and vices? As the name *Addicted* suggests, the web drama is no stranger to many other banned themes, such as drugs and violence, under the new censorship policy. The title "Addicted" (*shangyin*; 上瘾) directly refers to addiction, and combining the first names of the two main characters (Gu Hai; 顾海 and Bai Luoyin; 白洛因) constitutes "heroin" (*hai-luoyin*; 海洛因) in Chinese. Besides signaling the addictive nature of this fictive gay relationship, the name also suggests the series' addictive potential, evident in the

60 million views it attracted shortly after Valentine's Day.³ Besides the implied reference to illicit drugs, *Addicted* also depicts domestic violence, rape, battery, bribery, and abuses of power as productive forces behind the spotlighted gay relationship.

Belonging to the boys' love (BL hereafter) or *yaoi* genre historically created for a predominately female audience in Japan, *Addicted* was directed and produced by Chai Jidan (柴鸡蛋), a heterosexual Chinese female author who wrote the original novel published online. Far from being an activism-oriented project, *Addicted* focuses on the fantasized romance between men and its commodifiable pleasures, and its cast members and directors never publicly acknowledged any affiliation with LGBTQ groups or had any prior experience with other gay-themed projects. These conditions are drastically different from those of a gay film produced in the West or other Asian countries with more queer-friendly social atmospheres. Filmed in the streets of Beijing and in a society where homosexuality remains a tabooed discursive subject, *Addicted*'s BL elements are met with unique challenges, unintended consequences, and unpredictability. In analyzing the plot below, I will explain how the series' genre and the online media censors worked together to allow a queer utopianism to take place against a dystopian societal backdrop. I will also examine the critical themes of performativity, melancholia, and identification underlying the plot and reception of the series. Focusing on the relationship between the two main characters, this chapter also illustrates the role of grief in enabling their same-sex love and argues that the overcoming of their shared grief and precariousness works to threaten the heterosexual symbolic by resignifying norms of kinship and sexuality.

Genre, Censorship, and Queer Escapism

Taking place in contemporary Beijing, the story of *Addicted* revolves around the relationship of two high school students—Bai Luoyin and Gu Hai. Luoyin lives in a poor region of town and attends a low-performing high school, which suggests a bleak future because of China's infamous college entrance system. He lives with his caring but often careless dad, who works at a construction site. Luoyin's mom left them when he was little and, at the beginning of the plot, is about to marry again to a powerful and affluent military general who happens to be the father of Hai, whose first wife passed away due to a tragic accident when Hai was little. From the start, Hai expresses his strong discontent with the marriage arrangement and with the possibility that his stepmom would bring her own son (Luoyin) into the house. He dramatically rebelled and

---

3. See more at https://www.zhihu.com/question/40087662 and https://www.zhihu.com/question/40087662/answer/85421934.

decided to transfer to another high school, which, thanks to the orchestration of the author, happens to be the same school Luoyin attends. At this point, the two characters had no awareness of their family origins, and their story develops independently despite occasional pestering from their parents. In contrast to the unrealistic background story that would require incredible odds to occur in real life, the heterosexual symbolic permeates the plot environment through the assumption of heteronormativity that renders homosexuality invisible.[4] From the school uniforms students wear to the Northern dim sum sold on the streets, the everyday commonalities in the series signal a sense of normalcy and school-aged innocence. It is soon revealed that both characters have been in heterosexual relationships. This announcement, coupled with the desire of their single parents to recover their ideal nuclear family through remarriage, makes the homoerotic content later on more subversive and threatening to the symbolic order than if the heteronormative social world were repudiated from the very start.

More precisely speaking, the heterosexual symbolic comes less from the plot itself than from the larger social environment that made gay-themed filming in China's political center possible. To perform such a dangerous act, the imaginary plot must embed itself in the materiality of its surroundings and carefully negotiate norms of governmentality to pass the initial censors. The term "homosexual," or any identity marker that makes them categorically "abnormal," does not appear anywhere in the series, as if the characters have no conception of what that term might entail. Instead of depicting a form of abject homosexuality under state and cultural violence, the homoerotic love eventually developed between the two characters seemingly faces little disapproval from their families and friends, who mostly interpret their affections and attachment to each other as brotherly love or a deep same-sex friendship that should be encouraged. It is only when their girlfriends from their past intrude on their lives that the tension between the homosexual and the heterosexual becomes sharpened.

The dynamics between the BL couple and their heterosexual families and girlfriends in *Addicted* share certain similarities to the bromance TV/film genre that has gained increased popularity in American cinema. Bromance-themed American cinematic productions depicting strong, intimate bonds between heterosexual men, such as *Humpday* (dir. Lynn Shelton, 2009) and *I Love You, Man* (dir. John Hamburg, 2009), demonstrate how both a stabilizing domestic space

---

4. It is remarkable that the plot never portrays the sexualities of the BL couple as abnormal or perverse, and the characters have never struggled over their sexual attractions, thanks to the fact that they both had girlfriends before meeting each other. Thus, the heterosexual symbolic in the *Addicted* world does not actively repress queerness, but rather pretends that it is never present—which is less antagonistic and nihilistic than how queer negativity theories (Edelman 2004; Stanley 2011) would characterize the relation between heteronormativity and queerness.

and a shared, arguably misogynistic annoyance over "women problems" could be necessary anchoring grounds for male intimacy (DeAngelis 2014, 11–12). Both Hai and Luoyin display their annoyance over their ex-girlfriends, whose lingering presence in their lives poses a potential threat to their homoerotic bonds. The evidence of past heterosexual relationships helps establish their male intimacy as outwardly non-sexual, while at the same time rendering their sexual intimacy ineligible for full homosexual signification. Their ambiguous intimacy is further blurred by their parents' effort to reintegrate them into a stable heterosexual family through remarriage, where the pair would become legal stepbrothers. As such, the success of heterosexual family integration depends on the intimacy of the BL couple, even if it leads to incest. The parents' delight in and celebration of their sons' observed intimacy is another parodic iteration of compulsory heteronormativity. If bromance "queers" American cinema by rendering heterosexuality strange, BL in *Addicted* "queers" all fraternal relations as possibly incestuous.

The series' blurring of homosocial and homosexual desires also helps advance a plot where two young "straight" men could fall in love with each other. Their first impressions of each other are marked by antagonism and bickering. The two share certain personality traits: they are both stubborn, rebellious, even territorial. Yet their differences seem to resemble the *wen/wu* (文/武; literary/martial) dyad in Chinese masculinity studies first articulated by Kam Louie (2002), a male masculinity spectrum that has been popularized nowadays and widely deployed, if not exploited, in today's Chinese-language entertainment media (as evidenced through other case studies in *QTC*). *Wen* refers to cultural attainment, exemplified by highly educated Confucian officials in imperial China, whereas *wu* refers to physical prowess evident in the military class (Louie 2002). As the active "pursuer," Hai's first acts of "pursuit" are to annoy Luoyin and even set up traps to embarrass him in front of their teachers and classmates. His hypermasculine physicality, coupled with his military family background, suggests that Hai has a quintessential *wu* masculinity. In contrast, Luoyin is portrayed as more introverted and vulnerable, and, to Hai's chagrin, a much better student, highly skilled in calligraphy—making Luoyin a *wen* type. But despite the easy slippage that may read *wen* masculinity as effeminate and gay in a Western gender/sexual paradigm, Geng Song's (Song and Hird 2013) alternative *yin/yang* (阴/阳) framework helps explain why male same-sex eroticism was tolerated in premodern China if the man involved in such relationships can be both *yin* or *yang* without jeopardizing his masculinity. Song's study of Chinese literary masterpieces, *The Water Margins* (水浒传) and *Romance of the Three Kingdoms* (三国演义), further reveals the significance of homosociality in constructing Chinese masculinity, since the male heroes rarely exhibit sexual interest in women (Song and Hird 2013, 5). While the male homosocial intimacies in these classical novels are primarily between heroes of *wu* types, the *yin/yang* framework allows readings of same-sex intimacy between men who occupy opposite ends of the *wen/wu* spectrum. Given the gendered connotation of *yin/yang*, intimacies between *wen* and *wu* men could convey at least a romantic potential under certain circumstances.

If the *wen/wu* dyad can be understood as complimentary attributes of Chinese masculinity, not essentialist identities, then even acts of bickering and microaggressions could be interpreted or re-signified as touchy-feely closeness between male friends. Alvin K. H. Wong describes seemingly ordinary affects involving caring and frustration in *Addicted* as queer "affective overcoming," a protean force that "also reorders the kinship form, transforms the incest taboo and imagines a desire that borders between brotherhood and queer love" (2020, 510). In this light, affective exchanges between the pair can be understood as iterations of a "queering" that overcomes normative meanings of both quotidian and culturally significant affects and emotional bonds, infusing them with potential queer undertones. Upon learning serendipitously from another classmate that Luoyin's mother left him and his father for another man, Hai's acts of aggression take on predominately affectionate meanings. For example, in Episode 1, Hai tears away Luoyin's calligraphy homework assignment and brings it home. This is originally an act of revenge against Luoyin's condescending remarks about Luoyin's handwriting. However, as Hai studies the calligraphy, he becomes enchanted with the style and begins imitating it through practice. The knowledge of Luoyin's single-parent family background is also a key, deeper-level ingredient that makes Hai's enchantment with another man possible. He starts covertly following Luoyin to his home and, after seeing his poor living conditions, begins buying much-needed food and supplies for him. When Luoyin confronts him about the reason behind these acts of kindness, Hai admits that he is behind the pranks and revengeful acts, and justifies his presents as a way to redeem himself. Thus, over-generosity towards one's own sex is re-signified and rationalized through the language of confession and redemption as praiseworthy and noble. In this framing, there is no need for justification based on romantic longing or sexual orientation. The creative resignification itself is sufficient, without the need for disclosing or citing essential sexual identities.

Hence, it could be argued that neither heterosexuality nor homosexuality truly exist in the fictive world of *Addicted*. As Judith Butler argues in *The Psychic Life of Power* (1997) and elsewhere, heterosexuality and homosexuality have a co-constitutive relationship with one another. Heterosexuality is constituted through a repudiation of the possibility of homosexuality and vice versa. Thus, the absence of the idea of homosexuality in *Addicted* suggests that a conscious repudiation of the idea of homosexuality is impossible, so a heterosexual identity fails to be constituted coherently in the more Western sense of the term. The characters rarely have to or feel the need to give an account of their sexuality—forgoing the need for sexual confession that is a core technology of heteronormativity.[5] In contrast, other queer Chinese cinematic productions rarely bypass the tensions emerged in a highly heteronormative and regulative space. For example, Chris Berry's (2013, 248) analysis of the film *East Palace, West Palace* (东宫, 西宫; dir. Zhang Yuan, 1996) demonstrates how social minorities in China often find themselves fighting for their public visibility, as depicted in highly dramatized cinematic forms. The tensions between A Lan, a gay man, and the Beijing policeman with whom he is infatuated highlight the intensified power play between the homophobic state and the homosexual subject. In such an environment, the repudiation of homosexuality is both conscious and explicit, whereas the tensions between queerness and the heterosexual symbolic in *Addicted* are much more subtle. Nonetheless, this does not mean that an unconscious heteronormativity cannot still be operative. Butler argues that the "ritualized repetition of conventions" that produced gender is "socially compelled in part by the force of a compulsory heterosexuality" (1997, 144). Since heterosexuality is absent in the narrative of *Addicted*, a new term is needed to account for the ritualized social norms still operative in this fictive reality.

To this end, I propose the substitution of "heterosexuality" with "filial piety" in Confucianism. "Compulsory filial piety" regulates sexuality regardless of the existence of a sexual binarism. Here, I build on P. Steven Sangren's (2017) anthropological and psychoanalytical account of Chinese patriliny, which is a mode of desire production and "instituted fantasy" surrounding the filial son. A son is obligated, under compulsory filial piety, to form a family with a woman and produce heirs in order to fulfill his duties to his parents and ancestors. Thus, filial piety encompasses the heterosexual symbolic without naming it explicitly. Even heterosexual romance, when forged without immediate concerns of marriage and children, is ultimately enabled and encouraged by the possibilities of fulfilling one's duties of filial piety. This is consistent with the reality of the Chinese dating scene today, where the pressure to marry is magnified by the neoliberal ideals of financial security and social status solidified in marriage. It should also be noted that unlike the fictive world of *Addicted*, Western queer identity politics and cultures have been heavily shaping, and appropriated by, mainland Chinese society since the early 1990s (Rofel 2007). As more and more Chinese gain access to LGBTQ knowledge and the techniques of governmentality often associated with it, it is plausible that most production crew members and viewers have a basic awareness of gay identity in tension with the heterosexual symbolic. Still, the fictive world of the TV series itself, despite sharing a strong overlap with the

---

5. Here, I am referring to Michel Foucault's (1990, 2021) work linking confessional practices in Christian pastoral care to the emergence of perverse sexualities in Western modernity. To recount one's sexual life and fantasies in detail—in a clinical setting, for instance—contributes to the knowledge and normalization of sexuality. See Foucault's *The History of Sexuality, Vol. 1: An Introduction* (1990) and *Vol. 4: Confessions of the Flesh* (2021).

Chinese social world today, offers a rare escapism from the more salient sexual categories and subjugations intruding the Chinese society.

Grief, Precariousness, and Homosociality

Under the Chinese version of the heterosexual symbolic (in both the fictive and the social world), there also exist forms of power that render what is "grievable" and what is "ungrievable." Not all forms of loss are equally deserving of grief and mourning, thanks to the hierarchies the symbolic attributes to various bodies and ways of life.[6] The loss of Hai's mother is unequivocally grievable, as the loss signifies the brokenness of the heterosexual family unit, without which filial piety losses its meaning. Similarly, the early divorce in Luoyin's family is also a grievable loss of the same family ideal. The same logic can be extended to the loss of a girlfriend—the imagined significant other who plays an essential role in forming new heterosexual families under compulsory filial piety. Butler makes a counterintuitive claim that "the 'truest' lesbian melancholic is the strictly straight woman, and the 'truest' gay male melancholic is the strictly straight man" (1995, 177). This statement suggests that straight people suffer from the most severe form of gay melancholia, for they, unlike gay people, cannot even express grief over the loss of someone that they are not supposed to care very much about under heterosexual norms.[7] For those who identify with the exclusive "straight male" identity, the possibility of same-sex love is fully repudiated (and lost) from the start, yet its ungrievability prohibits grieving from happening. Since that loss cannot be recuperated, the lost object (homosexual desires) must be "incorporated"[8] into the ego and continues to haunt it—leading to the strongest form of gay male melancholia. The two "straight" characters in *Addicted* may not be the "truest" gay melancholics, but they still carry with them a repudiated possibility of same-sex love under compulsory filial piety, in which the loss of homosexual love makes too little sense to be grievable.

---

6. My analysis of grief builds on Butler's discussions in *Precarious Life: The Powers of Mourning and Violence* (2004) and "Melancholy Gender" (1995). See also *Frames of War: When Is Life Grievable?* (Butler 2009).
7. In the same section of "Melancholy Gender," Butler (1995) then argues that drag allegorizes heterosexual melancholy, formed from a refusal to grieve the same gender as a possible love object. Hence, straight people's refusal to love others of the same gender can be read as a kind of drag performance: they may still possess the potential for same-sex love, but the gendered matrix prohibits it. Since mourning and closure never happened, they cannot simply move on with their lives; instead, they incorporate that lost object deep in their psyche as gay melancholics.
8. I am referring to the idea of "melancholic incorporation" Butler discusses in relation to Sigmund Freud's 1949 publication, *The Ego and the Id*, in her paper "Melancholy Gender" (1995).

Unacknowledged under the Chinese heterosexual symbolic, same-sex desires are difficult to be recognized as real and legitimate desires. Even if same-sex desires were visibly performed under such a framing in *Addicted*, their desires still would not be recognized as homosexuality. Instead, only recognized forms of same-sex bonds, such as same-sex friendships and fraternal relationships, are celebrated, sometimes even invoked to capture same-sex desires. I argue that in *Addicted*, the homosocial dimension in the pair's relationship goes beyond the quintessential "erotic triangle" underlying most homosocial relations, as theorized by Eve Sedgwick (1985). Instead of basing homosocial bonds on erotic rivalry over a woman, the heterosexual socialization that Sedgwick recognizes as an integral goal of homosociality is achieved through a communion of powerful affects like grief shared by Hai and Luoyin. Given the significance of grief as a filial affect in Confucian and Chinese cultures, it doubly functions as a conduit for both filial and homoerotic desires in *Addicted*.

Thus, wrapping homoerotic content within honorable homosocial activities could be interpreted as an effective strategic maneuver on the part of the producers to evade TV censorship. In navigating an ambiguous regulatory field, queer TV productions in China often practice self-censorship, and the digital social platforms provide alternative outlets for homosexual content to reach a broader audience (Shaw and Zhang 2017). Given these unique conditions, rebranding or masquerading homoeroticism as homosociality may serve both the purpose of self-sanitization and the economic incentive to reach the largest audience possible. In *Addicted*, such covert operations are ubiquitous. For instance, Hai's desire to sleep in the same bed with Luoyin, even with clear sexual and romantic intent on Hai's part, never comes across as such in the perception of Luoyin's father, who regarded such desire as strong brotherly love that he himself envies. The father's own gay melancholia thus enables a reflexive resignification of the observed same-sex intimacy between his son and his friend. His own lack of same-sex intimacy, repudiated since childhood for reasons unknown, is redeemed through the same-sex intimacy his son enjoys. When Hai stops sleeping at his house after a serious confrontation, it is Luoyin's father who urges Luoyin to bring Hai back home, citing his own regrets for not ever having such a "good brother." This blurring of lines between gay love and brotherly love occurs frequently in *Addicted*. Their classmates regard them simply as best friends, as some female classmates attempt to win the heart of one of them by first talking to the other member of the pair for "insider tips." Much later in the series, when Luoyin's mother/Hai's stepmother witnesses their closeness, she becomes ecstatic, hopeful at the prospect of a happy second marriage that brings two boys who already love each other under the same roof as brothers. Such an "innocent" take on same-sex desire is, again, only possible in an utopian fantasy in which no strict binary between heterosexual and homosexual exists. Unlike the American brand of the heterosexual symbolic, which repudiates not only genital acts among the same sex but also suspiciously intimate same-sex friendships, the Chinese heterosexual symbolic has not yet repudiated male closeness in general (see, for example, Song 2019; Yang and Xu 2017). This nuanced symbolic thus recognizes the loss of brotherly love as legitimate grief.

Interestingly, these grievable losses, I argue, serve as a strong foundation from which homoerotic desires are made possible in *Addicted*. As indicated above, the grievable loss of a mother in their lives brings the two young men together in the first place. Their shared precariousness enabled them to overcome the barriers against same-sex intimacy imposed by compulsory filial piety. It is clearly shown in the series that Hai's expression of love toward Luoyin and Luoyin's gradual acceptance and return of Hai's love reach a new height during moments of shared precariousness and grief. For instance, following a malicious incident when a bully slanders Luoyin's family history in front of the whole class, Hai not only stands up for him, but also accompanies Luoyin to consume bottles of beer and street food. Hai confesses his own precariousness (in the form of his lost mother) to justify his obsession with Luoyin: "Did you see me act this way toward any other guy?" This rhetorical question reveals that Hai is experiencing a form of care and love previously absent (or repudiated) from his life, and it is the shared precariousness that allowed the slow awakening of a part of him that has been repudiated for too long. This is also the moment when Luoyin first learns about Hai's grief, and we start to see his reaction toward Hai's affection slowly transform from confusion and dismissal to acceptance and mutual desire from this point forward.

Under conditions of shared precariousness, the possibility of homosexual love no longer needs to be repudiated, as long as it can be camouflaged as recognized forms of same-sex bonds the culture still regards as useful for maintaining the Chinese heterosexual symbolic. As two guys with no previous history of same-sex relations, they too undergo the process of camouflage and slow awakening of desires as they come to terms with their relationship. Without any access to LGBTQ norms to cite and enact, the characters must work out their own understanding of same-sex desires by citing available norms from the heterosexual symbolic, often in the service of the symbolic. While sleeping in the same bed, Hai frequently attempts to embrace Luoyin in his arms and makes sexual jokes. These jokes sometimes justify same-sex sexual activities as a means to develop their sexual skills with women. One night, the conversation turns serious as Luoyin questions whether their behaviors and Hai's sexual demands are considered "normal." To respond, Hai confesses that:

> Is not because of this [sex] that I want to be together with you. I am also a normal guy, if I really wanted this [sex], why don't I find a female? It is because I really like you too much that I cannot control. In fact, you're too clean/pure in my head for me to touch you.

This is a rare incident in the entire series in which the question of sexual normalcy is brought up. Despite the mention of Hai being "a normal guy," it does not necessarily mean that the binary between heterosexuality and homosexuality emerges in the story. Instead, the normalcy could suggest one's ability to follow the norms of filial piety. Falling in love with someone of the same sex does not directly preclude one from fulfilling their duties. This is why Hai could maintain his love for Luoyin without completely renouncing his heterosexual relationship. When his girlfriend comes back to demand his attention, Hai seems to have lost interest in her. However, after a confrontation that ends up with Hai's girlfriend storming out of the building, it is Luoyin who urges Hai to chase after her to make sure that she will be safe. Hai complies out of his love for Luoyin. When the girlfriend sees Hai again, she stops crying and exclaims: "This is the first time that you ever chased out after me after a fight." Thus, this "improved" heterosexual behavior is made possible through homosexual love—demonstrating their symbiotic relationality.

In contrast, other Chinese queer films and dramas often highlight the tension between heterosexual and homosexual love, such as *Uncontrolled Love* (不可抗力; dir. Sun Cheng Zhi, 2016). Former girlfriends of main characters often openly confront their boyfriends' newfound taste in their own sex, and such dramatization frequently ends in tragedy. These shows also pit homosexual love directly against filial piety, forcing lovers to choose from a strictly binary option: to continue their love by rejecting all obligations, or fulfill their obligations and live in a loveless marriage. In *Addicted*, however, this binarism appears to be false. Rather, homoerotic love and filial piety seem to be mutually beneficial. The rare intimacy between Hai and Luoyin, after the big revelation that their parents are soon to be married, helps to justify the heterosexual marriage and the renewal of the ideal family structure under filial piety. In turn, the marriage arrangement also encourages their intimacy to flourish under the perfect disguise of legal fraternal bonds. Moreover, it is also due to Luoyin's expressed desire to gain independence and freedom that his father decides to marry another woman he has been in love with. Perhaps, because of limited space in Luoyin's house, his dad's remarriage implies that Luoyin must move out and live with Hai in their own apartment, one of many owned by Hai's affluent father. Moreover, the moment of marriage, followed by a permanent departure, constitutes another key moment of grief in *Addicted*. This time, it is the "loss" of his father that causes Luoyin to grieve with strong emotions. Unsurprisingly, this is also when Hai makes his promise to take care of him: "I will take good care of you, making up for the love you missed for the last 10 years."

Therefore, the absence of sexual essentialism in *Addicted* allows for queer desires and tensions to be resignified and masqueraded as acceptable same-sex bonds. However, how can we account for the strong reaction from the Chinese censors that banned the popular TV series and issued an official statement extending the ban to all productions with LGBTQ content? What is the source of anxiety and insecurity outside of the fictive world? As I briefly mentioned above, the heterosexual symbolic in the Chinese social world today differs from the fictive symbolic in the series in one substantial way: conceptions of a binary opposition between homosexuality and heterosexuality have taken root and a co-constitutive relationship has been established in the Chinese social world today. Therefore, the real Chinese symbolic operates through the exclusionary logic of repudiation that Butler names. This logic of repudiation is enacted to sustain heterosexuality as a coherent identity through an exclusion of an abject homosexuality. This logic forecloses "precisely the kind of complex crossings of identification and desire which might exceed and contest the binary frame itself" (Butler 1993, 103). That is to say, the working of the heterosexual symbolic prohibits fluid or incoherent identities from forming. Since the symbolic already anticipates a refusal to identify with hegemonic heterosexuality, forms of resistance that hinge on such a refusal cannot pose a sufficient threat to rework the symbolic. The logic of repudiation "presupposes a heterosexual relationality that relegates homosexual possibility to the transient domain of the imaginary" (Butler 1993, 111). In this domain, homosexual identification, especially as another coherent identity, cannot seriously challenge the working of the symbolic. Therefore, to truly challenge the symbolic, resistance must overcome both the abject status of homosexuality and the exclusionary logic of repudiation, in ways unanticipated by the symbolic itself.

The performative acts in the fictive world of *Addicted*, I argue, do precisely what is needed to pose a serious threat to the Chinese heterosexual symbolic. Most other Chinese and Sinophone LGBTQ productions, such as the film *Lan Yu* (蓝宇; dir. Stanley Kwan, 2001) and the TV drama *Crystal Boys* (PTS, Taiwan, 2003), adhere to the logic of repudiation by adopting coherent gay identities in direct conflict with compulsory filial piety[9]—tensions, rebellions, and tragedies already anticipated in the working of the symbolic. No matter how heroic and well-written the stories may be, these depictions of homosexual love fail to overcome the symbolic and operate only in the realm of the imaginary. In contrast, *Addicted* offers an alternative, utopian reality in which the exclusive logic is much less operative. The two characters in love never affirm their homosexuality, heterosexuality, or bisexuality. Nor could they give a clear account of their sexuality, since the linguistic system in their world does not allow such an articulation or a form of address to take place. Instead of completely repudiating their past heterosexual relationships and confronting compulsory filial piety, these characters learn to rework the symbolic through the citation and

---

9. According to Alvin K. H. Wong (2012), the tension between a Chinese hetero-patriarch and his child with non-normative sexuality is also depicted in lesbian films, such as Alice Wu's *Saving Face* (面子; 2005, USA).

performance of same-sex bonds already tolerated in the symbolic.[10] After citing norms of same-sex friendship and brotherly love as a foundation of their love relationship, the characters resignify these relationships by giving them new homoerotic meanings and possibilities. Consequently, the fictive world affords the opportunity for two young men to forge a profound, loving relationship with little pushback from their surroundings. This is a situation that completely defies the logic of repudiation that sustains the symbolic, and the resulting erotic possibilities transcend the abject status of homosexuality through creative resignifications that the symbolic fails to foresee.

Public Melancholia

Of course, these creative resignifications occur in an imagined reality and cannot truly challenge the symbolic without a strong connection to the larger Chinese social world today. The Chinese censors already preemptively deleted graphic sexual scenes between the two characters before allowing *Addicted* to air. The censors followed the logic of repudiation by refusing to recognize eroticized same-sex behaviors as part of the symbolic. But what they failed to anticipate is that, despite the forceful removal of sexual scenes, the non-sexual scenes that depict the affections and intimacy between Hai and Luoyin were sufficient to attract more than 100 million views shortly after its release (BBC 2016). Not only was the series able to act on multiple emotional registers of Chinese viewers by constructing an alternative, utopian reality, it also solicits grief as the common denominator to which everyone can relate, and masterfully resignifies it to transform the formally unspeakable, ungrievable love of homosexuality into something that is grievable and potentially valorized. This utopian same-sex erotics refuses to occupy a confined, predetermined social space of abjection and strives to occupy the space of ordinary friendships, classrooms, and families. In short, homosexuality could happen anywhere with anyone—a subversive effect that is arguably strengthened by the removal of sexual scenes, since leaving the sex out of the picture greatly expands the interpretive possibilities of same-sex intimacy depicted in *Addicted*.

Thus, it should come as no surprise that online forums on *Addicted* sometimes involve "straight" men confessing their enjoyment of watching *Addicted* and doubting their sexuality.[11] Some self-proclaimed straight male viewers admitted

---

10. It is notable that *Addicted* does not conform to either the Confucian family ethics or the Western liberal model that Chris Berry (2007) has compared. The BL couple's ambiguous lover-brother relationship was made possible precisely through their parents' desires to rebuild broken families. They do not desire to break away from their filial duties or entirely submit to the mandates from their parents.
11. A list of responses from self-identified straight male viewers can be found on Zhihu at https://www.zhihu.com/question/40565622.

that they initially regarded the two main characters as romantic rivals for a woman, only to be later mesmerized by their masculine yet homosexual love. "My sexual orientation is under merciless bombardment!" said one straight male blogger, who also warned others to watch the series with caution.[12] This is not to even mention the millions of straight female fans—the core intended audience of the genre—many of whom are believed to regard male homosexual love as "pure love" free from reproductive concerns and jealousy common in heterosexual relationships. This tendency to idealize BL has even manifested in a sub-BL genre involving incestuous father-son relations—which can be thought of as a superior form of romance that is also conducive to alternative conceptualizations of power dynamics in Chinese familial and political lives (Yang and Xu 2013).

Moreover, it should be noted that the resignifications in *Addicted* go beyond the realm of sexuality and into the political domain. Hai often expresses his love for Luoyin through leveraging his privileged personal connections. Since Luoyin's father works a low-wage construction job, Hai contacts a colleague of his father to help move Luoyin's father to a new position with a much higher wage and benefits. After learning about Auntie Zhou's (a family friend soon to be married to Luoyin's father) open-air food business being raided by corrupt local police, Hai pulls a few strings to allow Auntie Zhou to open a brand-new store in a safer location. These behaviors of favor asking are prevalent in Chinese society today, especially among corrupt politicians. Thus, to occupy the space of privilege and corruption for the purpose of expressing and manifesting homosexual love could have posed an embarrassing threat to the symbolic. It is difficult to know the extent to which these political concerns contributed to the decision to ban the series, since the official statement focuses much more on issues of sex than politics. But it is plausible that these additional concerns at least added to the anxiety felt by Chinese officials, who had more reasons to pull a newly released web series off of the Chinese cyberspace without delay.

After the abrupt online crackdown, a form of public melancholia emerged among the tens of millions of viewers and fans of *Addicted*. The first season contains only 15 episodes of a little more than 20 minutes each after censorship. They government pulled the plug around Episode 12, making it suddenly inaccessible on all Chinese websites. Viewers had to go to uncensored foreign websites or bypass the Chinese internet firewall to access YouTube, only to find out that the series ends with a cliffhanger—the sudden appearance of Luoyin's girlfriend, just returned from abroad. The return of Luoyin's girlfriend threatens the "brotherly-love" cover of the pair, since if Luoyin is forced to renounce his heterosexual love with his girlfriend, his homosexual relationship with Hai may need to be affirmed. Without the blurred intimacy protected under normative kinship, the entire queer utopian reality that had sustained the plot in all the

---

12. See https://freewechat.com/a/MzA3MDcyNTIyNA==/402664909/1.

available episodes would be on the verge of collapse. Indeed, in Chai Jidan's original literary account, the persistently inquisitive girlfriend eventually found out about their love affair but kept the secret to herself. It is around these chapters that terms like "homosexuality" appear explicitly in the text for the first time. Luoyin and Hai continued indulging in their unbridled desires after Luoyin's girlfriend gave up, but it becomes clear that it will only be a matter of time until *Addicted*'s narrative confronts the seismic clash between unveiled queerness and the hegemonic Chinese kinship order—a familiar queer fate that was deferred in infinite suspension by state censorship.

But given the sheer size of viewership during the airing period, most TV viewers of *Addicted* had likely never read the novel. Still mesmerized by and immersed in the utopian sensual world of *Addicted*, the ban violently deprived them of their access to such an alternative reality. When news broke out that the production crew had given up on the possibility of a second season and that the two leading actors had been prohibited from appearing in public together, a deep sense of grief permeated online Chinese forums. "It's like being forcibly stabbed in the chest," wrote one Zhihu user, who lamented over the ban that reminded him of the fragile reality of being gay in China.[13] Many gay viewers echoed similar sentiments that the ban was a painful wake-up call that their own lives would never come close to the utopian romance in *Addicted*, and yet many kept rewatching it years afterward on YouTube. English comments frequently confess viewers' incurable addiction to the series: "my heart cried like a baby" when the series was banned, and "rewatching this bring(s) back that devasted feeling I can't handle"; " I just finished the whole series for the 7th time . . . this is some kind of ADDICTION that no amount of rehab can ever cure."[14] This melancholic attachment to the series suggests that the ban helped sustain the utopian fantasy in many viewers' mind, despite the painful reality it violently invoked.

Meanwhile, the fictive world of *Addicted* quickly reached a foreign audience and gained huge popularity. Fans from Thailand to the United States hailed the Chinese gay-themed series as a rare LGBTQ milestone and joined the collective mourning across cultural and linguistic barriers.[15] When the cast traveled to Thailand for a big-stadium event dedicated to *Addicted* (reportedly sold out within five minutes), the two leading actors appeared on stage for interviews separately and only stood next to each other for less than three seconds before being pulled apart by stage staff.[16] This possibly suggests that state censorship has been internalized by the agencies overseeing the long-term career potentials of the two emerging stars. Since many fans expected to see the offstage friendship

---

13. See https://www.zhihu.com/question/40648505.
14. See some of the comments at https://www.youtube.com/watch?v=l74SxoKWgbs.
15. This is based on English comments on the episodes uploaded to YouTube and other discussions of the series on Reddit.
16. See https://item.btime.com/32mda9iu9cr8rmbgcqft2s26q3c?page=1.

between the two actors as a live continuation of the fictive world, their mandatory separation deepened the sense of loss and the melancholia it engendered.

Nonetheless, such public melancholia differs slightly from the Butlerian melancholia that centers on an ungrievable lost object. Rather, the lost object in this case is not only publicly grievable, but it can be effectively grieved among a massive number of people. This formerly ungrievable lost object has been significantly reworked through *Addicted* as intrinsically connected to a variety of relations worthy of grief. This fictive love relationship essentially incorporates same-sex erotic possibilities into the very structural fabric that sustains the symbolic. Thus, the ban exposes a weakness in the symbolic in dealing with an unpredictable phantom that takes too many possible forms. But to repudiate all such possible forms of queer love would require censorship of all forms of same-sex intimacy in subsequent TV productions—an impossible task to accomplish. What the ban of *Addicted* does achieve, however, is the materialization of grief from the fictive world into the Chinese social world. Instead of foreclosing the possibility of grieving homosexual love, it enables the grieving to happen on an unprecedented scale and creates an ethos of public mourning through online assemblies.

Conclusion

Perhaps, had the ban not happened and *Addicted* ran its natural course, there might not be a need for public mourning in the first place, since the story would likely provide a cathartic resolution even if the tragic elements unfolded later in the novel are adapted to the TV/computer screen. However, the ban essentially trapped the audience in a public melancholia that cannot be easily overcome—an unintended consequence that continues to haunt the hegemonic symbolic order. Without ever allowing the pivotal scene later on where Hai's father caught his son and stepson making out passionately to be TV-adapted, the queer cruising never comes to a stop, and the public forever mourns a loss that can never be fully articulated and incorporated into its psyche. Performatively, any pairs of brothers or male friends can be copies of Hai and Luoyin; the seemingly normative Chinese family is always undermined by the possibility of queer infiltration.

Put differently, the state helped extend the longevity of the queer utopianism in *Addicted* through the ban's temporal distortions. Recall that for Muñoz, queer futurity is forever deferred and always on the horizon, where radical queer potentiality is made possible through a collective temporal distortion. This messianic queer utopianism refutes the anti-queer present, placing hope in the "then and there." In contrast, the queer in *Addicted* and mainland China may not afford such a futurity, for Chinese filial obsessions insist on a reproductive future similar to the imaginary Child in Lee Edelman's *No Future* (2004). If neither the present nor the future is viable for queerness in the Chinese symbolic, what *Addicted* and the state censorship collaboratively achieved was essentially a queer utopianism in the present. The state became an unlikely ally in deferring the queer's tragic fate, opening up a temporal space where the hegemonic and the queer become indistinguishable in the here and now. By suspending and undermining the plot progression, the tragic queer future never materializes, while queer cruising of "heroin" continues indefinitely, along with other transgressive desires and vices.

Despite its ephemeral dominance over Chinese media platforms, *Addicted* has left an indelible impression on millions of enchanted Chinese viewers and on state officials who called for the crackdown. Through a reworking of grief and same-sex intimacy in the fictive world, homosexual love becomes possible in a variety of relational possibilities under compulsory filial piety. The lack of clear sexual binaries and of a logic of repudiation enabled the formation of complex subjectivities too amorphous to be completely subjugated in normative Chinese society. Although it may appear that the Chinese censors have won the battle and restored the abject status of homosexuality through the ban, such forms of state violence also produced forms of public mourning and melancholia that continue to pose a threat that may further destabilize the working of the symbolic. Since anything grievable is also something to be loved and desired, the sheer fact that a massive public mourning happened over banned same-sex love in China indicates a shift in public sentiment that refused to grieve AIDS patients not too long ago. If the Chinese heterosexual symbolic were to be challenged, it might be worthwhile to model any creative efforts after the script of *Addicted* by eschewing sexual essentialism and exclusionary logic all together and allowing broader coalitions and subjectivities to emerge and flourish.

5
Taming *The Untamed*
Politics and Gender in BL-Adapted Web Dramas

Jun Lei

The Untamed (陈情令), since its first release on Tencent Video on June 27, 2019, has remained the most popular and headline-generating web series in China. Set in a deliberately undefined ancient time, this costume drama features a refashioned "brotherhood" between two chivalrous male protagonists, Wei Wuxian (魏无羡; played by Xiao Zhan 肖战) and Lan Wangji (蓝忘机; played by Wang Yibo 王一博). The show not only topped Chinese domestic charts of popular web dramas for at least eighteen months, but also exerted a considerable impact on neighboring Asian markets and successfully reached an international (especially Anglo-American) audience through English-language sites, such as Netflix and YouTube. The show's capacity to break cultural barriers won praise from China's official media.

The Untamed is adapted from *Grandmaster of Demonic Cultivation* (魔道祖师, hereafter *Grandmaster*), an online boys' love (BL hereafter) novel. BL is a genre of homo-romance that originated in Japan and was introduced to China in the early 1990s (Feng 2013; Yang and Xu 2017). BL stories portray male-male homoerotic relationships, and BL fans mostly consist of heterosexual young women known as "rotten girls" (腐女). *Danmei* (耽美), the Chinese term for BL, clearly points to rotten girls' indulgence in male beauty. The use of "rotten" to describe BL fans indicates a negative evaluation of women whose enjoyment of homo-romance putatively ruins their desire for marriage and reproduction (Song 2022a). While online fiction is still a popular BL format among anime, comics/manga, games, and novels (ACGN), "BL-adapted web series" (耽改网剧) have become a more prominent cultural phenomenon in China. *The Untamed* was one such trendy adaptation that helped the BL genre and fandom to *chuquan* (出圈)—that is, to bring a niche genre to a mainstream audience and other fandoms who had no prior knowledge of it. BL was concomitantly exposed to more frequent public criticism and state censorship. In fact, regulatory policies targeted BL for "dual associations with homosexuality and pornography" (Yang and Xu 2017, 4).

Scholars of Chinese and Japanese BL have focused on three related topics. First, in terms of the assertion of female agency, researchers (Feng 2013; Galbraith 2011; Wood 2013; Yang and Xu 2016a, 2017) argue that the BL genre and its fan-based culture offer a unique affective space in which women more freely share opinions and feelings. They are thus empowered to challenge hierarchical gender order through creating and consuming male beauty. Second, regarding BL's capacity of queering gender expressions, they (Feng 2013; Wood 2013; Yang and Xu 2016b, 2017) also emphasize BL stories' discursive power in constructing a queer space that problematizes the fixed "nature" of sexes, genders, and sexualities. Lastly, in terms of subcultural fandoms' grassroots digital activism, scholars (Feng 2013; Wood 2013; Welker 2015; Yang and Xu 2016b, 2017) highlight BL communities' deftness with technology and flexible resistance to mainstream ideology and state censorship, and often optimistically deduce BL fandom as a "counter-public" that outsmarts official censors and subverts heterosexual norms.

Insightful as these views are, existing scholarship largely focuses on BL fiction (and on manga in the case of Japan), while in-depth analysis of web dramas remains lacking. Although the few scholarly publications on BL-adapted dramas (Hu and Wang 2020; Ng and Li 2020; Wang 2019) have all pointed out that in comparison with BL fiction, homosexual content is cleansed to appease censorship, they tend to follow BL fiction studies' view of narrative and fandom strategies. One most recent article breaks this academic inertia, focusing on the Chinese state's neoliberal and authoritarian governance of BL-adapted drama in fostering heteronormative consumer-subjects and social harmony (Ye 2022). Taking this research finding further, I propose that the "BL-adapted" (耽改) be studied as a genre related to but differentiated from BL. The two differ in narrative modes, fan objects, fan participation patterns, cultural function, and ideological positioning to dominant political and commercial forces. The study of the BL-adapted can also benefit from and contribute to existing debates on queerness in mainstream TV and media, in light of its crossover into mainstream genres such as campus, crime, suspense, history, *wuxia* (武侠; martial arts), and *xianxia* (仙侠; a Chinese fantasy about "cultivation" influenced by mythology, religious cultivations, and martial arts).

My discussion further suggests that the BL-adapted be studied as a survived but castrated mode of BL when media industry infiltration and state regulation have depleted sexual and homoerotic content of the BL-adapted genre and converted it into "bromance."[1] This chapter uses *The Untamed* as a starting point to discuss the potentials and limitations of BL-adapted dramas for fans and

---

1. "Bromance" is defined as an emotionally intense bond between straight men that allows certain physical intimacy such as cuddling and hugging without sex involved (Robinson, Anderson, and White 2018).

audiences to assert female agency and voice queer desire in the face of government censorship, commercial culture, and conservative gender ideologies. It first examines the fame and controversies revolving around the lead actors of *The Untamed* to reveal the BL-adapted as part of the Chinese entertainment industry's "pan-rotten" strategy for profit making, which relies on quickly manufacturing pop idols and effectively manipulating the audience's psychology and behavior. The chapter then extrapolates how the ideological expressions of BL-adapted dramas are shaped by state regulatory policies. Finally, the chapter analyzes four components of a commercially successful BL-adapted formula, as exemplified by *The Untamed*, which testifies to the limits within which queerness can be commodified on local entertainment TV without allowing for the tensions in the LGBTQ community to bubble over.

Cultivating the Audience for a "Pan-Rotten" Culture

The two male characters' chemistry in *The Untamed* not only excited the viewership of the show, but also inspired RPS (real person slash), a controversial subgenre of fanfiction featuring a film or television show's actors. One example is *Falling* (下坠), which caused controversies due to its homoerotic pairing of Xiao Zhan as a crossdressing sex worker and Wang Yibo as his underage customer. The story was initially serialized on Lofter.com, a Chinese blogging site, and AO3 (Archive of Our Own), a New York-based multi-fandom website for sharing and commenting on fanworks and fanarts. On February 24, 2020, a link to the novel was posted on Weibo, the second largest social media platform and the largest host of celebrity fanbases in China. Xiao's fans soon chastised the novel for "defaming" and feminizing their idol. On February 26, 2020, an opinion leader reported AO3 to Chinese authorities and posted a condemnation of the detrimental impact of underage prostitution and pornography on Weibo, appealing to the public: "freedom has limits!"[2] On February 29, AO3 was blocked in China. Having foreseen this consequence, AO3 and other fanwork creators and users started a Weibo trending hashtag "227 Great Unity" (227大团结) on February 27 to counterattack Xiao's fans and boycott the idol actor, which became known as the "227 Incident" (227事件). Its repercussions continue to haunt the entertainment business.

The responses of Xiao's fans to queer content have been inconsistent and puzzling. Keenly aware that their idol's rapidly growing fame largely depended on his "queer" role in *The Untamed*, many enthusiastically participated in official promotions of the show, passionately endorsing his ambiguous intimacy with Wang. However, the 227 Incident betrayed these fans' hostility to LGBTQ content, even though some fans are labeled or self-identified as rotten girls. Are

---

2. See https://www.sohu.com/a/377373166_391294.

they part of the "rotten culture" (腐文化), and how are they related to the BL fandom? After all, BL fans were once hit hard by government crackdowns; they stayed resistant to state regulations (Yang and Xu 2016b). Xiao's fans involved in the 227 Incident, instead, relied on state regulations for setting moral boundaries on speech.

This paradox becomes more intelligible if situated in what I call a "pan-rotten" culture with a complex audience composition. If rotten culture is a subculture with a pronounced queer taste based on BL fiction and constructed by Chinese rotten girls (Yang and Xu 2017), pan-rotten culture can be understood as a sphere of mainstream popular culture that the entertainment industry cultivates to profit from queer tastes among an audience with diverse sociocultural interests and identities. Popular pan-rotten products reappropriate subcultural gender nonconformity and adulterates such queerness with conventional light-hearted takes on homosociality. Pan-rotten culture depends on music and acting idols, so it often departs from rotten culture's obsession with ACGN characters. Rather, it vigorously attends to RPS of actors and semi-RPS of their TV roles. Finally, unlike rotten culture's aloofness, pan-rotten works are meant to generate positive energy to engage Chinese youth.

I use "clickbaiting" to describe the pan-rotten strategy deployed by creators of BL-adapted dramas and other pan-rotten products. The purpose of clickbaiting is to prompt clicks and increase digital traffic by appropriating nonheterosexual images and sentiments, while also maneuvering the polysemy of these representations and voices to appeal to a range of audiences. A similar term is "queer-baiting," used by fan communities and scholars to criticize media creators who intentionally suggest homoeroticism without the intention to follow through (Brennan 2018a; McDermot 2018). As Judith Fathallah points out, queerbaiting shows the possibility of queer representation but denies queer actualization and thus invalidates queer identities (Fathallah 2015). While both terms emphasize creators' exploitation of viewers' queer desire, this chapter uses "clickbaiting" because mainland China does not have a long tradition of fan activism for LGBTQ rights, and unlike Euro-American TV programs that mainly appeal to LGBTQ communities, "queer" viewers whom BL-adapted dramas intend to bait largely consist of heterosexual-identified BL fans.

Particularly, mainland Chinese talent TV shows in the 2000s, such as *Super Voice Girls* (超级女声) on Hunan TV (2004–2006) and *My Hero* (我型我秀) on Dragon TV (2006–2007), are the fledgling pan-rotten products that manufactured C-pop idols and idol groups and, to some extent, cultivated a pan-queer taste for BL-adapted dramas. Producers of these shows displayed idols' cuteness and sex appeal besides their talents and often staged same-sex intimate interactions that titillate audience's "queer" desire without being explicitly self-identified as "gay" or "lesbian" (Zhao 2018a). In recent years, male-male CPs (couplings) have grown to be a more popular and profitable form of queer pairing on Chinese TV.

Thorough research has yet to be done to reveal the psychological mechanisms surrounding audience reception, but I offer some hypotheses: first, a good-looking duo can compound the female viewers' scopophilic pleasure; second, male performance of cuteness and same-sex intimacy legitimates a female spectatorship that delinks women from being "objects of the gaze" and increases their sense of being in control; thirdly, pertaining to China and other countries with a rather conservative attitude towards female sexuality, consumption of male-male erotica reduces female audience's self-projection and subsequently their insecurity and guilt over enjoying norm-transgressive intimacies.

BL-adapted dramas starring well-known C-pop idols provide an extended stage for building a large and sustainable consumer base by drawing a high percentage of viewership from their fans. Idol fans' activities are disciplined by "fan circles" (饭圈), a new form of fan culture that emerged with the rise of C-pop idols and quick expansion of idol fans via social media in the 2010s, and has been jointly formed and formalized by idol agencies, corporate producers of idols' music and acting performances, and/or media platforms. Major revenue in the idol-fan economy comes from traffic data (流量) surrounding an idol, including clicks/views, comments, likes, and reposts, which are calculated algorithmically on media sites. As traffic data serve as the major quantitative evidence for an idol's popularity and influence, opinion leaders in fan circles motivate members' active digital participation in data contribution, in addition to traditional support, such as purchasing performance tickets and merchandise. Fans exercise a certain degree of agency by producing content, exerting influence on charts and traffic data, and bringing their idols to more mainstream attention (Tian 2020; C. Zhang 2016). However, self-expressions of individual fans are rarely allowed to contradict fan-circle agendas.

Besides idol fans, BL fans provide another important source of viewers for BL-adapted dramas. For creators of pan-rotten products, BL fans' "rotten" taste, their willingness to devote affection, money, and creativity, make them ideal consumers of BL-adapted dramas. As I will explain below, the pan-rotten mechanisms to trigger a psychological response from consumers mirror how BL elicits *moe* (萌; a euphoric response to male cuteness and homoeroticism) from its fans, except for a few differences.

Viewers of BL-adapted dramas overlap with and are more diverse than the BL fandom, which itself grows increasingly complex. A few trends in the BL fandom have affected the cultivation of the pan-rotten audience base (as seen in Figure 5.1). The early Chinese BL fandom in the 1990s and early 2000s largely consisted of fiction/novel fans, followed by ACGN fans. As a result, rotten girls' *moe* originated in virtual characters, and they shared *moe* among themselves in an enclosed space (圈地自萌, hereafter self-*moe*). However, the BL fandom can no longer remain self-*moe*-ing due to the aggression of fan circles, new technological developments, expansion of BL communities, and commercial and political interventions. A growing number of BL fans desired to *chuquan*, out of concern for survival, societal recognition, or commercial gain. I call this group "industry-driven fans" to emphasize their engagement with industry and compliance toward fan-circle and other industry regulations. They are also more easily converted to viewers of the BL-adapted. However, not all BL fans are fond of pan-rotten products. Hardcore BL fans, whom I roughly categorize as the "self-*moe*-ing branch," tend to resist fan-circle and other commercial practices whose thirst for exposure and profit differ from BL fans' original inclination for autonomy of self-expressions and public invisibility. Moreover, for the self-*moe*-ing branch, publicity may infringe copyright issues, as BL books are still illegal in mainland China and RPS can cause accusations of defaming actors (Yang and Xu 2016b). Most importantly, seeing content in BL-adapted drama as unacceptably diluted, they criticize Chinese bromance's betrayal of BL conventions by faking queerness and denying carnal desires.

These concepts help to illuminate the 227 Incident and other fandom wars in Chinese cyberspace. Xiao and Wang are both pop idols with preexisting fanbases.[3] Fan circles' supportive activities contributed to the show's success, which in turn helped enlarge their fanbases. Discord inevitably arose as the drama attracted a broader audience with greater variation in age and attitudes toward queer content. More importantly, the seemingly random 227 Incident was linked to fan-circle competition over resources. When actors in new series threaten the older ones' popularity, fan circles are likely to instigate online battles. This explains other skirmishes between Xiao's fans and those of the leading actors of *Guardian* (镇魂; Youku, 2018) and of *Words of Honor* (山河令, Youku, 2021).

Competition has also emerged between fans of same-sex idols starring in the same show. Marketing for *The Untamed* emphasized both the "Wang/Xian" CP of the characters Lan Wangji and Wei Wuxian, and "Bojun/Yixiao" (博君/一肖) CP, the pairing of their actors. After the marketing stage, however, the actors' interests conspicuously diverged, and their "solo fans" (唯粉; the type of Chinese

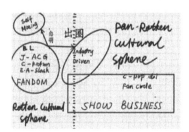

Figure 5.1: Rotten and pan-rotten culture

---

3. Xiao participated in the Chinese teen talent show *X-Fire* (燃烧吧少年; Zhejiang TV) in 2015 and debuted in the idol group X-NINE in 2016 as the main vocalist. Wang debuted in 2014 as a member of the South Korean-Chinese boy band group UNIQ, as the lead dancer and rapper.

idol fans who only like one member of a group but not others) divided into two hostile camps. Besides, solo fans and idol agencies, fearing queer readings might hinder their idols' long-term career development, began to reject CP fans and dismantle same-sex CPs so that their idols could quickly shed "queer" images and instead move toward more "straight" roles. By these accounts, many idol fans have always negotiated their queer desire with, if not directly compromised to, certain mainstream heterosexual norms.

The mainland Chinese entertainment industry has turned male idols into a highly marketable commodity, a bait for a predominantly heterosexual female audience. Meanwhile, audiences' and fans' emotional and financial investment are fueling the rapid development of local pop idol business and pan-rotten culture. Pan-rotten culture most certainly reflects Chinese women's growing financial ability to consume, different tastes for ideal masculinities, and changing views of gender norms and man-woman power dynamics. However, these changes are saturated with the capitalist logic of consumer culture—that is, the constant consumption of male beauty and male-male intimacy sustains rotten girls' feelings of power and autonomy. As long as they consume, they are made to believe that such desires and activities are autonomous, unaware of or indifferent to the fact that this "autonomy" is incorporated into a fan economy that both creates and caters to fans' desires. The fan-circle practice, as part and parcel of a digitalized Chinese entertainment industry, helps the industry to operate with a more comprehensive model that ties profit making to effective disciplining and emotional motivation of fans, and thus renders both pop idols and fans susceptible to the manipulation of capital.

From BL to the BL-Adapted: State Regulation and Ideological Implications

In the increasingly pan-rotten consumer culture, producers and investors have witnessed the power of female fans, especially the creative energy of rotten girls, the high mobilizability of idol fan circles, and the robust consumption ability of both. They have also observed, and to some extent, propelled the dissolution of borders between BL fandom, pop idol fans, and mainstream audiences, which subsequently feeds into this pan-rotten culture. Therefore, BL-adapted dramas, a cultural form that attracts BL fans and pop idol fans with the potential to expand to mainstream viewership, would predictably become a profitable model for the entertainment industry. The BL-adapted drama certainly owes its inception to the dual impetus of commercial culture and fan practices. However, it was the state regulation on "unhealthy" digital content that lent the final thrust.

Since President Xi Jinping came to power in China in late 2012, the official regulatory organ of the media and press has been reformed twice, from SARFT (State Administration of Radio, Film and Television) to SAPPRFT (State

Administration of Press, Publication, Radio, Film and Television) in 2013, and then to NRTA (National Radio and Television Administration) for tighter and more centralized control. In 2014, the CAC (Cyberspace Administration of China) was established as the central regulator for internet content. Besides these official censors, there is also the ISC (Internet Society of China), a semi-official organization with lower-level institutions across the country to monitor digital content. In a landmark talk at the Beijing Forum on Literature and Art in October 2014, Xi attacked vulgar culture and negative energy on the grounds that the media industry plays a key role in shaping the Chinese national spirit in the age of digitalization and globalization (hereafter Forum talk). Xi strongly disapproved of erotic, dark, and overly commercial productions, and stressed the state's key role in guarding the quality of Chinese culture and entertainment industries.

Since 2014, a series of new rules and laws have been inspired by Xi's Forum talk and other instructions on media control. Online publications were receiving increasing governmental scrutiny. CAC's new regulations on cyberspace information rehashed Xi's 2014 Forum talk. Certain rules particularly targeted BL and other erotic content, prohibiting infringing on reputation, distributing pornography, and inducing minors' immoral behaviors ("Wangluo" 2019). During anti-pornography campaigns, websites containing BL fiction had to remove a large number of titles (Yang and Xu 2016b; C. Zhang 2016). Self-publishing BL authors were arrested and sentenced to jail (Bai 2022; Tian 2020).

Another important change made to cybersecurity law is that the providers and operators of websites must ask users to provide real identity information. This reduced user anonymity and disturbed the online ecosystem of BL fans, who previously had fewer concerns about sharing taboo fantasies on relatively insulated online forums. Some websites hosting BL publications and fan activities did not survive, and those who did, such as Lucifer's Club, Jinjiang Literature City (晋江文学城; Jinjiang hereafter), and Lcread, had to implement stricter self-censorship. This in turn prompted subcultural fan communities, including BL fan groups and individuals, to migrate to fanwork sites based outside of China, such as AO3 and FanFiction.net. These migrant BL fans mostly prefer self-*moe*-ing to succumbing to ideological control and industry rules. Like other Chinese digital migrants on AO3, they stayed low-profile to keep themselves under the radar of Chinese censors until the aforementioned 227 Incident. At the same time, industry-driven BL writers and fans devoted their creative and consumptive energy to popularizing pan-rotten cultural products.

BL dramas, which emerged in cyberspace much later than BL novels, suffered a similar fate in the mid-2010s as legal developments and regulatory efforts began to impose barriers for erotic and homosexual TV programs. "General Rules for Content Production of TV Series" passed on December 31, 2015, for example, forbid a wide range of "abnormal" sexual relations ("Dianshiju" 2019). At an annual conference of the National Television Industry, high-ranking officials from SAPPRFT targeted vulgar and homosexual content, and proposed synchronizing regulations on web and satellite TV dramas (Y. Li 2016). Such policies snipped BL web series in the bud. TV studios had experimented in the early 2010s, but BL web dramas received little media coverage until *Counterattack* (逆袭) debuted on Tencent Video in the summer of 2015. This BL drama is based on a novel by famous BL author Chai Jidan (柴鸡蛋). Chai was also invited to write the scripts of *Counterattack* and two other BL dramas. *Addicted* (上瘾2016), the second BL series she scripted, became an immediate hit when it premiered on iQIYI and Tencent Video in early 2016. However, upon the order of SAPPRFT, the show was removed from online sites. Chai's third BL series, *Advanced Bravely* (盛势), was originally scheduled to debut in April 2017 on Tencent Video; it never showed up on the site but appeared later on YouTube, allegedly with deleted scenes.

In addition to harsh crackdowns, it is also necessary to consider the role of soft regulatory tactics. Researchers generally agree that despite the state's tightened control of media, it has increasingly used less oppressive and more sophisticated methods with strategic resilience and diversified control tactics (G. Yang 2014; Yang and Tang 2018). Chinese authorities also deployed soft tactics to exert influence through attraction rather than coercion (Luo and Voci 2018). Xi's administration has ridden on nationalist campaigns such as the "Chinese Dream," a rhetoric that reenvisioned a strong socialist nation with Chinese characteristics, unique Chinese traditions, and a promising future for Chinese people. As shown in messages delivered in the few far-reaching speeches since 2015,[4] soft tactics are intended to exert Chinese soft power domestically and globally. Domestically, the emphasis on common goals and positive energy helps to create consensus; globally, claiming the party-state's traditional Confucian cultural heritage helps to cultivate a more positive international image.

Following the state's regulation of media, a noticeable shift occurred in the mode of production that marked the change from BL to the BL-adapted. The BL-adapted, belonging to the pan-rotten cultural sphere, offers an alternative form that is more acceptable than a "rotten taste" to mainstream culture and state official media. The most obvious changes are, of course, de-sexualization and heterowashing. While BL dramas such as *Addicted* and *Advanced Bravely* do not contain as much explicit sexual content as the original novels do, they still allow viewers to get a glimpse of male-male physical intimacies such as

---

4. In Xi's aforementioned Forum talk in 2014, when cautioning against worship of foreign culture, he simultaneously encouraged domestic productions that enhance confidence in Chinese culture, exert Chinese spirit, and inherit and rejuvenate Chinese traditional culture. In yet another landmark speech delivered at the nineteenth National Congress in October 2017, Xi again emphasized the importance of Chinese cultural industries and markets, instructing that Chinese cultural soft power should draw on virtues, values, and moral principles of China's fine traditional culture.

kissing, hand-holding, and foreplay. BL-adapted dramas, however, cut off physical intimacies altogether and disguise homo-romance as bromance (as discussed in Chapter 4 in this volume, for example). Another noticeable change is the rearticulation of "deviant" desires (such as nonheterosexual desires or extramarital affairs) and dark energies (such as violence and immoral deeds) in state-sanctioned ways. For example, *Guardian*, the most popular BL-adapted drama prior to *The Untamed*, subdued the negative energy of the original fiction and embellished the drama with an uplifting outlook for a harmonious society (Wang 2019). Despite setbacks, *Guardian* racked up profits for the producers and media platforms and significantly elevated the two lead actors' celebrity status.

Four Components of a Winning Formula

Guardian's success motivated larger corporates to join in the production of BL-adapted dramas with bigger budgets. Since *Guardian*, major TV and film companies such as Enlight Media and Ciwen Media joined with Internet tech giants, such as Tencent, Ali, and iQIYI, to invest in producing new crops of idols and fans via online programs, turning idols into actors in BL-adapted dramas. The three most popular BL-adapted series, *Guardian*, *The Untamed*, and *Words of Honor*, denote a winning formula. In the rest of this chapter, I will use *The Untamed* to illustrate how this drama implements the formula's four key components—authorial reputation, masqueraded bromance, actor RPS, and a sublimated theme—to fill up the vacuum of "queer" representations left by the BL ban and actualize the clickbaiting strategy.

Authorial reputation

Production teams of BL-adapted dramas depend on the fame of the original novel and its author to boost revenue for the show. As mentioned earlier, industry-driven BL writers and fans, more accepting of diluted versions of homo-romance, are easier than the self-*moe*-ing ones to convert into viewers and even creators of the BL-adapted. Notably, famous BL writers can benefit from selling IPs (intellectual properties) to TV producers, and some also work with showrunners to co-write and co-market TV programs.

The industrialization of BL authors and works extends their impact from the rotten culture to a pan-rotten culture. Both *Guardian* and *Words of Honor* were based on BL fiction by Priest, a contracted and best-selling BL writer on Jinjiang. Priest is also among those BL writers who "experiment with diverse styles and themes and have incorporated elements of science fiction, sports, and other traditionally 'unfeminine' genres into their writings" (Yang and Xu 2017, 10). Her works have a wide appeal not only to BL and female-oriented (女性向) readers, but also to fans of martial arts, suspense, and science fiction. In the case of *The Untamed*, its original novel *Grandmaster* had topped the charts of BL fiction on Jinjiang, Lofter, and WeChat Read on Weibo Super Topic (微博超话; an interactive function added to Weibo in 2016). Its author, Moxiangtongxiu (墨香铜臭), like Priest, is a top BL writer with her own devoted fans. Meanwhile, the audio, manga, and anime based on *Grandmaster* had been released and well received before the drama series, so this large, cross-platform *Grandmaster* fanbase indicated a potentially lucrative market for *The Untamed*.

The relative safety of the subject matter in the original BL fiction is also a consideration. Even top-rated BL works cannot pass the scrutiny of production companies' own censors if they broach taboo topics such as sadomasochism (SM), underage sex, or incest (Wang 2019; Yang and Xu 2016b). Acceptable themes include martial arts, *xianxia*, detective work, and military settings. Easily recognizable and already popular among mainstream audiences of genre dramas, these thematic sub-genres help the BL-adapted drama disseminate outside of BL fans and idol fan circles. Moreover, these themes are compatible with another two components of the winning formula to be discussed below: they offer natural settings to masquerade bromance, where men's moderate emotional expressions and physical bonds are deemed normal and socially acceptable; and they accommodate a sublimated vision of social justice and harmony.

Masqueraded bromance

It is acknowledged that BL-adapted series masquerades homo-romance as platonic bromance to circumvent censorship (Hu and Wang 2020; Ng and Li 2020; Wang 2019). In fact, masqueraded bromance is also essential to clickbaiting. Creators encode messages about gay romance and sex, which send out signals nuanced enough for the general public to interpret as brotherhood, but strong enough for the BL fans and more aware audience to detect as romance. This way, the former can enjoy the text, and the latter can seek guilty pleasure in the subtext. As explained in detail in Chapter 6, the story in *The Untamed* unfolds mainly through the adventures of Wei Wuxian, a cultivator (修士) from the Jiang Clan and a mischievous rule-breaker. During a training course for young cultivators in Cloud Recesses, the residence of the Lan Clan, Wuxian is acquainted with Lan Wangji, the taciturn second young master of the clan and a strict rule follower. The two bond closely despite initial skirmishes due to their opposing personalities. Wuxian then becomes the primary suspect for the bloodbath in the Wen Clan's Never-Night Place (不夜天), where many are mysteriously slaughtered, and he himself falls off a cliff. Sixteen years later (thirteen years in the novel), Wuxian is resurrected as the grandmaster of demonic cultivation and reunited with Wangji. Together, they solve new murder mysteries and reveal the true killer who plotted the slaughter.

The drama follows the basic storyline of the original fiction, but the same-sex romance, as expected, is repackaged into bromance. In the novel, the tumultuous romance is made unmistakable by cuddling, listening to each other's heartbeats, kisses, and sex. For example, the chapter titled "Everyday is Everyday" (天天就是天天) depicts in graphic detail the sex between Wangji as the "top" (the dominant role in gay sex) and Wuxian as the "bottom" (the submissive role in gay sex). For readers of BL fiction, sex scenes not only signify the relationship being homosexual rather than homosocial, but also enhance the lovers' emotional bonds. In *Grandmaster*, when Wuxian kisses every inch of Wangji's skin, he discovers all the wounds in Wangji's body which he did not know existed. He is deeply touched, as each wound signifies an incident in which Wangji secretly protected him, bearing evidence to Wangji's willingness to suffer quietly for him.[5] Therefore, the phrase "Everyday is Everyday" is a widely discussed *moe* trigger among BL fans. The two characters in the drama, in contrast, never commit to being lovers or engage in any physical intimacy. Rather, the creators of *The Untamed* blend martial arts and *xianxia* elements into the drama, so male intimacy hides behind the masquerade of cultivators' brotherly love. Furthermore, they also arrange matters with Wen Qing (温情) and Mianmian (绵绵), two prop female characters with the potential for heterosexual relationships with Wuxian, so as to divert censors' and the audience's attention away from the connoted male same-sex romance.

To bait viewers, the drama is replete with candid interpersonal moments that fall along the homosocial and homosexual continuum to leave space for alternative interpretations. The Wang/Xian romance is insinuated via innuendos, micro facial expressions, and romantic instrumental music. However, such sentiments rely heavily on viewers' ability to infer from cues and subtexts. This is particularly true with the smart camera work that captures Wangji's micro expressions, as he rarely talks about his feelings. Viewers are frequently presented with eye-level shots of his soulful gazes at Wuxian, which creates an affective two-person cosmos. Viewers are also presented with close-ups of Wangji's face to reveal his inner emotions: how the lips turn up at the corner into a subtle smile that lights up and softens his entire face when Wuxian appears. For those who understand the reference to the BL fiction, these subtle hints evoke *moe*, but those without prior knowledge easily ignore or "misinterpret" them.

This Wang/Xian cosmos is further substantiated through other romantic allusions and symbolism. The rabbit and the headband, for example, signify the couple's physical intimacy and emotional connection. Initially, viewers are informed that Wangji's headband is sacred, only supposed to be touched by parents or a spouse (Episode 5). Soon, occasions emerge in which Wuxian touches the headband. On one occasion, when Wangji gets drunk, Wuxian

---

5. See Chapter 111 of the online fiction at https://www.enjing.com/modao/33606.htm.

reaches out to straighten his crooked headband. On another occasion, Wangji takes the headband off and binds his and Wuxian's wrists in a mysterious cave when he learns that only those wearing the clan's headbands can be protected from attacks by Killer Strings (Episode 6). It is also in this cave that rabbits first appear, all wearing headbands. Viewers without a "rotten" radar would understand Wangji's frequent rule-breaking and rescue missions as how a friend and teammate would normally respond to impending danger, and the rabbits and headband are simply everyday objects. However, for those steeped in rotten culture, they function as *moe* triggers: the rabbit as a symbol for queer love,[6] and untying the headband as a signature for setting sexual desire free, so that Wangji's behavior becomes proof of treating Wuxian as "the one and only."

Such ambiguity is a deliberate effort of the show's creators to stimulate fan activity and viewers' clicks. Titillated fans are eager to unravel the "true" Wang/Xian relationship, and they excel at locating telltale signs. Many have commented that since Wangji's headband is a sign of moral restriction, taking it off and offering it to Wuxian multiple times shows his willingness to shed restrictions and acknowledge Wuxian as his spouse (Chan 2019; Hudson 2020). A superfan,[7] Fefe, posted an audio on YouTube about two rabbits that Wuxian entrusts to Wangji upon his departure from Cloud Recesses.[8] In the audio, Wangji's brother observes the rabbits' personalities (one lively, one quiet), activities (the lively one makes new friends, while the quiet one watches him), and emotional responses (the quiet one is so jealous that he chases away new rabbits). Wangji then explains that the quiet rabbit (himself) is simply claiming what is his (Wuxian). This video gained nearly 100,000 views and 4,600 likes for Fefe's ingenious work that draws a parallel between the rabbit couple and the Wang/Xian CP.

On Chinese media sites (Douban, Weibo, Zhihu, Bilili) and English-language ones (Instagram, Reddit, and YouTube) alike, creative fanworks have greatly aroused users' curiosity in the Wang/Xian CP and the show. The official account of *The Untamed* on Zhihu posted a question about possible interpretations of the ending, and the top five answers received nearly 20,000 likes and over 1,000 comments. One respondent photoshopped a screen capture to make the homosexual theme explicit: Wuxian and Wangji appear to be a couple in a traditional Chinese wedding ceremony after their clothes are colored red and the two are tied with a red satin knot digitally added to the image.[9] Unfortunately, unlike what the authors of Chapter 2 find in *jiquan* fandom, the textual-poaching mainland Chinese fans, while "queering" images, audios, and texts, have never

---

6. Rabbit in Chinese, 兔子, is a local lexicon referring to gay men.
7. The term "superfan" refers to a fan with a large number of followers her/himself.
8. See https://www.youtube.com/watch?v=7EztT1kM3PA.
9. See https://www.zhihu.com/question/339460011/answer/782808259.

discussed gay marriages and LGBTQ rights—at least, never publicly—for fear of censorship.

Real person slash (RPS)

The Untamed's marketing team was well aware that the show had a dedicated female fanbase who watched it for the attractive male actors. Besides the character CP of Wang/Xian, the RPS of Wang Yibo and Xiao Zhan (Bojun/Yixiao) comprised another important step in expanding the show's pan-rotten appeal. Official accounts of the show and the actors on various media platforms joined with social media influencers and fan leaders to stage a series of two-person activities, such as interviews, variety shows, live broadcasts, concerts, and magazine cover shoots, suggesting attraction between the two actors in real life. These activities were meant to trigger *moe*, providing large doses of the actors' intimate interactions so that fans were enraptured about "shipping the intimacy" or *ketang* (磕糖; literally meaning "indulging in sweets" or "getting a sugar high"). Once the fans were stimulated enough, some would be motivated to share *moe* via creative fanworks and become unofficial yet effective promoters. During the course of the show's release in July and August 2019, RPS proved to be an effective marketing strategy, as Wang and Xiao each gained millions of new fans on Weibo alone.[10]

The official marketing campaign for Bojun/Yixiao officially commenced five days after the show was aired. On July 2, 2019, the team released a nine-minute behind-the-scenes video in which the two tease each other. Creators of the show systematically shot behind-the-scenes content, edited it into micro-videos, and regularly uploaded them onto platforms during the marketing stage. This nine-minute video immediately went viral and became the original source for fans' queer reading on social media, which resulted in a corpus of fanworks known as "Studies of Nine [minutes]." Fans shared *moe* traits of the two addressing each other as *laoshi* (老师; teacher) and bickering like two pupils. "Studies of Nine" flooded the screens of fan groups on Douban, who were eager to fill in the blanks of the story. One popular post asks: "What's bickering like after they have a child?"[11] Another post reads: "The unparalleled love between Lehua Prince Wang Yibo and his peace-making wife Xiao Zhan," which alludes to their romance despite the "running family feud" between the actors' respective

---

10. See "Comparing the Increase of Xiao Zhan's and Wang Yibo's Fans after *The Untamed*," which was posted on Douban on July 4, 2019, available at https://www.douban.com/group/topic/144851418/.
11. A Douban group, "Research Center of Nine," enthusiastically discussed the intimate interactions between Wang and Xiao from July 2019 to April 2021, available at https://www.douban.com/doulist/116357332/. When I last visited the site on July 21, 2021, some threads were deleted.

agencies Lehua and Jiwajiwa. The post also serves as a callback to complex clan feuds in the drama.

"Studies of Nine" is catalogued as elementary-level reading material in the "Curriculum for Bojun/Yixiao Studies" created by and for fans, a spoof of academic curricula.[12] Other categories of reading materials include advanced-level reading, intensive reading, required reading skills, and supplementary reading. "Studies of Sixteen (minutes)," for example, is placed on the advanced level because the intimacy requires more skill to decode. This title originates in a promotional event on *Happy Camp* (快乐大本营), a popular variety show broadcast by Hunan TV, on August 10, 2019. Wang and Xiao participated in a sixteen-minute game about garbage sorting, which inspired a large number of fanpics and fanvids that deftly identify the hidden "sugar-dense" interactions between Wang and Xiao. On the Chinese video-streaming site Bilibili alone, fours installments of fanvids titled "An In-Depth Research Report" garnered 3.38 million views and nearly 10,000 comments.[13] The installments consist of slow-motion edited footage of "sugary" moments during the sixteen minutes. Wang and Xiao's movements and facial expressions are scrutinized as evidence of their jealousy and care for each other. Like "Studies of Nine," "Studies of Sixteen" sent waves of ecstasy among fans, constantly evoking *moe* and more desire for the duo's public display of affection. Meanwhile, viewers' posts and other online activities are tracked and calculated algorithmically to contribute to the popularity of idol-actors and their shows.

Idols' agencies, showrunners, and fan circles deployed RPS marketing to motivate fans to influence metrics and semantic information on digital platforms and social media. This marketing ploy, motivated by clickbaiting, promotes a form of queer fantasy that does not directly subvert mainstream norms. *The Untamed*'s creators and actors provide ambiguous "raw materials" for fans to cook their *moe* with, but never confirm any gay identity or relationship. Fans, including those who self-identify as rotten girls, mostly adopt a heterosexual gaze when relishing RPS. This BL convention is extended to and further highlighted in male same-sex CPs in BL-adapted dramas and RPS of actors. Geng Song's brief analysis of *The Untamed* shows that that the two protagonists' personalities are "very much in line with that commonly found in the heterosexual relationships depicted in many contemporary TV dramas" (2022a, 77). Heterosexuality certainly does not stop with the queering of the show, as fans' comparison of Wang Yibo to a prince and Xiao Zhan to a princess has clear heterosexual implications. Fans also frequently call Wang the caring husband and Xiao the capricious wife,

---

12. One version of "Curriculum for Bojun/Yixiao Studies" is available in Liu and Jiang's paper "Anti-Structural Breakthrough" (2020, 13).
13. Bojun/Yixiao posted four installments in August 2019, available at https://www.bilibili.com/s/video/BV154411f7CT.

relishing the husband's dedication to and protectiveness of the wife in the CP. Male same-sex CPs, as both official creators' clickbaiting strategies and female fans' *moe* triggers, typify the female-oriented and heteronormative nature of pan-rotten cultural products.

Sublimated themes

Themes in BL-adapted dramas are sublimated so as to emphasize nationalistic content and greater social responsibilities. As described above, the state policies instruct that media products function as a cultural force domestically and globally. President Xi often uses the rhetoric of positive energy, social harmony, and peaceful rise for the regime's soft power strategy. Rebranding traditional Chinese culture, especially Confucianism, has become a guiding principle for old and new media.

The Untamed's showrunners carefully craft visuals of what state media defines as "Chinese national style," with ancient Chinese costumes, architecture, decor, and musical instruments. More than superfluous details, the show also highlights a uniquely Chinese style of culture that synthesizes Confucianism, Taoism, and martial arts culture. Wuxian's given name, Ying (婴; infant) is associated with the most desirable characteristics and eternal virtues of Taoism: purity, innocence, gentleness, and freedom from worldly attachments (Lao Zi, *Daode Jing*, Chapters 10, 20, and 27). Wuxian names his own sword "As You Wish" (如意) and lives under the motto "follow the heart and be free," both of which attest to Taoist principles. He is also guided by the spirit of martial arts to "restore justice." While the original fiction also contains the theme of justice, it emphasizes justice more as a self-motivated means to achieve freedom and romantic love. The drama, on the other hand, presents justice as a selfless means to achieve the common good. The series deliberately adds a "sky lantern" scene: Looking at the slowly rising lantern, Wuxian piously speaks his wish: "May I eradicate the evil, protect the weak, and have no regret in my heart." Wuxian's words catch Wangji's attention, making him realize for the first time that they are soulmates. This message, extending personal feelings to the common goal of fighting for justice, is a thread woven throughout the show.

While portraying Wuxian's pursuit of freedom and justice mostly in a positive light, the show raises issues about the consequences of his unrestrained spirit and pursuit of freedom guided by martial arts and Taoism. Wuxian's complete disregard for rules leads to "demonic tricks" that make him lose control and turn him into a damaging force. His dark energy thus needs to be tempered by Confucian virtues of moderation, self-restraint, loyalty, and sense of responsibility. Wangji turns out to be a "savior" with these virtues. The show reinforces Wangji's image as a talented gentleman who saves the chaotic world with his admirable morality and deeds. His honorary name, Light-Bearing Gentleman

(含光君), comes from a line in *The Book of Songs* (诗经), an anthology of ancient Chinese poetry and also one of the five Confucian classics, about a gentleman who excels in literary talents, good looks, and noble character (*Airs of the States* 国风, "Qi Yu from Wei" 卫国淇奥). Although Wangji similarly cherishes the martial spirit, he is simultaneously disciplined by the three thousand clan rules that resemble Confucian teachings. Through the two protagonists' contrasting personalities and common goals, the adapted drama promotes a positive and righteous Chinese energy nourished by the Taoist freedom principle, martial artists' mission of restoring justice, and, ultimately, Confucian moral restraint.

Unlike the original story that focuses on the development of the Wang/Xian romance with the cultivation world (修真界) as the background, the drama digs much deeper into the core of physical and moral cultivations of Chinese heroic spirit and young men's social responsibilities. These shifts of focus can be best illustrated by the changes to the ending. In the novel, they ultimately return to Cloud Recesses and live together happily ever after. In the version of the series on Tencent and YouTube, the two separate as amicable friends for the betterment of the world.[14] Wuxian continues to travel, while Wangji chooses to serve as the new leader of the cultivation world. The two endings thus embody two different values. The novel gratifies fans' wish to see fulfilled carnal desire and personal freedom as well as unchanging love and loyalty between lovers. It conveys the message that queer love is rewarding and individual happiness is achievable, at least in a sheltered place like Cloud Recesses. The ending of the show, however, denies such possibilities and implies that only when individuals are dedicated to unification under a wise leader can chaos be ended and peace be restored. Moreover, while the governance of the cultivation world needs a leader like Wangji, an untamed person like Wuxian can only be exiled to *jianghu* (江湖), a circle of wandering martial arts practitioners and outlaws that has a different set of rules of justice and governance.

The success of *The Untamed* in domestic and overseas markets exemplifies it as a model that aligns with the official ideology to establish cultural confidence, spread positive values, and erect Chinese heroic characters. Immediately after the release of the adapted drama in June 2019, an article was published by the official newspaper *People's Daily Overseas*. The author is extremely pleased with the drama's impressive attentiveness, not only to "the form of ancient Chinese style," but also to "the soul/spirit of the Chinese nation" (X. Hu 2019). According to the article, an essential component of the Chinese national spirit is embodied by young protagonists who are not restrained by "small love," but attuned to

---

14. In the version aired in Japan and Thailand, the two live happily together in Cloud Recesses, but more queer scenes are included in the Thai version. It would be worthwhile for future research to compare different marketing strategies in China and in Asian countries such as Japan and Thailand, where "rotten" culture is more acceptable to the audience and rotten content is less censored by the governments.

demands of "family, nation, and the world" (X. Hu 2019). Articles were also published online by *Enlightenment Daily* and the website of CCTV (China Central Television) around the same time, likewise commenting that besides traditional "Eastern concepts" centering around Confucianism, this drama attracts a large and often young audience by tuning into the "spirit of current times" (Tong 2019). These positive comments attest to the drama's tactful incorporation of mainstream elements to espouse state-approved messages to guide the public domestically and popularize positive images of China to international communities.

Since 2019, state media have invited idols such as Xiao Zhan, Wang Yibo, and Zhu Yilong (朱一龙; a male lead in *Guardian*) to perform on CCTV's annual *Spring Festival Gala* (春晚), a variety show that embeds the Party's policies and ideologies through ritualistic performances. These idols have also been recruited to play Chinese soldiers and communist members in propaganda films and TV series to attract younger audience.[15] These hypermasculine and heterosexual roles suggest a further "taming" of such BL-adapted dramas as *The Untamed*.

Conclusion

As BL content was increasingly censored and "rotten" pleasures discouraged, the entertainment industry quickly filled the void by cultivating new pan-rotten products and tastes. The BL-adapted web series, based on BL fiction but simultaneously "de-BL-ized" (去耽美化), has become the most prominent pan-rotten genre since the mid-2010s. Compared with BL, this derivative genre with watered-down and camouflaged queerness is more consumable for mainstream audience, more malleable by industry rules, and more accommodating to state indoctrination efforts. Using *The Untamed* as a case study, this chapter has reassessed optimistic scholarly claims about fans' digital dexterity, initiative, and capacity as a subversive force of heteronormativity and state ideology. It has revealed contentions and compliance between audience, industry, and state censors in "taming" BL-adapted wed dramas.

With state control and commercial appropriations, the BL-adapted TV genre does not necessarily break the shackles of conservative paradigms for gender and sexuality, nor does it liberate audience from gender hierarchy and

---

15. Zhu has been cast as a marine and flag raiser for the Hong Kong Handover Ceremony in *My People, My Country* (我和我的祖国; 2019), a film commemorating the seventieth anniversary of the People's Republic of China. His most recent role is in *The Rebel* (叛逆者; iQIYI, 2021), a historical drama series about the bildungsroman of a special agent originally trained by KMT (Kuomintang, or Chinese Nationalist Party) but converted to the CCP (Chinese Communist Party) in the 1930s and 1940s. Xiao plays a Chinese soldier in *Ace Troops* (王牌部队; iQIYI, 2021), a TV show for the CCP's 100th anniversary, according to the show's official Weibo account (https://weibo.com/u/5453172571?ssl_rnd=1607877500.9972&is_all=1).

heteronormativity. Rather, while gesturing towards new possibilities of queer representations and fantasies and of public agencies for female fans and viewers, this particular form of web dramas could distract attention from real, politically sensitive, and often severely censored lesbian and gay-themed media and cultural productions in China. The Chinese entertainment industry utilizes the queer subculture as a consumeristic tactic; its pan-rotten strategies and practices, seemingly more liberal about queer content and audience participation, bespeak a heteronormative conservatism and a manipulation of fans and viewers. In the current Chinese context, fans and audiences, many of whom are motivated by industry practices, can actually function as implementers or enhancers of existing mainstream gender ideologies rather than its attackers. For the regulatory authorities, by allowing TV producers and consumers to toe the line of what is acceptable, they can avoid criticism of Western media and project a positive image of an open-minded, modern nation and party while dampening attempts for actual political changes around LGBTQ issues.

6
Disjunctive Temporalities

Queer Sinophone Visuality across Mainland China, Hong Kong, and Taiwan[1]

Alvin K. Wong

Walking around the global Asian metropolises of Taipei, Shanghai, Hong Kong, and Singapore, one finds it hard to avoid the alluring presence of young male bodies with bright, flawless skins on advertisement billboards, giant LED screens, and the smaller screens of smartphones. In South Korea, young male celebrities who command a large female fanbase are usually referred to as "flower boys" (花美男), which refers to the broader pan-Asian regional circulation of soft masculinity. Sun Jung (2011), drawing on the work of Koichi Iwabuchi, defines "soft masculinity" as a form of odorless and border-crossing gender typology that might originate from the *bishōnen* (beautiful young boy) figure from Japan. According to Jung, "this *bishōnen* image has repeatedly appeared in pastiches and been commodified by various regional pop-stars, in the course of which this image has evolved to eventually create the 'shared imagination' of pan-East Asian soft masculinity" (2011, 30). Elsewhere, Sinophone theorist Shu-mei Shih (2007; see also Shih 1998) also notes the transnational geopolitics of desire, in which the bodies of mainland Chinese women assume loaded and often misogynist values across the transnational Chinese mediascapes, where they are often depicted as illegal new immigrants and alluring but dangerous seductresses of Hong Kong and Taiwanese married men.[2] While Jung and Shih focus on different gendered embodiments and mobilities across transnational boundaries, they both demonstrate the extent to which gender and sexuality assume new transactional meanings in the millennial age.

---

1. This research is supported by the GRF grant of the Research Grants Council of Hong Kong under the project code: 17613520.
2. I use the term Sinophone in a connotative and descriptive sense, which refers to "a network of places of cultural production outside China and on the margins of China and Chineseness, where a historical process of heterogenizing and localizing of continental Chinese culture has been taking place for several centuries" (Shih 2007, 4).

Alvin K. Wong

In the post-2000s mediascape, Boys' Love (BL) cultural commodities have taken transnational Asian popular cultures by storm. As Ling Yang and Yanrui Xu (2017) define,

> *Danmei* (耽美), or Boys' Love (BL), is a genre of male-male romance created by and for women and sexual minorities . . . First appearing in Japanese girls' comics in the 1970s, the genre has gained tremendous popularity in East Asia and worldwide via the spread of Japanese ACG (anime, comics, and games) culture. (Yang and Xu 2017, 3)

While the recent COVID-19 pandemic has led to increasing consumption of TV series, films, and online contents at home and enabled the successful wave of Thai BL television dramas, such as the 2020 series *2gether: The Series* (LINE TV), Taiwan cinema has also regained its previous success with gay youth films like *Formula 17* (17歲的天空; dir. Chen Yinjung, 2004) and *Eternal Summer* (盛夏光年; dir. Leste Chen, 2006). The queer "return" of Taiwan cinema is marked by the commercial success of *Your Name Engraved Herein* (刻在你心底的名字; dir. Patrick Kuang-Hui Liu, 2020), a heart-wrenching queer coming-of-age story centred on two young male high school students during the late martial law era in the 1980s. The film grossed more than one hundred million (TWD) locally and became the most successful LGBTQ film ever made in Taiwan (Arstin 2020).

Similarly, in recent years, BL cultural products like films, online media, and TV series also mushroomed in the People's Republic of China (also known as mainland China or the Mainland; PRC hereafter) and the postcolonial special administrative region of Hong Kong, often with a mixed result of great commercial success, toned-down gay content due to fear of censorship, or simply complete content shutdown after initial commercial success. For example, in 2016, the popular BL online drama *Addicted* (上癮; iQIYI) sparked much fanfare and popularity in the PRC. As discussed in detail in Chapter 4, the drama's narrative of two young men, Bai Luoyin (白洛因) and Gu Hai (顧海), who eventually overcome class and social differences in the postsocialist landscape, seems to promise a model of queer love and desire that is at odds with the otherwise heteronormative geopolitics of the PRC. However, such queer utopic content is contrasted sharply with the government reception of the series, as the show was forced to take off its content following the first 12th episodes in February 2016 (Yan 2016). The censorship of *Addicted* is followed by another incident in which a Chinese BL novelist with the pseudonym Tianyi was arrested and sentenced to ten years in prison. The reason of her arrest is that her novel *Occupy* (攻佔) depicts "obscene sexual behavior between males" with the themes of "violence, abuse, and humiliation" (Wang 2018).

In addition to the threat of censorship of queer media and BL content in particular, ideologically, the hypermasculinist, Confucianist, and heteronormative geopolitics of the PRC in the Xi Jinping era are often framed as less progressive in the domains of gay marriage, anti-discrimination law, and LGBTQ public spheres in comparison to post-martial law Taiwan (P. Liu 2007).[3] Charlie Yi Zhang also unpacks this hypermasculinity of PRC nationalism in the staging of the "national body" during public events and ceremonies as a heterosexualizing script, which "seamlessly reproduces the dimorphic gender paradigm, not only by endorsing its covert heterosexual premise . . . but also by the cross-referencing and reinforcing contrast between the robust, virile, and muscular male bodies and delicate, agile, and flexible female bodies" (2016, 7). As queer media studies scholars, how do we dissect and analyze the gap between the queer space and temporality depicted in BL cultural productions versus the actual geopolitics of gender and sexuality in the PRC and the broader Sinophone world? Building on Arjun Appadurai's theory of global disjuncture that pivots on "the *work of the imagination* as a constitutive feature of modern subjectivity" (1996, 3), I theorize the popularity, transregional circulation, and reception of BL media and visuality across the Sinophone public spheres through the concept of "disjunctive temporalities." Conceptually, disjunctive temporalities track the fast-shifting and malleable articulations of queer desire, embodiment, and intimacies as they manifest in distinct yet overlapping temporal modes across queer Sinophone mediascapes. While Chapter 4 and Chapter 5 of this volume examine BL and BL-adapted TV dramas through the concept of queer melancholia and the taming of queer desire via state censorship and the complicity of the media industry in the PRC, my chapter here expands the comparative scale by offering an analysis of the Sinophone geopolitics of queer visuality.

While *The Untamed* (陳情令; Tencent, 2019) in the BL mediascape of mainland China captures a form of "unhistorical queerness" whose queer appeal precisely lies in its portrayals of bromance and queer ambiguous desire in a non-historical world of *jianghu* (江湖; rivers and lakes of the heroic world), recent queer drama and films concerned with male homosexuality in postcolonial Hong Kong are by contrast more concerned with socially oriented issues such as aging, HIV prevention, and familial conflicts. The HIV-related online film *For Love, We Can* (愛，不難; dir. Chi-Lung Lam, 2014) and the recent hit TV drama *Ossan's Love* (大叔的愛; ViuTV, HK, 2021) thus visualize queer Hong Kong through what I coin "queer presentism." Finally, the legalization of gay marriage in Taiwan in 2019 has significantly impacted the queer imaginary of BL in films and media. In light-hearted BL films and TV dramas such as *Formula 17* (2004) and *Because of You* (因為愛你; LINE TV, TW, 2020), a world in which gay men (and, to a certain extent, lesbian, bisexual, and transgender people) no longer need to come out and can simply be as ordinary as any other Taiwanese citizen is highlighted again and again. Therefore, a certain "postliberal temporality" emerges in post-2019 Taiwan despite the continual social discriminations against transgender people,

---

3. Xi has served as president of the PRC since 2012.

sex workers, and other queer individuals. By delineating the three modalities of "unhistorical queerness" in mainland period dramas, "queer presentism" in postcolonial Hong Kong, and "postliberal temporality" in contemporary Taiwan, this chapter theorizes the overall disjunctive temporalities across queer Sinophone visuality and mediascapes.

Unhistorical Queerness across *Jianghu*: Queer Desire, Bromance, and the Postsocialist Mediascape

The Untamed depicts the highly homoerotic bonds between two courageous young men in the world of *jianghu*. According to Chinese literary scholar Chen Pingyuan, there are two meanings of the Chinese word *jianghu*: "1. a secret society within the real world that exists in opposition with the government, 2. a semi-Utopia where *xia* (俠) are free to defy authority and act on their conscience to punish evil and exalt goodness" (paraphrased in Teo 2009, 18). Whereas in Chinese dynastic eras heroes and heroines who roam across the world of *jianghu* might come from recognized sects such as Emei Sect (峨嵋派), Shaolin Sect (少林寺), Mount Hua Sect (華山派), and others that constitute the six major sects of the martial arts kingdom of *wulin* (武林), in the more recent popular TV series in the Mainland, the world of *jianghu* is usually divided by the forces of the fairies versus the evil that may not have any historical link. I coin the concept of "unhistorical queerness" to demonstrate how recent BL TV series in China have conjured a world of heroism, betrayal, reunion, and homoerotic bromance outside of and besides the real world of geopolitics in postsocialist China. Previous research on Sinophone BL cultural consumption demonstrates how Taiwanese young women recontextualize their queer fantasies in a non-Taiwanese imagined Japanese utopia (Martin 2012). Similarly, Jamie J. Zhao (2017c) demonstrates how queer fan fiction for the popular TV show *Super Voice Girl* (超級女聲; 2004–2006) imagines an alternate world that situates lesbian desire in non-Western, Chinese historical, and futuristic settings. Drawing on this body of scholarship on Sinophone BL and queer fantasy worlding, I show how unhistorical queerness can simultaneously open up a possibly utopian future wherein forms of queer desire deemed too "perverse" and unproper in the present geopolitics of China find intense emotional outlet, memorialization, and alternative visual mediation.

The Untamed narrates the queer bromance between the protagonists Wei Wuxian (魏無羨; played by Xiao Zhan 肖戰) and Lan Wangji (藍忘機; played by Wang Yibo 王一博) through a story of misunderstanding, trust, and the final recovery of true heroism. Wei's parents were killed when he was very young, and he was later adopted by Jiang Fengmian (江楓眠), the leader of the Yunmeng Jiang Sect (雲夢江氏). He grew up happily with Jiang's son, Jiang Cheng (江澄), and daughter, Jiang Yanli (江厭離). Just as they reach young adulthood, the world of *jianghu* enters into chaos as the evil forces of the Qishan Wen Sect (岐山溫氏) decide to take over the world. It is believed that whoever obtains the Stygian Iron (陰鐵) will be able to rule the world. Meanwhile, Wei befriends Lan Wangji when all other heroic sects visit the Gusu Lan Sect (姑蘇藍氏) to receive training. Lan is the most promising disciple and courageous fighter of the Lan Sect, and Wei is likewise the most skilful one in martial arts training within his sect. Wei is thought to be killed by the villain Wen Ruohan (溫若寒) in one battle, but later remerges as a most powerful fighter through mastering the secret power of the Stygian Tiger Amulet (陰虎符). Though the linkage between the Stygian Iron and the Stygian Tiger Amulet is never clearly explained in the story, one thing is clear at this point—Wei is no longer seen as a proper heroic fighter, but someone who practices demonic power akin to witchcraft. From this point on, Wei assumes the new name of Yiling Patriarch (夷陵老祖), and almost everyone from the morally righteous sects, including his childhood playmate Jiang Cheng, keep their distance from him except Lan. In one semi-final battle, in which everyone tries to fight over the Stygian Iron, Jiang Cheng is under peer pressure to kill Wei, and eventually finishes Wei with his sword. From then on, Wei/Yiling Patriarch disappears from the world of *jianghu* for 16 years. The series begins from the moment when Wei returns to the secular world with the mission of finding out the true villain who placed the blame on him 16 years ago and who is behind the evil scheme of causing chaos and betrayal among the sects.

What is more captivating to me as a queer critic and BL cultural consumer is the way in which this story of heroism, brotherhood, and betrayal is told through the intense emotional bond between the two male protagonists, Wei and Lan. In fact, this emphasis on the unbreakable bond of queer bromance across the chaotic spaces and temporalities of the world of *jianghu* forms the second aspect of the concept of unhistorical queerness—namely, a form of queer desire at the background of a timeless *jianghu*, but one whose power might *transcend the limit of time* itself. My reading of an unhistorical queerness and desire that transcend the limit of time is indebted to Rey Chow's (1999) deconstructive reading of togetherness and temporality in the queer Hong Kong film *Happy Together* (春光乍洩; dir. Wong Kar-wai, 1997). Commenting on the figuration of queer desire outside of cinematic time and shot in black-and-white color, Chow writes,

> It is, for sure, a moment of erotic passion, but it is also what we may call a moment of indifferentiation, a condition of perfect unity that was not only (perhaps) chronologically past but also seemingly *before difference and separation*. (Chow 1999, 34)

Similar to a cinematic queerness *before* and *beyond* time, the series visualizes unhistorical queerness through the most mundane and touching moment of togetherness and mutual respect between Wei and Lan. For instance, during Episode 3, the Jiang Sect sends Wei, his brother, and his sister to the Lan Sect to receive training; however, upon their arrival, Lan refuses their entrance by insisting to see an invitation letter. Wei argues with Lan relentlessly, leading Lan to use a magic spell to seal Wei's mouth from talking. The same night of their arrival, Wei breaks another strict rule of the Lan Sect by drinking at night on the rooftop! To teach the mischievous Wei a lesson, Lan engages in a sword fight with him, but the two keep on fighting without a clear victory emerging from either side. This fight under the shining moon at night is visually stunning in its onscreen composition (as shown in Figure 6.1). Gradually, we see the serious and morally uptight Lan beginning to loosen up. Specifically, one night, seduced by Wei for drinking, Lan gets seriously wasted. Lan even receives a harsh punishment from his master. From that point on, every time Wei runs into trouble or becomes forsaken by the whole sects of *jianghu*, Lan is always the first to come out and defend him.

The gradual blossoming of the Wei-Lan bond both depends on the ethics of heroism while pointing to moments of emotional outpour and ambiguous sexual urge. The narrative trajectory of turning the tough and serious Lan into a softened fighter capable of showing emotion thus illustrates the unhistorical queerness that exists side by side the more "proper" world of *jianghu*.

Another moment that cements the queer affective bond of Wei and Lan happens when Lan is seriously injured by the leader of the evil sect, Wen Ruohan; during a battle with a giant snake spirit, both men manage to kill the snake, resulting in another serious wound. Lan shows his affectionate side when he takes care of the shivering Wei, who has a fever. Lan tries to warm up Wei's body by transferring his *qi*/vital force to him, and during this moment, Wei requests that Lan

Figure 6.1: Lan Wangji (left) and Wei Wuxian (right) fighting under the moon

sing a song for him. Throughout the series, Lan is often painted as a serious and morally upright person whose heroism is marked by actions and not by words, whereas Wei often runs into trouble and likes to joke around. However, Lan only shows his soft side to Wei and, indeed, sings a song for him. During this affective and homoerotic moment, past scenes of them fighting, drinking, and laughing together replay through a flashback sequence. A moment like this powerfully captures the affective intensity and queer bond of the two men while suspending the brutal time and space of *jianghu*. It shows how, despite all the chaos, betrayal, and mistrust in the world, their queer attachment can transcend the limit of time and gesture toward an emotional togetherness that only Wei and Lan themselves can understand. In fact, during the first episode of the drama before Wei's resurrection, the disciples of Lan and the world of *jianghu* have jokingly described Lan as performing a virtuous ritual of widowhood for Wei, as he has been searching for Wei's whereabouts since he was killed by Jiang Cheng at the battle and fallen into the bottomless pit by the cliff.

Of course, over the course of adapting the *danmei* online serial novel into its current form as a TV series, *The Untamed* also has to negotiate with the danger of censorship of male-male homoerotic content that is much more sexually explicit in the original online text. Geng Song (2022a) perceptively analyzes this process of adaptation from the underground queer online literature scene to the popular TV cultural scene. He writes, "BL images and plots are retained out of commercial concerns, but appear in a rather ambivalent way, morphing into friendship or brotherhood rather than romance between the male characters" (Song 2022a, 78). While I largely agree with Song's analysis of how the process of adapting BL literature into popular TV series and cultural forms entails a process of containment, the overall narrative trajectory and ending of *The Untamed* also powerfully visualize a queer world of *jianghu*, one that transcends the spatial and temporal limit of both the televisual form and the geopolitics of postsocialism. Elsewhere, I have theorized this queer potential of BL in redressing the social upheavals of economic transition and disparity as a form of affective overcoming: "In other words, it frames queer affect as a possibility of reparation and redress for existing economic divisions in a globalizing China" (A. Wong 2020, 509).

The final episode is particularly arresting in its depiction of unhistorical queerness. After the ultimate villain, Jin Guangyao (金光瑤), is revealed to be the one who sets up the evil scheme of turning everyone against Wei, and who also kills his own sworn brother and father in order to rise to the top of the heroic world, the story is—at this point—coming to an end. But like any other ahistorical drama about the fairies and evil, it cannot end without some kind of transcendentalist landscape. Here, at the top of the mountain and at the edge of the cliff, Wei and Lan bid farewell, each marching to his own uncertain future in the world of *jianghu*. One thing is for certain: whenever there is evil in the world, the two will reunite. As they depart from one another amid the breathtaking landscape of pastoral greenery and blue sky, the feature song of the series is playing in the background. The lyrics tell of the bromance and loyalty of Wei and Lan in the following manner:

> Upon hearing the sound of the flute, one is lonely and the night has not ended. When right and wrong are all foregone, how can one pretend to be awake when the dream is over? In the mortal world, how does one measure loss and gain? . . . Let's boil a wine of life, death, happiness, and despair to worship the young hero. The bright moon will keep on shinning, so what's with the melancholy? Why not just face the wind and waves with a free style, and together we sing a song across the world.

When this song comes to an end, the final image is one of Wei taking a second glance with a slight smile, alluding to a possible reunion with Lan. The almost ideal merging of the song with homoerotic undertones in the ending echoes what I have been naming as the "unhistorical queerness" of BL TV drama in contemporary China. This unhistorical queerness calls forth a form of male-male and queer intimacy that is present in the original online text, but relatively toned down in the televisual form. Despite being subject to revision and negotiation, the relative openness of the visual form here gestures towards a queerness that transcends both the temporal and spatial limit of the visual form and the hypermasculine geopolitics of postsocialist China.

Queer Presentism in Postcolonial Hong Kong: *For Love, We Can* and *Ossan's Love*

So far, I have identified a televisual discourse of "unhistorical queerness" that circulates across the mainland Chinese popular representations of BL and homoeroticism, which is conditioned by the increasing censorship of queer and BL contents by the PRC's state media censorship organ NRTA (the National Radio and Television Administration). As Eve Ng and Xiaomeng Li point out,

> In 2007, the State Administration of Radio, Film and Television (the earlier incarnation of the NRTA) classified representations of homosexuality as obscene or "unhealthy" sexual content that should be deleted or selectively cut, but these regulations have been "unclear and complicated" in how they are understood and applied. (Ng and Li 2020, 481)

Compared to the Mainland, the social landscape for both queer activism and media representations seems to be more "liberal" and "progressive." For example, the city has decriminalized sodomy, a legal relic from the British colonial era, since 1991, and has been hosting the annual Pride Parade since 2008. During its tenth year anniversary of the LGBT parade, the number of participants reached 12,000 (Creery 2018). While the city has yet to pass any anti-discrimination ordinance that would protect LGBTQ individuals in the workplace and provide "equal protection" for all, it has a government-run organization called the Equal Opportunities Commission (EOC) that oversees discrimination cases related to sexual orientation and gender expressions. The EOC is supposed to work in a consultant role between the government and Hong Kong citizens in measuring the city's progress in gender democracy and social tolerance for sexual minorities.

More recently, Hong Kong witnessed a wave of legal cases that saw rulings in favor of the civil rights of LGBTQ subjects. For instance, in 2013, the Court of Final Appeal ruled in favor of a transwoman plaintiff, "Miss W," to marry in her affirmed gender rather than the one assigned at birth in the arena of heterosexual marriage. On June 6, 2019, the Court of Final Appeal also ruled in favor of a gay civil servant, Angus Leung, in a case that found the Civil Service Bureau in violation of Leung and his husband's rights as civil servants (which Leung is) to file for joint taxation and medical coverage. In March 2020, the High Court also adjudicated that "a Housing Authority policy that prevents same-sex couples who married abroad from applying for public housing is unconstitutional and unlawful" (R. Wong 2020). In my previous work, I have theorized Hong Kong as "a city of queer globalities where queerness evinces precisely the uneven experiments of working out transgender and queer identities in the relative absence of full legal protection, gay marriage, and queer liberalism" (Wong 2021, 109).

In terms of film and media representations, comedy shows by the Hui Brothers in the 1970s and gender parody and androgyny in 1980s Cantopop both pioneered mass camp queer aesthetics in Hong Kong culture (Chao 2020, 143–197). Furthermore, documentary films produced by the government-funded TV channel RTHK periodically survey the situations of LGBTQ Hong Kong individuals in a "realistic" manner, and a range of Hong Kong films, both commercial and arthouse, have depicted same-sex desire and queer genders and sexualities from the 1980s onward. In particular, Helen Hok-Sze Leung has analyzed such films as *Happy Together* (1997), *Portland Street Blues* (古惑仔情義篇之洪興十三妹; dir. Yip Wai Man, 1998), *Bishonen* (美少年之戀; dir. Yonfan, 1998), and *Butterfly* (蝴蝶; dir. Yan Yan Mak, 2004) as constituting what she terms the queer "undercurrents" of postcolonial Hong Kong culture. Leung remarks that "it is perhaps no coincidence that some of the most creative tales about the postcolonial city, and the most visionary stories of survival under its crisis-ridden milieu, are told through a queer lens" (2008, 6). While Leung's cultural studies approach in diagnosing undercurrents as the queer structure of feeling around the 1997 postcolonial handover resonates with my study of queer temporality here, I will also show that in the last ten years of so, a group of queer media cultural texts have also depicted the queer postcolonial city (the special administrative region of the PRC) in a queer temporal mode that is invested in the here, the quotidian, the ordinary, and the everyday. I coin the term "queer presentism" to name this quotidian everyday dimension of queer temporality.

The short film *For Love, We Can* was produced by the School of Film and Television at the Hong Kong Academy for Performing Arts, with funding by the HIV health advocacy NGO Red Ribbon Centre. The film was warmly received at the Hong Kong Lesbian and Gay Film Festival in 2014. It tells the love story between Jun Mok, a rebellious gay youth and hairdresser who lives with his widowed mother in a public housing estate, and his more "socially respectable" lover Michael, a local banker. Jun has multiple sexual partners before meeting Michael, the love of his life. Jun prefers the sexual practice of barebacking, and after one of his former sexual partners reveals to him that he is HIV+, Jun decides to break up with Michael while getting tested himself. Overall, the film narrates the drama-ridden life of Jun while imagining the possibility of queer love between Michael and Jun despite the social stigma of being HIV+.

The opening sequence of the film exudes the queer temporality of the everyday through a spatially raw depiction of what it means to live a working-class queer life in Hong Kong. The camera follows Jun's mother as she carries grocery bags with both hands. Her back is slouching slightly, showing how years of rough work at the local restaurant have taken a toll on her life. Here, the camera frames her back in the middle of a dim and long hallway that is a conventional look of the overcrowded but efficient public housing estate in Hong Kong. Before opening the door, however, she witnesses a bitchy verbal fight between her son Jun and a casual lover. Jun yells at the estranged boyfriend: "Wanna be my boyfriend? You're out of your mind!" The guy retorts: "Fuck you, Jun Mok." Overhearing this "gay drama," the local gossipy neighbor tells her daughter: "Mind your own business, kiddo. Don't listen to them."

The scene that quickly follows this one is when the protagonist Michael enters into the picture. On another night, Michael walks through the narrow corridors of the flat and enters Jun's room, which is only covered by a curtain. As they are having foreplay and moaning before sexual intercourse, Jun's mother is tossing and turning on her bed, separated only by a thin wall. Right before anal sex, Michael reaches for a condom and Jun says, "Forget that. It's too much trouble. I'd like to be closer." Michael then touches Jun's face lovingly and remarks: "I've never seen another guy with such beautiful eyebrows." Immediately after the night scene, the next is a long shot that captures the bright colors of the painted outer layer of the Choi Hung Estate, where Jun and his mother reside. Inside the flat, Michael runs into Jun's mother as he goes to work, and she remains silent. Another day, during lunchtime, Jun's mother visits Michael's branch at the Bank of China and deposits $250 (HKD) into her savings account. Another intimate scene shows Michael caressing Jun in his own flat, which is much brighter and more elegant in decoration and design. During this personal conversation, we learn that Michael's parents own printing companies in mainland China and that they are often not in Hong Kong. Michael also reveals to Jun that his mother visited his branch purposefully. Seeing that her bank account doesn't have a lot of money, Michael tells Jun to treat her nicer and "spend more time with her."

By visually juxtaposing the spaces of the dim public housing flat, the financial space of the Bank of China, and the elegant space of a middle-class home in Hong Kong, the film draws attention to the drastic differences between the two gay men in class and social backgrounds, what Ting-Fai Yu calls the uneven "spatialities of queer globalization" (2021). Furthermore, the film illustrates the queer presentism of Hong Kong, where queer people are not only visible in the gay bar scenes of Central and Causeway Bay but are, in fact, everywhere in the here and now. Queer presentism thus infuses the narrative as the two young men love and desire each other against the backdrop of a global city that has consistently ranked at the top for income inequality globally (Marques 2020). Beyond the affective undercurrents that predominated LGBTQ films and media around the 1997 handover, *For Love, We Can* portrays queer desire through the temporality of the everyday, thus pointing to the raw dimension of living in the global city. Furthermore, the film plays on the doubleness of the phrases "we can" in the English title. "We can" might be read as the queer affirmation of loving despite class differences; at the same time, it might also be read as the will to overcome the stigma of being HIV+ towards the later part of the film.

By the end of the film, Jun has tested positive, and the nurse comforts him with the fact that an early diagnosis can lead to better management of the illness. The pedagogical message seems to be that it is perfectly feasible to live a healthy life as a gay and HIV+ individual. Despite this medical advice, Jun has intentionally avoided Michael because Michael has never replied to his question: "Will you still love me if I am sick one day?" During a night when Jun refuses to come home, Michael has an intimate conversation with Jun's mother and basically promises her that he will always look after Jun no matter what. The next morning, Jun returns to the public housing estate while running into Michael. Jun wants a breakup, and Michael reveals that he is also HIV+ at this point. Michael stops Jun from talking back by emotionally kissing him in the fully public space, in front of another group of young men playing basketball from across a close distance. Their kissing happens under bright daylight, and Jun's mother witnesses it from across the street as well. This powerful and emotionally raw ending visualizes the queer presentism of Hong Kong. Beyond the commercial scenes of gay bars and the "undercurrent" scenes of sauna and hotel hookup, a testimony of queer love against all odds seems to be possible and imaginable because "for love, we can."

If *For Love, We Can* narrates gay male youth against the backdrop of HIV+ stigma and within the mundane temporality of Hong Kong, the recent popular TV drama *Ossan's Love* takes queer presentism further by visualizing the queer regionalism of Hong Kong across the transregional networks of Japan, Hong Kong, and Taiwan. The 2021 TV series is produced by ViuTV, a subscription-based television channel. It is adapted from the original 2018 Japanese TV drama with the same title. The Japanese series follows Soichi Haruta, a clumsy, humble, and hardworking real estate agent who finds himself straddled between the romantic pursuits by his boss Musashi Kurosawa and coworker Ryota Maki, who later on also becomes his roommate. The series went on to win numerous awards locally and became the biggest hit that year in Japan. Outside of Japan, the series was also warmly received in East Asia. Given the transnational success of *Ossan's Love*, the Hong Kong remake in 2021 came with high expectations. It is noteworthy that the main protagonists who assume the roles of Soichi and Ryota (whose names in the Hong Kong version are Tin and Muk) are played by Edan Lui (呂爵安) and Anson Lo (盧瀚霆), members of the highly popular 12-member boyband Mirror (Kwan 2021). The seasoned actor Kenny Wong (黃德斌), with a tall and muscular physique, plays the boss KK. Beyond the contemporary popularity of Mirror, which adds star appeal for the TV series, the drama also infuses queer presentism by narrating the blossoming of love between Tin and Muk through the logic of queer romance as a form of cohabitation. Indeed, the romance first begins as a form of cohabitation after Muk is introduced as the new real estate agent at Tin's workplace, the Q Realty. One night, after learning that Muk is a great chef and a homebody, Tin invites Muk to live with him because he has an extra room available. This form of bachelor cohabiting living arrangement is in fact quite common in Hong Kong, as the global city has one of the most expensive real estate markets in the world. Through cohabitation, Muk also finds out Tin's messy habits, which include tossing his underwear and socks all over the place, waking up late for work, and so forth. But the clumsiness and childish behaviors are also what mark Tin as particularly attractive to Muk, and in fact both Muk and the boss KK cannot quite articulate what attracts them to Tin besides the fact that he is a very "authentic" and kindhearted person. In other words, the series portrays the growing romantic bond between Muk and Tin through the most mundane aspect of dwelling in Hong Kong, and the queer presentism of Hong Kong is highly linked to the here and now—the ordinary lifestyle of bachelorhood in the city.

Beyond a heavy dose of queer contemporaneity that marks the queer time and place of Hong Kong, the TV series also powerfully maps the queer regionalism of Hong Kong through the theme of career-induced relocation to Taiwan. Elsewhere, Howard Chiang and I define "queer regionalism" as a concept that "reckons with the vertical logics of Euro-American empire, but at the same time a queer regional model signals greater attention to less orderly, bilateral, and horizontal intra-regional traffics of queerness across different countries and regions in Asia" (2016, 1645). *Ossan's Love* narrates the queer regionalism of Hong Kong through a narrative of queer love as a form of trial tested by temporary long-distance separation across Hong Kong and Taiwan. Specifically, by the 13th episode, Muk has one-sidedly suggested breaking up with Tin because he knows that Tin loves children, and their relationship can never result in a marriage with any conventional form of heterosexual reproduction (of course, the TV series does not yet entertain the queerer possibility of LGBT parenthood and adoption). Given this sudden heartbreak, Tin decides to take up his boss KK's offer to relocate to Taipei together to launch Taiwan's second headquarter location of Q Realty. While there, Tin encounters many problems as a new resident and worker in Taipei, which include a possible close encounter with a ghost when he examines a vacated flat for a new listing. KK "saves" Tin in that incident, and from there the two cohabit in Taipei happily for one year. After KK proposes marriage to Tin, Tin is dumbfounded but awkwardly accepts his proposal. Their Taipei officemates also congratulate the two. KK and Tin decide to go back to Hong Kong for two weeks to host a wedding. After being back in Hong Kong, Tin realizes that his heart still belongs to Muk. At the last minute, leading up to the wedding ceremony, KK forces Tin to confront his own feelings, and Tin runs all the way to the reclusive island of Tai O, where Muk's family home is located, to propose to Muk instead. The series ends with Muk and Tin fondling and kissing each other in a bright apartment space back in Tin's Hong Kong home (seen in Figure 6.2).

Spatially, the TV series mediates the queer presentism of a gay Hong Kong romance through the symbolic role of Taipei. Beyond its obvious status as another tiger economy in East Asia, it is noteworthy that in recent years, Taiwan also assumes a new status as a queer mecca as it hosts the largest gay parade in Asia. The Red House Theatre is another queer locale in Taipei, with numerous gay bars and shops frequented by the locals and tourists regardless of sexual orientation. Ideologically, Howard Chiang compares Taiwan and Hong Kong

Figure 6.2: Tin (left) kissing Muk (right) in a queer presentist mode

through the analytical rubric of transgender and argues that the current discourses of *tongzhi* and *ku'er* in Taiwan also need to account for the centrality of transgender activism. As Chiang writes,

> The global significance has been evinced by the fact that Taiwan became the twenty-ninth state in the world, and the first in Asia, to legalize same-sex marriage in May 2019 . . . The enduring plurality of Sinophone queering makes it unambiguous *why* and *how* the Taiwanese subversion of *tongzhi* constitutes a multidirectional form of resistance. (Chiang 2021, 205)

In other words, by comparing Hong Kong and Taiwan through the imaginary and actual geopolitics of queer liberalism and legal progressiveness in Sinophone Taiwan, *Ossan's Love* suggests that Tin's migratory experiences in Taipei also necessarily open up more queer horizons for Muk and himself in Hong Kong. It is only through the broadening of queer political imagination and the spatial entanglement of the two cities that the love between Tin and Muk can blossom in the end. As the TV drama ends on a queer presentist mode in Hong Kong within Tin's bright flat, they can finally love as who they are, not simply as coworkers who happen to cohabit together.

Towards a Postliberal Temporality: Queer Visuality in Post–Gay Marriage Taiwan

In the previous two sections, I explore different queer temporal logics that underline contemporary televisual modernity in the PRC and Hong Kong. Whereas *danmei* TV dramas in the Mainland exemplify "unhistorical queerness" that is at odds with the social reality of censorship and Confucian hypermasculine nationalism, in the case of postcolonial Hong Kong, a mode of queer presentism renders queer issues in the visual mode of everydayness and quotidian temporality that is increasingly trafficked in interregional queer discourses and regionalism. Meanwhile, queer Sinophone visual modernity has undergone significant changes before and after the 2019 benchmark of legalized gay marriage in Taiwan. In this last section, I offer a critical analysis of "postliberal temporality," a queer temporal worlding wherein gay male characters in films and TV drama find existence and presumably queer liberal freedom in an imaginary world where social discrimination is assumed to be receding from view. I identify the emergence of this postliberal temporality in the 2004 film *Formula 17*, directed by Chen Yinjung, and conclude with some brief comments on the 2020 Taiwanese BL drama *Because of You*.

Formula 17 cinematically announces the arrival of queer liberalism and a postliberal temporality by first setting up an imaginary spatial contrast between rural Taiwan and the urban gay mecca of Taipei. A brief plot summary might be useful here. Chou Tien Tsai (周天財; played by Tony Yang 楊祐寧) is a tanned and handsome country bumpkin who travels to Taipei to meet a summer online fling. After an unsuccessful date, he bumps into the number one playboy in town, Bai Tieh Nan (白鐵男; played by Duncan Chow 周群達). The Chinese name of "Tieh Nan" (鐵男) literally translates into English as "an iron man," alluding to Bai's heart of stone and his seasoned experiences in the dating and gay hookup scene in Taipei. Tien first bumps into Bai at the gay bar and sees him again at the gym. They run into each other again at a crossroads, and an older gay stranger helps to cement the bond between them by asking for Bai's business card and giving it to Tien. Eventually, Tien shows up on Bai's doorstep one night, and they have a night of passionate sex. The next morning, Bai disappears, and instead his friend Jun shows up at his apartment to explain to Tien that the situation has become more complicated. Misunderstanding the message and falsely assuming that Jun is a love rival, Tien thinks that Bai only treats him as a boy toy and decides to never see him again. It turns out that this all springs from a bigger misunderstanding—Bai only distances himself from Tien because in his childhood, a fortune teller revealed to him that all the things he treasures in his life will perish. The curse seems to repeat again and again as his flower, pet, and relatives all died. To fight against this curse, Bai would not let himself fall in love. Instead, he only has one-night stands. Eventually he develops a fear of falling in love. During the love-turned-hate ordeal between Bai and Tien, Bai leaves for a business trip; upon his return, he spots Tien on the street. He decides not to let go of his true love this time. The film ends with Bai revealing the truth to Tien and the two smiling at each other under the bright daylight in Taipei. Despite its uplifting mood, film critic Brian Hu detects a formulaic narrative: "What follows is essentially boy wants boy, boy gets boy, boy loses boy, boy regains boy. The turning points grind like clockwork, complete with flamboyant sidekicks who nurse heartache with flowers and romantic prose" (2005).

Symbolically, the film marks the arrival of postliberal temporality by contrasting the rural origin of Tien versus the queer cosmopolitanism of his Taipei friend Yu and his workplace, the gay bar where Tien first meets Bai. First, it is unclear where exactly Tien's hometown is. It is most likely in Tainan, the southern region of Taiwan, where the lifestyle seems to go at a slower pace than in Taipei. At the age of 17, Tien decides to take a train to meet his online date in Taipei. However, the guy turns out to be a disappointment for Tien, as the handsome but very vain man is only interested in having sex with him, whereas Tien wants to meet the love of his life. Tien then meets his best friend Yu at the bar. His entrance into the bar is quite visually symbolic, as he carries his luggage clumsily while effeminate gay boys and muscular guys are showing off their assets on the dance floor. Hilariously, during their brief catchup on life, Tien tells Yu that he is still a virgin, but the loud music has deafened Yu's hearing. When he asks Tien to repeat what he said again, Tien replies very loudly: "I am still a virgin!" This time, everyone at the bar overhears Tien's confession of virginity, thus marking his first awkward gay initiation into queer urban life in Taipei. By constructing Yu as the cosmopolitan "gay guide" at the bar and by discursively framing Tien as less modern, more "rural," but quite cute in his sexual innocence, *Formula 17* frames Tien's rural origin to be spatially incommensurable with Taipei. Furthermore, it sets the film off onto a journey of postliberal queer temporality, in which Tien's arrival to Taipei will propel him along a path toward gay maturity. Simply put, urban Taipei will transform Tien into a truly cosmopolitan young man through a queer telos of modernity.

If the film's postliberal temporality requires a strategic displacement of the rural in Tien, it also depends on an ideological displacement of feminism, transgender people, and everything that does not fit into the perfect picture of gay male cosmopolitanism. In his analysis of queer activism and Marxist critique in post–martial law Taiwan, Petrus Liu writes,

> Despite these apparent advances in queer human rights, however, sexual minorities remain subject to a strong form of queer illiberalism in Taiwan. The space of the queer is accessible only to those who have met the state's definition of the human. Prostitutes, people living with AIDS, gay men and lesbians who use recreational drugs, and transgendered people all fall outside the normative definition of a "gay but healthy" image promoted by the state and remain excluded if not outright persecuted. (Liu 2015, 158)

In Liu's view, the arrival of state feminism and the inclusion of some queer subjects into the fold of pink capitalism, rights-based cultural citizenship, and sexual respectability go hand in hand with the continual displacement and marginalization of anything outside of homonormativity (Duggan 2002). In this regard, *Formula 17* certainly reproduces the homonormative discourse of queer liberalism by marginalizing transgender people, women, and sex workers. Namely, these individuals simply do not exist in the diegesis of the film, and the only transgender character, the crossdresser C.C., simply serves as a laughingstock in the narrative.

The film exudes the postliberal temporality of queerness most powerfully through a narrative of luring Tien into a happy coupledom with the right guy, who is transnationally mobile, cosmopolitan, and linked to the capitalist modernity of Hong Kong. Specifically, Bai speaks Mandarin to Tien throughout the film, but occasionally he also speaks perfect Cantonese with Jun. This is a conscious filmmaking decision, and one reason to include both Hong Kong (Duncan Chow) and Taiwan actors might be to aim for wider commercial appeal and reception among Hong Kong audiences and especially young female and gay fans, given that most consumers of BL cultural products are in fact young girls who are often called "rotten girls," *funv* (腐女; Liu 2009). Ideologically, by framing Tien and Bai's overcoming of their misunderstanding only upon Bai's return from a business trip in Singapore, the film portrays Bai as a highly attractive gay cosmopolitan subject whose desirability springs from his ability to accrue transnational capital. Simply put, by ending the film with the queer romance between Bai and Tien, the film shows that with the help of a queer Sinophone cosmopolitan lover, Tien is able to transform into one just like him as well.

Because of You came out in 2020, just one year after Taiwan became the first country in Asia to legalize same-sex marriage. In this post–gay marriage world, how do mainstream media and televisual modernity translate the discourse of queer liberalism? What has changed since the emergence of postliberal temporality in *Formula 17* more than 15 years ago? Through a brief analysis of the discursive progression of the TV series, I aim to show how a heightened form of queer postliberal temporality has come into existence through a narrative of queer brotherhood cum gay male romance. *Because of You* begins with the airport scene where the oldest brother of the Yuan family, Yuan Jun Cheng (元君澄; played by Korean heartthrob Lee Shi Kang) arrives from Seoul. Jun Cheng comes to Taipei because his father, the owner of a Fortune 500 business, has called for his return. As the drama unfolds, we learn that the Yuan family business empire is being fought for among the three brothers and future heirs, who all have different biological mothers. Jun Cheng's Korean mother already passed away, and Yuan Jun Dao (元君道), the second brother, is not very ambitious about inheriting his father's empire. The youngest son, Yuan Jun Ping (元君平), is still in high school. Meanwhile, Jun Dao and Jun Ping all have very close male friends whom they secretly desire—namely, Yang Xiang Shi (楊翔實) and Yan Yue Rong (顏月戎). Upon his arrival at the airport, it turns out that Jun Cheng's chauffeurs are really gangsters hired by his uncle, who wants to kidnap him and force his father to surrender his business to him. Eventually, with the help of a handsome young man, Lin Xun (林尋), who can also speak Korean, Jun Cheng is able to escape to a safe place. Upon the death of his very ill mother, Lin finds a piece of paper with a phone number that his mother asked him to call. It turns out that the man who answers the call is Yuan Wei Zhi (元微知), the father of the three Yuan brothers and the owner of the business empire. Yuan at first mistakes Lin as his bastard child because Lin's mother was his estranged lover, Cui Ying (崔瑛). He then orders the oldest son, Jun Cheng, to capture Lin. Jun Cheng conducts a DNA test after releasing Lin, but the report actually shows that Lin is not the biological son of Yuan. Nonetheless, it is through this accidental encounter that Jun Cheng develops a peculiar queer feeling for Lin. The TV series thus maps the journey of Jun Cheng and Lin gradually falling in love with each other, and the ending of the drama shows the three brothers reconciling their differences and each bringing their boyfriends to a lovely dinner gathering.

Because of You both adheres to and departs from the conventional teen idol drama formula in Sinophone media. Ideologically, the romance story of someone (usually a young girl from a humble background) meeting a handsome young male heir and transforming each other's lives is a common theme running through post-2000 Sinophone TV dramas. The most obvious examples of the narratives of upward mobility through romance include *It Started with a Kiss* (惡作劇之吻; CTV, 2005) and *Fated to Love You* (命中注定我愛你; TTV, 2008) in Taiwan and *Boss & Me* (杉杉来了; Jiangsu TV, 2014) in the Mainland. These TV series also led to the rise in popularity of such border-crossing Sinophone stars such as Joe Cheng (鄭元暢), Ariel Lin (林依晨), Ethan Juan (阮經天), Joe Chen Chiao-en (陳喬恩), Hans Zhang (張翰), and Zhao Liying (趙麗穎), to give the most obvious examples (Ko 2004). So, the very fact that a young man like Lin Xun from a single-parent and working-class family is able to meet the love of his life, Jun Cheng, from a wealthy family is, in fact, nothing new. What is surprisingly arresting in the TV drama's representation of postliberal temporality with a queer twist is its dominant visual logics of "ordinary gayness" (Martin 1997). While *Formula 17* announces the arrival of queer liberalism by relegating the rural resident, the transgender individual, and the sex worker to the social margins, *Because of You* arguably exudes a postliberal logic more powerfully by depicting the three Yuan brothers and Lin Xun as young men who *only happen to be gay*. Previous works by Taiwan's queer theorists and feminists such as Jen-peng Liu and Ding Naifei (2005), and Josephine Chuen-juei Ho (2010) have respectively demonstrated how modes of sexual tolerance work complicitly with homophobia and how the post–martial law Taiwan state deploys anti-porn rhetoric through the global legality of protecting children in Taiwan. Yet, in the postliberal framing of queer desire in the TV series, the three brothers show no concern for LGBTQ rights and sexual radicalism. In other words, their gay identities (or lack thereof) do not translate into social burden and/or responsibility, and the series simply avoids any depiction of gay scenes, saunas, clubs, or social activism. Consequently, by constructing a televisual universe in which being gay simply does not matter anymore in post-2019 Taiwan, *Because of You* evinces postliberal temporality in which queerness is no longer that queer anymore.

Disjunctive Temporalities across the Sinophone Mediascape

In this chapter, I have laid out an interdisciplinary approach to track the differentiating logics of queer temporality across the televisual modernities of Sinophone mediascapes. While the concepts of "unhistorical queerness," "queer presentism," and "postliberal temporality" are each distinctively dominant in representations of queer desire and gay male intimacies across the three Sinophone geopolitical sites, the three frameworks are meant to be provocative rather than totalizing and prescriptive. In fact, it might even be more productive to unpack the overlapping relation across the three concepts in each Sinophone queer media cultural landscape. For instance, while *The Untamed* traffics in an ahistorical temporality of a queer *jianghu*, its ahistoricism might also assume that gay male homoeroticism is easily consumable as commodity and hence has entered into the postliberal order. Similarly, the overwhelming idealism of a queer cosmopolitan world dominated only by gay male youth and sexual fulfilment in *Ossan's Love*, *Formula 17*, and *Because of You* might also strike any critical queer theorist as largely "ahistorical," naively idealistic, if not outrightly apolitical. My work on the disjunctive temporalities across queer Sinophone media is heavily indebted to Audrey Yue and Helen Hok-Sze Leung's theory of queer Asia and disjunctive queer modernities. They note the simultaneous localizing and globalizing forces of global capitalism, local tradition, new urban spaces, and the creative industries in queer Asian cities like Singapore, Hong Kong, Taipei, and Bangkok. In other words, "the concept of disjunctive queer modernity provides a new starting point to account for the emergence of non-Western gay cities that do not follow the linear model of emancipation, rights, assimilation and equality" (Yue and Leung 2017, 761).

Taking my cue from Yue and Leung's theory of the queer Asian city, I show how the disjunctive logics of queer modernities across diverse geopolitical landscapes of postsocialist China, postcolonial Hong Kong, and post–martial law Taiwan have enabled the emergence of differential logics of queer desire as they are manifested in a range of cultural representations across online films, BL media, and TV dramas. These disjunctive temporalities of queer Sinophone visuality draw our attention to the wide-ranging practices of cultural commodification, stardom, fandom, and consumerism as we entangle ourselves across unhistorical, presentist, and postliberal social orders. We had better come up with more ambitious conceptual tools to track the fast-shifting mediascapes of queer Sinophone visuality.

III. Queer/ing Celebrities across Geocultural Boundaries

7
Queer Vocals and Stardom on Chinese TV
Case Studies of Wu Tsing-Fong and Zhou Shen

Linshan Jiang

This chapter examines the life experiences and TV performances of two pop singers, Taiwanese Wu Tsing-Fong (吴青峰; born in 1982) and mainland Chinese Zhou Shen (周深; born in 1992), as well as how people react to their images on Chinese TV. Wu and Zhou are special in the Sinophone entertainment industry because they both possess "androgynous" voices as male singers. At first glance, their appearances and personalities echo the popular soft masculinity—a hybrid form of Chinese Confucian *wen* (文) masculinity, Japanese *bishōnen* (美少年; rendered as "beautiful youth") masculinity, and global metrosexual masculinity—that scholars have identified in recent studies of stardom in East Asia (Jung 2011, 39; Louie 2014, 24; Louie 2015, 122; Song 2010, 410; Song and Hird 2013, 1; see also Chapters 3 and 6 in this volume). While the so-called "soft masculinity" may in itself be considered "effeminate," the voices of Wu and Zhou intensify this social stigma based on gender norms and are often denounced as unacceptable—indeed, queer. Their vocal queerness not only drew verbal abuse during the singers' teenage years, but also generated media sensation and public attention following each of their performing debuts. I use vocal queerness in these two cases to denote both a form of gender nonnormativity and a signifier of homosexuality for some audiences (although neither singer has declared himself as such).[1] Wu and Zhou continue to be targets of verbal abuse at present, despite their popularity. Nevertheless, I argue that their vocal queerness not only destabilizes the univocal male masculinity rooted in mainstream Chinese society, but also adds to the diverse representations of Chinese-speaking male gender personas in today's music, TV, and celebrity industries.

---

1. Wu wrote two songs, *Blue Eyes* (蓝眼睛) and *Left* (左边), in his third album, *Incomparable Beauty* (无与伦比的美丽), and dedicated them to his first love, a female cohort at the university. The female cohort also appeared in the music video of *Left*, and they kissed each other. This was reported by the Taiwan newspaper *Liberty Times* in 2007. See https://ent.ltn.com.tw/news/paper/168085.

Queerness is an overarching term which can refer concretely to LGBTQ individuals and communities as well as, more conceptually, a "process of formation" that is not within the sex-gender normative regime (Jagose 1996, 1). In post-2000 mainland China, there has been a "burgeoning 'queer pop' scene" (Zhao 2020a, 464). This queer scene is both celebrated and regulated in the mainstream media and public sphere of mainland China (Zhao 2020a, 464). Moreover, it expresses "queer ideologies and identities" on the one hand, and "capitalize[s] on queerness for profit" on the other (Wang 2015, 153). Particularly, when queer pop culture encounters Chinese TV, nonnormative forms of Chinese masculinity must often negotiate with both state propaganda and commercialization (Song 2010, 411). With TV as a public platform of entertainment and influence, Wu and Zhou continue to seek room for existence between "sissyphobia" (Song 2022a, 68), homophobia, transphobia, and voyeurism.

The age gap and geographical distance between Wu and Zhou point to the divergent entertainment industries in which they are situated and the different lived experiences they have had. When Wu debuted in 2004 as the lead vocalist for the indie band Sodagreen (苏打绿),[2] Taiwan led the entertainment industry across the Taiwan Strait. The internet was only one component among many available media streams, including TV, radio, mobile phones, face-to-face concerts, and musical festivals. When Zhou debuted in 2014 as a competitor on the third season of *The Voice of China* (中国好声音; Zhejiang TV, China, 2014), he was already an influential uploader on major Chinese online platforms for audio and video sharing as well as livestreaming. The convergence of TV and the internet is so prevalent in both mainland China and Taiwan nowadays that each of the TV shows discussed below can be viewed on both TV channels and online video sites.

In the rest of this chapter, I explore the two singers' active negotiations with the state and the market based on their queer masculinities. I conduct a close reading of Wu's and Zhou's TV performances, including singing, interviews, and awards ceremonies, through official TV channels and online-streaming TV platforms. I first review scholarship on Chinese masculinities and analyze how Wu and Zhou have coped with gender discrimination in their adolescence and professional careers through their TV presentations. As they navigate the mainstream media and face the commodification of queerness, I also explore how the performers play with popular culture through the incorporation of and resistance to consumerism in different social-political environments (such as mainland China and Taiwan). By so doing, I ask the following questions: How do these singers reconstruct alternative masculinities as they gain success and

---

2. In 2020, due to the dispute on the trademark registration with the producer, Sodagreen changed its name to Oaeen (魚丁糸). Since the songs I discuss in this chapter were released under the name of Sodagreen, I still use its original band name.

popularity? As they are gradually accepted by a larger audience in mainland China's mainstream media, how do Wu and Zhou display queerness as their artistic signature without being marginalized or censored?

Masculinities Reconsidered

The basic distinction between the concepts of man and masculinity is imperative in understanding the cases of Wu and Zhou. Studies of men and masculinities have developed since the 1980s (Kimmel, Hearn, and Connell 2005, 1; Louie 2014, 18). To decouple man from masculinity, C. J. Pascoe and Tristan Bridges explain that man refers to "a state of being" of those a society defines or perceives as male, while masculinity concerns "identity, performance, power, privilege, relations, styles, and structure" (2015, 3). Masculinity is "socially constructed" rather than being "biologically determined" (Pascoe and Bridges 2015, 3). This echoes the earlier distinction between biological sex and social gender roles, as the latter is "a term for the social construction of masculinity and femininity" (Goldie 2014, 6). In the cases of Wu and Zhou, although they both self-identify as male, the queerness of their voices—often labeled as "androgynous" or "effeminate"—is related to a range of social constructions of what it means to be a man or a woman, both, either, or neither. The binary distinction between man/manly/masculine and woman/womanly/feminine is still a common social assumption: men are assumed to have lower-pitched voices and women higher-pitched voices. When people's voices fail to match the normative expectations imposed on their bodies, they may be misidentified as the opposite sex.

Furthermore, there are different gendered connotations that accompany different gendered expressions. For example, androgyny may be framed as a "healthy phenomenon" which indicates "having" something unique or special (Li 2015, 77). Along these lines, the music critic Zheng Yang (郑洋) praised Wu's voice as "unique" in the TV singing competition program *Singer* (歌手; Hunan TV, China, 2019);[3] and the famous singer Na Ying (那英) commented on Zhou's voice as "a combination of *yin* (阴) and *yang* (阳)" in the TV singing competition program *Our Song* (我们的歌; Dragon TV, China, 2019–2020).[4] The philosophical concepts of *yin* (meaning "female essence, subordinate, passive, shaded") and *yang* (meaning "male essence, dominant, active, bright") in Daoism are closely related to Chinese gender culture (Edwards 2016, 90–91). It is also a man's privilege to achieve the perfect balance between *yin* and *yang* in premodern Chinese culture (Edwards 2016, 110). In contrast, words such as *niang* (娘) and *niangpao*

---

3. See the first episode of its 2019 season at https://w.mgtv.com/b/327378/4976960.html.
4. See the twelfth episode of the show, aired on January 19, 2020, at https://youtu.be/ebnHtmZhwjw.

(娘炮), rendered as "effeminate" or "sissy," are used as insults in the normative culture of contemporary Chinese-speaking world.

In research on men and masculinities in East Asia, the most prominent conceptualization is Kam Louie's *wen-wu* (文/武) dyad. Wu's and Zhou's life experiences also showcase this dyad. In the dyad, *wen* refers to "cultural attainment" and *wu* refers to "martial valor" (Louie 2002, 4; Louie and Edwards 1994, 135). Louie (2002) analyzes prominent figures in Chinese history who epitomize the "ideal masculinity in traditional Chinese culture" and sees how these figures demonstrate the *wen-wu* dyad. He (2002) also extends this dyad to modern representations of Chinese masculinity in fiction, films, and cultural phenomena (see also Song 2019, 111–12). While the ideal masculinity is achieved through a balance between *wen* and *wu*, in most of Chinese history, *wen* is given priority as "a sign of power and privilege" (Louie 2014, 22). In this sense, both Wu and Zhou fulfill the ideal of *wen*: Wu graduated from National Chengchi University in Taiwan with a good grasp of Chinese literature, and Zhou graduated from Lviv National Musical Academy in Ukraine as a professional *bel canto* singer. Through receiving higher education, they both possess the cultural knowledge that is expected in the *wen* component of the ideal masculinity.

Transposing the *wen-wu* dyad onto contemporary society, Louie (2015, 122, 124–25) situates Chinese masculinities in a global context and analyzes the ideal masculinity in Chinese, Japanese, and Korean popular cultures. He identifies a "softened" and "more 'feminine'" type of masculinity, which he attributes to the increasing "buying power of women" and the rise of youth culture. One typical example is the "Boys Over Flowers" (or "flower boy," as discussed in some other chapters of this book) phenomenon (Louie 2015, 129; Oh 2017, 126), which can be traced back to the Japanese manga *Boys Over Flowers* (花より男子, 1992–2004). Popularized through inter-Asian TV adaptations of the manga, "flower boy" nowadays has become a marker for this kind of masculinity and continues to be frequently represented in transnational Asian entertainment industry. In addition, soft masculinity—a form of male persona featuring "tender charisma, purity, and politeness"—is also prominent in South Korean TV dramas (Jung 2011, 52). Jung (2011, 28, 30) also notes that the soft masculinity popularized through South Korean popular culture has been shaped by the Chinese *wen* masculinity and the *bishōnen* image in Japanese popular culture.

However, the soft-masculinity type also faces criticism in mainland Chinese official media, which often manifests "sissyphobia" and "a fear of castration" (Song 2022a, 70). For example, it immediately generated a heated debate among the audience when male idols with soft-masculine personas were featured in the TV special *First Class of the New Semester* (开学第一课; CCTV, China) on September 1, 2018 (Ding 2018). Since the Ministry of Education required this special program to be shown on the first day of school, some parents feared that these "effeminate" celebrities would become "bad" role models for their sons; others believed that labeling these idols as "effeminate" was a form of gender stereotyping. Even the mainstream media joined the debate. The official media outlet Xinhua News Agency described the phenomenon as "a crisis of masculinity" and a symptom of "sick culture" and the idols' image as "slender and weak" (Ding 2018). The party-state newspaper *People's Daily* called for respect for diversity and criticized the usage of derogatory words, such as "sissy" and "neither male nor female" (不男不女); at the same time, however, celebrities were exhorted to show a "more positive and upbeat image" (Ding 2018). As Chapter 3 also finds, this debate unfolding in mainland Chinese official media commentaries on alternative forms of masculinity, which Geng Song (2022a, 70) refers to as "sissyphobia" or "a fear of castration," covering "a wider scope than homophobia" and operating "in a heterosexual context," illustrates indoctrinated normative understandings of male masculinity, as well as the underlying premise that masculinity is presumed to be the binarist opposite of femininity.

Derogatory epithets, such as "neither male nor female," echo what Eva Cheuk-yin Li analyzes as a negation of gender (2015, 77). These comments can also be found in Taiwan. On the front cover of the Taiwan-published Chinese-language translation of C. J. Pascoe's *Dude, You're a Fag: Masculinity and Sexuality in High School*, it states that "the worst word to insult a boy is '*niang*'" (2020). In the Chinese language, *niang* has a similar connotation as "fag" and "sissy" in English. In the foreword, Wang Hongren (2020), a Taiwan-based sociologist, shares his gendered experience in adolescence when, as a boy, he had to confirm his macho masculinity in a heteronormative society among his male peers. Even though same-sex marriage was legalized in Taiwan in 2019, Wang, as a self-identified gay man, has persistently experienced gender discrimination. This echoes Derek Hird's ethnographic finding in Beijing between 2004 and 2011 that even if androgyny is "tolerated as a social phenomenon," young people still reject it in their daily life (2012, 63; see also Louie 2014, 25). Here, androgyny is conflated with effeminacy, even though they have different connotations, which again demonstrates the discrepancy between everyday life and media representations (Li 2015, 77). As my later analysis reveals, Wu and Zhou began to face social stigma when they were young, before becoming well known. Following each of their rises to stardom, the stigma has intensified through audiences' reactions to their celebrity images on screen.

Besides the soft masculinity that is popular on mainland Chinese TV (Song and Hird 2013, 10), Song adds three other types of ideal masculinities in TV dramas, including the "wartime heroic man," "metrosexual urbanites," and Chinese men following "a cosmopolitan fashion" that is characterized as "transnational business masculinity" (2018, 27, 28). Song (2018) also explains the extraordinary popularity of TV in contemporary Chinese popular culture. Originally, Chinese TV had been solely state-owned and designed for propaganda; however, commercialization has put "an end to the government monopoly of TV production"

(Song 2010, 411). Nowadays, while the major television networks in mainland China are still owned by the central or provincial governments, Chinese TV is under the triple influence of the government's "guiding culture," everyday culture, and intellectuals' "elite culture" (Song 2010, 412). Along with the globalization of Chinese social and media environments in more recent years, there has been an "interplay between nationalist sentiments and cosmopolitan desires" and "complicity between state agenda and global capitalism" (Song 2018, 27, 28). Chinese TV also draws greater attention from younger generations with the "digitalization and convergence of media" (Song 2018, 28). People can watch these programs in "downloaded forms on the laptop or cell phone" (Song 2018, 28). As information and communication technology continues to develop, all these programs are readily available on streaming services. In this sense, pop singers need to navigate among different media, and audiences have more ways to interact with their favorite singers in the increasingly complex digital landscape.

Vocal Queerness on TV

In 2019 and 2020, respectively, Wu and Zhou were invited to compete in the mainland Chinese singing competition TV program *Singer*. Since *Singer* is one of the most popular reality TV shows in mainland China (Cheung 2017, 91; Li 2019, 38), it offers Wu and Zhou another round of tremendous exposure. The TV program shows footage of not only the actual contest but also the processes of preparation and rehearsal in order to visualize the "immediacy and authenticity of the broadcasting content" (Cheung 2017, 93). *Singer* can be analyzed both as a "televisual musicscape" and a "lingualscape" with gorgeous presentations of musical performances on TV (Cheung 2017, 93; Li 2019, 37). During the time they participated in *Singer*, Wu and Zhou also participated in other TV programs and gave more interviews to tell their personal stories. These interviews serve as spin-off media sources that contribute to the audience's imaginaries of the singers. The gendered personas of Wu and Zhou are *not* limited to one TV program *but* shaped by multimedia and cross-textual constitution (Redmond and Holmes 2007, 6).

While *Singer* was aired from January to April of 2019, Wu gave an interview in February on a mainland Chinese online TV show called *See You at 9PM* (今晚九点见; Tencent Video, 2019). Wu shared his teenage experience of being bullied by other students because he was shy, physically thin and small, with a rather "strange" voice.[5] Similarly, while competing on *Singer* between February and April 2020, Zhou gave an interview on a mainland Chinese TV program entitled

---

5. See https://v.qq.com/x/cover/qr2451wbga9e055/a00297w5rd6.html.

People in News (新闻当事人; Hunan TV, 2020) in March.[6] During the interview, Zhou recalled that he was hurt by his high school classmates when they made jokes about his voice because it was different from his male peers. While their voices became low during puberty, Zhou's voice remained high-pitched. Both Wu and Zhou chose to be silent in their adolescence when experiencing social stigma due to their appearances, behaviors, and voices. Despite this, both decided to continue singing and launched their singing careers. During the two interviews, the interviewers were considerate and sensitive when asking questions. However, the performers had a different experience during their first few years on stage. Both of them received malevolent criticism in the public space in response to the queerness of their voices, together with their relatively petite builds.

While Zhou's and Wu's appearances and behaviors seem to fit the characteristics of soft masculinity like other actors in TV dramas, their voices, or a combination of their appearance and voices, problematizes their placement in that category. Their voices are not simply costume elements they can put on and then take off, or a performance that can be switched off when they are off-stage. This is a point of difference from other singers, such as Li Yugang (李玉刚), who is a mainland Chinese male performer proficient in cross-gender singing and dancing (He 2013, 155). Li's queerness has been largely accepted and celebrated by the audience and mainland Chinese official media because he can "change from his female costumes back to normal male clothes and stop singing in a falsetto but use his normal male vocal to sing a pop song to prove his gender normality" (Wang 2015, 163). However, Wu and Zhou have to pretend and perform the "normal male" vocal range because they have naturally "effeminate" voices. While "falsetto" is a vocal style that allows a performer to sing beyond the vocal range of their "full" modal voice—referred to as a "fake voice" (假声) in Chinese—Wu and Zhou are not faking their voices. Instead, the relatively higher pitch compared to other men's voices that people are more familiar with is natural and genuine for them as part of their bodies. As singers, they are capable of switching from their modal voice register to their falsetto register. However, their modal voice is not considered to be "normal" based on the general public's "common assumptions." Their voices can be incorporated into and appreciated by the mainstream because Chinese culture has a tradition of males performing in a female voice, such as the ones often seen in traditional Peking opera performances. At the same time, Wu and Zhou are also distinct from the traditions of Peking opera that are more often associated with Li's cross-dressing performances, because they do not try to match their own high voices with female costumes.

---

6. See https://w.mgtv.com/b/334730/7716445.html.

In 2009, Wu responded to mainstream society's judgment on his band Sodagreen's fifth full-length album after a long period of depression following his debut in 2001 due to disparaging comments made about his voice. He wrote a song entitled "Peter and the Wolf" (彼得与狼), explicitly criticizing individuals who follow others blindly without reflecting on a certain issue. He sings:

> You say I am sissy
> But I dare to say you are more cowardly than me
> Others say something today
> You say the same thing tomorrow
> Yet think yourself thoughtful
> This collective is hysterical, hysterical, hysterical
>
> 你说我娘
> 但我说你比我懦弱
> 人家今天说什么
> 你明天就说什么
> 还以为自己真有满脑子的思想
> 这集体歇斯底里歇斯底里歇斯底里[7]

This song is an outright response to the criticism of his voice. On a 2019 online mainland Chinese talk show entitled *Ai Si Bu Si* (爱思不si), Wu further explains that "if, one day, those people encounter the abusive language that I have encountered, they would be even more fragile than I was; so, I don't care what they think."[8] This tactic of questioning the attacker frees him from self-pity. Furthermore, he questions the use of *niang* as a negative word. Originally, *niang* simply meant "mother." When the detractors use *niang* to disparage someone, they are insulting the feminine features of that person. Wu asks, "Why is it not good to have feminine features? Is it not good to be a woman?" Both questions highlight the fundamental concept of hegemonic masculinities, which both "embodies the currently accepted answer to the problem of the legitimacy of patriarchy" and "guarantees (or is taken to guarantee) the dominant position of men and the subordination of women" (Connell 2005, 77). Wu not only becomes more self-confident, but shows concerns about everyday violence toward the so-called "effeminate" group. In their live performance of "Peter and the Wolf" in the Taipei Arena in 2016, Sodagreen displayed a portrait of Yeh Yung-chih (叶永志) at the end of the performance, accompanied by the lyric "How many people were killed by the heat?" (有多少人被热死).[9] Yeh Yung-chih was found dead in his middle school bathroom on April 20, 2000 after enduring constant bullying for his "effeminate" behaviors. The cause of his death is disputed, but

---

7. This is the sixth track in the album *Fever* (狂热), produced by Willin Music.
8. See https://krcom.cn/7315375944/episodes/2358773:4434632943597604. The quote in the following sentence is from the same interview.
9. See https://www.youtube.com/watch?v=3hE-sWLkqfU.

the school violence surrounding this incident generated legal and educational changes in Taiwan. In 2018, celebrity singer Jolin Tsai (蔡依林) also released a song entitled "Womxnly" (originally titled "Rosy Boy" [玫瑰少年] in the Chinese version) to memorialize Yeh and call for justice for minorities. When this song was used on the celebrity girl-group manufacturing show *Sisters Who Make Waves* (乘风破浪的姐姐; Hunan TV, China, 2020; see Chapter 2 for a detailed discussion of the show), one group appropriated "Womxnly," turning it into a self-affirming feminist song for women. However, the lyrics that originally encouraged "rosy boys" like Yeh were omitted, making its connotation of queer mourning invisible.[10]

Meanwhile, Wu constantly finds himself in a situation where he needs to explain his voice to others. In one episode of one of the most famous Taiwan-based talk shows, *Kangsi Coming* (康熙来了; CTi Variety, 2004–2016; see Chapter 8 for an in-depth study of the show), Wu encountered questions about his voice from the two hosts, Dee Hsu (徐熙娣) and Kevin Tsai (蔡康永). In this show, Tsai and Hsu constantly teased Wu for his queer voice, possibly on behalf of the audience. For example, after Wu finished singing Sodagreen's most famous track, "Little Love Song" (小情歌), Tsai asked him if he can sing without a falsetto or a "fake voice." Wu said he was not using a "fake voice," and Tsai even confirmed this with another professional singer. When Hsu asked him if he had a "lower voice, that is like 'real voice' (真音)," he denied the insinuation again and answered that he was born with such a voice.[11]

Since *Kangsi Coming* is a talk show, the hosts and the guests are performing in a comedic way that can make people laugh (even when using offensive language). For example, the two hosts kept using female appellations to refer to Wu, including "Old Lady" (老娘), "Little Queen" (小天后), "Aunt" (大婶), and "Girl" (少女). He performed according to these words, but later rejected these appellations. As this game of referring to him by female appellations continued for another three episodes of the same show between 2011 and 2012, Wu began to encounter fans calling him by the same terms. He finally explained to the hosts that he no longer wanted to be referred to in this way. While he considered it a joke among his acquaintances, it was annoying to be referred to in this way by fans. Instead, he encouraged fans to refer to him in a cute and affectionate way, such as "Cutie" (可人儿) and "Little Smartie" (小聪明), which have no gender markers. His negotiation of these appellations shows his insistence upon his male identity and his open attitude toward combating social stigma. By playing this language game on

---

10. The rendering of this song on the show *Sisters Who Make Waves* can be found at https://w.mgtv.com/b/338497/9668010.html?lastp=v_progdtl.
11. This episode is entitled "A-Mei Concert in *Kangsi Coming*" (阿妹康熙来了演唱会) and was aired on September 28, 2011.

a comedy talk show, Wu deconstructs the abusive label of "effeminacy" applied to him and gains more visibility through this popular TV show.

Similar to Wu, Zhou has also encountered gendered social stigma since his debut. He first gained notice in the mainstream media in 2014, when he participated in the third season of *The Voice of China*, one of the most influential reality TV singing competitions at the time. Unlike *Singer*, which is a stage for established singers, *The Voice of China* aims to discover ordinary people who have a talent for singing. The program adopts a blind audition at the beginning of the competition, meaning that the four judges select contestants solely based on their voice. This is one of the biggest selling points of the show (Jiang 2018, 1238), and Zhou's misidentification as a girl turned into a point of intrigue for his first episode. Two famous mainland Chinese singers, Na Ying and Yang Kun (杨坤), served as judges and members of the coaching panel. As Zhou sang the Taiwanese female singer Chyi Yu's (齐豫) song "Smiling Face" (欢颜), both Na and Yang thought that the song was sung by a girl. The two judges expressed their surprise after discovering Zhou's gender identity, and Zhou was tagged as the "male version of Chyi Yu" with his performance.[12]

Even though both Yang and the voiceover emphasized that Zhou's voice "transcends age and gender," the media drew attention to the "effeminate" quality of his voice. For example, Tencent Entertainment, one of the major platforms for entertainment news, adopted a striking headline: "Interview with Zhou Shen: 'female voice' was ridiculed by female classmates as shemale" (Pan 2014). In this interview, when Zhou mentioned that his classmates would make derogatory comments about his voice, the interviewer asked for some examples, which Zhou declined to mention. However, upon further questioning, Zhou hesitantly offered the word "Thai shemale" (泰国人妖).[13] The media's voyeuristic sensationalism forced Zhou to reveal his traumatic experiences. Even though the majority of the interview focused on his later life, the interviewer capitalized on this part of the conversation in the interview title and even twisted the classmates in general into "female classmates" in the title. This showcases what Sara Ahmed (2014, 163) defines as the "commodification of queer." Drawing on Rosemary Hennessy's (1994, 31) discussion of how gayness becomes visible and commodified in consumerism, Ahmed emphasizes that "the 'non' of the 'non-normative' is not outside existing circuits of exchange, but may even intensify the movement of commodities, which converts into capital" (2014, 163). Zhou's

---

12. This is from the second episode of the third season of *The Voice of China*, which can be found at https://v.qq.com/x/cover/tw1zspbe633stws.html.
13. Calling *kathoey* or *katoey* (transgender woman in Thailand) as Thai *renyao* is also a showcase of gender discrimination. Howard Chiang (2014a, 206) translates *renyao* as "human prodigy" and streamlines the historical archives of *renyao* in both traditional Chinese culture and in Taiwan. By combining Thailand and *renyao* together, it is related to the burgeoning "*renyao* show" as a selling point of Thai tourism.

vocal queerness was converted into a commodity as the audience was invited to share their surprise, as the two coaches had done. Media outlets whipped up the sensation even further by applying social stigma back to Zhou. As a result, when the performer searched through the comments on him, he often found reactions like, "What?! Zhou Shen is a man!" He felt very unhappy and was confused about why everyone focused solely on his gender identity. The TV program, the news, and the audience all joined the carnival by turning Zhou into a "spectacle," and they were satisfied through this hunt for novelty without caring about Zhou's feelings.

This queer spectacle became even more exaggerated when Zhou participated in the first and third seasons of *Masked Singer* (蒙面歌手; Jiangsu Satellite TV, China) in 2016 and 2018 respectively. This singing competition requires singers to wear elaborate masks and full-body costumes in order to hide their identity, and then asks the celebrity judges and the audience to guess who the singer is. Zhou emphasized both in the show and the interview that his singing was not a cross-gender performance, and he hoped that audiences would instead focus on his singing talent (Huang 2016). He emphasized this point because his typical performance, without masking, would often be considered a cross-gender performance because of his vocal queerness, as in the aforementioned case of Li Yugang. Since Zhou's face would be covered with a mask and he would be dressed up in a costume during his performance on the *Masked Singer*, he thought that the audience would focus on the performance itself. However, as this program provided him with a dress to wear on stage, he was once again misidentified as a girl. In the interview, Zhou mentioned a comment made about him on the show, "I think the 'moth' (Zhou's costumed persona) sings pretty well; but I would reject it if it was sung by Zhou Shen" (Huang 2016). The TV show and the audience yet again conspired against Zhou's self-identification. His way of reconciling with these kinds of comment is to adopt the attitude that "it is better to be insulted than have nobody watching it" (Huang 2016).

His self-reconciliation can also be put in a larger context to understand the commodification of queer cultures. While it must be admitted that his voice turns into a queer spectacle for the audience's voyeurism or is even utilized as a form of homo/transphobic freakshow exploitation, the commodification also equips Zhou with the stage to make queer bodies visible (Jackson 2009, 368). In this process, he gradually learns to reconcile with himself, navigate the game of entertainment capitalism, and demonstrate his agency in the coming TV shows. When the audience once again admitted their surprise that "Zhou Shen is a man" on *Singer* in 2020, he felt happy about it because more people recognized his talent. The producers finally showed respect for his singing ability and offered him a stage on which to sing rather than simply creating a media sensation. Unlike Wu's outspokenness toward the verbal abuse, Zhou has never explicitly responded in his songs in the face of persisting criticism. Instead, Zhou finds other venues by encouraging other people who may also have similar experiences, which can also be seen as a way of countering sissyphobia. In another interview during his appearance on *Singer*, he commented that there must be a lot of people who have a voice similar to his, and he hoped that his existence and performance could be a source of encouragement for them.[14] At the same time, his repeated insistence on his male identity ensures that the audience will not misgender him, or draw inferences on his sexual identity from his voice or physical appearance. It also helps to avoid being censored and scolded in the mainstream media.

Queer Stardom

Even if they continue to face gendered social stigma, it is undeniable that singers like Wu and Zhou are becoming more popular and stepping into the mainstream. Wu, as a relatively senior singer, has created countless musical products for himself, Sodagreen, and other singers. He has won major Chinese-language music awards and participated in a variety of TV shows both in mainland China and Taiwan. On Weibo, he has more than 15 million followers. Zhou has also gained more popularity in recent years and has released numerous songs every year since his debut. He has received many awards and participated in various TV shows. On Weibo, he has more than 7 million followers.

Becoming popular and mainstream means a larger audience for these performers, and they cannot avoid being commodified. Researching the Taiwanese indie music scene, Shih-Lun Chang points out that Sodagreen, as an indie band, openly embraces "the glamour and the vanity of commercial success without hesitation" (2010, 91). However, embracing the market does not mean that Wu's intention in writing music is for the sake of popularity. Wu expressed this concern in the interview *See You at 9PM*. Sodagreen's first hit, "Little Love Song," has long been judged as a pop song originally written for the sake of becoming popular. Because of this judgment, Wu refused to sing this song for a long time. He finally reconciled with himself and started to sing it again by concluding, "If I follow other people's misunderstanding and refuse to sing this song, I am also wronging this song." This reconciliation also extends to a 2019 performance in *Singer*, where he sang "Return in Songs" (歌颂者). This song, whose title is literally translated as "the person who sings and chants," is an intertextual response to "Little Love Song," and the two share similar lyrics and pieces of melody. Therefore, "Return in Songs" serves to look back at his singing career and to recall where he started from. When Wu performed "Return in Songs" on *Singer*, the band showed huge emotional investment in the piece. As Wu finished the final note of the song, Kay Liu (刘家凯), one of Sodagreen's members, hugged

---

14. See https://youtu.be/_cDvnP0af6A.

him as Wu burst into tears. The host He Jiong (何炅), guest singer Jolin Tsai, and audience members were all moved by the performance and wept with him. There was a sense of shared joy at this moment on stage as his friends and fans bore witness to, and accompanied him through, all his difficulties along the path of his singing career. In 2020, when Wu was awarded the Best Male Mandarin Singer at the Golden Melody Awards ceremony, he offered an affirming acceptance speech: "I want to selfishly say to myself: thank myself for not being beaten down; thank myself for continuing singing and chanting desperately; you have worked very hard, thank you."[15]

Besides the Yeh incident discussed above, Sodagreen also participated in the charity concert for marriage equality, "Love Is King, It Makes Us All Equal," in 2016 to promote equal rights for same-sex marriage. They sang three songs from their album *Winter Endless* (冬未了), including "He Raised His Hand to Make a Roll Call" (他举起右手点名), "Rainy Night" (下雨的夜晚), and "Beyond the Wall" (墙外的风景). The major theme of the album is about the human life cycle. This album relates to the city of Berlin and addresses issues of the Holocaust, but it can also extend to other historical and social issues. For example, in the lyrics for "Beyond the Wall," the wall can refer to the Berlin Wall or any wall that hinders us from walking freely outside. Wu explains that the song is dedicated to his friends whose love "cannot be exposed to the sunlight."[16] Therefore, it makes sense that Sodagreen chose to perform this song in the concert. As this statement was made and the concert was held before the legalization of same-sex marriage in Taiwan, it was particularly significant for celebrities to speak up in support of queer issues in public through the concert. In Taiwan, it is only after years of fighting for their rights in all kinds of forms, through literature, film, popular culture, law, demonstrations, and so on, that people find it easier to express their support of LGBTQ rights, and people who are sexual minorities can stand in the sunshine (Chiang 2019, 241).

In mainland China, the situation is quite different, and it is hard to tackle these issues directly in the mainstream media. Major media platforms deploy self-censorship regarding nonnormative appearances and performances. For example, tattoos needed to be covered, and male dancers could not wear earrings or dresses in the third season of *Street Dance of China* (这！就是街舞; Youku, 2020). However, Zhou has maintained his own style of queerness before and after his debut. As a fan of Animation, Comics, and Games (ACG) culture, he frequently finds ways to bring this subculture to his performance in the mainstream media. While ACG culture has no direct relationship to LGBTQ issues,

---

15. This is part of Wu's speech when he was awarded the Best Male Mandarin Singer. See https://youtu.be/jzJ8tzVc8AQ.
16. This quote is from Sodazine 9 in the package of the preorder CD. Sodazine is a bonus journal in the CD package to narrate the stories behind each song.

the nonnormative components of the subculture, such as BL/GL cultures, can also serve as inspiration for people to explore further and even challenge the mainstream culture (Martin 2016, 197).

On *Singer* in 2020, Zhou sang a song that originated from ACG culture, ilem's "Dalabengba" (达拉崩吧), which was first posted on Bilibili (one of the major video sharing websites in mainland China) in 2017 and became an instant hit in the ACG community. Zhou featured his remarkable vocal ability by playing five different roles in this song, including a little girl, a boy, a king, a dragon, and the voiceover. While the voiceover was his usual voice, he also performed male characters (the boy and the king), a female character (the little girl), and even the supernatural character (the dragon), from young (the boy and the little girl) to old (the king and the dragon). With this vocal roleplay, Zhou goes beyond the rigid gender binary between the masculine and the feminine. In one of the intermezzi, he also sang in the style of *bel canto*, which demonstrates his musical mastery beyond the pop music genre. In another intermezzo, his choreography was based on the Japanese pop singer Garnidelia's "Paradise Land" (極楽浄土), which was one of the most popular songs within the ACG circle. This combination of ACG subculture, pop culture, and high culture also suggests the possibility of connecting different types of (sub)culture and breaking down hierarchies among them. Zhou's performance made "Dalabengba" even more popular and turned it into one of the greatest hits of the year. His singing not only attracted an audience who were ACG fans, but also a general popular culture audience. ACG culture is usually called "two-dimensional space," and real life is called "three-dimensional space" (Wu 2017). In this way, Zhou broke the walls of different dimensions by bringing the ACG subculture into broader public view.

Zhou is also an influential uploader of Bilibili, a hub for fans of ACG culture to share videos. The site's users can submit "bullet subtitles" (弹幕), a layer of comments that float over the video, as opposed to "clustering ... in as special comments section" (Wang 2020a, 16). These "bullet subtitles" can include interpretations of, or debates on, a given video (Wang 2020a, 16). They help form a sense of community among fans of Zhou through a "pseudo-synchronic setting" that offers fans "a collective watching experience" (Wang 2020a, 19). During the eleventh anniversary ceremony of Bilibili in 2020, Zhou expressed his love of the site by referring to it as a "home" for people with similar hobbies. The video of his speech is full of "bullet subtitles" that echo his words by cheering "welcome home."[17] Even though it is a form of virtual communication mediated by an online platform, Bilibili is also an emerging method for creating affective bonds in the internet age. On this platform, when someone questions Zhou's voice, there are users who teach each other the right way to treat him. For example, when users surprisedly remarked "What? A boy?" or used "she" to address

---

17. See https://www.bilibili.com/video/BV1SK4y1477d?p=6.

Zhou, other users would clarify who Zhou is. In this sense, Zhou and his fans are creating a more queer-friendly community of mutual respect together. This bonding is based on the basic understanding of Zhou's vocal queerness as a gift rather than a source of stigma. In light of this, it is reasonable to assume that Zhou's audience would also demonstrate more friendly attitudes toward similar cases.

Conclusion

As Jamie J. Zhao (2020a, 463) suggests, popular culture can be the "front line" for a wholesale queering of culture. There is a "multivalent potential of 'queer' in forming disruption to and negotiation with normative media imaginaries of desiring, being, and belonging" (Zhao and Wong 2020, 476). Singers like Wu and Zhou may not be as radical as activists in local and transnational queer and feminist movements. In order to mediate and sustain their alternative masculinities under the public scrutiny, they have actively adopted a male identity to legitimize themselves. However, their bodies become the "situations" undermining the normative imaginaries of popular culture (Butler 1986, 45). As Judith Butler notes, "the body is a material reality which has already been located and defined within a social context" (1986, 45). Interpretations of these performers' vocal queerness already exist and may continue to proliferate and develop. At the same time, "the body is a field of interpretive possibilities" (Butler 1986, 45). That is, their existence and performances have the power to reinterpret the relationship between their gender identity and voice, for themselves as well as their fans and audiences.

Mainland China and Taiwan are two locales with shared cultural roots, values, and norms, yet different historical trajectories, especially in the social pursuit of queer visibility in the public space. While Taiwan tends to be more progressive in terms of legal rights and activism around gender and sexuality, changing the everyday opinions of the masses still takes time. My above analysis demonstrates that Wu and Zhou intersect with queerness in two main ways: first, in respecting and using their high voices, they represent for many listeners a nonnormative masculinity, and second, although they do not explicitly reference a minority sexuality, some audience members' interpretation of each of them as "sissy" points to the complexities around such a persona and its all-too-frequent reaction as "sissyphobia." In this sense, the formation of audiences' affective bonds surrounding pop singers like Wu and Zhou can be understood as a moderate way of effecting queer-centered cultural changes. While finding a broad audience in the Chinese-language mainstream media and public spaces, Wu and Zhou maintain queer-charged voices and personas.

Acknowledgments

I would like to express my heartfelt gratitude to the book editor, Jamie J. Zhao, for guiding me through the journey of writing this chapter. Her encouragement and critical response helped me to persist. My appreciation also goes to Sabine Frühstück and Fran Martin, as well as my friends, Yuan Gao, Kun Huang, Keyun Tian, and Shiqi Lin, for sharing their invaluable ideas and suggestions. I also thank the reviewers for their helpful comments. Finally, I would like to say "I love you" to my idols, Wu Tsing-Fong and Zhou Shen, for offering me the courage to face the stigma of having a low-pitched voice as a woman.

8
Gay Men in/and *Kangsi Coming*

Oscar Tianyang Zhou

Introduction

In September 2015, I interviewed Tiger-Girl, a 32-year-old Chinese gay man in Beijing, who was a video game designer.[1] Like many other Beijing drifters, he came from an industrial city in the northeast of Hebei province, China, and moved to the city to seek a better life. Tiger-Girl was a loyal fan of TV entertainment. When asked about memorable images of gay men in the Chinese-language media, he cited two male entertainers, Mix Xiao (肖骁, a gender-nonconforming Chinese TV celebrity) and Edison Fan (樊野, a hunky Chinese influencer and gay model) from the popular Chinese online talk show *U Can U Bibi* (奇葩说; iQIYI, 2014–2021), to exemplify the two most common ways gay men have been constructed by Chinese-language media and popular culture, as either "sissy" or "outstanding" (which refers to the "macho" men).[2] Tiger-Girl explained that being gay means "two men love each other in a manly way." Therefore, by lacking masculinity, effeminate gay men like Mix Xiao "have a negative impact on the Chinese gay community, who only reinforce the stereotypes of gay men as 'sissies' (娘娘腔)." By contrast, Tiger-Girl highly commended Edison Fan for his masculine images and viewed him as a positive role model for Chinese gay men. Tiger-Girl's story led me to wonder what the social meanings of the new "gay" images on entertainment media screens, such as Mix Xiao and Edison Fan, are, and how these representations can create new meanings of Chinese gay sexualities. How and why do these new gay representations differ from their precursors in the Chinese-language media?

---

1. This interview stems from my recent research project that examines the cultural politics of gay men's everyday media practices in China, which included semi-structured ethnographic interviews with self-identified Chinese gay men in Beijing between 2015 and 2016.
2. *U Can U Bibi* is one of China's most popular online talk shows, aired on iQIYI since 2014, which features a debate competition joined by both influential celebrities and newcomers of entertainment industry to discuss contemporary socio-cultural issues in China.

The representation of gender and sexual minorities matters, for as Richard Dyer has written, "how social groups are treated in cultural representation is part and parcel of how they are treated in life" (2002, 1). "How we are seen," he expands, "determines in part how we are treated; how we treat others is based on how we see them; such seeing comes from representation" (Dyer 2002, 1). Representation is vitally important for queers, particularly when they lack the support of queer communities. Lianrui Jia and Tianyang Zhou (2015) argue that severe restrictions have been imposed on the spread of content relating to homosexuality in the mainland Chinese media. This is a result of longstanding discrimination against gay men and lesbians in the local society, which views homosexuality as socio-culturally abnormal and perverted. The visibility of LGBTQ communities within popular culture has increased in recent years, however, thanks to the digitization of media and changing social conditions in a globalized China (Bao 2018; Wang 2015; Wei 2010; Zhao 2020a; T. Zhou 2018, 2020).

Whereas academic discussions of male homosexuality in Chinese media and popular culture frequently attends to cinematic representations (see, for example, Berry 1998; Bian 2007; Lim 2006; Robinson 2013; Zhou 2014), this chapter focuses on entertainment TV, particularly talk shows. I take two of the most influential Chinese-language talk shows—*Kangsi Coming* (康熙来了; CTi Variety, Taiwan, 2004–2016) and its successor, *U Can U Bibi*—as case studies to investigate how gay men are (mis)represented in Chinese-language media and popular culture, looking at the (non-)normative sexual identities that are associated with these new (mis)representations. This chapter is different from previous studies on "queering" Chinese mainstream TV (for example, Yang and Bao 2012; Zhou 2017), which focus on queer fans' negotiation and resistance. Instead, I use a contextual approach to look at how the representations of gayness in the two talk shows can be used to help us understand what it is like being gay in mainland China and Taiwan today.

I begin by outlining the rise and fall of *Kangsi Coming* in the context of Chinese-language TV in transition. Despite remaining under certain regulation and censorship, TV has become increasingly dynamic, digitized, heterogeneous, and transcultural in the Chinese-speaking world. In this context, I explore the discussion of "gay typification" in popular media, which is, as Dyer argues, "a near necessity for the representation of gayness, the product of social, political, practical and textual determinations" (2002, 20). I examine two dominant gay types represented in *Kangsi Coming* and *U Can U Bibi*: the "sissy" and the "macho," which each signifies both a gay subject and object of desire. The new gay representations analyzed in this chapter show how popular culture both creates and constrains gay identities. Nevertheless, they do not exhaust the range of gay types in Chinese-language media. In conclusion, I argue that it is impossible to treat the issue of gay visibility and representation in isolation from the actual consumers of queer media cultures. Hence, I call for a reflexive ethnographic approach that is able to unpack the incompatible expectations and outcomes at stake in the increasing queer visibility enabled by digital media technologies.

The Rise and Fall of *Kangsi Coming*

I became aware of the Mandarin variety-comedy talk show named *Kangsi Coming* while studying for my bachelor's degree in mainland China during 2007. Watching the show quickly became one of my most cherished queer experiences, and I have seen every single episode released online. Inaugurated in Taiwan in 2004 and continuing until 2016, it became the longest-running and most successful variety talk show in the Chinese-speaking world. Recorded in a small studio, the show was fast-moving, uncontrived, and humorous. It centered around conversations on a range of different (and often controversial) topics that two hosts, Kevin Tsai (蔡康永) and Dee Hsu (徐熙娣), conducted with entertainers, celebrities, and politicians from Taiwan, mainland China, Hong Kong, and elsewhere.

In 2005, Chinese Entertainment TV (CETV) became the first TV channel to introduce *Kangsi Coming* to audiences in mainland China. As a non-mainland broadcaster, however, CETV was subject to mainland Chinese broadcasting regulations, which restricted its operations to cities in southern China. Demand from mainland audiences led to widespread informal circulation. As a result, it became available on the black market, along with other Taiwanese and Hong Kong TV programs (E. Zhao 2016). It was not until 2011 that Tudou.com, a leading Chinese online video network, was awarded the exclusive rights to broadcast the show on the Mainland. These were then sold to iQIYI, another popular Chinese online video platform, in 2013. This ensured that the show was available on both sides of the Taiwan Strait. Featuring a range of novelties and unrestrained discussions of the personal lives of guest celebrities and its two hosts, *Kangsi Coming* was unprecedented when compared with coetaneous variety shows on the mainland TV, which strictly adhered to state guidelines. This brought the show even greater success (in terms of Internet ratings) in mainland China than it had enjoyed in Taiwan. In addition, the show has also engaged with mainland Chinese fans by means of the *Kangsi* Gala Concert (康熙盛典). As it toured major mainland cities between 2008 and 2010, it showcased celebrities from both mainland China and Taiwan. Thus, *Kangsi Coming* became not only a competitive stage on which Taiwanese celebrities could enter the mainland entertainment market, but also the most effective platform for local celebrities to promote their films, dramas, and music to audiences in other parts of the Chinese-speaking world.

Kevin Tsai and Dee Hsu are at the heart of the show. In fact, the show's title is a combination of their names. As its producer Wei-Chung Wang stated, "*Kangsi* only belongs to Kevin Tsai and Dee Hsu" (*NetEase Entertainment* 2015). Their personal chemistry appears natural, and the show relies on their almost symbiotic relationship. Paris Shih (2015) observes that *Kangsi Coming* is secretly loved by gay men because of their connection to Dee Hsu, who is known as "Little S" (小S) because of her hourglass figure. Having risen to fame in the 1990s as a singer in the duo S.O.S., Little S is one of the best-known female comedians and hosts in the Chinese-speaking world. She joined *Kangsi Coming* in 2004, rapidly becoming a top comedian owing to her fast wit and caustic humor. Importantly, Little S consistently supported same-sex marriage at a time when this was rare among celebrities, thus winning her the devotion of legions of gay fans.

Arguably, gay subjectivities on Chinese-speaking TV (and among its audiences) and Little S's stardom have mutually constructed one another. Her performances on TV are seen as camp practices, containing strong elements of theatricality and reflexive parody. Her stardom has arguably supported the notions of "being as if playing a role" and "life as theatre," presenting a comic version of the world (Sontag 2018). More importantly, her exaggerated and pretentious performances on TV have been appropriated and imitated by many gay men to express their queer effeminacies and challenge "the local gay male agenda inscribed by moralistic, assimilationist and sissy-phobic tendencies" (Lin 2006, 284). For example, in 2002, Little S created the character of "Teacher Hsu" (徐老师), who was inspired by the 1980s American fitness guru Jane Fonda. Teacher Hsu rapidly became one of the most well-known characters in local gay cultural history. Shih (2015) defines her as a site of a politics of the body, which simultaneously advocates for and mocks fitness and bodily management, and their inevitable failure. Little S's extravagant televised impersonations subvert the boundaries between beauty and ugliness, good and evil, and desirable and undesirable. In so doing, she has opened up a cultural space between "coming out" and "staying in the closet," in which gay men can express themselves, communicate with each other, and build communities. Little S's gay fans become "gay" by imitating her. She welcomes this and (re)impersonates their sissiness on TV in turn. Gay men and Little S, in other words, are intimately interconnected, with each becoming the other (Shih 2015).

Little S's co-host, Tsai, is one of the best-known TV hosts and writers in the Chinese-speaking world. Between 2003 and 2008, he was nominated for the Best Host in a Variety Program award at the Golden Bell Awards no less than six times. He and Little S eventually won this influential annual Taiwanese TV production award in 2005. Tsai is also one of the few openly gay celebrities in the Chinese-speaking world, becoming a prominent LGBTQ role model after acknowledging his sexual orientation on a talk show in 2002. Because of this, the "gay" agenda of *Kangsi Coming* is very clear. The entertainment industry has praised Tsai, who graduated with a master's degree in TV production from the University of California, Los Angeles, for being "an intellectual within the entertainment circles" (娱乐圈里的读书人). He first appeared in mainland Chinese variety shows in 2014, as a host of the popular talent talk show *U Can U Bibi*. Like many in Taiwan's entertainment industry, he thereby transferred his focus from Taiwan to mainland China in pursuit of a larger market. In 2015, the second season of *U Can U Bibi* featured an episode discussing whether gay men and lesbians should come out to their parents. Tsai's own emotional description of his experience of being an openly gay celebrity, in which he tearfully insisted that "we are not monsters," subsequently went viral online.

Tsai's success in *U Can U Bibi* indicates how the Taiwanese and mainland entertainment industries are interrelated. Indeed, as Elaine Jing Zhao has written, "collaborations between Taiwanese and mainland creative workers . . . have a better chance of tailoring to the local culture and audience taste than direct import of Taiwanese content" (2016, 59). In addition, Tsai's decision to pursue his career in mainland China served as a catalyst for Taiwanese entertainment professionals to move from Taiwan's declining local entertainment industry (Huang 2015). Against this backdrop, *Kangsi Coming* was closed down in 2015, marking the end of the golden age of Taiwanese variety shows. By then, however, both Little S and Tsai were actively engaged in mainland Chinese online video platforms. Little S started her own food talk show *S-style Show* (姐姐好饿; 2016–2017) and celebrity reality show *I Fiori Delle Sorelle* (小姐姐的花店; 2018–2019) on iQIYI, an online video platform based in Beijing, while Tsai continued to host *U Can U Bibi*. Since 2018, they have co-hosted a lifestyle talk show titled *The Truth of the Prismatic Universe* (真相吧! 花花万物; 2018–2020)—the mainland version of *Kangsi Coming*—on Youku, a top Chinese online video and streaming service platform. It is in this context that this chapter uses *Kangsi Coming* and its successor *U Can U Bibi* as case studies to investigate how gay men are (mis)represented in Chinese-language media and popular culture.

Sissy "Gay" Men

Kangsi Coming's defining theme has always been gay sensibilities, its particular strength being how it humorously plays with signs of gayness. The most popular representations of gayness in the show tend to be the trope of the sissy gay pretender. This illustrates the importance of gender in gay representations in media and popular culture, particularly in relation to comedy (Raymond 2003; Wei 2010; T. Zhou 2020). In *Kangsi Coming*, a notable example of the "sissy gay" trope appears in a 2009 episode titled *"Kangsi* Tender Men Dance Contest*"* (康熙温柔汉舞蹈大赛), in which five male entertainers (whose sexualities are never revealed) are invited to compete. The key to winning is to embrace and display one's inner male effeminacy, which serves as the comedic device. The most overtly effeminate entertainer is the news reporter Kelvin Hsu (许建国), who becomes the episode's focus. The two hosts introduce a short farcical sketch, in which Hsu is matched with Ryan Kuo (郭晋东), a tall and muscular entertainer.

As Kuo embraces Hsu slowly from behind and calls him "baby," streaming loving-heart bubbles render the screen cloudy pink. The farce is clearly homoerotic, with Hsu and Kuo presented as a gay couple to comedic effect.

The gendered humor continues focusing on Hsu, not least by having him engage in a "sexy" jazz dance with two young male dancers while wearing heavy eye makeup and black leggings. Hsu's embarrassed and reluctant movements contrast with the professional dancers' fluid and confident performances. This invites further caustic interjections from Little S and reduces Tsai to tears of laughter. Tsai calls Hsu "an old, dispirited madam" (心灰意冷的老妈妈桑), thus attributing his embarrassment to a self-rejection of his own inner sissiness. Pretending to help him overcome this, the two hosts implore him to shout "I am a sissy" (我就是娘们儿) loudly and dance again. As one would expect, Hsu continues to move awkwardly, seemingly reluctant to embrace his feminine inner self. Little S mocks him for performing not like "a seductive bitch" (小贱货) but "an exhausted housewife" (被事务压垮的家庭主妇).

One possible reading of this scene suggests that such performances subvert the essentialist way in which the boundary between heterosexual and homosexual identities is often imagined. They may serve to empower effeminate gay men to disrupt gender and sexual norms and fight against effeminophobia (Lin 2013). As such, these performances can be seen to echo a queer agenda, according to which it is "either that we're all queer or that there's a little queer in each of us" (Raymond 2003, 107). The "queer" performances in *Kangsi Coming* are tightly intertwined with local LGBTQ rights movements in Taiwan (Lin 2006; Shih 2015). The show was launched one year after the first Taiwan Pride—the largest LGBTQ pride parade in Asia—that was held in Taipei in 2003. More than three decades of the LGBTQ social movement has led to a shift towards greater social acceptance of gender and sexual minorities in Taiwan (Lee 2017). As a result, in general, the Taiwanese entertainment industry is much more queer-friendly than its mainland Chinese counterpart.

Kangsi Coming teaches its viewers that there is a little sissiness in each of us, which should be embraced rather than suppressed and denigrated. It could also be argued, however, that the gendered humor that arises from performances such as the "*Kangsi* Tender Men Dance Contest" is made possible by the audience's knowledge that the heterosexuality of these male entertainers is never in doubt. The viewers tend to have "an epistemological advantage," providing them "not only with a certain degree of distance but also with reinscribed boundaries between the gay and the straight" (Raymond 2003, 108). This advantage and certainty allow the male entertainers that feature in the program to play with the effeminate and sissy stereotypes of gay men without worrying that their performances will be read as homophobic. The result is a comedy of misreading.

Kangsi Coming exploits the trope of the sissy gay pretender purposefully to position male entertainers as "gay." This is demonstrated by the abovementioned Taiwanese celebrity Kuo, who is well-known for having a fictional gay relationship with his male model roommate. On the show, he often talks about their everyday life in a homoerotic way, although it is almost certain that *Kangsi Coming* has scripted his "gay" performances (Taiwan's social acceptance of LGBTQ people greatly encouraged local entertainment TV, especially talk shows, to explore and commercialize issues of gender and sexuality). Through these performances, the show explicitly plays with sexuality, allowing the audience to access male entertainers' eroticism. Arguably, *Kangsi Coming* creates a fantasy world in which gay men, far from being victims of legal discrimination and social exclusion, are more powerful than their heterosexual counterparts. These inverted performances, to a large extent, echo the fact that Taiwan has the most progressive gay rights climate in Asia, generating a lot of humor. They might, however, "mask the ways that power operates" and "make the mechanisms of power even more covert" (Raymond 2003, 108). These comedic gay performances exist amid the reproduction of an unequal social system: whereas the viewers of Chinese-language entertainment TV are able to tune in or out of specific programs, this remains impossible when it comes to broader structural social inequalities. In addition, it is also important to consider the power of the "sexual hierarchy" of media representations (Lin 2013), which privileges gay pretenders' sissy comedies and some gay men's non-confrontational storytelling, while further marginalizing and stigmatizing queer people's more flamboyant and radical performances.

Moreover, these representations of gayness should not be understood solely in relation to media practices; they are also closely related to the broader gay social movement. Indeed, the gendered gay performances in *Kangsi Coming* (along with their associated sissiness humor) have caused controversy, which has crystallized into a public debate in Taiwan about the televisual appropriation of (gay) male effeminacy as a comedic device. This recalls the furor surrounding one of the most successful mainland Chinese commercial filmmakers, Xiaogang Feng, who was criticized by Chinese gay activists for his stereotypical depiction of gay men as "sissy" in the 2008 Chinese romantic comedy film *If You Are the One* (非诚勿扰; Wei 2010). The controversy surrounding gay sissiness humor led to criticism of *Kangsi Coming* in general and Tsai in particular. Critics have argued that, as a gay public figure, Tsai should not mock male effeminacy to increase ratings, because it could reinforce the "sissy" stereotype of gay men. His supporters, however, have argued that he was simply doing his job and did not intend the offensive humor to be personal.

In response to this criticism, Tsai wrote an article on his blog titled "When I am calling a guy 'sissy'" (当我说一个男生"娘"的时候):

Are we mocking and condemning him when we call a guy effeminate? Many people will say "yes, of course." But I don't think so. For me, it is definitely okay for a guy to be effeminate, and to shout loudly about being sissy if that makes them more self-confident and interesting. In my dictionary, "effeminate" is not a negative term, what's wrong with guys being effeminate? . . . Presuming guys should not be effeminate is a heterosexist bias. Presuming guys should not be called "sissies" is being strung along by this heterosexist bias . . . Therefore, when I call a guy effeminate . . . I wish the audience to feel the uniqueness of him, rather than judging him. (Tsai 2009, translated by the author)

Tsai views male effeminacy as nothing to be ashamed of, criticizing those who cast it in a negative light. Negative interpretations of comedic sissy performances along the lines of the hetero/homo dichotomy, he argues, fail to acknowledge the diversity within gay communities. Tsai defends himself and the show by attributing these interpretations to a heterosexual bias. To win the audience over to his side, he employs the rhetoric of intentionality, according to which "meaning resides with the speaker" (Pérez and Greene 2016, 269). In asserting that his intention is to challenge negative understandings of sissiness, he puts himself above criticism.

Tsai's article, however, provoked criticism from Taiwanese gender education scholars, including the feminist activist Jau-Jiun Hsiao (2009), who points out that Tsai's defense prioritizes his intention over viewers' personal experiences. She argued that Tsai failed to acknowledge that different people may have unequal access to societal resources, which means that not everyone can overcome bullying based on gender non-conformity and make something positive of their experiences. In addition, the show romanticizes the terms "effeminate" and "sissy," neglecting how historically they have been used to verbally abuse and bully effeminate schoolboys. Tsai strongly disagreed with this criticism, referencing Voldemort from the *Harry Potter* series to illustrate his interpretation of sissiness: "if we don't dare to call him Voldemort, instead calling him 'He Who Must Not Be Named', will he make a concession? [No], he will only become more aggressive" (Tsai 2010). Yet, this can also be seen as a defense for his own elite gayness that embodies an emerging *gaymi* (meaning women's gay male friends) masculinity with "gentility and impeccable tastes" (Wang, Tan, and Wei 2019, 911).[3]

Humor can mediate and reinforce the meanings imposed by hegemonic gender relations as well as forms of resistance to them (Weaver, Mora, and Morgan 2016). The controversy over gay sissiness humor demonstrates the identity work and politics performed by those who were concerned to defend or

---

3. *Gaymi is* "discursively constructed as a genteel and fashionable gay man who accommodates women's emotional needs" in China, which "indexes progressive social change"; at the same time, it also indicates stereotypes about gay men (Wang, Tan, and Wei 2019, 911).

condemn *Kangsi Coming*. What is more, it brings the rhetorical and political nature of sissy jokes into focus. Tsai sees his deliberate sissiness banter as equivalent to heroes courageously violating the taboo against pronouncing Voldemort's real name, which suggests a rebellion against heteronormativity and conformity. He thus presents sissy humor as close to what we might call "rebellious humor"—a momentary escape from restrictive social norms. Unlike conservative humor, which mocks rule-breakers, rebellious humor targets power (in Tsai's case, this would be heteronormativity). This humor sees to it that "authority is challenged and the guardians of rules are mocked" (Billig 2005, 208). Some scholars have highlighted the rebellious potential of *Kangsi Coming*'s gay sissiness humor. For example, Dennis C. Lin (2013) provides a "queer" reading of gender performances in *Kangsi Coming*, foregrounding the ways in which campness figures a means of combating assimilationist tendencies in gay culture and social movements. Similarly, Po-Han Lien (2015) defends the show by highlighting its emancipatory power, which cuts against the excessive rhetoric of victimization and the reservedness that is enforced by political correctness.

Such readings, however, run the risk of engaging in "a fetishism of resistance . . . a tendency in cultural studies to celebrate resistance *per se* without distinguishing between types and forms of resistance" (Kellner 1995, 38). Arguably, work in this mold can

> lose sight of the manipulative and conservative effects of certain types of media culture, and thus serve the interests of the culture industries as they are presently constituted and those groups who use the culture industries to promote their own interests and agendas. (Kellner 1995, 38–39)

In the context of late capitalism, commercial entertainment media has come to value liberating and rebellious humor highly. Comedic sissy performances in *Kangsi Coming* may have made gay pretenders famous, but they have also contributed to the emergence of a new "sissy media business." For example, as a result of his popular "gay" role on the show, Ryan Kuo (in partnership with his male roommate) has launched a variety talk show, *Sissies Coming* (娘娘驾到) in Taiwan, created by the *Kangsi Coming* production team. This venture further exploits the trope of the gay pretender and explicitly advertises "gay" sissiness as its distinct selling point. Although this new talk show was cancelled after just seven months, it was popular especially among local female audiences.

U Can U Bibi, one of the most popular online talk shows in mainland China, presents a similar scenario. In the show, a popular entertainer, Mix Xiao, has won over legions of young fans (in particular, post-90s Chinese viewers) with his sissy performances. On account of his hyper-feminine tone and V-shaped facial contours, some viewers see him as *"shejing nan"* (蛇精男; meaning the male version of a seductive and dangerous snake fairy) whose sissy performances "confound conventional and established binary gender categories of male vs.

female" in China (J. Li 2016, 78). However, the representations of sissy "gay" men in *U Can U Bibi* are best understood in terms of what Qian Wang (2015, 163) calls "a 'one stone, two birds' strategy for the government and the creative industries... allowing a politically neutralised cult of queerness benefits China's economy without generating 'real' social change." *U Can U Bibi* deliberately hints at how Mix Xiao's effeminate and exaggerated performances position him as gay, successfully monetizing his "sissy" label. At the same time, however, it explicitly informs the audience that offscreen he behaves in a more traditionally masculine manner (a message that is reinforced by his female associates). Mix Xiao (2017) once explained that "there is a real man (纯爷们儿) alive in my soul." In this way, he prioritized an essentialized masculine interior over his performative effeminate behaviors. Moreover, the show also emphasizes his cleverness as if it were an exceptional quality for a sissy performer, as well as his individualistic, anti-mainstream attitude.

Equating enjoying sissy humor/performance on TV with the radical politics of rebellion, then, can be problematic. Indeed, Michael Billig (2005, 209) observes that:

> These [entertainment] products do not encourage their audiences to become rebels in an absolute sense, for their rebelliousness conforms to the standards of the times. At the flick of a switch (and after the proper payment by credit card), we can enjoy regular programmes of fun and mockery. Dutiful consumption encourages us to mock apparent authority, enabling us to enjoy the feeling of constant rebelliousness in economic conditions that demand continual dissatisfaction with yesterday's products. (Billig 2005, 209)

In her critical analysis of *Queer Eye for the Straight Guy*, a popular American makeover reality show that features a team of gay professionals performing a makeover, usually on a straight man, Katherine Sender (2006, 133) argues that the show "entices heterosexual men into a gay-inflected contemporary sphere of intimate consumption." While acknowleging its queerness, Sender points out that "the show suggests that the appropriate place to negotiate gender and sexual politics is the commercial realm, leaving its progressive message vulnerable to the vagaries of audience ratings and marketers' patronage" (2006, 138). Difference is capable of being monetized both on and offscreen. Presenting sissy "gay" performances in the media as opposing heteronormativity, without fully evaluating their impact, can simply contribute to promoting new "queer" styles and artifacts. It can reinforce a form of identity politics that tends to overlook the structural forces of oppression such as capitalism.

As Wei Wei (2010) argues, a heteronormative commercial media tends to undermine the queer potentials of Chinese popular culture. Although there has been a dramatic increase in the number of queer images on Chinese entertainment media screens since 2005, these new queer performances do not legitimize homosexuality in Chinese public culture (Zhao 2020a). Instead, they feature, in Jamie J. Zhao's (2018b, 483) words, "an extremely ambivalent queer potential by emphasizing nonnormative culture's performative and playful, yet also sometimes manipulative and pejorative nature." It is therefore vital to acknowledge the disciplinary functions of seemingly rebellious sissy humor/performance in Chinese media and popular culture. Undoubtedly, audiences can engage with their favorite talk shows in a reflexive way. However, this reflexivity, as Sender (2012, 25) argues, "does not afford audiences unlimited agency or freedom to self-define, but can also be considered a new type of habitus that comes with demands and expectations."

The "Ideal Man"

Reflecting on the role of camp in Western gay cultural history, Andy Medhurst (1997) puts forward the following observation:

> in gay men's myth of our past we like to think it was some screaming queen. Thus an emblematic camp individual became an enshrined community figurehead, but this queen's starring role was simultaneously her farewell performance—all she did, in the long run, was to usher in the hyper-masculine gay culture of the 1970s, where effeminacy was stigmatized. (Medhurst 1997, 278)

Indeed, camp has been used as a survival mechanism not only in the West but also in the Chinese-speaking world. Many gay men in Taiwan see gender performances in *Kangsi Coming* as camp practices with emancipatory power (Lien 2015; Lin 2013; Shih 2015). While acknowledging the significance of televised camp practices for local gay community, we should also nevertheless recognize that what they have ushered in, as Medhurst (1997) suggests, is an emergent hyper-masculine gay culture. This development has crystallized into a new gay type onscreen—namely, the "macho." This transformation is best understood in the broader context of the global proliferation of male bodies as desired and objectified commodities (Forrest 1994; Gill, Henwood, and McLean 2005; Song and Hird 2013). David Forrest (1994, 104) points out that "we may be witnessing the proliferation of certain identities based on sexual practices, fashion, life-styles or certain fetishes, but these revolve around the athletic male body."

The way in which *Kangsi Coming* presents the "macho" gay type is exemplified by an episode from 2014 titled "A Survey of Male Celebrities' Popularity among Gay Men" (男明星同志好感度大调查). This episode included a competition among ten male celebrities, whose attractiveness was assessed by gay audiences. The competition demonstrated "both what it is like to be gay and what it is gay people find attractive" (Dyer 2002, 28). 150 local gay men from outside the entertainment industry were invited to give their opinions on which celebrity they considered to be the most desirable—indeed, the "ideal man" (同志天菜). The show also featured two guest judges: (1) the well-known gay illustrator Sunny Face, who represented an authoritative gay insider, and (2) the popular female TV anchor Patty Wu, a straight female ally. This episode ignited a heated online discussion and the entertainment industry came to value the contest's winner highly, as part of the pink economy.

As the episode begins, Little S and Tsai attempt to predict which of the celebrities will be voted the top five most attractive among gay men. They choose five male entertainers with muscular and athletic bodies, expressing confidence that their prediction will be reflected in the voting. They then focus on the low end of the ranking, and in particular on Hao-Ping Huang (黃豪平), a young, petite Taiwanese comedian whom they consider the least masculine of the group and therefore least attractive to gay men. Although Huang does not acknowledge his sexuality, everyone in the studio takes his effeminate attributes (such as his physique, voice, and behavior) as incontestable evidence of his gayness. He is depicted as a gay man, betrayed by his sissiness while being unwilling to come out. This is also reflected in the interviews that the show conducts with gay audiences. They disparagingly label him a "sissy sister" and "lesbian," reflecting enduring sissyphobia in Chinese-speaking gay communities (Lin 2006, 2013; Zheng 2015; T. Zhou 2020, 2021). One effeminate gay voter dislikes him intensely on the grounds that "similar poles repel each other" (同性相斥), suggesting that an ideal gay relationship should conform to dominant heteronormative gender norms, with one partner being masculine and the other feminine.

The body is the principal site at which masculinities are reified. Forrest argues that "whatever its contradictions or changing characteristics, 'male masculinity' is tied to a masculine body" and that "this body is hard, muscular and athletic; a symbol (if not a guarantee) of power within a hierarchically gendered society" (1994, 104). Similarly, Zhiqiu Benson Zhou (2020, 576–77) points out that masculine built bodies in the Chinese gay world "represent movement toward the 'right' advancement to the superior [Western] modernity," which "symbolize certain people's economic capital to reshape their bodies." The desirability of masculine bodies is confirmed by the male celebrities whom *Kangsi Coming*'s gay audience voted the top three most desirable of those presented to them. Each has a muscular, lean, and athletic body, the signs of eroticism. More importantly, the show assembles an extensive gay "wish list," producing a cartoon character named the "ideal man." Designed by the guest judge, Sunny Face, the "ideal man" is comprised of short hair; bushy eyebrows; a clipped beard; a big chest; thick arms; toned abs; firm buttocks; a "big package"; and plump legs. This "ideal man" is reminiscent of the "clones" found in gay America during the 1970s:

> The clone was, in many ways, the manliest of men. He had a gym-defined body; after hours of rigorous body building, his physique rippled with bulging muscles, looking more like competitive body builders than hairdressers or florists . . . He kept his hair short and had a thick moustache or closely cropped beard. (Levine 1998, 7)

This "ideal man" represents the most desirable masculine body, which only a small number of gay winners could attain. As Sunny Face suggests, the "ideal man" differentiates himself from "snowy little egrets"—a gay slang term referring to those with a developed upper-body build and very slender legs. Striving to achieve the ideal masculine body can be detrimental. As Daryl Higgins (2006, 91) points out, "the body becomes the site for competition, and for the losers in the race the object of shame and self-loathing." This can result in gay men focusing on dieting and muscle-building rather than "the primal need for connection and intimacy with others" (Higgins 2006, 91). Indeed, in Taiwan, hitting the gym and building muscles has become an integral part of gay subculture, leading to many gay men facing massive anxiety over their body image; moreover, this anxiety is further fueled by taking and sharing smartphone gym selfies among local gay communities (Jhuo 2020).

The "ideal man" visualizes various expressions of masculinity to which gay men may be attracted. It may encourage *Kangsi Coming*'s gay viewers to sculpt their bodies so as to dilute their femininity. Through this masculinization, is the "macho" gay type that is emerging in media and popular culture simply reinforcing the very stereotypes and gender norms that are the origin of so much prejudice and oppression? Shaun Cole (2000, 128) argues that "the macho-man is a reaction against effeminacy, and this means that the masculine/feminine binary structure has not gone away, but only been redistributed." Within Chinese gay communities, hypermasculine built bodies may serve to "prioritize heteromasculinity, while marginalizing other types of masculinities that deviate from this normative masculinity" (Z. Zhou 2020, 566). On the other hand, however, Raewyn Connell (1992) argues that the gendered eroticism that gay men direct toward stereotypical masculinity can challenge the gendered social system. In this vein, gay masculinity can be seen simultaneously as "both subversive (in that it challenges orthodox masculinity) and reactionary (in that it reinforces gender stereotypes—a crucial factor in the oppression of gay sexuality)" (Forrest 1994, 105).

The "ideal man" does not simply embrace traditional, stereotypical heterosexual masculinity. It can also be seen as signifying the "macho" man who is marked off from the simply straight man by both a gay sensibility and "an excess of masculinity" (Dyer 2002, 38). As the guest judge Sunny Face argued, whereas a straight man might leave his facial hair scruffy and scraggly, the "ideal man" always keeps his hair short, eyebrows trimmed, and beard clipped. Arguably, this brings "a gay sensibility to a gendered attire" (Levine 1998, 60). The "ideal man" proves his masculinity by building an exaggeratedly manly body: whereas a straight man might work out to get leaner and fitter, the "ideal man" aims to be shredded, chiseling his serratus muscles in addition to his V-cut abs. Like the queer satire put forward in *Kangsi Coming*, the "ideal man" arguably indicates what Martin P. Levine (1998, 59) has termed "the doubleness of clone style," which contains both "self-conscious, almost parodying references to stereotypically traditional masculinity" and a "self-conscious embracing of that very stereotype at the same time."

The mainland gay Internet celebrity and model Edison Fan, with his exaggerated masculinity, can be seen as a real-life representation of the cartoon "ideal man." In 2015, Edison Fan shared his coming out story on *U Can U Bibi*. His personal appearance differed considerably from heterosexual entertainers'. His hair was slick and his moustache trimmed, his clothing perfectly matched and designed to accentuate his athletic physique. More importantly, he deployed macho fashion in a sexual way so as to express "hotness." In a departure from the conventional suits of his heterosexual counterparts, Edison Fan often dresses in string vests to call viewers' attention to his well-built chest and biceps. Even when he wears a suit, Edison Fan deliberately highlights his musculature by unbuttoning his shirt. His sense of fashion serves to perform not only gender but class, in that it emphasizes good taste, consumerism, and elitism. This echoes Geng Song and Derek Hird's (2013, 74) observation that "Chinese hypermasculine sexuality is constructed as a privilege of the rich, just like other forms of consumption." At the same time, Edison Fan's rough masculine identity also has something of the working class to it. Indeed, in one selfie, which has circulated widely across Chinese social media platforms, he resembles a skillful construction worker. Here, his macho stylization recalls hypermasculine "clone" fashion, which embraces a "rougher, coarser masculinity of the common laborer" (Levine 1998, 60).

In emphasizing exaggerated masculine images and physiques, the "ideal man" and his living counterpart Edison Fan are both a parody and emulation of heterosexual masculinity, with a camp sensibility. They echo Cole's (2000, 129) description of the "tightrope" that some gay men walk "between straight imitation and an interpretation that could identify them not only as real men but as real *gay* men." Seen in this light, macho looks may serve "a dual purpose, in that whilst attracting other gay men it also acted as a form of self-protection." This is particularly important in mainland Chinese society, which goes on stigmatizing and discriminating against homosexuality. In its liberating aspect, the "macho" man is closer to camp, which "constantly draws attention to the artifices attendant on the construction of images of what is natural" rather than "expressing a sense of what is natural" (Dyer 2002, 40). The new macho gay type in *Kangsi Coming* (and elsewhere) can arguably be seen as self-conscious performance of the signs of masculinity and gender. This is important, for "it is in the play and exaggeration that an alternative sexuality is implied—a sexuality, that is, that recognizes itself as in a problematic relationship to the conventional conflation of sexuality and gender" (Dyer 2002, 40). This is not to suggest that the "macho" man presented in media and popular culture is the foremost way in which gay men in Taiwan and mainland China present themselves. These representations are context-specific, which need to be understood as tightly intertwined with indigenous political regulation, media industry, and the pink economy. Gay men in the Chinese-speaking world have exhibited diverse ways of doing masculinities. Accordingly, more empirical research is needed to capture the differences—including those concerning race, class, gender, and age—that challenge attempts to construct a unitary identity for Chinese gay men.

Conclusion

In this chapter, I have explored the issues of gay visibility in the media, illuminating the ways that media and popular culture create and constrain gay identities. The images and discourses of homosexuality flow from and through Chinese-speaking media, particularly TV entertainment genres, shaping how gay men understand themselves and the world around them. I have examined some representative cases of gayness in *Kangsi Coming* and *U Can U Bibi*, highlighting the heterogeneity and transculturality of Chinese-language TV. While acknowledging the trans-regional circulation of queer TV in mainland China and Taiwan, it is important to note that the televised cultural representations in question are specific to the local context, including media and political regulations, pink economy, social movements, and changing social attitudes toward gender and sexuality. Together, they shape the production, consumption, and circulation of gay images in the two major Chinese-speaking societies. The evolving queer mediascapes in the Chinese-language world, especially the rise of gay social networking services (Wang 2020; Li and Lu 2020; Zhou 2021), promise to enhance the visibility of gay men. That said, it has never been simply visibility that is at stake here, but rather only a specific kind of visibility. Thus, the new gay cultural representations that emerge through digitization may "cultivate a narrow but widely accepted definition of gay identity as a marketing tool and help to integrate gay people as gay people into a new marketing niche" (Hennessy 2000, 137). Although the market is not necessarily the unpardonable enemy of queers, when gay visibility and cultural practices become a good business prospect in a digital age, the question we need to ask is "Who is profiting from these new markets?"

With the "queer turn" in Chinese-language media studies (Zhao and Wong 2020), a growing body of scholarship seeks to examine the new representations of nonnormative sexualities in China, contributing to the de-Westernization of queer theory and LGBTQ activism in the transnational context. Interpreting these texts critically may be a necessary part of the project of queering Chinese media studies, but it should not be its ultimate goal. This highlights the need for a reflexive ethnographic approach if we are to be able to unpack the incompatible expectations and outcomes that surround the increase in queer visibility brought on by digital technologies. This need is particularly pressing in the light of scholars' difficulties with connecting with the queer communities about whom "we" write. Gay (in)visibility in Chinese popular culture is paradoxical. Although it commences "from assertions accepted as true about a positive good—progress, financial means, acceptance, and digital prowess," the value of these goods "turns out to be at least partly negative, contrary to expectation" (Barnhurst 2007, 2). Therefore, I close this chapter by inviting further critical reflection on the diverse cultural politics that shape (and are shaped by) gay men's everyday media practices in China.

9
Queer Motherly Fantasy

The Sinophone Mom Fandom of Saint Suppapong Udomkaewkanjana

Pang Ka Wei

> "My baby boy, be bold and take wing. Mama will always back you up. Be yourself and stay happy." (Luna, 24 years old, Shandong, mainland China)
>
> "Don't drain yourself out. Take enough rest. Mama loves you. [blow a kiss]" (Guoguo, 20 years old, Jiangsu, mainland China)
>
> "Really wanna spank him for staying up late! Not going to bed, huh!" (Hami, 33 years old, Guangdong, mainland China)

This baby boy who always stays up late is Suppapong Udomkaewkanjana, more widely known by his nickname Saint (hereafter, Saintsup). Saintsup is no baby boy, but—at the time—a twenty-two-year-old Thai actor, singer and entrepreneur that has gained popularity worldwide. In an Instagram live session in 2019, he pouted, saying that he was afraid of his moms not loving him. The moms he referred to are in fact his fans. Like the above quotes, many of his fans see Saintsup as "son," "hijo," ("son" in Spanish) or "zaizai" ("son" in Chinese)[1] while calling themselves mom. They are the mom fans, stanning for their darling boy Saintsup, who gained his fame playing leading roles in Thai boys' love (BL) TV series.

In two years, Saintsup attracted more than 2 million followers on Instagram and 1 million on Weibo (as of September 5, 2020). He named his fandom MingEr and often addresses his fans as moms. With his smiling cherubic face, Saintsup delights his mom fans with his occasional childlike behavior. His Chinese descent also appeals to the Sinophone fans, especially those in mainland China. Despite the geo-blocking, state censorship of homoerotic works and language barrier, mainland Chinese fans continue to support Saintsup by all means. For many months in 2020, Saintsup was voted one of the top ten celebrities in the

---

1. It happens that the pronunciation of the words "崽崽" in Mandarin, as well as "囝囝" and "仔仔" in Cantonese, can all be Romanized as *zaizai* despite their different Romanization systems and characters.

Asia-Pacific superstar chart on Weibo. In reciprocity, Saintsup also publicly acknowledges his "Chinese moms" for their tremendous support, and increasingly gears towards the mainland China market.

This imaginary kinship between fans and idols, as Qing Yan and Fan Yang (2021) term it in their exploration of the parakin fans of "cultivated idols" in mainland China, is a parakin relationship that is distinctive from the nonreciprocal parasocial ones. Parakin fans of "cultivated idols" are keen on "co-creating" their idols, as if they are playing "raising sims." Analyzing social media posts and interviews, Yan and Yang (2021) classify the motivations of the parakin fans into a dual (self-oriented and idol-oriented) motivation model. Their proposition, to a large extent, is based on a heterosexist family imagination and presumes that fans establish such a parakin relationship out of the lack of or discontent at their own family relationship, arguing that mainland Chinese fans become mother fans because of escapism and compensation. It is on this that the transnational Sinophone mom fandom of "non-cultivated" BL actor Saintsup could offer a more sophisticated picture.

As the mom fan has become a growing fandom of young Asian idols, this chapter looks more closely into how the family metaphor is at work among the trans-Asian Sinophone mom fans of Saintsup by means of survey and in-depth interviews: how they negotiate their identity with respect to sexuality, fantasy and desire, age, national/ethnic identity, East Asian/Southeast Asian imaginations, as well as the fan-idol relationship. If we see the transnational fandom as "a product (and a further trigger) of overseas fan communities' voluntary and purposeful cultural and linguistic mediation" (Lee 2014, 198), I argue that this motherly fan identity is derived from the heteropatriarchal family structure as a result of a negotiation of their desire and fantasy towards a young male queer subject.

Sinophone Fandom and Queer Fantasies

This chapter approaches the term Sinophone in both its denotative and connotative senses. Since most fandoms, and transnational ones in particular, are largely online communities, fans of different linguistic backgrounds communicate with each other online in a certain lingua franca. In Saintsup's fandom, English, Chinese, and Spanish are the three major linguae francae besides Thai. Here, the term "Sinophone" is seen as a counterpart of Anglophone and Hispanophone. The Sinophone is used denotatively to refer to the fans who primarily communicate with written Chinese—or, to be more precise, Sinitic scripts. Owing to the unpromising quality of machine and amateur translations, the language barrier leaves much room for interpretation and contestation, as well as imagination and fantasy.

Meanwhile, this Sinophone fandom is comprised of Chinese-speaking/writing fans whose heterogeneity is oftentimes rendered invisible in the multicultural fandom. In Saintsup's fandom, for example, they are collectively known as "Chinese moms." It is in this sense that it is necessary to bring in the notion of the Sinophone as an interrogation of China-centrism in understanding the "Chinese" fandom. In understanding the concept of "Sinophone," there are two main approaches: one is by Shu-mei Shih and another by David Der-wei Wang. Seeing Chineseness as an ethnicized reductive Han-centric construction, Shih (2011) employs "the Sinophone," the polyphonic and polyscriptic notion, as a critique of it. While I share this use of the Sinophone as a critical framework that interrogates the hegemonic call for an essentialist, monolingual, and Han-centric Chineseness, I hope to differ on the use of the term by a majority of queer Sinophone studies scholars that adopt Shih's (2007) definition of the Sinophone as only Chinese-speakers outside mainland China. Unlike literary studies in which writers, may they be Chinese settlers, diasporic, or exilic subjects, could more easily be categorized as outside China proper based on their place of residence, the online fannish subjects are far more hybrid. In order to adequately address and engage with the heterogeneous body of the Sinophone fandom, I would follow Wang's (2017) usage of the term to include not only the geopolitically peripheral subjects but also those within China proper. To put it more clearly, in this chapter, the Sinophone mom fans include Chinese-speaking/writing ethnic Chinese both outside and inside mainland China who self-identify themselves as mom fans.

Sharing this anti-essentializing and anti-normativizing attempt with the Sinophone is queer theory (Chiang and Wong 2020b; Heinrich 2014). These Sinophone mom fans assume a motherly role rooted in a heteropatriarchal family imagination while paradoxically queering it. This imagination in the Sinophone context is largely a Confucian one that sees family relationships as primarily hierarchical with respect to sex, age, and generation (Lai 2020) that coincide with heterosexisim, cisgenderism, and monogamy. Therefore, in addition to the homoeroticism in BL works, the shifting identificatory positions and queer fantasy manifested by these mom fans in trans-Asian fanning and BL consumption can also be regarded as queer. The queerness transgresses, if not necessarily resists, the stability of these familial hierarchies and thus the normativizing forces of the heteropatriarchy. Putting into question China-centrism and heteropatriarchy, this chapter offers a queer Sinophone reading of Saintsup's mom fandom against the background of the blooming Y-series production in Thailand.

From Y-series to Taifu

Taking after the success of the film *Love of Siam* (dir. Chookiat Sakveerakul, 2007), Thailand has seen a bloom in the male homoerotic youth TV genre, the Y-series, in the second decade of the twenty-first century. Y-series, more commonly known as BL series by the Anglophone audience, is the local abbreviated term for Thai TV adaptations of *yaoi* (and also *yuri*) stories (Saejang 2019, 72). The production of these Y-series has grown from one per year in the early 2010s to over 40 in 2020. Starring good-looking young men, these Y-series often plot their stories as a coming-of-age schoolyard romance among urban Thai boys.

As part of the ongoing high-tech low-end "gloBLisation" (Yang and Xu 2017, 3–4), many of these Y-series, such as *SOTUS* (One31, LINE TV and GMM 25, 2016), *2Moons* (One31 and GMM One, 2017), *Love By Chance* (LINE TV and GMM 25, 2018), *TharnType* (One31 and LINE TV 2019), *Until We Meet Again* (LINE TV, 2019), *Why R U?* (One31 and LINE TV, 2020), *2gether* (GMM 25 and LINE TV, 2020), and *I Told Sunset About You* (LINE TV and Vimeo, 2020), are being circulated worldwide facilitated by the streaming media and file-sharing technology. Y-series as an expanding niche market draws a growing transnational fandom. Like Saintsup, his personal and series-related fan clubs can be found in not only Thailand, but also in East Asia (in places like mainland China, Japan, Taiwan, South Korea, and Hong Kong), Southeast Asia (for example, Laos, Myanmar, Vietnam, Singapore, Malaysia, and the Philippines), Europe (France, Spain, and Germany), North America, Latin America (Argentina, Mexico, El Salvador, and Peru) on top of the many unaffiliated fans in the Middle East, South Asia, and so on. Among them, Sinophone fans form a huge, probably the largest, fanbase of the Y-series.

This huge Sinophone fanbase is made up of mostly ethnic Chinese fans in mainland China, Taiwan, Hong Kong, Singapore, Malaysia, and other parts of the world. Take the viewership of Y-series in mainland China as an example; the majority are themselves female *fujoshi* who are lovers of male homoerotic stories, and some of them have been watching Y-series for years. In my online survey held in July 2020, 80 percent of the 344 Sinophone Saintsup fans have experience with consuming BL works. The large base of Chinese *fujoshi* also made possible well-established Thai-Chinese subbing groups that offer timely Chinese subtitles of Y-series. Among them, Tianfu Taiju (8.9 million followers on its Weibo @tfthaimovie) and CFanGroup (3.5 million followers on its Weibo @CFanGroup) are the most prominent. While many credit the latter with its very faithful translation, the former is known for its vivid localized translation and its collaboration with Thai production houses so that many of its subbed *Taifu* episodes can be aired in synchronous with its premiere in Thailand (Limpongsatorn 2020, 65–76). Here, *Taifu* (*Tai* means Thai, while *fu* refers to *fujoshi*) is an abbreviated translation of *Taiguo Fuju* (Thai BL series) among Sinophone, especially mainland Chinese, netizens.

Taifu has spread to a wider audience among the Sinophone audience thanks to the "commons-based" "shared economy" (Ito 2012, 182) in the fandom and digital technology. Whereas those who live outside mainland China enjoy greater liberty in viewing these series on YouTube, LINE TV, Netflix, and other sites, those within the Mainland may need extra effort despite its well-established *Taifu* subbing mechanism. They may either access the unwalled internet world with a VPN or be more resilient in the face of state censorship. To disseminate the Chinese-subbed *Taifu* episodes, the above-mentioned subbing groups adopt various guerilla tactics: they used to upload only the clean version of the episode, mosaicking the allegedly sensitive scenes, to streaming sites such as Bilibili.com and Dilidili.com, then share URLs and passcodes via popular mainland Chinese social platforms and apps, such as Weibo and WeChat, so that interested parties could access the unmosaicked videos on the cloud (Limpongsatorn 2020, 132–33). The tightening state controls on foreign media broadcast and homoerotic content could not halt the passion of *Taifu* lovers.

From *Taifu* Fans to Mingming's Fans

Many *Taifu* lovers become active participants as media fans. They are prosumers who contribute to promoting *Taifu*, producing fanvids, and forming a strong *Taifu* fanbase that provides a reserve of Chinese resources to people inside and outside the fandom. This includes a bewildering array of Chinese-subbed fanvids and translated/subbed interviews and a database of actors, images, and fanfics that could be easily accessible on various streaming and social media platforms. The approachability of Thai actors makes celebrity-fan interactions easier than those with the distant stars in South Korea and mainland China, subsequently enriching the resources reserve. Benefiting from the fan expertise and epistemophilia within the fandom (Duffett 2013, 40), curious ordinary viewers could have easily found their own gems and been drawn to particular Thai actors, one of whom is Saintsup.

Saintsup made his debut playing the role of Pete in *Love by Chance* (2018) and gained further momentum with his leading role in *Why R U?* (2020), where he plays the role of Tutor. In mainland China, both series were great hits among *Taifu* fans, and Saintsup has become one of the most loved Thai celebrities on Weibo. On March 23, 2020, for example, Saintsup ranked first on Weibo's Asia-Pacific superstar chart. Five months later, on August 28, even when none of his series were being aired, Saintsup ranked second on Weibo's Asia-Pacific superstar chart after Lisa (Lalisa Manoban), a Thai member of the Korean girl group Blackpink that topped the chart. Whereas other Y-series actors such as Mew (Suppasit Jongcheveevat) and Gulf (Kanawut Traipipattanapong) are also well-liked worldwide, Saintsup has an extraordinarily high proportion of Sinophone fans. For instance, on August 18, 2020, Saintsup initiated two unannounced live sessions on Yizhibo and Instagram consecutively; the former yielded 459,000 viewers, while the latter racked up 3,300. Whereas the fewer views of the latter could be due to the different time zones, work hours, and differing readiness and connectivity for livestreaming among overseas fans, the huge number of viewers on this mainland Chinese livestreaming site reflects the very high proportion of his active followers in mainland China.

In order to better understand the Sinophone fandom of Saintsup, a questionnaire was distributed online in late July 2020 and collected data from 344 eligible respondents.[2] These respondents are Sinophone fans who started following Saintsup as early as in January 2018 and as lately as in July 2020.[3] Their ages range from 15 to 50 years old. Out of the 344 respondents, 338 are female (the other six are male). 72 percent self-identify as heterosexual. They live in mainland China, Taiwan, Hong Kong, Malaysia, Singapore, the United States, Germany, Japan, and other places. Within these 344 fans, three-quarters of them used to call Saintsup by his Chinese given name, Mingming, in addition to his nickname, Saint. Since these Sinophone fans share a similar Sinitic writing system (predominantly in Simplified Chinese characters), the Chinese language is highly visible in not only Weibo pages and forums, but also in Twitter tweets and Instagram comments; even non-Sinophone fans could easily identify and call these fans "Chinese moms."

Who are Chinese moms? How do these Sinophone fans view themselves? Why do they identify themselves with the title "Chinese moms," or why not? What does it mean to be a mom fan? Why do they relate themselves with Saintsup as a next-of-kin? How does this kinship/family metaphor affect their understanding, desire, affection and performance of themselves? To understand more about the Sinophone mom fandom, I conducted online interviews in August 2020 with ten mom fans of Saintsup, among the respondents of the aforementioned online survey. To ensure a more diverse sampling, interview invitations were sent to mom fans of different sexes, ages, places of residence, occupations, sexual orientations, and sub-fandoms. However, it turned out that all ten of the favorable replies were from female fans, 20 to 50 years of age, who primarily or partially identified themselves as both mom fans of Saintsup and CP fans of ZaintSee.[4] Two of the interviewees started following Saintsup in 2018, three in 2019 and five in 2020. If we see fandom as an "affinity space" for fans to connect, negotiate, and explore pleasures in the context of a shared media culture at a given time (Duffett 2013, 288), this mother-son parakin imagination within the transcultural

---

2. Special thanks to Wong Tak Yin Yumi for her invaluable assistance in processing the questionnaire data and preparing the interview transcription.
3. The survey recruited self-identified *Huaren* (華人) as informants.
4. ZaintSee CP fans are shipper stans who adore the pairing of Saintsup and his partner Zee Pruk Panich in *Why R U?*, which aired from January to April 2020. While "shipper stan" is a common English term, synonymous with CP fans in Chinese and referring to the fans who are keen on pairing up two real people or fictional characters as a couple in a romantic relationship, many ZaintSee CP fans reiterate that they do not intentionally ship Saintsup and Zee, but are drawn by the chemistry between them.

Asian fandom elicits and embodies queer fantasies that consistently transgress the kinship dynamics. Listening to these shipper-stan mom fans of Saintsup could possibly shed light on how the queerly motherly identification of these Sinophone fans negotiates with the heteropatriarchal family ideology.

Fans as Moms

When Saintsup had his debut in 2018, he was only 20 years old. Until now, his fandom has been comprised of mostly female fans older than him. Unlike the stereotype of fans as immature teenage girls idolizing a hero (Hills 2014, 11), Saintsup's fandom paints a very different picture: Saintsup often addresses his fans as *Phi* (พี่, elder sister/brother) when meeting them in person and call them *Mae* (แม่, mother) as a collective noun referring to his fans in general. Likewise, apart from solo stans and shipper stans,[5] there is another common set of classifications that is based on the fan's self-identification in relation to the idol: mom fans, elder-sis fans and girlfriend fans.

Most of my interviewees easily distinguish themselves from the girlfriend fans who see the idol as their boyfriend. In their perception, girlfriend fans are often more possessive due to the monogamous heterosexual romantic ideal. They are usually of a similar age to or younger than the idol, seeing their idol as an object of desire and fantasizing about developing a romantic relationship with the idol. Limpongsatorn (2020, 124) also adds that girlfriend fans tend to be more hostile to other women, whether it be their peers or the idol's work partners. In short, girlfriend fans are thought to be seeking heterosexual romance with the male idol, and tend to expect more attention, care, and love from the idol. Nine out of my ten interviewees drew a clear line between themselves and being girlfriend fans except one, which I will discuss later.

Girlfriend fans seem to be a sub-group in the fandom that can be easily defined, but the distinction between mom fans and elder-sis fans is not as clear-cut. One may easily attribute this mother-child imagination of the fan-idol relationship to the older age of these female fans, thinking that the positioning of themselves as mom fans is because of them being mothers or having already reached the age of a mother. Limpongsatorn (2020) too suggests that the key difference between mom fans and elder-sis fans is age. According to her interviewees, it is mostly

---

5. Solo stans and shipper stans are two categories of stans on Stan Twitter. Whereas "stan" used to be known as a portmanteau of "stalker" and "fan" to refer to overzealous, obsessive fans, it has become a common term that is synonymous in its noun form with "zealous fan," while its verb form means "to support and stand by." As illustrated in footnote 4, shipper stans are fans who are particularly interested in the romantic relationship of the real persons or fictional characters concerned (Duffett 2013, 299). Solo stans, in contrast, emphasize their support for an individual celebrity. Despite the possible hostility between the two stan groups, they are not mutually exclusive identities.

because "mother" seems to be associated with the image of an older woman; young women are reluctant to relate themselves to old age, so they choose to position themselves as elder sisters, the elder-sis fans. Nevertheless, from my survey, among the 169 respondents (around 49.1 percent of the 344 respondents) who self-identified themselves as mom fans, 29.6 percent are younger than or the same age as Saintsup, with the youngest born in 2004—six years younger than him. Only 18.9 percent are older than Saintsup by more than ten years. The largest group (32.0 percent) is made up of fans who are four to ten years older, followed by those who are one to three years older (19.5 percent). And despite the small number of male respondents, a couple of them partially identify themselves as mom fans as well. From this, we could tell that the assumption of mom fans as older female is not the full picture.

It is, in a way, right to say that age is a consideration of the fan's positioning, but to become a mom fan is more than just age concern. Instead of the different motives gathered by Yan and Yang (2021),[6] mom fans and elder-sis fans in this case are overlapping identities distinguished by different affects. A few interviewees were hesitant about calling themselves mom fans and preferred to be called "elder-sis". Luna (24, Shandong, mainland China, fan since December 2019) said,

> I was in fact an elder-sis fan in the beginning and rejected the label "mom fans," for I thought we were about the same age, how could I be a mom? It's disrespecting. However, after following him for some while, I could barely hold myself back. Mingming is way too lovable. He is a hardworking child, and he is so kind. I wanted to love him fondly and give him the best, just like a mom. That's how I became a mom fan.

Almost every interviewee told me that age does not matter, and that there is no age limitation to becoming a mom fan. They said that it is a matter of mentality. Summarizing their descriptions, mom fans love Saintsup unconditionally as if he were their own child. They would worry about whether Saintsup has eaten well and slept well. They would also try their hardest to provide the best means of support to Saintsup, ready to spend money on him and not to do anything that might defame him.

Compared to elder-sis fans, different interviewees opined that mom fans worry a lot more. Elder-sis fans are more like peers who play with Saintsup, but mom fans worry about literally everything. And yet, mom fans and elder-sis fans are not mutually exclusive. While most younger-in-age but older-than-Saintsup female fans did struggle between whether or not to claim themselves as mom fans, considering how the term denotes an older woman, Hsuching, a

---

6. In their study of parakin fans of "cultivated idols" in mainland China, Yan and Yang (2021) gather that mother fans are driven more by escapism and compensation while sister fans are driven more by self-achievement, entertainment, satisfaction, and physical attractions.

50-year-old mother (Tainan, Taiwan, fan since May 2018), shifts between the two identities for a different reason. She said that when Saintsup is happy, she sees herself as an elder-sis fan who can have fun with Saintsup; when he is upset, she would be a mom fan hoping to console him at her best. This "generational difference" matters because it is not just about age, but also the role that they play: the elder-sis fans are the peers who support and have fun with the idol, and the mom fans are the parents who unconditionally care for and are concerned about their child. The most frequently used verb to describe the characteristic of mom fans is *caoxin* (操心, worry and concern), never-ending *caoxin*. As Jiepin (26 years old, Shenzhen, mainland China, March 2020) summed up, the mom fan is a combination of *shiye fen* (事業粉; career fans) and *shengming fen* (生命粉; life fans) that hope the best for Saintsup's career prospects and overall well-being. To them, a girlfriend's love may die down, but a mom's love lasts.

This imaginary kinship, nonetheless, is full of elasticity. In the Sinophone setting, kinship is a rather inelastic order and category (Heinrich 2014). As Hsuching put it, she would not claim herself as Saintsup's mom but as his mom fan because, to her, M'Nuk, Saintsup's biological mother, is his one-and-only mom. This insistence may not be articulated clearly by my other informants, but it is apparent that in such a trans-Asian fandom, "mom" becomes a handy identity and a voluntary choice that queerly grows out of the rigidity and their perception of the heteropatriarchal kinship.

Saintsup the *Ke'ai*

What turned fans of all ages into mom fans? Most interviewees, like Luna, said it is Saintsup's *ke'ai* (可愛; cute, adorable, lovable) demeanor that triggers their maternal instinct, their impulse to love and protect him. *Ke'ai* has been a signature of Saintsup. For the survey question where fans were asked to describe Saintsup with three adjectives, 248 out of the 344 put in the word *ke'ai* or its variants, making it the most commonly agreed-upon attribute. In search of the English equivalent of *ke'ai*, I discussed the matter with Bagel (24 years old, Taipei, Taiwan, fan since July 2019), who is proficient in both Chinese and English, and she reckoned that "lovable" is the most faithful translation that could address the complexity of Saintsup's *ke'ai* without denying his cuteness and adorability.

To his fans, Saintsup is a cuteness overload. Many love Saintsup's chubby cheeks so much that there was once a Twitter trend with the hashtag #SaintLovelyCheek dedicated to them. Another favourite of his fans is his angelic smile that, according to several interviewees, melts their hearts. Many compare the cuteness of Saintsup to that of a bunny, which is a mascot of him taken from *Why R U?*. Instead of a meek bunny, fans often juxtapose pictures of Saintsup with pictures of the expressive and sometimes mischievous bunny character Snowball from the animation *The Secret Life of Pets* (2016) and its sequel. To many, the way Saintsup eats, sulks, and plays pranks are all cute. Saintsup knows his cuteness well, and he would strike *aegyo* poses in front of the camera and his fans. Yet, unlike the "queered *ke'ai*" explored in Shih-chen Chao (2017) that revolves around performing femininity, the *ke'ai* Saintsup embodies is not necessarily feminine cuteness, but babyish/boyish cuteness as well. In the eyes of his fans, Saintsup is a versatile young actor who could be both cute and handsome, hot and cool, coy and assertive, boyish and manly—showcasing diverse masculinities.

To his fans, it is this showcase of diverse masculinities of Saintsup that makes him unique and appealing. One may say that this versatile yet simultaneously contradictory soft masculinity is similar to the *kawaii* masculinity performed by many *chogukjeok* K-pop idol boys (Jung 2011), and it is no denying that Saintsup makes reference to K-pop idols, but Saintsup's *ke'ai* exceeds a strategic star persona. In my interview, I invited the mom fans to share with me pictures of Saintsup that impressed them the most. It turned out that most photos could be classified into four categories: the lovely (Saintsup eating or smiling), the handsome (Saintsup striking hot poses), the family-loving (Saintsup with his mother or baby cousin), and the devout and kind-hearted (Saintsup chanting in the temple or making merit). In a 2019 interview with Domundi TV, Saintsup said that he prefers to be called "cute" more than "handsome" because cuteness comes from not only his appearance, but also his actions and personality. And this is exactly why many fans adore Saintsup.

To all the mom fans I interviewed, Saintsup is beyond cute, but lovable. Here are some of the positive traits of Saintsup they mentioned: kind, caring, warm, family-loving, courteous, respectful, humble, positive, talented, strong, determined, courageous, responsible, mature, hardworking, professional, visionary, and enterprising. A few shared similar stories of how much perseverance Saintsup has while experiencing smearing and defaming in his early career, how wise and compassionate he is to have set up his own business to facilitate community economy, and how wonderful he is being a devout Buddhist who joins the showbiz industry for a good cause: to spread happiness and mobilize more people to do good deeds. As Datong (25 years old, Guangxi, mainland China, fan since March 2020) described, "he is literally an angel on earth." She particularly admired his persistence in doing voluntary work and making merit. To mom fans, it is this emotional, mental, and spiritual maturity of Saintsup that makes him particularly lovable. However, despite their acknowledgement of his maturity, mom fans often look at Saintsup as though he were a young kid.

Mom fans adore Saintsup so much that they tend to infantilize him. In the interviews, mom fans—regardless of age—referred to Saintsup as *xiaohai*, *haizi*, or *siupangjau*, all of which are synonyms of "child." They are aware that Saintsup is a grown-up and that he is maturing day by day, but as Luna said, "in the eyes of the mother, her child is always a child." When fans claim a mother position, they immediately take up a nurturing role that justifies their emotional and financial investment in Saintsup, making them more involved in supporting, caring for, and protecting him. All these could easily be seen on the comments on Saintsup's various social media accounts. Some mom fans share the happiness of Saintsup when he is comfortable being who he is when he is with his loved ones. Some are ready to defend him against anyone who may take advantage of him. Some are happy seeing him enjoying his food. Some would dissuade him from building too much muscle. And almost every mom fan worries about his health, knowing how hard he has been working and studying. This tendency of infantilizing the idol pictures Saintsup as vulnerable and naive despite his maturity. Assuming a mother role, some mom fans may have crossed the idol-fan boundary, intruding on Saintsup's privacy and undermining the bodily autonomy of their imaginary son, an "intimate stranger" in Duffett (2013)'s term, in the MingEr family.

The MingEr Family

Saintsup's fandom name, MingEr, is a transliteration of the Chinese name 明兒. According to Saintsup the Official (2018)'s account of the term, this name is made up of Saintsup's Chinese name, "Ming," and "-er", meaning (1) every fan is Saintsup's "tomorrow" (the Chinese compound word *ming'er* means "tomorrow"), (2) "Ming" (Saintsup) is our "son" (taking the meaning of the Chinese word *er*), and (3) all fans are the people of Ming (taking the meaning of the English suffix -er). How do Sinophone fans perceive this name, then? All my interviewees think that this name sounds *ke'ai*. Half of them see in *er* a hint of childlikeness, as if the fans are young children. And this infantilizing hint to them is again very *ke'ai* because "mothers need to be pampered by their children too," said Luna. A few, like Guoguo (20 years old, Jiangsu, mainland China, fan since August 2018), did hesitate, wondering if a CP fan like her is eligible to be a MingEr, and was soon relieved by knowing that fans of all sub-fandoms too are MingEr. If a fandom name is meant to forge a closer bond between the idol and the fans (Linden and Linden 2017, 170), what is this bond between Saintsup and his mom fans like?

Saintsup used to say that MingEr is like a family. If taking the second meaning of the fandom name, he would be the "son" in this family. This family metaphor legitimizes his fans' identification of themselves as Saintsup's next of kin, especially as the mother. Do mom fans agree with this family metaphor? Most said yes and trusted that Saintsup sees all his fans equally as MingEr. While Hami (33 years old, Guangdong, mainland China, fan since March 2020) was pessimistic about the possibility of harmony among the sub-fandoms in mainland China, Mani (23 years old, Jiangsu, mainland China, fan since March 2020) saw it in a different light. Mani said, "In a family, there are parents who are stern, like those MingErs who dislike shipping (i.e. coupling); some are loving, like our kind; we would love whoever Mingming loves to be with. There are different voices in a family, so is the MingEr community." This MingEr family is comprised of fans from different social, cultural and linguistic backgrounds, but they cross paths with each other all because of their idol, Saintsup.

Despite the differences among mom fans, they all share a similar affection toward Saintsup, forming an affective alliance. As an affective alliance, fans share an invigorated passion towards the same subject within a specific cultural context. This contextual affective life allows them to construct relatively stable moments of identity as well as imagination and enactment of their own projects and possibilities out of their own volition (Grossberg 1992, 59). In the case of the Sinophone mom fandom, Saintsup becomes the baby boy among son-centric mom fans and sister fans. Mom fans relate this motherly affection to their maternal instinct, but as Chodorow (1999) argues, women's mothering is more a product of socialization and social reproduction than biological inevitability. In other words, instead of a universal maternal instinct, women mother according to their own perception of what a mother should be like and should do in their own cultural and social context. In this sense, mom fans, or more specifically, Sinophone mom fans, are all contextually moulded, and yet these Sinophone mom fans are most of the time being homogenized as "Chinese moms." So, who are "Chinese moms"?

Who Are Chinese Moms?

"Chinese moms" (แม่จีน) is an umbrella term to denote Sinophone fans in the MingEr fandom, and the Thai fandom at large. On Twitter and Instagram, the two most frequently used social media platforms of Saintsup, many followers comment in the Chinese language. These Sinophone followers are known as Chinese moms, or *Zhongguo mama* (中國媽媽; China mothers). A majority of them are China nationals who could be easily identified by the China flag emoji next to their screen names or in their bios. Besides mainland Chinese, there are also Singaporean and Malaysian *huaren*, Taiwanese, Hongkongers, and others. So, what is the common characteristic of Chinese moms? High spending power. As agreed upon by all interviewees, Chinese moms are known as big spenders. However, are all Sinophone mom fans "Chinese moms"? To many Sinophone fans, "Chinese moms" refer to only mainland Chinese mom fans.

When Saintsup addresses his Chinese fans in Mandarin, the term *Zhongguo fensi* (中國粉絲; China fans) instead of *huaren fensi* (華人粉絲; ethnic Chinese fans) is being employed. While the two may seem interchangeable to the mainland Chinese, it makes a big difference to the larger ethnic Chinese outside mainland China. As reflected in the survey, less than 10 percent of the non-mainland

Chinese fans outside of mainland China identify themselves with the name *Zhongguo fensi* or *Zhongguo mama*. Aside from the possible stereotype, the sense of uneasiness in identifying with this name largely comes from the perceived difference between *Zhongguoren* and *huaren*; the former refers to a heavily coded national identity, and the latter an ethnic identity across nations. As Fran Martin (2014, 36) elucidates, *huaren* is a specific term that "indexes a de-nationalised Chineseness that is transnational in reach" and includes Sinophone communities inside and outside mainland China. Overseas ethnically Chinese people like Saintsup are more often known as *huaren*, or sometimes *huaqiao* or *huayi*, rather than *Zhongguoren*. Therefore, *huaren fensi* and *huaren mama* in this case would be more inclusive alternatives in addressing the Sinophone fandom at large. While ethnic Chinese fans in Southeast Asian countries could shout out their dissimilarity with pride, fans in predominantly Chinese regions such as Taiwan and Hong Kong choose to downplay their uneasiness. Despite feeling aggrieved, they see this silence necessary in order not to affect their beloved idol's reputation and his mainland China market with any unnecessary dispute triggered by the nationalistic zeal of other parties.

In a way, it is also some kind of nationalistic zeal that fosters a strong bond between the mainland Chinese mom fans and Saintsup. As abovementioned, many Sinophone fans call Saintsup by his Chinese name, Mingming. Being of Chinese descent in Thailand, Saintsup was given the Chinese name Huang Mingming at birth. If the Saintsup-MingEr relationship is bonded by the family metaphor, the Chinese ancestry of Saintsup reinforces the imaginary kinship of many mainland Chinese mom fans. Chineseness is seen as an essentially and hermetically shared trait of the ethnic Chinese across time and space (Heinrich 2014). Among the Sinophone mom fans I interviewed, mainland Chinese fans particularly feel closer to Saintsup or proud because of the same cultural root; they feel like they are the same deep down, to the bone and the blood. They are also more inclined to attribute his positive traits, such as his business mind and efficiency, to his Chinese, or more specifically Teo-Swa, origin. It is this seemingly uncontested yet imaginary trans-Asian kinship that calls for scrutiny with a critical lens of Sinophonicity.

Likewise, Saintsup's love for the dragon could also arouse this kindred feeling among many mainland Chinese fans. Most mom fans I interviewed interpreted this dragon as the Chinese dragon when asked to compare it with Saintsup. Contrary to the bunny that is associated with Saintsup's cuteness, almost all mainland Chinese fans relate Saintsup's dragon obsession to his Chineseness, evident that he has not forgotten his Chinese lineage, for Chinese people are often said to be the descendants of the dragon. Prioritizing this shared cultural root of Saintsup, these mainland Chinese fans displace Saintsup's Sino-Thai identity from a Chinese ethnicity of Thai national to become an essentialized Chinese in

Thailand (and somehow disregard his Thai-ness).[7] Owing to this association of Saintsup with Chineseness, together with Saintsup's compassionate personality, mainland Chinese mom fans are particularly eager to offer generous support to Saintsup.

Due to the geographical distance and impossibility of visiting Thailand during the COVID-19 pandemic, mainland Chinese moms translate their love into material support. Means of material support include mass purchase of Saintsup's own brand SaanSook, sending extravagant gifts and food support, buying airtime in the huge LED billboards outside landmark shopping malls in downtown Bangkok, registering stars in the sky in Saintsup's name, being top spenders of the products endorsed by Saintsup, sending money garlands and bouquets in fan-meetings, and so on. On the one hand, this could be seen as an engagement of conspicuous support among (sub-)fandoms; on the other hand, there is no denying that this very generous support is a labor of love (Duffett 2013, 23), or in the Chinese fannish term, "powered by love." Like what Hami said, they always want to give the best to Saintsup: the best gifts, the best support. They see consumption as their duty to support their idol in the showbiz industry and themselves as active, accountable contributors to their idol's marketability and media exposure both outside and inside the Great Firewall (GFW).

The language barrier, in addition to the resolutions and connectivity compromised due to the GFW, are inevitable hindrances for fans in mainland China to being in touch with Saintsup. Even though most *Taifu* are translated by semi-professional Thai-Chinese subbing groups, other live events or online communications depend on fans' amateur translations out of passion—again, as a labor of love—to fill this gap. As Hye-Kyung Lee (2014) argues, fans in the transnational setting act as "both gate-opener and gate-keeper via choosing, mediating, circulating and promoting cultural texts beyond its country of origin" (201). Such selective and sometimes biased translation was particularly apparent when it comes to issues such as social movements and sexuality. On top of being gate-openers and gatekeepers that construct and shape the Sinophone fandom, fans and amateur translators could sometimes be also gate-twisters. When the decontextualized snippet translations with varying accuracy are further circulated online, words may be twisted due to partial translation, mistranslation, out-of-context translation and interpretation, or different interpretations of the translation. The distorted information, in this age of cyber-Balkanization, becomes rumours archived in the social media database and further breeds toxicity, haters and antis in the *Taifu* fandom. Inter- or intra- fandom flame wars could thus be easily triggered in the name of "love" and "protection."

---

7. Interestingly, mainland Chinese fans also tend to overlook Saintsup's Teochew proficiency, as if Chinese language equates monolingually to only Mandarin.

Despite that the Sinophone mom fans may have differing perceptions of the term "Chinese moms" and varied desired means of support, their views on Saintsup's move towards the mainland China market are surprisingly in tune with each other. Whilst most mom fans understand and are happy for Saintsup's success in the mainland China market, they also show concern and worries. Snowy (31 years old, Hong Kong, fan since January 2019) worried that Saintsup's health will be compromised, for work-life balance is not valued in her understanding of the mainland China showbiz industry. Jiepin, who is an artist manager, an insider of the mainland China showbiz industry, shared a different concern: despite the trend of *danmei* TV adaptations (TV series adapted from BL novels) in China, she reckoned that people both inside and outside the mainland China showbiz industry look down on BL actors, so it will be better if Saintsup enters the mainland China market in a different capacity. Also aware of the different circumstances of the mainland China showbiz industry and fandom is Bagel. Considering Saintsup's will to bring happiness to everyone, Bagel worried that Saintsup will be overstressed when he needs to cater to the many different stakeholders there, which is an impossible mission.

Although many Sinophone mom fans are drawn closer by the imaginary kinship reinforced by what they believe as the common Chinese heritage and culture they share, they are not unaware of Saintsup's Thai-ness, as he has been dedicated to helping the Thai community, as well as promoting Thai industries, tourism, and economy. The differences and distance are sometimes necessary, especially when fans need to rationalize certain visuals, aesthetics, or practice on which they differ. Many mainland Chinese fans would use the othering term *Tatai* (They, the Thai) to dismiss the differences as cultural differences. It is this simultaneous closeness and distance that helps create the unique Saintsup in the eyes of his Sinophone mom fans, differentiate him from other local and overseas actors, as well as catalyze the many queerly motherly fantasies surrounding him.

The Queerly Motherly Fantasy

If it is a kindred feeling that arouses the stronger affections of the mom fans toward Saintsup, it is possibly the distance and foreignness of him that fulfill the fantasy for them. As Martin (2017) illustrates with the BL scene in Taiwan, the double foreignness in both gender and national-cultural identification in Japanese BL texts "enables a pleasurable exploration of an expansive imaginative, affective and erotic space" (210–11). This "double foreignness" could also shed light on understanding the transnational Sinophone fandom of Saintsup.

Tracing the origin of the Sinophone mom fans' affection to Saintsup, it is no surprise that what first drew their attention is Saintsup's *Taifu*. Many Thai directors, actresses, and actors, Saintsup included, said they participate in Y-series in a bid to contribute to the LGBTQ community. In series *Love By Chance* (2018),

Why R U? (2020) and *Let's Fight Ghost* (2021), as well as *lakorns* such as *The Leaves* (2019) and *My Mischievous Fiancée* (แม่ครัวคนใหม่) (2021), Saintsup embodies different gender roles and gender identities. Along with his own character, fans could see in him an alternative boyhood or young manhood: one that does not sever himself from love, communication, and compassion, and not (yet) fully moulded by or succumbed to the oftentimes toxic patriarchal masculinity that despises cuteness, femininity, queerness, and interdependency. It is these alternative and diverse masculinities that capture the hearts of mom fans besides the homoerotic fantasy they seek.

Homoerotic fantasy is key to the *fujoshi* as an escape from the heteropatriarchy, exploration to transgressive sex and sexuality, and aspiration for ideal romance (Welker 2006). Like most other BL texts, Y-series can both reinforce and contest the conventional masculinity (Jenkins 2013, 206). They, at the same time, reinforce the homonormativity of cosmopolitan masculine "white Asian" (Kang 2013) and open up possibilities to reimagine manhood and transgress sexuality. The double foreignness of Y-series is likely to facilitate and inspire further imagination and fantasy of the viewers' ideal partnership with their favorite "one-and-only" BL pairing—in the case of my interviewees, TutorFighter in *Why R U?* and, subsequently, ZaintSee in real life. These mom fans shared with me how much they adore the couple with non-rigid gender roles, how strong the chemistry is between them, and how complementary the two are that they make each other a better person.[8] In ZaintSee, they see their ideal, reciprocal, equal partnership that is to a certain extent liberating from the rigid hierarchical heteropatriarchy.

What's intriguing here is: how would these fans, who identify as Saintsup's mom fans, view the homoerotic love scenes in the series? These mom fans are delighted to see Saintsup happy being with someone he likes, but they view the love scenes differently. Jiepin, Bagel, Shasha (30 years old, Kuala Lumpur, Malaysia, fan since July 2020), Datong, and Guoguo found themselves retreating back to an ordinary viewer and/or *fujoshi* and shipper stan position, viewing Saintsup as the character in the series. Datong added that her mom fan identity emerges mostly when watching ZaintSee's everyday interactions. She also wondered what it would be like for a mother watching her child playing love scenes. Perhaps Hsuching, Mani, and Hami could explain this mindset a bit. Hsuching said she did watch from the perspective of a mother, and that was

---

8. Most of my interviewees explained that they adore ZaintSee, for Saintsup and Zee are a strong/strong pair (強強 or 強強配) both in the series and in real life (as seen from their interactions in behind-the-scene footage, events, and livestreams). Instead of the stereotypical dominant *seme* and subordinate *uke* roles, fans see in ZaintSee mutual understanding, love, and support. Datong even said that she found watching ZaintSee happier than being in a romantic relationship herself. In other words, the relationship between Saint and Zee are more equal. Both of them are strong, and they are both versatile instead of taking a clear and rigid seme/uke role.

why she would sometimes shy away from the scene. Also watching them as a mother are Mani and Hami. Hami said she would appreciate the hot kissing scenes, and Mani was caught in a dilemma between "Babe, you are too young. You shouldn't be doing this!" and "My babe is so good at this." Luna has more complex feelings about the situation. She thought that she would have multiple identifications while enjoying the scenes; following her feelings, she could be watching from the perspective of mother, elder sister, girlfriend, or even boyfriend. This also shows that the mom fan identification is malleable.

The mom fan identification can be seen as a primary identity that fans use to relate themselves to Saintsup. Against the homoerotic backdrop of *Taifu*, rarely do *fujoshi* fans project themselves into the scene. In real life, intergenerational heterosexual romance with older women is not encouraged, if not condemned, so positioning oneself as the mother or elder sister is more legitimate when showing their tremendous affection towards a younger male idol. Whereas the so-called traditional Chinese culture is rather ambiguous about mothers projecting their desires towards their sons, the modern policing of sexuality conditions these mom fans, provoking the incest taboo when claiming the mom fan position and desiring this son figure. Nevertheless, as mentioned early on, the boundary between mom fans and girlfriend fans is not as rigid as some mom fans have described it. Luna noted that when Saintsup looks tempting and "boyfriendable," her fannish position would transpose from a mom to a girlfriend. From the fact that 32.5 percent of the mom fans in the survey also identify themselves as girlfriend fans at the same time, it is clear that multiple identificatory positions are possible in the fandom.

To cut a long story short, this queerly motherly fantasy is multilayered. It begins with the queer fantasy of the *fujoshi* watching BL TV series. Fantasizing the male same-sex romance in the series, these media fans are drawn by the chemistry of the BL couple ZaintSee in addition to Saintsup's versatile masculinities and *ke'ai* personality to become celebrity fans of Saintsup. Due to Saintsup's *ke'ai*, fans of different age and sex transgress or defy the "natural order" of the heteropatriarchal kinship and queerly assume a motherly position that is further buttressed by an imaginary shared cultural root. This motherly position, at fans' disposal, then challenges the supposedly immutable mother identity with its fluid and multiple identificatory positions and its conditional unconditional love.

The Conditional Unconditional Love

From *Taifu fujoshi* audience to Saintsup's mom fans, these fans position themselves primarily as a mother. This position shapes their fannish affection and performance. In projecting onto the idol their personal hopes and fantasies (Hills 2002, 65), mom fans perform, in their own conception, as the best mom, unconditionally loving their best boy Saintsup. This *Taifu*-based fan-as-mother/ idol-as-son imagination endorses a young man's need for tender loving care and acknowledges the fluidity of sexuality. This mom position, at its best, allows the mother identity to break free from biology, whether it be age, biological sex, or blood tie, sexual orientation, as well as the heterosexist binary subject/object model of desire. However, since this mother-son imagination is very much within the capitalist heteropatriarchal formulation of the family and parenting, at its worst, it breeds material parenting, domineering mothers, and helicopter mothers that cosset the idol to a point where the behavior might become manipulating or overprotective. The protectiveness might develop into manipulation that at some point becomes a hindrance to the idol's socialization and career (Yan and Yang 2021). The tremendous investment of fans' affection and money also makes many prone to emotional blackmail that demands the idol's returns of their "unconditional" devotion. This dissolves the claim that mom fans' love is unconditional.

Mom fans are fans, so their love is conditional. Fans' passion oscillates in response to how much the idol realizes their fantasized ideal; so does the passion of mom fans. In the case of Saintsup, the unprecedented 2020 pandemic lockdown provided the best time and space for many Sinophone fans to indulge in *Taifu* and his online fandom, resulting in an intense devotion in immense affective labour during the period. Months later, when fans have gone back to their daily routine, and/or witnessed the ridicule and hostility within the fandom, their engagement and identification with the fandom may be gradually undermined. Since engaging in a transnational fandom is more demanding, fans would be less eager to spend as much time and effort when their volition drops off. As Duffett (2013, 279) puts it, some fans have lasting dedication and some are more nomadic, whether they be mom fans, elder-sis fans, girlfriend fans, solo stans, or shipper stans. For this parakin identity is a projective identification, fans could readily disclaim this identity just as easily as they claim it. That is to say, Saintsup does not need to be afraid: it is not a case of his moms not loving him anymore, but that they are moms no more.

Individual fans identifying themselves as the idol's mother may not be new, but mom fandoms have become prominent among young Asian male idols, and more visible thanks to social media. In the case of Saintsup's mom fandom, we may understand it as a group of fans—female, male, and non-binary, young and old, straight and queer, local and overseas—realizing their fantasy towards a young Thai actor beyond the heterosexist definition by claiming the mother position, rationalizing their strong affection as motherly love. And this imaginary mother-child bond is strengthened among many Sinophone mom fans due to Saintsup's Chinese lineage. This queerly mother position could be an expedient resolution to the nonnormative intergenerational romance taboo, homoerotic fantasy, or a conscious choice of these desiring subjects.

Since this motherly love is shaped by individual fans' own conception of maternity from their unique experience and specific culture, the Sinophone mom fandom of Saintsup illustrates a manifold and distinctive picture of a transnational, transmedia, transcultural queer affective alliance framed in a heteropatriarchal envisioning of kinship that begins with their queer TV viewing experience. From watching *Taifu* to stanning Saintsup, Sinophone mom fans take up and perform the motherly role by infantilizing and cosseting their idol, as well as engaging in affective labour and consumption. The very queer nature of this mom fandom transforms the supposedly inelastic kinship in the Sinophone setting and liberates these mom fans from the norms and taboos of the heteropatriarchy, so that fantasies of all sorts can be played out. Now, Saintsup is moving beyond the Y-series, venturing upon different genres of series and films, and managing his own artist management company cum production house, IdolFactory, but his mom fandom will continue to make and queer spaces in the media, cyberspace, and everyday life to unceasingly interrogate the norms with their motherly love and fantasy.

Appendix 9.1: Online Questionnaire[9]

Part 1

1. When did you start following Saint?
2. From which online platforms do you receive updates about Saint?
3. Which official accounts of Saint have you followed or subscribed to?
4. How much do you like Saint's role in the following series?
5. Are you looking forward to watching Saint's upcoming series "Let's Fight Ghost"?

Part 2

1. Please use three adjectives to describe Saint.
2. Which names do you like to use when talking about Saint?
3. By what means do you support Saint?
4. Which of the following fan types are you identified with?
5. Which of the following fandoms are you identified with?
6. When Saintsup addresses his fans with the following names, do you think you are one of them?
7. Do you have other fannish experiences?

Part 3

1. Sex
2. Sexual orientation
3. Year of birth
4. BL viewing experience
5. Place of current residence
6. Place of origin
7. Occupation
8. Language

---

9. This is an online questionnaire entitled "Saint 黃明明華人粉絲研究" [A study on Saint Huang Mingming's Sinophone fandom], opened from July 15 to July 25, 2020 at https://cloud.itsc.cuhk.edu.hk/mycuform/view.php?id=553897. The questionnaire was originally in Traditional Chinese characters, and this is an English translation of its questions.

Appendix 9.2: Interview Questions

Part 1

1. When and how did you start adoring Saint?
2. What do you like him the best?
3. Do you talk about Saint with your colleagues, friends, or family?
4. In what ways do you think he is different from other stars or celebrities?
5. Please share your favourite photos or video clips of Saint.
6. What is your most unforgettable scene/anecdote of Saint?
7. What are your least favourite photos of his?

Part 2

1. Do you have the habit or prior experience of watching Thai series? How long have you watched them?
2. In what ways do you think Thai series are different from series of other regions?
3. In what ways do you think Thai stars are different from stars of other regions?
4. What do you think about the following roles played by Saint in different series?
5. Which one do you like the best? Which CP? Why?
6. Is this your favourite plot and persona in BL stories?
7. Having watched these series, have you learnt more about the situation of the sexual minority in Thailand? As far as you know, what is it like?
8. Among these roles and Saint himself, which personality do you like more? Why?

Part 3

1. Did you sign up for more social media accounts because of Saint? Which one do you prefer to use for receiving the latest news and information about Saint? Why?
2. What are the pros and cons of using these different online platforms? Are there any differences in terms of fan discussion and atmosphere among them?
3. What is the biggest problem you encounter? How do you usually solve it? Are you worried or scared about bypassing state censorship and viewing BL?

4. Which accounts do you follow? In which language(s) are the posts you read most often written? Chinese, English, or Thai?
5. Do you know any other fans personally?
6. What do you think is unique about Saint's fandom?
7. Would you spend money on supporting Saint? Is there an upper limit?
8. There are haters and anti-fans on the internet; do you read their posts? Would you try to defend Saint?
9. Are there any kinds of support that you would not do?
10. What kinds of support do you appreciate? What kind of support do you not appreciate?
11. What kind of support do you think Saint would like to see the most from his fans?
12. Do you plan to watch the online fan-meeting on September 20?

Part 4

1. Many often compare Saint to a bunny; do you think he is like a bunny? In what ways do you think he is similar to and different from a bunny?
2. Saint often compares himself to a dragon; what do you think? Is he like a dragon?
3. Is Saint's Chinese lineage special to you?
4. Do you think the #Newwy incident has affected the relationship between Saint's Chinese and Thai fans?

Part 5

1. What do you think about mom fans? What is the mentality of mom fans? What would mom fans do and not do? Is there an age limit for mom fans? Are mom fans necessarily older female fans?
2. What are the differences among mom fans, girlfriend fans, and sister fans?
3. How did you decide to become a mom fan?
4. Are there solo fans and CP fans among mom fans? Are there conflicts among these identities?
5. If your favourite CP no longer work together, will this affect your adoration of Saint?
6. One day when Saint matures and no longer acts as cute as he is now, will it affect your love for him or your position as a mom fan?
7. Are there different types of mom fans?
8. As a mom fan, do you view Saint's love scenes from the position of a mom?
9. What are your thoughts on Saint's Chinese mom fans? Saint's Chinese mom fans? How are they different from the mom fans of other regions?

10. Saint says that MingEr is a family. Do you think so? How are the two similar to or different from each other?
11. Saint's fandom is known as MingEr. What do you think about this name?
12. Has Saint changed your attitude, style, or ways of being a fan?
13. Besides your fannish habits, what else do you think Saint has changed about you?
14. What do you think a good mother should be like when it comes to nurturing children?
15. What would you do if your child comes out of the closet to you one day?

Final Question: If you could leave a message to Saint as a mom fan, what would you like to say to him?

References

Abate, Michelle Ann. 2011. "Introduction: Special Issue on Tomboys and Tomboyism." *Journal of Lesbian Studies* 15, no. 4: 407–11. https://doi.org/10.1080/10894160.2011.532026.
Agha, Asif. 2011a. "Meet Mediatization." *Language & Communication* 31, no. 3: 163–70. https://doi.org/10.1016/j.langcom.2011.03.006.
Agha, Asif. 2011b. "Large and Small Scale Forms of Personhood." *Language & Communication* 31, no. 3: 171–80. https://doi.org/10.1016/j.langcom.2011.02.006.
Ahmed, Sara. 2014. *The Cultural Politics of Emotion*. New York: Routledge.
Amar, Nathanel. 2018. "'你有 Freestyle 吗?' (Do You Freestyle?): The Roots of Censorship in Chinese Hip-Hop." *China Perspectives*, no. 1–2. Accessed July 1, 2021. https://www.cefc.com.hk/article/ni-you-freestyle-ma-roots-chinese-hip-hop-censorship/.
Ang, Ien. 2001. *On Not Speaking Chinese*. New York: Routledge.
Appadurai, Arjun. 1996. *Modernity at Large: Cultural Dimensions of Globalization*. Minneapolis: University of Minnesota Press.
Arstin. 2020. "Tanwan shoubu poyi tongzhi dianying, 《Kezai Ni Xindide Mingzi》 shifou jishen jingdian dianying de shentan?" 台灣首部破億同志電影,《刻在你心底的名字》是否擠身經典電影的神壇? [The first tongzhi film in Taiwan reached 0.1 billion box office, whether *Your Name Engraved Herein* can be considered a classic film]. *The News Lens*. Last modified December 11, 2020. https://www.thenewslens.com/article/144487.
Bacon-Smith, Camille. 1992. *Enterprising Women: Television Fandom and the Creation of Popular Myth*. Philadelphia: University of Pennsylvania Press.
Bai, Meijiadai. 2022. "Regulation of Pornography and Criminalization of BL Readers and Authors in Contemporary China." *Cultural Studies* 36, no. 2: 279–301. https://doi.org/10.1080/09502386.2021.1912805.
Bai, Ruoyun. 2015a. "'Clean Up the Screen': Regulating Television Entertainment in the 2000s." In *Chinese Television in the Twenty-First Century: Entertaining the Nation*, edited by Ruoyun Bai and Geng Song, 69–86. New York: Routledge.
Bai, Ruoyun. 2015b. *Staging Corruption: Chinese Television and Politics*. Hong Kong: Hong Kong University Press.
Bai, Ruoyun, and Geng Song. 2015. "Introduction." In *Chinese Television in the Twenty-First Century: Entertaining the Nation*, edited by Ruoyun Bai and Geng Song, 1–14. New York: Routledge.

Bai, Ruoyun, and Geng Song, eds. 2015. *Chinese Television in the Twenty-First Century: Entertaining the Nation*. New York: Routledge.

Balding, Christopher. 2017. "The Soft Power of Chinese Censorship." *The Asia Dialogue*, November 6, 2017. Accessed July 1, 2021. https://theasiadialogue.com/2017/11/06/the-soft-power-of-chinese-censorship/.

Banet-Weiser, Sarah. 2012. *Authentic TM: The Politics and Ambivalence in a Brand Culture*. New York: New York University Press.

Banet-Weiser, Sarah. 2018. *Empowered: Popular Feminism and Popular Misogyny*. Durham, NC: Duke University Press.

Banet-Weiser, Sarah, Rosalind Gill, and Catherine Rottenberg. 2019. "Postfeminism, Popular Feminism and Neoliberal Feminism? Sarah Banet-Weiser, Rosalind Gill, and Catherine Rottenberg in Conversation." *Feminist Theory* 21, no. 1: 3–24. https://doi.org/10.1177/1464700119842555.

Bao, Hongwei. 2018. *Queer Comrades: Gay Identity and Tongzhi Activism in Postsocialist China*. Denmark: NIAS Press.

Bao, Hongwei. 2020. *Queer China: Lesbian and Gay Literature and Visual Culture under Postsocialism*. London: Routledge.

Bao, Hongwei. 2021. *Queer Media in China*. London: Routledge.

Barlow, Tani E. 2004. *The Question of Women in Chinese Feminism*. Durham, NC: Duke University Press.

Barnhurst, Kevin G. 2007. "Visibility as Paradox: Representation and Simultaneous Contrast." In *Media/Queered: Visibility and Its Discontents*, edited by Kevin G. Barnhurst, 1–20. New York: Peter Lang.

Bassi, Camila. 2016. "What's Radical About Reality TV? An Unexpected Tale from Shanghai of a Chinese Lesbian Antihero." *Gender, Place and Culture: A Journal of Feminist Geography* 23, no. 11: 1619–30. https://doi.org/10.1080/0966369X.2015.1136809.

Baudinette, Thomas. 2019. "*Lovesick, The Series*: Adapting Japanese 'Boys Love' to Thailand and the Creation of a New Genre of Queer Media." *South East Asia Research* 27, no. 2: 115–32. https://doi.org/10.1080/0967828X.2019.1627762.

BBC. 2016. "Zhongwen zouhong tongxinglian ticai wangluoju beipo xiajia" 中国走红同性恋题材网络剧被迫下架. [Popular Chinese gay-themed web series forcibly pulled]. *BBC News* 中文. Last modified February 24, 2016. https://www.bbc.com/zhongwen/simp/china/2016/02/160224_online_gay_drama_china.

BBC. 2021. "China NPC: Three-Child Policy Formally Passed into Law." Last modified August 20, 2021. Accessed September 1, 2021. https://www.bbc.com/news/world-asia-china-58277473.

Benjamin, Walter. 2010. "The Work of Art in the Age of Its Technological Reproducibility." Translated by Harry Zohn and Edmund Jephcott. In *The Norton Anthology of Theory and Criticism*, 2nd ed., edited by William E. Cain et al., 1051–71. New York: W. W. Norton & Company.

Berry, Chris. 1998. "East Palace, West Palace: Staging gay life in China." *Jump Cut: A Review of Contemporary Media*, no. 42: 84–89. https://www.ejumpcut.org/archive/onlinessays/JC42folder/EastWestPalaceGays.html.

Berry, Chris. 2000. "Happy Alone? Sad Young Men in East Asian Gay Cinema." *Journal of Homosexuality* 39, no. 3/4: 187–200. https://doi.org/10.1300/J082v39n03_07.

References

Berry, Chris. 2007. "The Chinese Side of the Mountain." *Film Quarterly* 60, no. 3: 32–37. https://doi.org/10.1525/fq.2007.60.3.32.

Berry, Chris. 2013. "Staging Gay Life in China: Zhang Yuan and East Palace, West Palace." In *Chinese Cinema: Critical Concepts in Media and Cultural Studies*, edited by Chris Berry, 242–53. New York: Routledge.

Berry, Chris, Fran Martin, and Audrey Yue, eds. 2003. *Mobile Cultures: New Media in Queer Asia*. Durham, NC: Duke University Press.

Bian, Jing 边静. *Jiaopian miyu: Huayu dianying zhong de tongxinglian huayu* 胶片密语: 华语电影中的同性恋话语. [Celluloid secrets: The discourses of homosexuality in Chinese cinemas]. Beijing: Communication University of China Press, 2007.

Billig, Michael. 2005. *Laughter and Ridicule: Towards a Social Critique of Humor*. London: Sage.

Boyd, David John. 2016. "'Nonsensical Is Our Thing!': Queering Fanservice as 'Deleuzional' Desire-Production in Studio Trigger's Kiru ra Kira/Kill la Kill." *Queer Studies in Media & Popular Culture* 1, no. 1: 61–83. https://doi.org/10.1386/qsmpc.1.1.61_1.

Bradley, Peri. 2012. "The Exotic Erotic: Queer Representations in the Context of Postcolonial Ethnicity on British TV." In *LGBT Transnational Identity and the Media*, edited by Christopher Pullen, 161–80. London: Palgrave Macmillan.

Brennan, Joseph. 2018a. "Queerbaiting: The 'Playful' Possibilities of Homoeroticism." *International Journal of Cultural Studies* 21, no. 2: 189–206. https://doi.org/10.1177/1367877916631050.

Brennan, Joseph. 2018b. "Slashbaiting, an Alternative to Queerbaiting." *The Journal of Fandom Studies* 6, no. 2: 187–204. https://doi.org/10.1386/jfs.6.2.187_1.

Brownell, Susan, and Jeffrey N. Wasserstrom. 2002. "Part Five: The Gender Rebels." In *Chinese Femininities, Chinese Masculinities: A Reader*, edited by Susan Brownell and Jeffrey N. Wasserstrom, 251–53. Berkeley, CA: University of California Press.

Burn, Shawn Meghan, A. Kathleen O'Neil, and Shirley Nederend. 1996. "Childhood Tomboyism and Adult Androgyny." *Sex Roles* 34, no. 5/6: 419–28. https://doi.org/10.1007/BF01547810.

Butler, Judith. 1986. "Sex and Gender in Simone de Beauvoir's Second Sex." *Yale French Studies* 72: 35–49. https://www.jstor.org/stable/2930225.

Butler, Judith. 1990. *Gender Trouble: Feminism and the Subversion of Identity*. New York: Routledge.

Butler, Judith. 1993. *Bodies that Matter: On the Discursive Limits of "Sex."* New York: Routledge.

Butler, Judith. 1995. "Melancholy Gender—Refused Identification." *Psychoanalytic Dialogues* 5, no. 2: 165–80.

Butler, Judith. 1997. *The Psychic Life of Power: Theories in Subjection*. Stanford: Stanford University Press.

Butler, Judith. 2004. *Precarious Life: The Powers of Mourning and Violence*. London: Verso.

Butler, Judith. 2009. *Frames of War: When Is Life Grievable?* London: Verso.

Cai, Shenshen. 2016. *Television Drama in Contemporary China: Political, Social, and Cultural Phenomena*. London: Routledge.

Califia, Patrick. 2004. "Androgyny." In *Encyclopedia of Lesbian, Gay, Bisexual and Transgender History in America*, edited by Marc Stein, 58–61. Detroit, MI: Charles Scribner's Sons.

Campbell, John. 2005. "Outing PlanetOut: Surveillance, Gay Marketing, and Internet Affinity Portals." *New Media and Society* 7, no. 5: 663–83. https://doi.org/10.1177/1461444805056011.

Carr, C. Lynn. 2005. "Tomboyism or Lesbianism? Beyond Sex/Gender/Sexual Conflation." *Sex Roles* 53, no. 1/2: 119–31. https://doi.org/10.1007/s11199-005-4286-5.

Chan, Jocelin. 2019. "6 Times *The Untamed* Was Like, 'Censorship Who?' and Gave the Gays Their Rights." *PULP*. Last modified November 15, 2019. https://www.pulp-usu.com/pop/2019/11/15/6-times-the-untamed-was-like-censorship-who-and-gave-the-gays-their-rights.

Chang, Shih-Lun. 2010. "The Face of Independence? A Visual Record of Taiwanese Indie Music Scene." *Inter-Asia Cultural Studies* 11, no. 1: 89–99. https://doi.org/10.1080/14649370903403611.

Chao, Antonia. 2000. "Global Metaphors and Local Strategies in the Construction of Taiwan's Lesbian Identities." *Culture, Health & Sexuality* 2, no. 4: 377–90. https://doi.org/10.1080/13691050050174404.

Chao, Shi-Yan. 2020. *Queer Representations in Chinese-Language Film and the Cultural Landscape*. Amsterdam: Amsterdam University Press.

Chao, Shi-Yan. 2021. "The Signifying Tomboy and the Thai TV Series *Club Friday To Be Continued: She Changed*." *Communication, Culture & Critique*, September 20 (online first). https://doi.org/10.1093/ccc/tcab060.

Chao, Shih-chen. 2017. "Cosplay, Cuteness, and *Weinang*: The Queered *Ke'ai* of Male Cosplayers as 'Fake Girls'." In *Boys' Love, Cosplay, and Androgynous Idols: Queer Fan Cultures in Mainland China, Hong Kong, and Taiwan*, edited by Maud Lavin, Ling Yang, and Jing Jamie Zhao, 20–44. Hong Kong: Hong Kong University Press.

Chasin, Alexandra. 2000. *Selling Out: The Gay and Lesbian Movement Goes to Market*. New York. St. Martin's.

Chen, Xu, and Wilfred Yang Wang. 2019. "How China Is Legally Recognizing Same-Sex Couples, But Not Empowering Them." *The Conversation*, October 1, 2019. Accessed July 1, 2021. http://theconversation.com/how-china-is-legally-recognising-same-sex-couples-but-not-empowering-them-122270.

Cheung, Carlos K.F. 2017. "Trans-Border Televisual Musicscape: Regionalizing Reality TV *I Am a Singer* in China and Hong Kong." *Global Media and China* 2, no. 1: 90–108. https://doi.org/10.1177/2059436417695815.

Chiang, Feichi. 2016. "Counterpublic but Obedient: A Case of Taiwan's BL Fandom." *Inter-Asian Cultural Studies* 17, no. 2: 223–38. https://doi.org/10.1080/14649373.2016.1170311.

Chiang, Howard, ed. 2012. *Transgender China*. New York: Palgrave MacMillan.

Chiang, Howard. 2014a. "Archiving Peripheral Taiwan: The Prodigy of the Human and Historical Narration." *Radical History Review* 120, October: 204–25. https://doi.org/10.1215/01636545-2704110.

Chiang, Howard. 2014b. "Queering China: A New Synthesis." *GLQ* 20, no. 3: 353–78. https://doi.org/10.1215/10642684-2422701.

Chiang, Howard. 2019. "Gay Marriage in Taiwan and The Struggle for Recognition." *Current History* 118, no. 809: 241–43. https://doi.org/10.1525/curh.2019.118.809.241.

Chiang, Howard. 2021. *Transtopia in the Sinophone Pacific*. New York: Columbia University Press.

References

Chiang, Howard, and Alvin K. Wong. 2016. "Queering the Transnational Turn: Regionalism and Queer Asias." *Gender, Place & Culture* 23, no. 11: 1643–56. https://doi.org/10.1080/0966369X.2015.1136811.

Chiang, Howard, and Alvin K. Wong. 2020a. "Introduction—Queer Sinophone Studies: Interdisciplinary Synergies." In *Keywords in Queer Sinophone Studies*, edited by Howard Chiang, and Alvin K. Wong, 1–15. New York: Routledge.

Chiang, Howard, and Alvin K. Wong, eds. 2020b. *Keywords in Queer Sinophone Studies*. London: Routledge.

Chiang, Howard, and Ari Larissa Heinrich, eds. 2014. *Queer Sinophone Studies*. New York: Routledge.

Chin, Bertha, and Lori Hitchcock Morimoto. 2013. "Towards a Theory of Transcultural Fandom." *Participations* 10, no. 1: 92–108. https://www.participations.org/Volume%2010/Issue%201/7%20Chin%20&%20Morimoto%2010.1.pdf.

China Daily. 2012. "Up Young! Had a Perfect Ending." Last modified September 5, 2012. Accessed July 1, 2021. https://web.archive.org/web/20160304231800/http://www.chinadaily.com.cn/hqpl/yssp/2012-09-05/content_6925569.html.

China Entertainment Network. 2016. "Liu Yuxin's Professionalism Dominanted the Stage and Won the Praises of Nicky Wu and Su Hong." Last modified May 5, 2016. Accessed July 1, 2021. https://m.sohu.com/n/447783978/.

Chodorow, Nancy. 1999. "Why Women Mother." In *The Reproduction of Mothering: Psychoanalysis and the Sociology of Gender (with a New Preface)*, 11–39. Berkeley: University of California Press.

Chow, Rey. 1999. "Nostalgia of the New Wave: Structure in Wong Kar-wai's *Happy Together*." *Camera Obscura* 14, no. 3: 30–49. https://doi.org/10.1215/02705346-14-3_42-30.

Christian, Aymar Jean. 2016. "Video Stars: Marketing Queer Performance in Networked Television." In *Intersectional Internet: Race, Sex, and Culture Online*, edited by Safiya Umoja Noble and Brendesha M. Tynes, 95–114. New York: Peter Lang.

Chun, Allen. 1996. "Fuck Chineseness: On the Ambiguities of Ethnicity as Culture as Identity." *Boundary 2* 23, no. 2: 111–38. https://doi.org/10.2307/303809.

CNSA. 2017. "Zhongguo wangluo shiting jiemu fuwu xiehui fabu 'wangluo shiting jiemu neirong shenhe tongze'." 中国网络视听节目服务协会发布《网络视听节目内容审核通则》 [China Netcasting Services Association issues "internet and television programming censorship policy]. *CNSA*. Last modified June 30, 2017. http://www.cnsa.cn/art/2017/6/30/art_1505_26038.html.

Cole, Shaun. 2000. "'Macho Man': Clones and the Development of a Masculine Stereotype." *Fashion Theory* 4, no. 2: 125–40. https://doi.org/10.2752/136270400779108735.

Connell, Raewyn W. 1992. "A Very Straight Gay: Masculinity, Homosexual Experience, and the Dynamics of Gender." *American Sociological Review* 57, no. 6: 735–51.

Connell, Raewyn W. 2005. *Masculinities*. Berkeley: University of California Press.

Coonan, Clifford. 2016. "Women in China: Family Panning Rules Relaxed." *Irish Times*. Last modified December 29, 2016. Accessed June 1, 2021. https://radiichina.com/after-the-international-hype-chinas-beyonce-fails-to-make-produce-101-cut/.

Craig, Traci, and Jessica LaCroix. 2011. "Tomboy as Protective Identity." *Journal of Lesbian Studies* 15, no. 4: 450–65. https://doi.org/10.1080/10894160.2011.532030.

Creery, Jennifer. 2018. "In Pictures: 'Call for the Law, Equality for All'—Hong Kong Pride Attendees Demand Greater LGBT+ Legal Protection." *Hong Kong Free Press*. Last modified November 18, 2018. https://hongkongfp.com/2018/11/18/pictures-call-law-equality-hong-kong-pride-attendees-demand-greater-lgbt-legal-protection/.

Davies, Gloria, and M. E. Davies. 2010. "Jin Xing: China's Transsexual Star of Dance." In *Celebrity in China*, edited by Louise Edwards and Elaine Jeffreys, 169–91. Hong Kong: Hong Kong University Press.

Davis, Glyn, and Gray Needham, eds. 2009. *Queer TV: Theories, Histories, Politics*. New York: Routledge.

Day, Faithe, and Aymar Jean Christian. 2017. "Locating Black Queer TV: Fans, Producers, and Networked Publics on YouTube." *Transformative Works and Cultures* 24. http://dx.doi.org/10.3983/twc.2017.867.

DeAngelis, Michael. 2014. "Introduction." In *Reading the Bromance: Homosocial Relationships in Film and Television*, edited by Michael DeAngelis, 1–26. Detroit: Wayne State University Press.

Deleuze, Gilles, and Félix Guattari. 1987. *A Thousand Plateaus: Capitalism and Schizophrenia*. Translated by Brian Massumi. Minneapolis: University of Minnesota Press.

Derrida, Jacques. 1992. "'The Strange Institution Called Literature': An Interview with Jacques Derrida." Translated by Geoffrey Bennington and Rachel Bowlby. In *Acts of Literature*, edited by Derek Attridge, 33–75. New York: Routledge.

"Dianshiju neirong zhizhong tongze" 电视剧内容制作通则 [General rules for content production of TV series"]. 2019. *China TV Drama Production Industry Association*. Last modified August 20, 2019. http://www.ctpia.com.cn/index/xhzcq/detail?id=178.

Ding, Yi 丁一. 2018. "Yidang jiemu yinfa de niangbao zhi zheng." 一旦节目引发的"娘炮之争" [Debate on *niang* through a TV program] *China Daily*, September 13, 2018. https://language.chinadaily.com.cn/a/201809/13/WS5b9a2e3ca31033b4f4655ebc.html.

Domundi TV. 2019. "10 คำถามที่คุณอยากรู้ กับ เซ้นต์ kissboys." Facebook video, 4:25. February 3, 2019. https://www.facebook.com/1136090346464096/videos/146673829571470.

Doty, Alexander. 1993. *Making Things Perfectly Queer*. Minneapolis: University of Minnesota Press.

dramapotatoe. 2021. "A New Chapter in C-Ent and Fan Culture: Summary of 'Qinglang' Clear Internet Campaign + 10 New Measure." August 30, 2021. Accessed April 1, 2022. https://dramapotatoe.com/a-new-chapter-in-c-ent-and-fan-culture-summary-of-qinglang-clear-internet-campaign-10-new-measures/.

Duffett, Mark. 2013. *Understanding Fandom: An Introduction to the Study of Media Fan Culture*. New York: Bloomsbury.

Duggan, Lisa. 2002. "The New Homonormativity: The Sexual Politics of Neoliberalism." In *Materializing Democracy: Towards a Revitalized Cultural Politics*, edited by Russ Castronovo and Dana D. Nelson, 175–94. Durham: Duke University Press.

Dyer, Richard. 1993. *The Matter of Images: Essays on Representations*. New York: Routledge.

Dyer, Richard. 1997. "The White Man's Muscles." In *Race and the Subject of Masculinities*, edited by Harry Stecopoulous and Michael Uebel, 286–314. Durham, NC: Duke University Press.

Dyer, Richard. 2002. *The Matter of Images: Essays on Representations*. 2nd edition. London: Routledge.

Edelman, Lee. 2004. *No Future: Queer Theory and the Death Drive*. Durham, NC: Duke University Press.

References

Edwards, Louise. 2016. "Aestheticizing Masculinity in *Honglou meng*: Clothing, Dress, and Decoration." In *Changing Chinese Masculinities: From Imperial Pillars of State to Global Real Men*, edited by Kam Louie, 90–112. Hong Kong: Hong Kong University Press.

Elfish. 2020. "Liu Yuxin Becomes the Center Position of the Theme Song of *Youth With You 2!*" *Goody25* (blog). April 6, 2020. Accessed July 1, 2021. https://www.goody25.com/mind7483993.

Ellis-Petersen, Hannah. 2016. "China Bans Depictions of Gay People on Television." *The Guardian*, March 4, 2016. Accessed July 1, 2021. https://www.theguardian.com/tv-and-radio/2016/mar/04/china-bans-gay-people-television-clampdown-xi-jinping-censorship.

Engebretsen, Elisabeth L. 2014. *Queer Women in Urban China: An Ethnography*. London: Routledge.

Engebretsen, Elisabeth L., and William F. Schroeder (with Hongwei Bao), eds. 2015. *Queer/Tongzhi China: New Perspectives on Research, Activism and Media Cultures*. Copenhagen: NIAS Press.

Evans, Harriet. 1997. *Women and Sexuality in China*. Oxford: Polity Press.

Fathallah, Judith. 2015. "'Moriarty's Ghost: Or the Queer Disruption of the BBC's Sherlock." *Television & New Media* 16, no. 5: 490–500. https://doi.org/10.1177/1527476414543528.

Feng, Jiayun. 2018. "Internal Memo Reveals Tighter Regulations on Chinese Films and Television Dramas." *Sup China*, June 12, 2018. Accessed July 1, 2021. https://supchina.com/2018/06/12/internal-memo-reveals-tighter-regulations-on-chinese-films-and-television-dramas/.

Feng, Jin. 2013. *Romancing the Internet: Producing and Consuming Chinese Web Romance*. Leiden: Brill.

Forrest, David. 1994. "'We're Here, We're Queer, and We're Not Going Shopping': Changing Gay Male Identities in Contemporary Britain." In *Dislocating Masculinity: Comparative Ethnographies*, edited by Andrea Cornwall and N. Lindisfarne, 97–110. London: Routledge.

Foucault, Michel. 1978. *The History of Sexuality: Volume I: An Introduction*. Trans. By Robert Hurley. New York: Pantheon Books.

Foucault, Michel. 1990. *The History of Sexuality. Vol. 1. An Introduction*. New York: Vintage Books.

Foucault, Michel. 2021. *Confessions of the Flesh: The History of Sexuality Volume 4*, edited by Gros Frédéric. Translated by Robert Hurley. New York: Pantheon Books.

French, David, and Michael Richards, eds. 2000. *Television in Contemporary China*. London: Sage.

Freud, Sigmund. 1949. *The Ego and the Id*. London: The Hogarth Press.

Fung, Carman. 2021. "TBG and Po: Discourses on Authentic Desire in 2010s Lesbian Subcultures in Hong Kong, China, and Taiwan." *Journal of Lesbian Studies* 25, no. 2: 141–58. https://doi.org/10.1080/10894160.2019.1694787.

Galbraith, Patrick. 2011. "Fujoshi: Fantasy Play and Transgressive Intimacy Among 'Rotten Girls' in Contemporary Japan." *Signs* 37, no. 1: 211–32. https://doi.org/10.1086/660182.

Galbraith, Patrick W, and Jason G. Karlin. 2012. *Idols and Celebrity in Japanese Media Culture*. London: Palgrave Macmillan.

Gater, Bruce, and Jasmine B. MacDonald. 2015. "Are Actors Really Real in Reality TV? The Changing Face of Performativity in Reality Television." *Fusion Journal* 7. Access July 1, 2021. https://fusion-journal.com/issue/007-fusion-mask-performance-performativity-and-communication/are-actors-really-real-in-reality-tv-the-changing-face-of-performativity-in-reality-television/.

Gill, Rosalind. 2007. "Postfeminist Media Culture: Elements of a Sensibility." *European Journal of Cultural Studies* 10, no. 2: 147–66. https://doi.org/10.1177/1367549407075898.

Gill, Rosalind. 2017. "The Affective, Cultural and Psychic Life of Postfeminism: A Postfeminist Sensibility 10 Years On." *European Journal of Cultural Studies* 20, no. 6: 606–26. https://doi.org/10.1177/1367549417733003.

Gill, Rosalind, and Christina Scharff, eds. 2011. *New Femininities: Postfeminism, Neoliberalism, and Subjectivity*. Hampshire: Palgrave Macmillan.

Gill, Rosalind, Karen Henwood, and Carl McLean. 2005. "Body Projects and the Regulation of Normative Masculinity." *Body & Society* 11, no. 1: 37–62.

Goffman, Erving. [1976] 1979. *Gender Advertisements*. London: The Macmillan Press.

Goldberg, RL. 2019. "Even This Review Is a Dildo: On Paul B. Preciado's *Countersexual Manifesto*." *Los Angeles Review of Books*, February 16, 2019. https://lareviewofbooks.org/article/even-this-review-is-a-dildo-on-paul-b-preciados-countersexual-manifesto/.

Goldie, Terry. 2014. *The Man Who Invented Gender: Engaging the Ideas of John Money*. Vancouver: University of British Columbia Press.

Gong, Haomin, and Xin Yang. 2018. *Reconfiguring Class, Gender, Ethnicity and Ethics in Chinese Internet Culture*. London: Routledge.

Gong, Yuan. 2017. "Media Reflexivity and Taste: Chinese Slash Fans' Queering of European Football." *Communication, Culture and Critique* 10, no. 1: 166–83. https://doi.org/10.1111/cccr.12140.

Gorfinkel, Lauren. 2018. *Chinese Television and National Identity Construction: The Cultural Politics of Music-Entertainment Programmes*. London: Routledge.

Green, Adam Isaiah. 2002. "Gay but Not Queer: Toward a Post-Queer Study of Sexuality." *Theory and Society* 31, no. 4: 521–45. https://www.jstor.org/stable/3108514.

Griffin, Gabriele. 2017. *A Dictionary of Gender Studies*. Oxford: Oxford University Press.

Gross, Larry. 2001. *Up from Invisibility: Lesbians, Gay Men, and the Media in America*. New York: Columbia University Press.

Grossberg, Lawrence. 1992. "Is There a Fan in the House? The Affective Sensibility of Fandom." In *The Adoring Audience: Fan Culture and Popular Media*, edited by Lisa A. Lewis, 50–65. London: Routledge.

Gui, Conglu 桂从路. 2018. "Shenme shi jintian gai you de 'nanxing qizhi'" 什么是今天该有的"男性气质" [What is the right masculinity for today's men]. *Renmin ribao* 人民日报, September 6, 2018. https://www.sohu.com/a/252524543_157164.

Guo, Shaohua. 2017. "When Dating Shows Encounter State Censors: A Case Study of *If You Are the One*." *Media, Culture & Society* 39, no. 4: 487–503. https://doi.org/10.1177/0163443716648492.

Hains, Rebecca C. 2012. *Growing Up With Girl Power: Girlhood on Screen and in Everyday Life*. New York: Peter Lang.

Halberstam, Judith. 1998. *Female Masculinity*. Durham, NC: Duke University Press.

Halberstam, Judith. 2012. "Global Female Masculinities." *Sexualities* 15, no. 3/4: 336–54. https://doi.org/10.1177/1363460712436480.

Halperin, David. 2003. "The Normalization of Queer Theory." *Journal of Homosexuality* 45, no. 2/3/4: 339–43. https://doi.org/10.1300/J082v45n02_17.

Hart, Kylo-Patrick R., ed. 2016. *Queer TV in the 21st Century: Essays on Broadcasting from Taboo to Acceptance*. Jefferson, NC: McFarland and Company.

He, Chengzhou. 2013. "Trespassing, Crisis, and Renewal: Li Yugang and Cross-Dressing Performance." *differences* 24, no. 2: 150–71. https://doi.org/10.1215/10407391-2335094.

He, Chengzhou. 2014. "Performance and the Politics of Gender: Transgender Performance in Contemporary Chinese Films." *Gender, Place & Culture* 21, no. 5: 622–36. https://doi.org/10.1080/0966369X.2013.810595.

Hebdige, Dick. [1979] 2002. *Subculture: The Meaning of Style*. London: Routledge.

Heinrich, Ari Larissa. 2014. "'A Volatile Alliance': Queer Sinophone Synergies Across Literature, Film and Culture." In *Queer Sinophone Cultures*, edited by Howard Chiang, and Ari Larissa Heinrich, 3–16. Hoboken: Taylor and Francis.

Hennessy, Rosemary. 1994. "Queer Visibility in Commodity Culture." *Cultural Critique*, no. 29: 31–76. https://www.jstor.org/stable/1354421.

Hennessy, Rosemary. 2000. *Profit and Pleasure: Sexual Identities in Late Capitalism*. 1st ed. New York: Routledge.

Higgins, Daryl. 2006. "Narcissism, the Adonic Complex, and the Pursuit of the Ideal." In *Gendered Outcasts and Sexual Outlaws: Sexual Oppression and Gender Hierarchies in Queer Men's Lives*, edited by Chris Kendall and Wayne Martino, 79–100. Binghamton: Harrington Park Press.

Hill, Annette. 2005. "Reality TV: Performance, Authenticity, and Television Audiences." In *A Companion to Television*, edited by Janet Wasko, 449–67. Oxford: Blackwell.

Hills, Matt. 2002. *Fan Cultures*. Sussex Studies in Culture and Communication. London: Routledge.

Hills, Matt. 2014. "Returning to 'Becoming-a-Fan' Stories: Theorising Transformational Objects and the Emergence/Extension of Fandom." In *The Ashgate Research Companion to Fan Cultures*, edited by Linda Duits, Koos Zwaan, and Stijn Reijnders, 9–22. Farnham, UK: Ashgate.

Hinsch, Bret. 1990. *Passions of the Cut Sleeve: The Male Homosexual Tradition in China*. Berkeley: University of California Press.

Hird, Derek. 2012. "The Paradox of Pluralisation: Masculinities, Androgyny and Male Anxiety in Contemporary China." In *Understanding Global Sexualities: New Frontiers*, edited by Peter Aggleton, Paul Boyce, Henrietta L. Moore, and Richard Parker, 49–65. London: Routledge.

Hird, Derek, and Geng Song. 2018. "Transnational Chinese Masculinities in a Global Age." In *The Cosmopolitan Dream: Transnational Chinese Masculinities in a Global Age*, edited by Derek Hird and Geng Song, 1–24. Hong Kong: Hong Kong University Press.

Hird, Derek, and Geng Song, eds. 2018. *The Cosmopolitan Dream: Transnational Chinese Masculinities in a Global Age*. Hong Kong: Hong Kong University Press.

Ho, Josephine Chuen-juei. 2010. "Queer Existence under Global Governance: A Taiwan Exemplar." *positions* 18, no. 2: 537–54. https://doi.org/10.1215/10679847-2010-013.

Ho, Loretta Wing Wah. 2009. *Gay and Lesbian Subculture in Urban China*. Oxon: Routledge.

Ho, Michelle H.S., Eva Cheuk-Yin Li, and Lucetta Y.L. Kam. 2021. "Editorial Introduction: Androgynous Bodies and Cultures in Asia." *Inter-Asia Cultural Studies* 22, no. 2: 129–38. https://doi.org/10.1080/14649373.2021.1927568.

Ho, Petula Sik Ying, Stevi Jackson, Siyang Cao, and Chi Kwok. 2018. "Sex with Chinese Characteristics: Sexuality Research in/on 21-st Century China." *Journal of Sex Research* 55, no. 4–5: 486–521. https://doi.org/10.1080/00224499.2018.1437593.

Hockx, Michel. 2015. *Internet Literature in China*. New York: Columbia University Press.

Hong Fincher, Leta. 2014. *Leftover Women: The Resurgence of Gender Inequality in China*. London: Zed Books.

Honig, Emily. 2002. "Maoist Mappings of Gender: Reassessing the Red Guards." In *Chinese Femininities/Chinese Masculinities: A Reader*, edited by Susan Brownell and Jeffrey N. Wasserstrom, 255–68. Berkeley: CA: University of California Press.

Horvat, Anamarija. 2020. "Crossing the Borders of Queer TV: Depictions of Migration and (Im)mobility in Contemporary LGBTQ Television." *Critical Studies in Television* 15, no. 3: 280–301. https://doi.org/10.1177/1749602020934091.

Hsiao, Jau-Jiun 蕭昭君. "'Niangniangqiang' shi zanmei ma?" 「娘娘腔」是讚美嗎? [Is 'sissy' a compliment?] *Taiwanese Feminist Scholars Association*, July 15, 2009. http://web.nanya.edu.tw/gec/news_detail.aspx?nno=52.

Hu, Brian. 2005. "*Formula 17*: Testing a Formula for Mainstream Cinema in Taiwan." *Senses of Cinema*, no. 34. Last modified February 2005. https://www.sensesofcinema.com/2005/feature-articles/formula_17/.

Hu, Kelly. 2016. "Between Informal and Formal Cultural Economy: Chinese Subtitle Groups and Flexible Accumulations in the Age of Online Viewing." In *Routledge Handbook of East Asian Popular Culture*, edited by Koichi Iwabuchi, Eva Tsai, and Chris Berry, 45–54. New York: Routledge.

Hu, Tingting, and Cathy Yue Wang. 2020. "Who is the Counterpublic? Bromance-as-Masquerade in Chinese Online Drama—S.C.I. Mystery." *Television & New Media* 22, no. 6: 671–86. https://doi.org/10.1177/1527476420937262.

Hu, Xin 胡鑫. 2019. "Zhanshi Zhongguo yuansu" 展示中国元素 [Display of Chinese elements]. *People's Daily Overseas*. Last modified June 28, 2019. http://media.people.com.cn/n1/2019/0628/c40606-31200385.html.

Hu, Yu-Ying. 2019. "Mainstreaming Female Masculinity, Signifying Lesbian Visibility: The Rise of Zhongxing Phenomenon in Transnational Taiwan." *Sexualities* 22, no. 1–2: 182–202. https://doi.org/10.1177/1363460717701690.

Huang, Angus. 2015. "Wo'men rang Caikangyong gudan de hezhi chugui zhejian shi" 我们让蔡康永孤单的,何止出柜这件事 [Coming-out is not the only thing we have done to make Kevin Tsai feel lonely] *Sanli Xinwenwang* 三立新聞網. Last modified June 23, 2015. https://www.setn.com/News.aspx?NewsID=81780.

Huang, Xiaohe 黄小河. 2016. "Ta cai bushi shenme yao'ezi, ta shi yizhi renzhen change de Zhou Shen" 他才不是什么幺蛾子,他是一只认证唱歌的周深 [He is not a moth, he is Zhou Shen who has kept singing]. *Pengpai* 澎湃. Last modified October 24, 2016. https://www.thepaper.cn/newsDetail_forward_1548289.

Huang, Xiaohe 黄小河. 2020. "*Yundongba shaonian* zong daoyan Li Chao: Mei ge ren dou kao shili, er bushi yanzhi bipin" 《运动吧少年》总导演李超:每个人都靠实力,而不是颜值比拼 [The chief director of *Let's Exercise, Boys*, Li Chao: Everyone replies on his or her ability, not how good s/he looks]. *Pengpai* 澎湃. Last modified July 25, 2020. https://www.thepaper.cn/newsDetail_forward_8434034.

Huang, Xin. 2013. "From 'Hyper-Feminine' to Androgyny: Changing Notions of Femininity in Contemporary China." In *Asian Popular Culture in Transition*, edited by John A. Lent and Lorna Fitzsimmons, 133–55. New York: Routledge.

Huang, Yu. 1994. "Peaceful Evolution: The Case of Television Reform in Post-Mao China." *Media, Culture and Society* 16, no. 2: 217–41. https://doi.org/10.1177/016344379401600203.

Hudson, Nikki. 2020. "All the Symbolism behind the WangXian ship in 'The Untamed'." *Film Daily*. Last modified January 20, 2020. https://filmdaily.co/news/the-untamed-wangxian-symbolism/.

"Hunan weishi *Yundongba shaonian* zhongbang fabu zhu shijue gainian, Z shidai yundongxi shaonian jijiang chaoran laoxi" 湖南卫视《运动吧少年》重磅发布主视觉概念，Z世代运动系少年即将超燃来袭 [The premiere event for Hunan TV's *Let's Exercise, Boys* emphasized the concept of visuality, the sports youth of generation Z is burgeoning and forthcoming]. 2020. *Hunantv.com*, June 15, 2020. http://zixun.hunantv.com/hntv/20200615/173501935.html.

Hyde, Janet Shibley. 1991. *Half the Human Experience: The Psychology of Women*. Lexington: D. C. Heath & Company.

Ito, Mizuko. 2012. "Contributors versus Leechers: Fansubbing Ethics and a Hybrid Public Culture." In *Fandom Unbound: Otaku Culture in a Connected World*, edited by Mizuko Ito, Daisuke Okabe, and Izumi Tsuji, 179–204. New Haven: Yale University Press.

Iwabuchi, Koichi. 2002. *Recentering Globalization: Popular Culture and Japanese Transnationalism*. Durham, NC: Duke University Press.

Iwabuchi, Koichi, ed. 2004. *Feeling Asian Modernities: Transnational Consumption of Japanese TV Drama*. Hong Kong: Hong Kong University Press.

Iwabuchi, Koichi, Eva Tsai, and Chris Berry, eds. 2017. *Routledge Handbook of East Asian Popular Culture*. London: Routledge.

Jackson, Peter A. 2009. "Capitalism and Global Queering: National Markets, Parallels among Sexual Cultures, and Multiple Queer Modernities." *GLQ: A Journal of Lesbian and Gay Studies* 15, no. 3: 357–95. https://muse.jhu.edu/article/266701.

Jackson, Sue, and Elizabeth Westrupp. 2010. "Sex, Postfeminist Popular Culture and the Pre-Teen Girl." *Sexualities* 13, no. 3: 357–76. https://doi.org/10.1177/1363460709363135.

Jaffe, Alexandra. 2011. "Sociolinguistic Diversity in Mainstream Media: Authenticity, Authority and Processes of Mediation and Mediatization." *Journal of Language and Politics* 10, no. 4: 562–86. https://doi.org/10.1075/jlp.10.4.05jaf.

Jagose, Annamarie. 1996. *Queer Theory: An Introduction*. New York: New York University Press.

Jenkins, Henry. 1992. *Textual Poachers: Television Fans and Participatory Culture*. New York: Routledge.

Jenkins, Henry. 2013. *Textual Poachers: Television Fans and Participatory Culture*. 2nd ed. New York: Routledge.

Jhuo, Ching-O 卓菁莪. 2020. "Wo pai gu wo zai: nantongzhi yu jianshenfang zibai de shequn shenti zhanyan" 我拍故我在：男同志於健身房自拍的社群身體展演 [I take selfies, therefore I am: Gay men's gym selfies as body presentation on social media]. MA diss., National Chengchi University. https://ah.nccu.edu.tw/item?item_id=150342&locale=en-US.

Ji, Yuqiao. 2020. "Hit Chinese Reality Show 'Sisters Who Make Waves' Fails to Live up to Feminist Goals." *Global Times*. Last modified September 7, 2020. https://www.globaltimes.cn/content/1200147.shtml.

Jia, Lianrui, and Tianyang Zhou. 2015. "Regulation of Homosexuality in the Chinese Media Scene." *The Asia Dialogue*. Last modified July 28, 2015. https://theasiadialogue.com/2015/07/28/regulation-of-homosexuality-in-the-chinese-media-scene/.

Jiang, Xinxin. 2018. "Illusionary Fairness and Controlled Democracy: A Critical Examination of Blind Audition and Voting System in *The Voice of China*." *Media, Culture & Society* 40, no. 8: 1237–51. https://doi.org/10.1177/0163443718798905.

Jiang, Xinxin, and Alberto González. 2021. "<China Dream> and <Root-Seeking>: The Rhetoric of Nationalism in *The Voice of China*." *Journal of Contemporary China* 30, no. 132: 1014–26. https://doi.org/10.1080/10670564.2021.1893553.

Jiao, Lin. 2021. "Reconciling Femininities and Female Masculinities: Women's Premarital Experiences of Breast-Binding in the Maoist Era." *Modern China* 48, no. 2: 321–52. https://doi.org/10.1177/0097700421992314.

Johnson, David K. 2019. *Buying Gay: How Physique Entrepreneurs Sparked a Movement*. New York: Columbia University Press.

Joyrich, Lynne. 2014. "Queer Television Studies: Currents, Flows, and (Main)streams." *Cinema Journal* 53, no. 2: 133–39. https://muse.jhu.edu/article/535712.

Jung, Jaehee. 2018. "Young Women's Perceptions of Traditional and Contemporary Female Beauty Ideals in China." *Family & Consumer Sciences* 47, no. 1: 56–72. https://doi.org/10.1111/fcsr.12273.

Jung, Sun. 2011. *Korean Masculinities and Transcultural Consumption: Yonsama, Rain, Oldboy, K-Pop Idols*. Hong Kong: Hong Kong University Press.

Kam, Lucetta Y. L. 2013. *Shanghai Lalas: Female Tongzhi Communities and Politics in Urban China*. Hong Kong: Hong Kong University Press.

Kam, Lucetta Y. L. 2014. "Desiring T, Desiring Self: 'T-Style' Pop Singers and Lesbian Culture in China." *Journal of Lesbian Studies* 18, no. 3: 252–65. https://doi.org/10.1080/10894160.2014.896613.

Käng, Dredge Byung'chu. 2013. "Conceptualizing Thai Genderscapes: Transformation and Continuity in the Thai Sex/Gender System." In *Contemporary Socio-Cultural and Political Perspectives in Thailand*, edited by Pranee Liamputtong, 409–29. Dordrecht: Springer Netherlands.

Kang, Wenqing. 2009. *Obsession: Male Same-Sex Relations in China, 1900–1950*. Hong Kong: Hong Kong University Press.

Keane, Michael. 2004. "A Revolution in Television and a Great Leap Forward for Innovation: China in the Global Television Format Business." In *Television across Asia: TV Industries, Programme Formats and Globalization*, edited by Albert Moran and Michael Keane, 88–104. London: RoutledgeCurzon.

Keane, Michael. 2015. *The Chinese Television Industry*. London: Palgrave.

Keane, Michael, Anthony Y.H. Fung, and Albert Moran. 2007. *New Television, Globalization, and the East Asian Cultural Imaginations*. Hong Kong: Hong Kong University Press.

Keane, Michael, and Bonnie Liu. 2009. "Independent Television Production, TV Formats and Media Diversity in China." In *TV Formats Worldwide: Localizing Global Programs*, edited by Albert Moran, 241–54. Bristol: Intellect.

Keane, Michael, and Joy Danjing Zhang. 2017. "Where Are We Going? Parent–Child Television Reality Programs in China." *Media, Culture & Society* 39, no. 5: 630–43. https://doi.org/10.1177/0163443716663641.

Kellner, Douglas. 1995. *Media Culture: Cultural Studies, Identity and Politics between the Modern and the Post-Modern*. London: Routledge.

Kim, Gooyong. 2019. *From Factory Girls to K-Pop Idol Girls: Cultural Politics of Developmentalism, Patriarchy, and Neoliberalism in South Korea's Popular Music Industry*. Lanham: Lexington Books.

Kim, Yeran. 2011. "Idol Republic." *Journal of Gender Studies* 20, no. 4: 333–45. https://doi.org/10.1080/09589236.2011.617604.

Kimmel, Michael S., Jeff R. Hearn, and Robert W. Connell. 2005. "Introduction." In *Handbook of Studies on men and masculinities*, edited by Michael S. Kimmel, Jeff R. Hearn, and Robert W. Connell, 1–12. Thousand Oaks, CA: Sage Publications.

Ko, Yu-fen. 2004. "The Desired Form: Japanese Idol Dramas in Taiwan." In *Feeling Asian Modernities: Transnational Consumption of Japanese TV Dramas*, edited by Iwabuchi Koichi, 107–28. Hong Kong: Hong Kong University Press.

Kohnen, Melanie. 2016. *Queer Representation, Visibility, and Race in American Film and Television: Screening the Closet*. New York: Routledge.

Kong, Travis S.K. 2020. "The Pursuit of Masculinity by Young Gay Men in Neoliberal Hong Kong and Shanghai." *Journal of Youth Studies* 23, no. 8: 1004–21. https://doi.org/10.1080/13676261.2019.1646893.

Lai, Jocelyn Yi-Hsuan. 2020. "Divergent Staging of East Asian Patriarchy Within the Confucian Order in Taiwan's Transnational Television Drama Co-productions." *Continuum: Journal of Media & Cultural Studies* 34, no. 5: 651–64. https://doi.org/10.1080/10304312.2020.1812215.

Lao Zi 老子. 1990. *Daode Jing* 道德经. Hefei, Anhui: Anhui renmin chubanshe.

Lavin, Maud. 2015. "Tomboy in Love: Korean and U.S. Views of Heterosexual Eroticism in the K-Drama *First Shop of Coffee Prince*." *Situations* 8, no. 1: 45–69. http://situations.yonsei.ac.kr/product/data/item/1535539292/detail/f4aaafaaa8.pdf.

Lavin, Maud, Ling Yang, and Jing Jamie Zhao, eds. 2017. *Boys' Love, Cosplay, and Androgynous Idols: Queer Fan Cultures in Mainland China, Hong Kong and Taiwan*. Hong Kong: Hong Kong University Press.

Lee, Haiyan. 2007. *Revolution of the Heart: A Genealogy of Love in China, 1900–1950*. Stanford: Stanford University Press.

Lee, Hye-Kyung. 2014. "Transnational Cultural Fandom." In *The Ashgate Research Companion to Fan Cultures*, edited by Linda Duits, Koos Zwaan, and Stijn Reijnders, 195–208. Farnham, UK: Ashgate.

Lee, Jieun, and Hyangsoon Yi. 2020. "*Ssen-Unni* in K-Pop: The Makings of 'Strong Sisters' in South Korea." *Korean Journal* 60, no. 1: 17–39. https://doi.org/10.25024/kj.2020.60.1.17.

Lee, Po-Han. 2017. "Queer Activism in Taiwan: An Emergent Rainbow Coalition from the Assemblage Perspective." *Sociological Review* 65, no. 4: 682–98. https://doi.org/10.1177/0038026116681441.

Lei, Jun. 2015. "'Natural' Curves: Breast-Binding and Changing Aesthetics of the Female Body in China of the Early Twentieth Century." *Modern Chinese Literature and Culture* 27, no. 1: 163–223. https://www.jstor.org/stable/24886589.

Leung, Helen Hok-Sze. 2008. *Undercurrents: Queer Culture and Postcolonial Hong Kong*. Vancouver: University of British Columbia Press.

Levine, Martin P. 1998. *Gay Macho: The Life and Death of the Homosexual Clone*, edited with an introduction by Michael S. Kimmel. New York: New York University Press.

Lewis, Tania. 2007. "'He Needs to Face His Fears with These Five Queers!': *Queer Eye for the Straight Guy*, Makeover TV, and the Lifestyle Expert." *Television & New Media* 8, no. 4: 285–311. https://doi.org/10.1177/1527476407306639.

Lewis, Tania, Fran Martin, and Wanning Sun. 2016. *Telemodernities: Television and Transforming Lives in Asia*. Durham, NC: Duke University Press.

Li, Eva Cheuk-yin. 2015. "Approaching Transnational Chinese Queer Stardom as Zhongxing ('Neutral Sex/Gender') Sensibility." *East Asian Journal of Popular Culture* 1, no. 1: 75–95. https://link.gale.com/apps/doc/A414645984/AONE?u=anon~cfb8ea60&sid=googleScholar&xid=8e51c833.

Li, Eva Cheuk-yin. 2017. "Desiring Queer, Negotiating Normal: Denise Ho (HOCC) Fandom before and after the Coming-Out." In *Boys' Love, Cosplay, and Androgynous Idols: Queer Fan Cultures in Mainland China, Hong Kong, and Taiwan*, edited by Maud Lavin, Ling Yang, and Jamie Jing Zhao, 131–56. Hong Kong: Hong Kong University Press.

Li, Jin. 2016. "Gender Malleability and the Discursive Construction of Wo-man and Ladyboy in Media." In *Texas Linguistics Forum 59: Proceedings of the 24th Annual Symposium about Language and Society, Austin*, 71–78. April 15–16, 2016. http://salsa.ling.utexas.edu/proceedings/2016/Li.pdf.

Li, Po-Wei, and Chia-Rung Lu. 2020. "Articulating Sexuality, Desire, and Identity: A Keyword Analysis of Heteronormativity in Taiwanese Gay and Lesbian Dating Websites." *Sexuality & Culture*, no. 24: 1499–521. https://doi.org/10.1007/s12119-020-09709-5.

Li, Tian. 2019. "'Bang Bang Bang' – Nonsense or an Alternative Language? The Lingualscape in the Chinese Remake of *I Am a Singer*." *China Perspectives*, no. 3: 37–45. https://doi.org/10.4000/chinaperspectives.9417.

Li, Yannan. 2009. "Japanese Boy-Love Manga and the Global Fandom: A Case Study of Chinese Female Readers." Master thesis, Indiana University Bloomington. http://dx.doi.org/10.7912/C2/439.

Li, Yun 李芸. 2016. "Quanguo dianshiju hangye nianhui" 全国电视剧行业年会 [Annual conference of Chinese tv industry]. *Wechat*. Last modified February 28, 2016. https://mp.weixin.qq.com/s?__biz=MjM5MjEwOTc3Nw==&mid=401680163&idx=4&sn=457f9375989a4ac4c4a4d032d29a3b5a&3rd=MzA3MDU4NTYzMw==.

Lien, Po-Han 連柏翰. 2015. "Fuqian zhengzhi: *Kangxilaile* de xinao fengge yu buzhengque jiefang kongjian" 膚淺政治:《康熙來了》的嬉鬧風格與不正確解放空間 [Non-serious politics: *Kangsi Coming*'s comedic style and the liberating force of its political incorrectness]. *Pop Culture Academy*, December 14, 2015. https://popcultureacademytw.com/2015/12/14/skindeeppolitics/.

Liew, Kai Khiun, and Natasha Ismail. 2018. "In/appropriate, Ir/retrievable: Dragging Out Singapore's Queer Televisual Archives." *Queer Studies in Media & Popular Culture* 3, no. 2: 175–89. https://doi.org/10.1386/qsmpc.3.2.175_1.

Liew, Kai Khiun, Nidya Shanthini Manokara, and Lizawati Mohd T'a'at. 2016. "Televised Minority Beauties: Ethnocultural Mobility and Femininity in Singapore's Television Beauty Contests." *Critical Studies in Television* 11, no. 3: 330–47. https://doi.org/10.1177/1749602016662045.

Lim, Song Hwee. 2006. *Celluloid Comrades: Representations of Male Homosexuality in Contemporary Chinese Cinemas*. Honolulu: University of Hawai'i Press.

Limpongsatorn, Kongkiat. 2020. "A Study of Thailand's Boys Love Drama and Its Transnational Chinese Audience." MA thesis, National Taiwan Normal University. https://www.proquest.com/openview/8f1dcc1c3843236f3b4523b9869f3733/1?pq-origsite=gscholar&cbl=2026366&diss=y.

Lin, Dennis C. 2006. "Sissies Online: Taiwanese Male Queers Performing Sissinesses in Cyberspaces." *Inter-Asia Cultural Studies* 7, no. 2: 270–88. https://doi.org/10.1080/14649370600673938.

Lin, Dennis C. 林純德. 2013. "'C/Niang' de zhanzheng zhishe, guaitai zhanyan yu fankang nengdongxing: jianshi 'Caikangyong C/Niang shijian' zhong de 'xingbie pingdeng jiaoyu nvxing zhuyi' lunshu" 「C／娘」的爭戰指涉、怪胎展演與反抗能動性：檢視「蔡康永C／娘事件」中的「性別平等教育女性主義」論述 [C/*Niang*'s contested signification, queer performativity and resistant agency: Rethinking gender equity education feminist discourses within the Kang-Yung Tsai C/*Niang* Event] *Taiwan: A Radical Quarterly in Social Studies*, no. 90: 163–214.

Lin, Kai, Deeanna M. Button, Mingyue Su, and Sishi Chen. 2016. "Chinese College Students' Attitudes Toward Homosexuality: Exploring the Effects of Traditional Culture and Modernizing Factors." *Sexuality Research and Social Policy* 13, no. 2: 158–72. https://doi.org/10.1007/s13178-016-0223-3.

Lin, Lilian, and Chang Chen. 2016. "China's Censors Take Another Gay-Themed Web Drama Offline." *The Wall Street Journal*. Last modified February 24, 2016. https://www.wsj.com/articles/BL-CJB-28737.

Linden, Henrik, and Sara Linden. 2017. *Fans and Fan Cultures: Tourism, Consumerism and Social Media*. London: Palgrave Macmillan UK.

Liu, Guoqiang 刘国强, and Jiang Xiaomei 蒋效妹. 2020. "Fan jiekouhua de tuwei" 反结构化的突围 [Anti-structural breakthrough]. *Guoji xinwen jie* 国际新闻界 [International News], no. 12: 6–25. http://cjjc.ruc.edu.cn/CN/Y2020/V42/I12/6.

Liu, Ian Yuying. 2018. "The Chinese Dream, Neoliberalism, and International Legal Ideology." *The Chinese Journal of Global Governance* 4, no. 2: 81–121. https://doi.org/10.1163/23525207-12340033.

Liu, Jen-peng, and Ding Naifei. 2005. "Reticent Poetics, Queer Politics." *Inter-Asia Cultural Studies* 6, no. 1: 30–55. https://doi.org/10.1080/1462394042000326897.

Liu, Jieyu. 2007. *Gender and Work in Urban China*. New York: Routledge.

Liu, Lydia H., Rebecca E. Karl, and Dorothy Ko, eds. 2013. *The Birth of Chinese Feminism: Essential Texts in Transnational Theory*. New York: Columbia University Press.

Liu, Petrus. 2007. "Queer Marxism in Taiwan." *Inter-Asia Cultural Studies* 8, no. 4: 517–39. https://doi.org/10.1080/14649370701567971.

Liu, Petrus. 2015. *Queer Marxism in Two Chinas*. Durham, NC: Duke University Press.

Liu, Petrus, and Lisa Rofel, eds. 2010. "Beyound the Strai(gh)ts: Transnational and Queer Chinese Politics." Special issue of *positions: asia critique* 18, no. 2: 281–89. https://doi.org/10.1215/10679847-2010-001.

Liu, Ting. 2009. "Conflicting Discourses on Boys' Love and Subcultural Tactics in Mainland China and Hong Kong." *Intersections*, no. 20. http://intersections.anu.edu.au/issue20/liu.htm.

Louie, Kam. 2002. *Theorizing Chinese Masculinity: Society and Gender in China*. Cambridge: Cambridge University Press.

Louie, Kam. 2014. "Chinese Masculinity Studies in the Twenty-First Century: Westernizing, Easternizing and Globalizing *Wen* and *Wu*." *NORMA: International Journal for Masculinity Studies* 9, no. 1: 18–29. https://doi.org/10.1080/18902138.2014.892283.

Louie, Kam. 2015. *Chinese Masculinities in a Globalizing World*. New York: Routledge.

Louie, Kam, ed. 2016. *Changing Chinese Masculinities: From Imperial Pillars of State to Global Real Men*. Hong Kong: Hong Kong University Press.

Louie, Kam, and Louise Edwards. 1994. "Chinese Masculinity: Theorizing 'Wen' and 'Wu'." *East Asian History*, no. 8: 135–48.

Lovelock, Michael. 2019. *Reality TV and Queer Identities: Sexuality, Authenticity, Celebrity*. Cham: Palgrave Macmillan.

Lu, Sheldon. 2016. "The Postsocialist Working Class: Male Heroes in Jia Zhangke's Films." In *Changing Chinese Masculinities: From Imperial Pillars of State to Global Real Men*, edited by Kam Louie, 59–72. Hong Kong: Hong Kong University Press.

Lu, Sheldon. 2018. "Transnational Chinese Masculinity in Film Representation." In *The Cosmopolitan Dream: Transnational Chinese Masculinities in a Global Age*, edited by Derek Hird, and Geng Song, 27–39. Hong Kong: Hong Kong University Press.

Lu, Yi-Ting, and Yu-Ying Hu. 2021. "Who Are the *Zhongxing Nu Hai*? Gender, Sexuality, and the Configuration of Gender-Neutral Identity in Contemporary Taiwan." *Inter-Asia Cultural Studies* 22, no. 2: 178–95. https://doi.org/10.1080/14649373.2021.1927570.

Luo, Hui, and Paola Voci, eds. 2018. *Screening China's Soft Power*. New York: Taylor & Francis.

Ma, Alexandra. 2018. "Grueling Diets, 12-Hour Training Days, and Monthly Exams: Here's What It Takes to be a Pop Star in China." *Business Insider*. Last modified July 8, 2018. Accessed July 24, 2021. https://www.businessinsider.com/china-pop-idol-training-shows-absurd-beauty-standards-for-women

MacDermot, Michael. 2018. "The Contest of Queerbaiting: Negotiating Authenticity in Fan–Creator Interactions." *The Journal of Fandom Studies* 6, no. 2: 133–44. https://doi.org/10.1386/jfs.6.2.133_1.

Malici, Luca. 2014. "Queer TV Moments and Family Viewing in Italy." *Journal of GLBT Family Studies* 10, no. 1–2: 188–210. https://doi.org/10.1080/1550428X.2014.857234.

Maris, Elena. 2016. "Hacking *Xena*: Technological Innovation and Queer Influence in the Production of Mainstream Television." *Critical Studies in Media Communication* 33, no. 1: 123–37. https://doi.org/10.1080/15295036.2015.1129063.

Marques, Clara Ferreira. 2020. "Hong Kong Must Tackle Its Worsening Wealth Gap." *Bloomberg*. Last modified November 16, 2020. https://www.bloomberg.com/opinion/articles/2020-11-17/hong-kong-needs-to-tackle-its-worsening-inequality.

Martin, Jr., Alfred L. 2021. *The Generic Closet: Black Gayness and the Black-Cast Sitcom*. Indianapolis: Indiana University Press.

Martin, Biddy. 1997. *Femininity Played Straight: The Significance of Being Lesbian*. New York: Routledge.

Martin, Carol Lynn. 1990. "Attitude and Expectations about Children with Nontraditional and Traditional Gender Roles." *Sex Roles*, no. 22: 151–66. https://doi.org/10.1007/BF00288188.

Martin, Fran. 2008. "That Global Feeling: Sexual Subjectivities and Imagined Geographies in Chinese-Language Lesbian Cyberspaces." In *Internationalizing Internet Studies*, edited by Gerard Goggin and Mark McLelland, 285–311. New York: Routledge.

Martin, Fran. 2010a. *Backward Glances: Contemporary Chinese Cultures and the Female Homoerotic Imaginary*. Durham, NC: Duke University Press.

Martin, Fran. 2010b. "Feminist Girls, Lesbian Comrades: Performances of Critical Girlhood in Taiwan Pop Music." In *Girlhood: A Global History*, edited by Jennifer Helgren and Colleen Vasconcellos, 83–102. London: Rutgers University Press.

Martin, Fran. 2012. "Girls Who Love Boys' Love: Japanese Homoerotic Manga as Transnational Taiwan Culture." *Inter-Asia Cultural Studies* 13, no. 3: 365–83. https://doi.org/10.1080/14649373.2012.689707.

Martin, Fran. 2014. "Transnational Queer Sinophone Cultures." In *Routledge Handbook of Sexuality Studies in East Asia*, edited by Mark McLelland, and Vera Mackie, 35–48. London: Routledge.

Martin, Fran. 2016. "Queer Pop Culture in the Sinophone Mediaspehere." In *Routledge Handbook of East Asian Popular Culture*, edited by Koichi Iwabuchi, Eva Tsai, and Chris Berry, 191–201. Abingdon: Routledge.

Martin, Fran. 2017. "Girls Who Love Boys' Love: BL as Goods to Think with in Taiwan (with a Revised and Updated Coda)." In *Boys' Love, Cosplay, and Androgynous Idols: Queer Fan Cultures in Mainland China, Hong Kong, and Taiwan*, edited by Maud Lavin, Ling Yang, and Jing Jamie Zhao, 195–220. Hong Kong: Hong Kong University Press.

Martin, Fran, Peter A. Jackson, Mark McLelland, and Audrey Yue, eds. 2008. *AsiaPacifiQueer: Rethinking Genders and Sexualities*. Urbana and Chicago: University of Illinois Press.

Martin, Fran, Koichi Iwabuchi, Grace Gassin, and WaiLing Seto. 2020. "Transcultural Media Practices Fostering Cosmopolitan Ethos in a Digital Age: Engagements with East Asian Media in Australia." *Inter-Asia Cultural Studies* 21, no. 1: 2–19. https://doi.org/10.1080/14649373.2020.1728921.

McCarthy, Anna. 2001. "Ellen: Making Queer Television History." *GLQ: A Journal of Lesbian and Gay Studies* 7, no. 4: 593–620. https://muse.jhu.edu/article/12189.

McCarthy, Michael. 2015. "#SONGOFTHEDAY/REVIEW: JOLIN TSAI – 'I'M NOT YOURS' FEAT. NAMIE AMURO." *Love is Pop* (blog). Accessed July 1, 2021. https://loveispop.com/reviews/songoftheday-review-jolin-tsai-im-not-yours-feat-namie-amuro/.

McDermott, Michael. 2018. "The Contest of Queerbaiting: Negotiating Authenticity in Fan-Creator Interactions." *Journal of Fandom Studies* 6, no. 2: 133–44. https://doi.org/10.1386/jfs.6.2.133_1.

McIntyre, Joanna. 2016. "Transgender Idol: Queer Subjectivities and Australian Reality TV." *European Journal of Cultural Studies* 20, no. 1: 87–103. https://doi.org/10.1177/1367549416640535.

Medhurst, Andy. 1997. "Camp." In *Lesbian and Gay Studies: A Critical Introduction*, edited by Andy Medhurst, and Sally R. Munt, 274–93. London: Cassell.

Meng, Bingchun. 2009. "Who Needs Democracy if We Can Pick Our Favorite Girl? *Super Girl* as Media Septable." *Chinese Journal of Communication* 2, no. 3: 257–72. https://doi.org/10.1080/17544750903208996.

McNicholas-Smith, Kate, and Imogen Tyler. 2017. "Lesbian Brides: Post-Queer Popular Culture". *Feminist Media Studies* 17, no. 3: 315–31. https://doi.org/10.1080/14680777.2017.1282883.

McRobbie, Angela. 2008. *The Aftermath of Feminism: Gender, Culture and Social Change*. London: SAGE Publications.

Miller, Quinn. 2014. "Queer Recalibration." *Cinema Journal* 53, no. 2: 140–44. https://www.jstor.org/stable/43653575.

Miller, Quinlan. 2019. *Camp TV: Trans Gender Queer Sitcom History*. Durham, NC: Duke University Press.

Miller, Stephen D. 2000. "The (Temporary?) Queering of Japanese TV." *Journal of Homosexuality* 39, no. 3–4: 83–109. https://doi.org/10.1300/J082v39n03_03.

Moran, Albert, and Michael A. Keane, eds. 2004. *Television across Asia: Television Industries, Programme Formats and Globalization*. London: Routledge Curzon.

Morimoto, Lori Hitchcock. 2013. "Trans-cult-ural Fandom: Desire, Technology, and the Transformation of Fan Subjectivities in the Japanese Female Fandom of Hong Kong Stars." *Transformative Works and Cultures* 14. https://doi.org/10.3983/twc.2013.0494.

Mulvey, Laura. 1975. "Visual Pleasure and Narrative Cinema." *Screen* 16, no. 3: 6–18. https://doi.org/10.1093/screen/16.3.6.

Muñoz, José Esteban. 2005. "Queer Minstrels for the Straight Eye: Race as Surplus in Gay TV." *GLQ: A Journal of Lesbian and Gay Studies* 11, no. 1: 101–2.

Muñoz, José Esteban. 2009. *Cruising Utopia: The Then and There of Queer Futurity*. New York: New York University Press.

Namaste, Ki. 1994. "The Politics of Inside/Out: Queer Theory, Poststructuralism, and a Sociological Approach to Sexuality." *Sociological Theory* 12, no. 2: 220–31. https://doi.org/10.2307/201866.

Negra, Diane. 2008. *What a Girl Wants? Fantasizing the Reclamation of Self in Postfeminism*. New York: Routledge.

NetEase Entertainment. 2015. "Wangweizhong queding *Kangxi* jiang tingbo: jiemu zhi shuyu tamenliang" 王伟忠确定《康熙》将停播: 节目只属于他们俩 [Weizhong Wang confirmed that *Kangsi Coming* will be closed down: The show only belongs to them] *NetEase Entertainment*, October 16, 2015. http://ent.163.com/15/1016/17/B62KQUH800031GVS.html.

Ng, Eve. 2008. "Reading the Romance of Fan Cultural Production: Music Videos of a Television Lesbian Couple." *Popular Communication* 6, no. 2: 103–21. https://doi.org/10.1080/15405700701746525.

Ng, Eve. 2013. "A 'Post-Gay' Era? Media Gaystreaming, Homonormativity, and the Politics of LGBT Integration." *Communication, Culture & Critique* 6, no. 2: 258–83. https://doi.org/10.1111/cccr.12013.

Ng, Eve. 2017. "Between Text, Paratext, and Context: Queerbaiting and the Contemporary Media Landscape." *Transformative Works and Cultures* 24. http://dx.doi.org/10.3983/twc.2017.917.

Ng, Eve. 2021. "The 'Gentleman-Like' Anne Lister on Gentleman Jack: Queerness, Class, and Prestige in 'Quality' Period Dramas." *International Journal of Communication* 15: 2397–417. https://ijoc.org/index.php/ijoc/article/view/17218/3448.

Ng, Eve, and Xiaomeng Li. 2020. "A Queer 'Socialist Brotherhood': *The Guardian* Web Series, Boys' Love Fandom, and the Chinese State." *Feminist Media Studies* 20, no. 4: 479–95. https://doi.org/10.1080/14680777.2020.1754627.

Ng, How Wee. 2015. "Rethinking Censorship in China: The Case of *Snail House*." In *Chinese Television in the Twenty-First Century: Entertaining the Nation*, edited by Ruoyun Bai and Geng Song, 87–103. New York: Routledge.

Oh, Chuyun. 2017. "'Cinderella' in Reverse: Eroticizing Bodily Labor of Sympathetic Men in K-Pop Dance Practice Video." In *East Asian Men: Masculinity, Sexuality and Desire*, edited by Xiaodong Lin, Chris Haywood, and Mairtin Mac an Ghaill, 123–41. London: Palgrave Macmillan.

Ong, Aihwa, and Li Zhang. 2011. "Introduction: Privatizing China, Powers of the Self, Socialism from Afrar." In *Privatizing China: Socialism from Afar*, edited by Aihwa Ong and Li Zhang, 1–19. New York: Cornell University Press.

Pan, Junliang 潘俊良. 2014. "Dujia zhuanfang Zhou Shen" 独家专访周深 [Interview with Zhou Shen]." *Tencent Entertainment*. July 26, 2014. https://www.bilezu.com/html/82444846.html.

Pascoe, C.J. 2020. *Ni zhege niangpao* 你这个娘炮 [*Dude, You're a Fag*]. Translated by Yi Li. Taipei: Yeren Publisher.

Pascoe, C.J., and Tristan Bridges. 2015. *Exploring Masculinities: Identity, Inequality, Continuity and Change*. New York: Oxford University Press.

Peele, Thomas, ed. 2007. *Queer Popular Culture: Literature, Media, Film, and Television*. New York: Palgrave MacMillan.

Peng, Altman Yuzhu. 2020. *A Feminist Reading of China's Digital Public Sphere*. New York: Palgrave Macmillan.

Penley, Constance. 1997. *NASA/Trek: Popular Science and Sex in America*. New York: Verso.

Pérez, Raúl and Viveca S. Greene. 2016. "Debating Rape Jokes vs. Rape Culture: Framing and Counter-Framing Misogynistic Comedy." *Social Semiotics* 26, no. 3: 265–82. https://doi.org/10.1080/10350330.2015.1134823.

Peters, Wendy. 2011. "Pink Dollars, White Collars: *Queer as Folk*, Valuable Viewers, and the Price of Gay TV." *Critical Studies in Media Communication* 28, no. 3: 193–212. https://doi.org/10.1080/15295036.2011.559478.

Preciado, Paul B. 2018. *Countersexual Manifesto*. Translated by Kevin Gerry Dunn. New York: Columbia University Press.

Qian, Colin, and Ryan Woo. 2021. "Chinese Plan to Boost 'Masculinity' with PE Classes Sparks Debate." *Reuters*. Last modified February 3, 2021. https://www.reuters.com/article/us-china-society-masculinity-idUSKBN2A30LV.

RADII China. 2018. "'China's Beyonce' Wang Ju Fails to Make 'Produce 101' Cut." June 25, 2018. Accessed July 1, 2021. https://radiichina.com/after-the-international-hype-chinas-beyonce-fails-to-make-produce-101-cut/.

Raymond, Diane. 2003. "Popular Culture and Queer Representation: A Critical Perspective." In *Gender, Race and Class in Media: A Text-Reader*, edited by Gail Dines and Jean M. Humez, 98–110. London: Sage.

Redmond, Sean, and Su Holmes. 2007. "Introduction: What's in a Reader?" In *Stardom and Celebrity: A Reader*, edited by Sean Redmond and Su Holmes, 1–11. London: Sage.

Robinson, Luke. 2013. *Independent Chinese Documentary: From the Studio to the Street*. London: Palgrave Macmillan.

Robinson, Stefan, Eric Anderson, and Adam White. 2018. "The Bromance: Undergraduate Male Friendships and the Expansion of Contemporary Homosocial Boundaries." *Sex Roles*, no. 78: 94–106. https://doi.org/10.1007/s11199-017-0768-5.

Rocha, Leon. 2010. "*Xing*: The Discourse of Sex and Human Nature in Modern China." *Gender & History* 22, no. 3: 603–28.

Rofel, Lisa. 2007. *Desiring China: Experiments in Neoliberalism, Sexuality, and Public Culture.* Durham, NC: Duke University Press.

Rubin, Gayle S. 2011. *Deviations: A Gayle Rubin Reader.* Durham, NC: Duke University Press.

Russ, Joanna, ed. 1985. *Magic Mommas, Trembling Sisters, Puritans & Perverts: Feminist Essays.* New York: The Crossing Press.

Saejang, Jooyin. 2019. "The Subtitling and Dubbing into Chinese of Male Homosexual and Ladyboy Roles in Thai Soap Operas." PhD diss., University College London. https://discovery.ucl.ac.uk/id/eprint/10071750/.

Saintsup the Official (@_saint_official). 2018. "เกร็ดน่ารู้ : 明兒 (หมิงเอ๋อ) ในภาษาจีน จะมี 3 นัยยะ คือ." Twitter, October 2, 2018. https://twitter.com/_saint_official/status/1046847807091499009.

Salmons, Janet. 2015. *Qualitative Online Interviews: Strategies, Design, and Skills.* Thousand Oaks: Sage Publications.

Sang, Tze-lan D. 2003. *The Emerging Lesbian.* Chicago: University of Chicago Press.

Sangren, P. Steven. 2017. *Filial Obsessions: Chinese Patriliny and Its Discontents.* London: Palgrave Macmillan.

Sedgwick, Eve Kosofsky. 1985. *Between Men: English Literature and Male Homosocial Desire.* New York: Columbia University Press.

Sedgwick, Eve Kosofsky. 1993. *Tendencies.* Durham: Duke University Press.

Sender, Katherine. 2004. *Business, Not Politics: The Making of the Gay Market.* New York: Columbia University Press.

Sender, Katherine. 2007. "Dualcasting: Bravo's Gay Programming and the Quest for Women Audiences" In *Cable Visions: Television beyond Broadcasting*, edited by Sarah Banet-Weiser, Cynthia Chris, and Anthony Freitas, 302–18. New York: New York University Press.

Sender, Katherine. 2006. "Queens for a Day: Queer Eye for the Straight Guy and the Neoliberal Project." *Critical Studies in Media Communication* 23, no. 2: 131–51. https://doi.org/10.1080/07393180600714505.

Sender, Katherine. 2012. *The Makeover: Reality Television and Reflexive Audiences.* New York: New York University Press.

Shaw, Gareth, and Xiaoling Zhang. 2018. "Cyberspace and Gay Rights in a Digital China: Queer Documentary Filmmaking under State Censorship." *China Information* 32, no. 2: 270–92. https://doi.org/10.1177/0920203X17734134.

Shi, Liang. 2014. *Chinese Lesbian Cinema: Mirror Rubbing, Lala, and Les.* New York: Lexington.

Shih, Paris 施舜翔. 2015. "Zongyi tianhou: XiaoS de hunzhong ganbao meixue yu nantongzhi yule zhengzhi" 綜藝天后: 小S的混種敢曝美學與男同志娛樂政治 [Popular Diva: the camp aesthetics of Xiao S and the entertainment politics of gay men]. *Pop Culture Academy*, December 14, 2015. https://popcultureacademytw.com/2015/12/14/divaofentertainments/.

Shih, Shu-mei. 1998. "Gender and a New Geopolitics of Desire: The Seduction of Mainland Women in Taiwan and Hong Kong Media." *Signs* 23, no. 2: 287–319. https://www.jstor.org/stable/3175092.

Shih, Shu-mei. 2007. *Visuality and Identity: Sinophone Articulation Across the Pacific*. Berkeley: University of California Press.
Shih, Shu-mei. 2011. "The Concept of the Sinophone." *PMLA* 126, no. 3: 709–18.
Simpson, Mark. 2014. "The Metrosexual is Dead. Long Live 'the Spornosexual'." *The Telegraph*. Last modified June 10, 2014. https://www.telegraph.co.uk/men/fashion-and-style/10881682/The-metrosexual-is-dead.-Long-live-the-spornosexual.html.
Skeggs, Beverley, and Helen Wood. 2012. *Reacting to Reality TV: Performance, Audience and Value*. Oxon: Routledge.
Skerski, Jamie. 2011. "Tomboy Chic: Re-Fashioning Gender Rebellion." *Journal of Lesbian Studies* 15, no. 4: 466–79. https://doi.org/10.1080/10894160.2011.532031.
Sohu. 2018. "The MV Release of LadyBees's Queen Bee; Entering a New Age of Girl Power as Queens." Last modified November 29, 2018. Accessed June 28, 2021. https://www.sohu.com/a/278498346_115487.
Sohu. 2020. "Chris Lee's 'For Every Girl' Dominates the Internet! *People's Daily*: May You Be Treated Tenderly by the World……." Last modified March 9, 2020. Accessed July 1, 2021. https://www.sohu.com/a/378823410_627450.
Song, Geng. 2010. "Chinese Masculinities Revisited: Male Images in Contemporary TV Drama Serials." *Modern China* 36, no. 4: 404–34. https://doi.org/10.1177/0097700410368221.
Song, Geng. 2016. "All Dogs Deserve to Be Beaten: Negotiating Manhood and Nationhood in Chinese TV Dramas." In *Changing Chinese Masculinities: From Imperial Pillars of State to Global Real Men*, edited by Kam Louie, 204–19. Hong Kong: Hong Kong University Press.
Song, Geng. 2018. "Cosmopolitanism with Chinese Characteristics: Transnational Male Images in Chinese TV Dramas." In *The Cosmopolitan Dream: Transnational Chinese Masculinities in a Global Age*, edited by Derek Hird and Geng Song, 27–39. Hong Kong: Hong Kong University Press.
Song, Geng. 2019. "Masculinizing *Jianghu* Spaces in the Past and Present: Homosociality, Nationalism and Chineseness." *NAN NÜ* 21, no. 1: 107–29. https://doi.org/10.1163/15685268-00211P04.
Song, Geng. 2022a. "'Little Fresh Meat': The Politics of Sissiness and Sissyphobia in Contemporary China." *Men and Masculinities* 25, no. 1: 68–86. https://doi.org/10.1177/1097184X211014939.
Song, Geng. 2022b. *Televising Chineseness: Gender, Nation, and Subjectivity*. Ann Arbor: University of Michigan Press.
Song, Geng, and Derek Hird. 2013. *Men and Masculinities in Contemporary China*. Boston: Brill.
Song, Mingwei. 2015. *Young China: National Rejuvenation and the Bildungsroman, 1900–1959*. Cambridge, MA: Harvard University Press.
Sontag, Susan. 2018. *Notes on Camp*. London: Penguin Classics.
Spurlin, William J. 2014. "Queering Translation." In *A Companion to Translation Studies*, edited by Sandra Bermann, and Catherine Porter, 298–309. Chichester: Wiley Blackwell.
Spurlin, William J. 2017. "Queering Translation: Rethinking Gender and Sexual Politics in the Spaces between Languages and Cultures." In *Queer in Translation*, edited by B. J. Epstein and Robert Gillett, 172–83. Abingdon and New York: Routledge.

Stanley, Eric. 2011. "Near Life, Queer Death: Overkill and Ontological Capture." *Social Text* 29, no. 2: 1–19. https://doi.org/10.1215/01642472-1259461.

Straayer, Chris, and Tom Waugh. 2005. "Queer TV Style: Introduction." *GLQ: A Journal of Lesbian and Gay Studies* 11, no. 1: 95. https://muse.jhu.edu/article/176323/pdf.

Su, Lezhou. 2018. "A Free Life: Transnational Reconstruction of Chinese Wen Masculinity." In *The Cosmopolitan Dream: Transnational Chinese Masculinities in a Global Age*, edited by Derek Hird and Geng Song, 87–101. Hong Kong: Hong Kong University Press.

Sun, Wanning, and Lauren Gorfinkel. 2015. "Television, Scale and Place-Identity in the PRC: Provincial, National and Global Influences from 1958 to 2013." In *Television Histories in Asia: Issues and Contexts*, edited by Jinna Tay and Graeme Turner, 19–37. New York: Routledge.

Tan, See-Kam. 2000. "The Cross-Gender Performances of Yam Kim-Fei, or the Queer Factor in Postwar Hong Kong Cantonese Opera/Opera Films." *Journal of Homosexuality* 39, no. 3/4: 201–11. https://doi.org/10.1300/J082v39n03_08.

Tan, See-Kam. 2007. "Huangmei Opera Films, Shaw Brothers and Ling Bo—Chaste Love Stories, Genderless Cross-Dressers and Sexless Gender-Plays?" *Jump Cut*, no. 49 (online). Accessed March 30, 2022. https://www.ejumpcut.org/archive/jc49.2007/TanSee-Kam/text.html.

Tao, Talia, and Alicia Liu. 2021. "China Cracks Down on Digital Fandom: Behind the 'Qinglang' Operation." *Glimpse from the Globe*, October 5, 2021. Access April 1, 2022. https://www.glimpsefromtheglobe.com/regions/asia-and-the-pacific/china-cracks-down-on-digital-fandoms-behind-the-qinglang-operation/.

Tay, Jinna, and Graeme Turner, eds. 2015. *Television Histories in Asia: Issues and Contexts*. New York: Routledge.

Teo, Stephen. 2009. *Chinese Martial Arts Cinema: The Wuxia Tradition*. Edinburgh: Edinburgh University Press.

Thornber, Karen Laura. 2014. "Rethinking the World in World Literature: East Asia and Literary Contact Nebulae." In *World Literature in Theory*, edited by David Damrosch, 460–79. Chichester: Wiley Blackwell.

Tian, Xi. 2020. "More than Conformity or Resistance: Chinese 'Boys' Love' Fandom in the Age of Internet Censorship." *Journal of the European Association for Chinese Studies*, no. 1: 189–213. https://doi.org/10.25365/jeacs.2020.1.189-213.

Tong, Wejing 童薇菁. 2019. "Guofeng zhimei" 国风之美 [Beauty of national style]. *CCTV*. Last modified July 3, 2019. http://news.cctv.com/2019/07/03/ARTIXEKsAFmlA8XXzpdACs2O190703.shtml.

Tsai, Kevin 蔡康永. 2009. "Dang wo shuo yige nansheng 'niang' de shihou" 当我说一个男生'娘'的时候 [When I am calling a guy "sissy"] *Caikangyong de boke* 蔡康永的博客 [Kevin Tsai's blog] (blog), *Sina*, July 7, 2009. http://blog.sina.com.cn/s/blog_4c69db7d0100dy7i.html.

Tsai, Kevin 蔡康永. 2010. "'Fodimo'? haishi 'nageren'? erlun duikang xingbie qishi" 「佛地魔」？還是「那個人」？二論對抗性別歧視 ['Voldemort'? or 'that guy'? Revisiting fighting against gender discrimination]. *Caikangyong de boluoge* 蔡康永的部落格 [Kevin Tsai's blog] (blog), *Sina*, October 26, 2010. https://tsaikangyung.pixnet.net/blog/post/32340115.

Tsui, Lokman. 2003. "The Panopticon as the Antithesis of a Space of Freedom: Control and Regulation of the Internet in China." *China Information* 17, no. 2: 65–82. https://doi.org/10.1177/0920203X0301700203.

van Leeuwen, Theo. 2001. "What Is Authenticity?" *Discourse Studies* 3, no. 4: 392–97. https://doi.org/10.1177/1461445601003004003.
Villarejo, Amy. 2014. *Ethereal Queer: Television, Historicity, Desire*. Durham, NC: Duke University Press.
Wang, Cathy Yue. 2019. "Officially Sanctioned Adaptation and Affective Fan Resistance: The Transmedia Convergence of the Online Drama *Guardian* in China." *International Journal of TV Serial Narratives* 5, no. 2: 45–58. https://doi.org/10.6092/issn.2421-454X/9156.
Wang, David Der-wei. 2017. "Introduction: Worlding Literary China." In *A New Literary History of Modern China*, 1–28. Cambridge, MA: Harvard University Press.
Wang, Di, and Sida Liu. 2020. "Performing Artivism: Feminists, Lawyers, and Online Legal Mobilization in China." *Law & Social Inquiry* 45, no. 3: 678–705. https://doi.org/10.1017/lsi.2019.64.
Wang, Hongren. 2020. "Ni zhege niangpao tuijian xu: wo de yinan yangcheng ji—yanggang kongtong yu 'deng' daren" 《你这个娘炮》推荐序：我的异男养成记——阳刚、恐同与『登』大人 [Foreword to dude, you're a fag: My growing-up to be a strange man—macho, homophobia, and becoming man]. *The News Lens*. Last modified June 2, 2020. https://www.thenewslens.com/article/135742.
Wang, Qian. 2015. "Queerness, Entertainment, and Politics: Queer Performance and Performativity in Chinese Pop." In *Queer/Tongzhi China: New Perspectives on Research, Activism and Media Cultures*, edited by Elisabeth L. Engebretsen, William F. Schroeder, and Hongwei Bao, 153–78. Copenhagen: NIAS Press.
Wang, Serenitie. 2018. "Chinese Writer Sentenced to 10 Years in Prison for Homoerotic Book." *CNN*. Last modified November 19, 2018. https://edition.cnn.com/2018/11/19/china/chinese-erotic-fiction-writer-prison-intl/index.html.
Wang, Shuaishuai. 2020. "Chinese Affective Platform Economies: Dating, Live Streaming, and Performative Labor on Blued." *Media, Culture & Society* 42, no. 4: 502–20. https://doi.org/10.1177/0163443719867283.
Wang, Vivian, and Joy Dong. 2021. "This Boy Band is the Joy that Hong Kong Needs Right Now." *The New York Times*. Last modified August 12, 2021. https://www.nytimes.com/2021/08/12/world/asia/hong-kong-mirror-band.html.
Wang, Xin, Chris K.K. Tan, and Yao Wei. 2019. "*Gaymi*: Emergent Masculinities and Straight Women's Friendships with Gay Male Best Friends in Jinan, China." *Sexualities* 22, no. 5–6: 901–15. https://doi.org/10.1177/1363460718773689.
Wang, Yiran. 2021. "'Passionate Aesthetics': T-P Gender Practices and Discourses, and the Hierarchies within Lesbian (Lala) Communities in Contemporary Mainland China." *Journal of Gender Studies* 30, no. 5: 561–72. https://doi.org/10.1080/09589236.2021.1929094.
Wang, Yiwen. 2020a. "Homoeroticising Archaic Wind Music: A Rhizomatic Return to Ancient China." *China Perspectives*, no. 2: 15–23. https://doi.org/10.4000/chinaperspectives.10096.
Wang, Yiwen. 2020b. "The Paradox of Queer Aura: A Case Study of Gender-Switching Video Remakes." *Feminist Media Studies* 20, no. 4: 496–514. https://doi.org/10.1080/14680777.2020.1754628.
Wang, Zixu, Xin Chen, and Caroline Radnofsky. 2021. "China Proposes Teaching Masculinity to Boys as State is Alarmed by Changing Gender Roles." *NBC News*. Last modified March 5, 2021. https://www.nbcnews.com/news/world/

china-proposes-teaching-masculinity-boys-state-alarmed-changing-gender-roles-n1258939?tm_medium=10today.media.fri.20210305.436.1&utm_source=email&utm_content=article&utm_campaign=10-for-today---4.0-styling.

"Wangluo xinxi neirong shengtai zhili guiding" 网络信息内容生态治理规定 [Provisions on ecological management of network information content]. 2019. Cyber Administration of China. Last modified December 20, 2019. http://www.cac.gov.cn/2019-12/20/c_1578375159509309.htm.

Weaver, Simon, Raúl Alberto Mora, and Karen Morgan. 2016. "Gender and Humour: Examining Discourses of Hegemony and Resistance." *Social Semiotics* 26, no. 3: 227–33. https://doi.org/10.1080/10350330.2015.1134820.

Webber, Michael, Mark Wang, and Ying Zhu. 2002. "Knocking on WTO's Door." In *China's Transition to a Global Economy*, edited by Michael Webber, Mark Wang, and Ying Zhu, 1–13. New York: Palgrave Macmillan.

Wei, Wei 魏伟. 2010. "Cong fuhaoxing miejue dao shengchaxing gongkai: *Feichengwurao* dui tongxinglian de zaixian" 从符号性灭绝到审查性公开:《非诚勿扰》对同性恋的再现 [From symbolic extinction to open under censorship: The representations of homosexuality in *If You Are the One*] *Kaifang shidai* 开放时代 [*Open Times*], no. 2. http://www.opentimes.cn/Abstract/1222.html.

Welker, James. 2006. "Beautiful, Borrowed, and Bent: 'Boys' Love' as Girls' Love in Shôjo Manga." *Signs* 31, no. 3: 841–70. https://doi.org/10.1086/498987.

Welker, James. 2015. "A Brief History of Shōnen'ai, Yaoi, and Boys Love." In *Boys Love Manga and Beyond: History, Culture, and Community in Japan*, edited by Mark McLelland, Kazumi Nagaike, Katsuhiko Suganuma, and James Welker, 42–75. Jackson: University of Mississippi Press.

Wen, Huike. 2014. *Television and the Modernization Ideal in 1980s China*. Lanham, MD: Lexington Books.

Wolfman, Greg. 2017. "Metrosexual, Hipster, Spornosexual: Why Do We Keep Redefining Men?" *The Conversation*, May 5, 2017. https://theconversation.com/metrosexual-hipster-spornosexual-why-do-we-keep-redefining-men-72444.

Wong, Alvin K. 2012. "From the Transnational to the Sinophone: Lesbian Representations in Chinese-Language Films." *Journal of Lesbian Studies* 16, no. 3: 307–22. https://doi.org/10.1080/10894160.2012.673930.

Wong, Alvin K. 2020. "Towards a Queer Affective Economy of Boys' Love in Contemporary Chinese Media." *Continuum* 34, no. 4: 500–13. https://doi.org/10.1080/10304312.2020.1785078.

Wong, Alvin K. 2021. "Beyond Queer Liberalism: On Queer Globalities and Regionalism from Postcolonial Hong Kong." In *Sexualities, Transnationalism, and Globalization*, edited by Yanqiu Rachel Zhou, Christina Sinding, and Donald Goellnicht, 107–20. New York: Routledge.

Wong, Rachel. 2020. "Hong Kong's Homophobic Public Housing Policy Ruled Unconstitutional and Unlawful by High Court." *Hong Kong Free Press*. March 4, 2020. https://hongkongfp.com/2020/03/04/hong-kongs-homophobic-public-housing-policy-ruled-unconstitutional-unlawful-high-court/.

Wood, Andrea. 2013. "Boys' Love Anime and Queer Desires in Convergence Culture: Transnational Fandom, Censorship and Resistance." *Journal of Graphic Novels and Comics* 4, no. 1: 44–63. https://doi.org/10.1080/21504857.2013.784201.

Wood, Helen. 2009. *Talking with Television*. Chicago: University of Illinois Press.

Wu, Angela Xiao, and Yige Dong. 2019. "What Is Made-in-China Feminist(s)? Gender Discontent and Class Friction in Post-Socialist China." *Critical Asian Studies* 51, no. 4: 471–92. https://doi.org/10.1080/14672715.2019.1656538.

Wu, Changchang. 2020. "Sisters' Act: The Hollow Feminism of China's Hottest New Show." *Sixth Tone*. Last modified June 26, 2020. https://www.sixthtone.com/news/1005852/sisters-act-the-hollow-feminism-of-chinas-hottest-new-show.

Wu, Jinna 吴晋娜. 2017. "'erciyuan' wenhua, cong xiaozhong zouxiang dazhong" "二次元"文化，从小众走向大众 [Two-dimensional culture, from minority to majority]. *Guangming ribao* 光明日报, June 27, 2017. https://epaper.gmw.cn/gmrb/html/2017-06/27/nw.D110000gmrb_20170627_2-08.htm.

Wu, Xiaoyi 吴潇怡. 2020. "*Yundongba shaonian*: Zai tiyu jingji zhong zhanxian rexue zhumeng qingchun" 《运动吧少年》：在体育竞技中展现热血逐梦青春 [*Let's Exercise, Boys*: Chasing the dreams of youth in sports competitions]. *Guangming ribao* 光明日报, July 29, 2020. https://wap.gmdaily.cn/article/1d06432772e24867b6f2774ec182f13c.

Xiao, Hui Faye. 2012. "'Androgynous Beauty, Virtual Sisterhood': Stardom, Fandom, and Chinese Talent Shows under Globalization." In *Super Girls, Gangstas, Freeters, and Xenomaniacs: Gender and Modernity in Global Youth Culture*, edited by Susan Dewey and Karen J. Brison, 104–24. Syracuse: Syracuse University Press.

Xiao, Hui Faye. 2014. *Family Revolution: Marital Strife in Contemporary Chinese Literature and Visual Culture*. Seattle: University of Washington Press.

Xiao, Hui Faye. 2020. *Youth Economy, Crisis, and Reinvention in Twenty-First-Century China*. London: Routledge.

Xiao, Mix 肖骁. "Zhuanfang 'Qipazhiwang' Xiaoxiao: qishi wo you yige hen MAN de linghun" 专访 "奇葩之王" 肖骁：其实我有一个很MAN的灵魂 [Mix Xiao: There is a real man alive in my soul]. Filmed June 2017 at v.ifeng.com 凤凰网视频. Video, 20:35. https://v.ifeng.com/c/015c1046-4cab-4085-924f-9ecb38af43bc.

Xin, Shiping 辛识平. 2018. "'Niangpao' zhi feng dang xiu yi" "娘炮"之风当休矣 [The "sissy" style should be stopped]. *Xinhuanet*. Last modified September 6, 2018. http://www.xinhuanet.com/politics/2018-09/06/c_1123391309.htm.

Yan, Alice. 2016. "Chinese Gay Drama Pulled from Internet, Sparking Backlash." *South China Morning Post*. Last modified February 23, 2016. https://www.scmp.com/news/china/society/article/1915975/chinese-gay-drama-pulled-internet-sparking-backlash.

Yan, Qing, and Fan Yang. 2021. "From Parasocial to Parakin: Co-creating Idols on Social Media." *New Media & Society* 23, no. 9: 2593–615. https://doi.org/10.1177/1461444820933313.

Yan, Yunxiang. 2010. "The Chinese Path to Individualization." *The British Journal of Sociology* 61, no. 3: 489–512. https://doi.org/10.1111/j.1468-4446.2010.01323.x.

Yang, Guobin. 2014. "Internet Activism & the Party-State in China." *Daedalus* 143, no. 2: 110–23. https://doi.org/10.1162/DAED_a_00276.

Yang, Guobin. 2022. *The Wuhan Lockdown*. New York: Columbia University Press.

Yang, Jie. 2007. "'Re-Employment Stars': Language, Gender and Neoliberal Restructuring in China." In *Words, Worlds, and Material Girls: Language, Gender, Globalization*, edited by Bonnie S. McElhinny, 73–102. Berlin: Mouton de Gruyter.

Yang, Ling. 2009. "All for Love: The Corn Fandom, Prosumers, and the Chinese Way of Creating a Superstar." *International Journal of Cultural Studies* 12, no. 5: 527–43. https://doi.org/10.1177/1367877909337863.

Yang, Ling. 2014. "Reality Talent Shows in China." In *A Companion to Reality TV*, edited by Laurie Ouellette, 516–40. Malden, MA: John Wiley & Sons.

Yang, Ling. 2022. "Zhongguo mingxing fendu yanjiu de wenti yu lujing" 中国明星粉都研究的问题与路径 [The questions and routes in the studies of China's celebrity fandom]. *Zhongguo shehui kexue pingjia* 中国社会科学评价 [*China Social Science Review*], no. 1: 138–47. http://ex.cssn.cn/index/dkzgxp/zgshkxpj/2022nd1q_129972/202204/t20220418_5404097.shtml.

Yang, Ling, and Hongwei Bao. 2012. "Queerly Intimate: Friends, Fans and Affective Communication in a *Super Girl* Fan Fiction Community." *Cultural Studies* 26, no. 6: 842–71. https://doi.org/10.1080/09502386.2012.679286.

Yang, Ling, and Yanrui Xu. 2013. "Forbidden Love: Incest, Generational Conflict, and the Erotics of Power in Chinese BL Fiction." *Journal of Graphic Novels and Comics* 4, no. 1: 30–43. https://doi.org/10.1080/21504857.2013.771378.

Yang, Ling, and Yanrui Xu. 2016a. "*Danmei*, Xianqing, and the Making of a Queer Online Public Sphere in China." *Communication and the Public* 1, no. 2: 251–56. https://doi.org/10.1177/2057047316648661.

Yang, Ling, and Yanrui Xu. 2016b. "The Love that Dare Not Speak Its Name, the Fate of Chinese *Danmei* Communities in the 2014 Anti-Porn Campaign." In *The End of Cool Japan: Ethical, Legal, and Cultural Challenges to Japanese Popular Culture*, edited by Mark McLelland, 163–83. Abingdon: Routledge.

Yang, Ling, and Yanrui Xu. 2017. "Chinese *Danmei* Fandom and Cultural Globalization from Below." In *Boys' Love, Cosplay, and Androgynous Idols: Queer Fan Cultures in Mainland China, Hong Kong, and Taiwan*, edited by Maud Lavin, Ling Yang, and Jing Jamie Zhao, 3–19. Hong Kong: Hong Kong University Press.

Yang, Mayfair Mei-Hui. 1999. "From Gender Erasure to Gender Difference." In *Spaces of Their Own: Women's Public Sphere in Transnational China*, edited by Mayfair Mei-Hui Yang, 35–67. Minneapolis: University of Minnesota Press.

Yang, Peidong, and Lijun Tang. 2018. "'Positive Energy': Hegemonic Intervention and Online Media Discourse in China's Xi Jinping Era." *China: An International Journal* 16, no. 1: 1–22. https://muse.jhu.edu/article/688045.

Yang, Yue. 2022. "When Positive Energy Meets Satirical Feminist Backfire: Hashtag Activism during the COVID-19 Outbreak in China." *Global Media and China* 7, no. 1: 99–119. https://doi.org/10.1177/20594364211021316.

Ye, Shana. 2022. "Word of Honor and Brand Homonationalism with 'Chinese Characteristics': The *Dangai* Industry, Queer Masculinity and the 'Opacity' of the State." *Feminist Media Studies* (online): 1–17. https://doi.org/10.1080/14680777.2022.2037007.

Yu, Haiqing. 2009. *Media and Cultural Transformation in China*. New York: Routledge.

Yu, Haiqing. 2011. "*Dwelling Narrowness*: Chinese Media and Their Disingenuous Neoliberal Logic." *Continuum* 25, no. 1: 33–46. https://doi.org/10.1080/10304312.2011.538466.

Yu, Ting-Fai. 2021. "Spatialities of Queer Globalization: Middle- and Working-Class Hong Kong Gay Men's Subjective Constructions of Homophobia." *Sexualities* 24, no. 4: 636–53. https://doi.org/10.1177/1363460720936466.

Yue, Audrey, and Haiqing Yu. 2008. "China's *Super Girl*: Mobile Youth Cultures and New Sexualities." In *Youth, Media and Culture in the Asia Pacific Region*, edited by Usha M Rodrigues and Belinda Smaill, 117–34. Newcastle: Cambridge Scholars Publishing.

Yue, Audrey, and Helen Hok-Sze Leung. 2017. "Notes Towards the Queer Asian City: Singapore and Hong Kong." *Urban Studies* 54, no. 3: 747–64. https://doi.org/10.1177/0042098015602996.

Yuen, Shu Min. 2011. "*Last Friends*, Beyond Friends—Articulating Non-Normative Gender and Sexuality on Mainstream Japanese Television." *Inter-Asia Cultural Studies* 12, no. 3: 383–400. https://doi.org/10.1080/14649373.2011.578796.

Zhang, Charlie Yi. 2016. "Queering the National Body of Contemporary China." *Frontiers* 37, no. 2: 1–26. https://doi.org/10.5250/fronjwomestud.37.2.0001.

Zhang, Charlie Yi. 2017. "When Feminist Falls in Love with Queer: Dan Mei Culture as a Transnational Apparatus of Love." *Feminist Formations* 29, no. 2: 121–46. https://muse.jhu.edu/article/671720.

Zhang, Charlie Yi, and Adam K. Dedman. 2021. "Hyperreal Homoerotic Love in a Monarchized Military Conjuncture: A Situated View of the Thai Boys' Love Industry." *Feminist Media Studies* 21, no. 6: 1039–43. https://doi.org/10.1080/14680777.2021.1959370.

Zhang, Chunyu. 2016. "Loving Boys Twice as Much: Chinese Women's Paradoxical Fandom of 'Boys' Love' Fiction." *Women's Studies in Communication* 39, no. 3: 249–67. https://doi.org/10.1080/07491409.2016.1190806.

Zhang, Qingfei. 2014. "Transgender Representation by the *People's Daily* Since 1949." *Sexuality & Culture* 18, no. 1: 180–95. https://doi.org/10.1007/s12119-013-9184-3.

Zhang, Qingfei. 2015. "Sexuality and the Official Construction of Occidentalism in Maoist and early Post-Mao China." *European Journal of Cultural Studies* 18, no. 1: 86–107. https://doi.org/10.1177/1367549414557807.

Zhang, Xindong, no. (@运动吧少年-张鑫栋). 2020. "Shou gong. Haohao xiuxi" 收工。好好休息 [Done with work. Have good rest]. Weibo photo, August 10, 2020. https://weibo.com/6325666375/Jfk6plAlB?filter=hot&root_comment_id=0&ssl_rnd=1611098261.182&type=comment#_rnd1611098262913.

Zhang, Yanhua. 2014. "Crafting Confucian Remedies for Happiness in Contemporary China: Unraveling the Yu Dan Phenomenon." In *The Political Economy of Affect and Emotion in East Asia*, edited by Jie Yang, 31–44. Abingdon, Oxon: Routledge.

Zhang, Yiqian. 2018. "Woman Not Slim and Fair Shoots to Phenomenal Stardom with LGBT, Feminist Fan Base." *Global Times*. Last modified June 5, 2018. https://www.globaltimes.cn/page/201806/1105683.shtml.

Zhao, Elaine Jing. 2016. "Collaboration Reconfigured: The Evolving Landscape of Entertainment TV Markets between Taiwan and Mainland China." *Media International Australia* 159, no. 1: 53–62. https://doi.org/10.1177/1329878X16638936.

Zhao, Jamie J. 2014. "Fandom as a Middle Ground: Fictive Queer Fantasies and Real-World Lesbianism in *FSCN*." *Media Fields Journal* 10. http://mediafieldsjournal.squarespace.com/fandom-as-a-middle-ground/.

Zhao, Jamie J. 2016. "A Splendid Chinese Queer TV? 'Crafting' Nonnormative Masculinities in Formatted Chinese Reality TV Shows." *Feminist Media Studies* 16, no. 1: 164–68. https://doi.org/10.1080/14680777.2016.1120486.

Zhao, Jamie J. 2017a. "A Queerly Normalized Western Lesbian Imaginary: Online Chinese Fans' Gossip about the Danish Fashion Model Freja Beha Erichsen." *Feminist Media Studies* 17, no. 1: 42–58. https://doi.org/10.1080/14680777.2017.1261839.

Zhao, Jamie J. 2017b. "Queering the Post-*L Word* 'Shane' in the 'Garden of Eden': Online Chinese Fans' Gossip about the American Actress Katherine Moennig." In *Boys' Love, Cosplay, and Androgynous Idols: Queer Fan Cultures in Mainland China, Hong Kong, and Taiwan*, edited by Maud Lavin, Ling Yang, and Jing Jamie Zhao, 63–90. Hong Kong: Hong Kong University Press.

Zhao, Jamie J. 2017c. "Queerly Imagining 'Super Girl' in an Alternate World: The Fannish Worlding in *FSCN* Femslash Romance." *Transformative Works and Cultures* 24. https://doi.org/10.3983/twc.2017.0870.

Zhao, Jamie J. 2018a. "Censoring 'Rainbow' in China." *The Asia Dialogue*, June 1, 2018. Accessed July 1, 2021. https://theasiadialogue.com/2018/06/01/censoring-rainbow-in-china/.

Zhao, Jamie J. 2018b. "Queer, Yet Never Lesbian: A Ten-Year Look Back at the Reality TV Singing Competition Show *Super Voice Girl*." *Celebrity Studies* 9, no. 4: 470–86. https://doi.org/10.1080/19392397.2018.1508957.

Zhao, Jamie J. 2018c. "The Ebb and Flow of Female Homoeroticism in the Online Chinese Queer Fandom of *Super Voice Girl* (2006)." *Journal of Fandom Studies* 6, no. 1: 33–45. https://doi.org/10.1386/jfs.6.1.33_1.

Zhao, Jamie J. 2019a. "Queer TV China as an Area of Critical Scholarly Inquiry in the 2010s." criticalasianstudies.org/ Commentary 26. https://criticalasianstudies.org/commentary/2019/12/25/201926-jamie-zhao-queer-tv-china-as-an-area-of-critical-scholarly-inquiry-in-the-2010s.

Zhao, Jamie J. 2019b. "The Emerging 'National Husband'." In *Love Stories in China: The Politics of Intimacy in the Twenty-First Century*, edited by Wanning Sun and Ling Yang, 205–25. New York: Routledge.

Zhao, Jamie J. 2020a. "It Has Never Been 'Normal': Queer Pop in Post-2000 China." *Feminist Media Studies* 20, no. 4: 463–78. https://doi.org/10.1080/14680777.2020.1754626.

Zhao, Jamie J. 2020b. "Queerness within Chineseness: Nationalism and Sexual Morality on and off the Competition Show *The Rap of China*." *Continuum* 34, no. 4: 484–99. https://doi.org/10.1080/10304312.2020.1785077.

Zhao, Jamie J. 2021a. "Blackpink Queers Your Area: The Global Queerbaiting and Queer Fandom of K-Pop Female Idols." *Feminist Media Studies* 21, no. 6: 1033–38. https://doi.org/10.1080/14680777.2021.1959373.

Zhao, Jamie J. 2021b. "Doing It Like a Tomboy on Post-2010 Chinese TV." *Communication, Culture and Critique* (online first, tcab053): 1–7. https://doi.org/10.1093/ccc/tcab053.

Zhao, Jamie J. 2021c. "Introduction: Global Queer Fandoms of Asian Media and Celebrities." *Feminist Media Studies* 21, no. 6: 102–32. https://doi.org/10.1080/14680777.2021.1959374.

Zhao, Jamie J., and Alvin K. Wong. 2020. "Introduction: Making a Queer Turn in Contemporary Chinese-Language Media Studies." *Continuum* 34, no. 4: 475–83. https://doi.org/10.1080/10304312.2020.1785076.

Zhao, Jing Jamie, Ling Yang, and Maud Lavin. 2017. "Introduction." In *Boys' Love, Cosplay, and Androgynous Idols: Queer Fan Cultures in Mainland China, Hong Kong, and Taiwan*, edited by Maud Lavin, Ling Yang, and Jamie J. Zhao, xi–xxxiii. Hong Kong: Hong Kong University Press.

Zhao, Shumei 趙淑梅, Shuyang Wang 王書洋, Shuhong Tang 唐淑宏, and Xueying Zhang 張雪英. 2018. *Liangan dazhong wenhua Bijiao* 兩岸大眾文化比較 [Comparing mass culture between Taiwan and Mainland China]. Taipei: Songbo Press.

Zhao, Yuezhi. 2008. *Communication in China: Political Economy, Power, and Conflict*. Lanham, MD: Rowman & Littlefield.

Zheng, Tiantian. 2015. *Tongzhi Living: Men Attracted to Men in Postsocialist China*. Minneapolis: University of Minnesota Press.

Zheng, Xiqing. 2019. "'Revolution Plus Love?' Online Fandom of the Television Drama Series *The Disguiser*." In *Love Stories in China: Politics of Intimacy in the Twenty-First Century*, edited by Wanning Sun and Ling Yang, 352–79. London: Routledge.

Zhong, Xueping. 2010. *Mainstream Culture Refocused: Television Drama, Society, and the Production of Meaning in Reform-Era China*. Honolulu: University of Hawaii Press.

Zhou, Shuyan. 2017. "From Online BL Fandom to the CCTV Spring Festival Gala." In *Boys' Love, Cosplay, and Androgynous Idols: Queer Fan Cultures in Mainland China, Hong Kong, and Taiwan*, edited by Maud Lavin, Ling Yang, and Jing Jamie Zhao, 91–110. Hong Kong: Hong Kong University Press.

Zhou, Tianyang. 2018. "Jack'd, Douban Group, and Feizan.com: The Impact of Cyberqueer Techno-Practice on the Chinese Gay Male Experience." In *Exploring Erotic Encounters: The Inescapable Entanglement of Tradition, Transcendence and Transgression*, edited by John T. Grider and Dionne van Reenen, 27–43. Leiden: Brill.

Zhou, Tianyang. 2020. "'Chinese Top, British Bottom': Becoming a Gay Male Internet Celebrity in China." In *Queer Intercultural Communication: The Intersectional Politics of Belonging in and across Differences*, edited by Shinsuke Eguchi and Bernadette Marie Calafell, 79–95. Lanham, MD: Rowman & Littlefield.

Zhou, Tianyang. 2021. "Communicating 'Race' in A Digitized Gay China." In *Queer Sites in Global Contexts: Technologies, Spaces, and Otherness*, edited by Regner Ramos and Sharif Mowlabocus, 162–78. New York: Routledge.

Zhou, Yuxing. 2014. "Chinese Queer Images on Screen: A Case Study of Cui Zi'en's Films." *Asian Studies Review* 38, no. 1: 124–40. https://doi.org/10.1080/10357823.2013.865703.

Zhou, Zhiqiu Benson. 2020. "(Un)Naturality and Chinese Queer Masculinities on *Ailaibulai*." *Feminist Media Studies* 20, no. 4: 565–81. https://doi.org/10.1080/14680777.2020.1754634.

Zhu, Ping, and Hui Faye Xiao. 2021. "Feminisms with Chinese Characteristics: An Introduction." In *Feminism with Chinese Characteristics*, edited by Ping Zhu and Hui Faye Xiao, 1–34. Syracuse, New York: Syracuse University Press.

Zhu, Ying. 2008. *Tamelevision in Post-Reform China: Serial Dramas, Confucian Leadership, and the Global Television Market*. London: Routledge.

Zhu, Ying. 2012. *Two Billion Eyes: The Story of China Central Television*. New York: The New Press.

Zhu, Ying, and Chris Berry. 2009. "Introduction." In *TV China*, edited by Ying Zhu and Chris Berry, 1–11. Bloomington: Indiana University Press.

Zhu, Ying, Michael Keane, and Ruoyun Bai, eds. 2008. *TV Drama in China*. Hong Kong: Hong Kong University Press.

Contributors

Aobo DONG is a doctoral candidate in the Department of Women's, Gender, and Sexuality Studies (WGSS) and a teaching associate at Emory University, USA. His research interests include queer kinship, queer of color critique, law and religion, and Asian diasporic studies. Focused on North American and Indonesia, his dissertation seeks to theorize diasporic Chineseness as a simultaneously hegemonic and perverse in relation to queerness in an age of heightened Sinophobia and queerphobia. His book chapter, "Till Death Do Us Kin," is forthcoming in 2022 in *Queer Kinship: Race, Sex, Belonging, Form* published by Duke University Press.

Jia GUO is a PhD candidate in the Department of Gender and Cultural Studies, University of Sydney, Australia. Her research interests include feminist media studies, social media, and transnational popular culture. The topic of her PhD thesis is "Contextualizing Postfeminism in China: Cosmopolitan Young Women, Aesthetic Labor and Social Media."

Wangtaolue GUO is a translator and PhD candidate in transnational and comparative literatures at the University of Alberta, Canada. His research interests include queer translation, sexuality and translation, and translingual writing. His academic work has appeared in *TranscUlturAl*, *New Voices in Translation Studies*, and *The Routledge Handbook of Translation, Feminism and Gender*.

Linshan JIANG is a postdoctoral associate in the Department of Asian and Middle Eastern Studies at Duke University, USA. She received her PhD in East Asian languages and cultural studies from the University of California, Santa Barbara, USA, where she also obtained a PhD emphasis in translation studies. Her research interests are modern and contemporary literature, film, and popular culture in mainland China, Taiwan, and Japan, trauma and memory studies, gender and sexuality studies, queer studies, as well as comparative literature and translation studies. Her primary research project focuses on female writers' war experience and memories of the Asia-Pacific War, entitled "Women Writing War Memories: Hayashi Fumiko, Nieh Hualing, and Zhang Ling." Her second research project explores how queerness is performed in the Sinophone queer cultural productions. She has published articles about gender studies and queer studies in literature and culture as well as translations of scholarly and popular works in Chinese and English.

Shaojun KONG is a PhD candidate in the Department of Gender and Cultural Studies, University of Sydney, Australia. Her research interests include gender and mobility, feminist geography, and Chinese studies. The topic of her PhD thesis is "Chinese Women on the Move: Generation Yer's Negotiation of Freedom, Pleasure and Tradition in Mobility."

Jun LEI is an associate professor of Chinese at Texas A&M University, USA. Her research interests include gender studies, history of sexuality, and contemporary Chinese literature and media. She co-authored *First Step: An Elementary Reader for Modern Chinese* (Princeton University Press, 2014). She has published articles in *Modern Chinese Literature and Culture*, *Modern China*, and *Contention of Literature and Arts* among others, as well as book chapters. Her monograph *Mastery of Words and Swords: Negotiating Intellectual Masculinities in Modern China, 1890s–1930s* was recently published by Hong Kong University Press (2022).

PANG Ka Wei is a lecturer in cultural studies at the Department of Cultural and Religious Studies, The Chinese University of Hong Kong, HKSAR, China. Her research interests are gender and sexualities, life stories, and health humanities. Her recent publications include "The Making of Chinese Medicine in Hong Kong" (2018), published in *Social Transformations in Chinese Societies*, as well as book chapters on breast cancer metaphors in Hong Kong pink ribbon campaigns (2020), and the oral history of a female Chinese worker at the Regional Seminary for South China (2021).

Jennifer QUIST is a PhD candidate in transnational and comparative literatures at the University of Alberta, Canada. She is the author of three novels, one of which was longlisted for the International Dublin Literary Award. Her critical work has been published in *New Left Review*, and in other academic and journalistic venues. Along with popular culture, she specializes in translation and creative writing studies.

Alvin K. WONG is an assistant professor in comparative literature and the director of the Center for the Study of Globalization and Cultures at the University of Hong Kong, HKSAR, China. His research and teaching interests include Hong Kong culture, Chinese cultural studies, Sinophone studies, transnational feminism, and queer theory. Wong is writing a book titled *Queer Hong Kong as Method*. He has published in journals such as *Journal of Lesbian Studies*,

Gender, Place & Culture, Culture, Theory, and Critique, Concentric, Cultural Dynamics, Continuum, and *Interventions* and in edited volumes such as *Transgender China* (Palgrave, 2012), *Queer Sinophone Cultures* (Routledge, 2014), *Filming the Everyday: Independent Documentaries in Twenty-First-Century China* (Rowan & Littlefield, 2016), and *Fredric Jameson and Film Theory* (Rutgers University Press, 2022). He also coedited the volume *Keywords in Queer Sinophone Studies* (Routledge, 2020). Wong is an associate editor of *Journal of Intercultural Studies* and coeditor of the HKU Press book series "Entanglements." He is currently the vice chair of the Society of Sinophone Studies.

Jamie J. ZHAO is currently an assistant professor in media and cultural studies in the School of Creative Media at City University of Hong Kong. She holds a PhD in gender studies from the Chinese University of Hong Kong, HKSAR, China, and obtained another PhD in film and TV studies from the University of Warwick, UK. Her research explores East Asian media and public discourses on female gender and sexuality in a globalist age. She coedited the anthologies *Boys' Love, Cosplay, and Androgynous Idols: Queer Fan Cultures in Mainland China, Hong Kong, and Taiwan* (Hong Kong University Press, 2017), *Contemporary Queer Chinese Art* (Bloomsbury, 2023), and the *Routledge Handbook of Chinese Gender and Sexuality* (Routledge, 2023). She is also the coeditor of the "Queering China" book series published by Bloomsbury and the "Transdisciplinary Souths" book series published by Routledge. In addition, she serves on the editorial board of *Communication, Culture & Critique* and the *International Journal of East Asian Studies*, as well as Bloomsbury's "Asian Celebrity and Fandom Studies" book series.

Oscar Tianyang ZHOU is a lecturer in media at the School of Arts at the University of Kent, UK. His research uses the lenses of cultural studies, feminist, and queer theory to investigate how LGBTQ communities engage with media technologies, texts, and practices in their everyday life. His work has been published in journals such as *Communication, Culture, & Critique, Sexualities, Feminist Media Studies,* and *China Media Research,* as well as in edited volumes such as *Queer Sites in Global Contexts* (Routledge, 2021), *Queer Intercultural Communication* (Rowman & Littlefield, 2020), *Exploring Erotic Encounters* (Brill, 2019), and *Chinese Social Media* (Routledge, 2018). He is the president of UK-China Media and Cultural Studies Association (UCMeCSA).

Index

Note: Page numbers in italics refer to figures.

Acker, Amy, 54
act of talking on TV, 46
Addicted (web series): absence of sexual essentialism, 98–99; ban of, 87–88, 89, 101, 102, 103–4; censorship of, 15–16, 20, 87–88, 100, 101, 102, 103–4, 125; characters of, 90, 93; events dedicated to, 102; filial piety and grief in, 94, 95, 97, 99; gay melancholia in, 95, 96; genre of, 90, 91–92; homoerotic desires in, 20, 92, 93–94, 96, 97–98; impact on viewers, 100–101, 103, 104; online forums on, 100–101; online video-streaming, 15, 101, 102; plot of, 90–91; political domain of, 101; popularity of, 102, 113; precariousness trope, 97; production of, 90; public melancholia about, 101–3; queer utopianism in, 88–89, 99–100, 102, 103, 125; themes of, 89–90
Advanced Bravely (BL drama), 113
aging women: cultural stereotypes about, 62–63; empowerment of, 52, 54
Airs of the States, 121
Amuro, Namie, 47
"androgynous" beauty, 31, 44
"androgynous" images, 11, 17, 18, 29, 33, 35, 37–38, 39, 45, 73
"androgynous" performers, 53, 69
"androgynous" voices, 22, 145, 147
"androgyny," 17, 33, 35–36, 147, 149
Animation, Comics, and Games (ACG) culture, 57, 105, 108, 109, 125, 157–58

anti-fans, 44, 47–48
AO3 (Archive of Our Own) website, 107, 112
Appadurai, Arjun, 126
Approaching Homosexuality (talk show), 13
Arabic number 1: in Chinese gay subculture, meaning of, 81, 82

Baidu Forums (social media platform), 89
Baihe (百合), 57
Because of You (TV series), 21, 126, 137, 140–41, 142
Beijing Forum on Literature and Art, 112
Benjamin, Walter, 68
Bie Girls (Chinese we-media channel), 56
"big sister" personas: fan culture and, 52, 54, 55; as ideal feminist image, 56, 59, 60, 62, 66; manufacturing of, 19, 56, 62
Bilibili, 75, 119, 158, 181
bishōnen (beautiful young boy), 124, 145, 148
Bishonen (film), 132
Blackpink (South Korean girl group), 45, 181
BL-adapted dramas: audience of, 105, 111; authorial reputation, 114–15; broadcasting of, 58; censorship of, 125–26; in Chinese-speaking societies, 21; comparison to BL fiction, 106, 122; C-pop idols in, 109; dissemination of, 115; fans of, 109–10, 113–14; genre of, 106, 122–23; homosociality in, 58; ideological expressions of, 107; lack of physical intimacies in, 113–14;

masqueraded bromance, 115–18; popularity of, 17, 114; rearticulation of "deviant" desires, 114; regulatory efforts, 112–13; studies of, 4, 8, 20, 106; web series, 105
Blanchett, Cate, 54
BL (boys' love) fiction: acceptable themes, 115; censorship of, 112; dissemination of, 125; film adaptations of, 105; outside of China, 112; production of, 21
BL TV, 3, 17, 25, 127, 131, 193; in Thailand, 4, 22
Book of Songs, The, 121
Boss & Me (TV series), 141
bromance, 20, 91, 106n1
bullet subtitles, 158
"butchness": adult lesbian identity of, 34
Butler, Judith, 20, 72, 88, 95, 95n7, 159; *The Psychic Life of Power*, 93
Butterfly (film), 132

Cai Xukun, 44, 45–46, 47, 48
campness, 169
camp practices, 119, 132, 164, 171, 174
Carol (film), 54
censorship: of BL genre, 125–26; in cyberspace, 14, 14n1; of homoerotic works, 177; of homosexual content, 7, 10, 15, 58, 82; of media, 1, 19, 23, 53; official policies, 14–15, 71, 73, 87–88, 131; overcoming of, 181; social reality of, 137. *See also* self-censorship
Central Cyberspace Affairs Commission, 14n1
CFanGroup, 180
Chai Jidan, 90, 102, 113
Chen, Joe Chiao-en, 141
Chen Chia-hwa (a.k.a. Ella), 44–45
Cheng, Joe, 141
China, People Republic of (PRC): beauty cultures, 31; demographic policy, 30–31; gender and sexuality in, 10–11, 50; globalization and, 36; heteronormative ideology, 1, 13, 16, 21, 126; hypermasculine sexuality, 174; market reforms, 70; masculinity crisis, 69, 149; media regulations, 89, 104; nationhood and manhood in, 71; performing arts in, 10; policies on homosexuality, 1, 12–13, 89; political-ideological manipulations, 23, 31; popular culture, 170–71, 176; regulatory bodies, 111–12; sexual minorities in, 37, 89; social media platforms, 43–44
China Central TV (CCTV), 11, 122
China-centrism, 4, 7, 179
Chinese Classification of Mental Disorders, 12
Chinese Dream, 31, 40, 113
Chinese Entertainment TV (CETV), 163
Chinese heterosexual symbolic, 99, 104
Chinese-language media studies, 7–8, 175–76
Chinese moms: affection to their idol, 190, 191, 193–94; vs. elder-sis fans, 183–84; homoerotic fantasy of, 192–93, 194; identification of, 182, 188–89, 193; imaginary kinship of, 191
Chineseness, 3–4, 7, 9–10, 23, 24, 179
Chinese TV: commercialization of, 11; entertainment programs, 11–12; gendered aspects of, 6; as global phenomenon, 1; government control of, 11, 149–50; homoerotic content production, 10, 16–17; studies of, 1, 6; vocal queerness on, 150–56; younger generations and, 150
Chow, Duncan, 138
Christian pastoral care: emergence of sexualities and, 94n5
Chuquan (出圈), 105, 110
cinematic queerness, 128–29
clickbaiting, 108
compulsory filial piety, 20, 94, 95, 97, 99, 104
Confucianism, 26, 94, 120
Counterattack (BL drama), 113
C-pop idols, 108–9, 110–11
CPs (couplings), 108, 110–11, 117, 118, 119–20, 182, 187
Crystal Boys (TV drama), 99
cultivation reality shows, 41, 43, 44, 48, 52, 52n1, 55, 59
cultivation world, 121
Cultural Revolution, 11, 35, 36

cyberspace: censorship of, 14–15; fandom wars in, 110; mom fandom in, 195; regulations on, 112
Cyberspace Administration of China (CAC), 112

danmei (耽美), 2, 105, 125, 191; TV adaptation of, 130, 137
Deceit, Desire, and the Novel (Girard), 76
de-Westernization of queer theory, 175
dildo: concept of, 71–72
dildonic assemblage, 19, 68, 69, 71–72
Dilidili.com, 181
disjunctive queer modernity, 142
disjunctive temporalities, 126
Douban, 43, 53n5, 54, 57, 80, 118
duality, 77

East Palace, West Palace (film), 94
elder-sis fans, 194; vs. mom fans, 183–85, 184n6
Ella (Chen Chia-hwa), 44–45
Equal Opportunities Commission (EOC), 132
Eternal Summer (film), 125
Euro-American-centric celebrity-fan economy, 25
Euro-American-centric same-sex erotism, 34

Falling (web fiction), 107
falsetto, 151, 153
Fan, Edison, 161, 174
fan circles, 14n1, 109–10, 111, 115, 119
fans: classification of, 183, 183n5; imaginary kinship between idols and, 178; as moms, 183–85
Fated to Love You (TV series), 141
female masculinity, 18, 34–35, 36, 37–38, 43, 54, 59–60. *See also* male masculinity
female-oriented cultural products, 120
female-oriented readers, 114
female same-sex, 34, 65
femininity, 9, 30, 34, 38, 43, 45, 54, 60, 65, 75, 80, 147
feminism in China, 10–11, 31, 32–33
filial piety, 94, 95, 97, 99
First Class of the New Semester (TV special), 148

"flower boys," 67, 124
flower-like men, 17
Fonda, Jane, 164
For Love, We Can (film), 21; characters of, 133–34; HIV theme, 126, 134; plot of, 133–34; portrayal of queer desire, 126, 134; production of, 133
Formula 17 (TV series), 21, 125; characters of, 137–39; cosmopolitanism of, 139–40, 142; plot of, 137–39; postliberal temporality in, 126, 138–39, 140, 141; queer liberalism of, 137
Foucault, Michel, 72, 94n5
fujoshi, 180, 192, 193

gay melancholia, 95, 96
gay men: cultural representation of, 22, 161–62, 166–67, 175; empowerment of, 167; masculinity, 173
gay sissiness humor, 168–69
gender melancholia, 20, 88, 95n7
girlfriend fans, 183, 194
girl pop: rise of, 30
global disjuncture theory, 126
globalization, 3, 36, 112, 130, 142, 162; of Chinese media and TV, 2, 10, 30, 49, 70, 150; sexual, 33, 134
glocalization, 21, 30, 33, 34
Go Princess Go (web series), 17
Grandmaster of Demonic Cultivation (BL fiction), 105, 115, 116
grief, 94, 95, 97, 99
Guardian (BL-adapted drama), 114

Han Hong, 34
Happy Together (film), 128, 132
He Jiong, 157
heterosexuality: filial piety and, 94; grief and, 95; vs. homosexuality, 93–94, 98–99
historical dramas, 16–17
homosexuality: Chinese term for, 11; government's policies on, 1, 12–13, 89; vs. heterosexuality, 93–94, 98–99; in premodern China, 92; Western conception of, 8
homosociality, 1, 24; attitude toward female, 58; in construction of Chinese

masculinity, 92–93; sexual desire and, 76; socialization as goal of, 96
Hong Kong: BL culture in, 8, 21; China's sovereignty over, 12; gender democracy, 131–32; queer activism in, 131, 132, 135, 137; vs. Taiwan, 136–37
Hong Kong Lesbian and Gay Film Festival, 133
Hsu, Dee (a.k.a. "Little S"): career of, 165; as talk show host, 163, 164, 166, 172
Hsu, Kelvin, 165–66
Hui Brothers comedy shows, 132
Humpday (film), 91
Hunan TV, 38, 67
hyper-femininity, 43
hyper-masculinity, 171

"ideal man" (同志天菜): stereotypes of, 172–74
idol-fan economy, 109
idol group cultivation reality shows, 52n1. See also girl group cultivation reality shows
I Fiori Delle Sorelle (reality show), 165
If You Are the One (film), 167
If You Are the One (TV show), 17
I Love You, Man (film), 91
"I'm Not Yours" (song), 47
International Women's Day, 49, 50
iQIYI (online video platform), 113, 114, 161n2, 163, 165
iron-T, 38, 40, 44, 47, 59, 59n14, 60, 60n18
ISC (Internet Society of China), 112
I Told Sunset About You (TV series), 17, 180
It Started with a Kiss (TV series), 141

jianghu: meanings of, 127, 130
Jinjiang Literature City, 112, 114–15
Jin Xing, 13, 40–41
jiquan (姬圈; lesbian circle) fandom: approach to female gender and sexuality, 55, 59–62; discussion themes, 57–58; formation and growth of, 19, 53–54, 57–60; lesbian culture and, 55, 57; participants of, 57; popular feminist rhetoric, 65–66; support of LGBTQ rights, 61–62

Jiquan Gossip Group, 54; discussion themes, 61–62, *62*, 64–65; members of, 57–58
Jony J, 44, 45
Juan, Ethan, 141

Kangsi Coming (talk show), 22, 153; "A Survey of Male Celebrities' Popularity among Gay Men" episode, 171–72; closure of, 165; criticism of, 167, 168–69; hosts of, 163–64; humor, 166, 167, 169; image of "ideal man," 172–75; "*Kangsi* Tender Men Dance Contest" episode, 165–66; popularity of, 162, 163–65; representation of gay men, 162, 164, 165, 166–67, 175; themes of, 165
ke'ai (可爱; cuteness), 185–86
kinship: in Sinophone culture, 185
K-pop, 186
Kuo, Ryan, 165–66, 167, 169

LadyBees (girl group cultivation show), 41–42
LadyBees girl band, 43
Lan Wangji, 110
Leaves, The (TV series), 192
"leftover women," 25, 30
lesbianism, 33–34, 35, 37, 53, 55, 57, 61
lesbians, 34, 40, 55, 57, 59. See also iron-T
Les Sky Group, 57, 58
Let's Exercise, Boys (sports reality show), 19; bodily images, 74, 78; censorship system and, 71, 76, 82; contestants of, 74, 78, 79–80; criticism of, 68; as a dildonic assemblage, 71–73; fan-edited videos of, 75–76; female audience, 75, 76; format of, 67; launch of, 67, 74; narrative of masculinities, 69, 75, 77, 82, 83; opening monologue, 74–75; promotion of, 67–68, 78–79; queer readings of, 82, 83; reception of, 68; screenshot of the logo, *83*; social media and, 78–79; spornosexuality of, 68, 77; success of, 83; training grounds, 76–77
Let's Fight Ghost (TV series), 192
letter "S": in Chinese gay subculture, meaning of, 81, 82

Index 237

LGBTQ issues: media censorship of, 12–13; neoliberal ideologies and, 56; in public discourse, 13–14, 15–16, 162; "Three No's" rule, 12–13
Li Sidanni, 60–61
little fresh meat (小鲜肉), 44, 67, 70, 71, 73, 74, 77, 83
Little Tigers band, 42
Liu Yuxin, 18, 29, 31–32, 33, 59
Li Yuchun (a.k.a. Chris Lee): acting career of, 29, 41, 42, 45–49; anti-fans of, 44; backstage interview, 48; queer persona of, 31; tomboyism of, 41, 42–43, 46, 47, 50; winner of the *Up Young!* competition, 45
Li Yugang, 151, 155
Lofter.com (Chinese blogging site), 107
Love By Chance (TV series), 180, 181, 191
Love of Siam (film), 179
Lucifer's Club, 112
Lu Keran, 47, 60

"macho" men: in popular culture, 161, 162, 173, 174–75
male-male CPs (couplings), 108–9
male masculinity: body and, 172; Chinese ideals of, 68–71; concept of man vs. concept of, 147; crisis of, 69, 149; homosociality in construction of, 92–93; media representation of, 70, 73; as social construct, 147; studies of, 70, 147; types of, 83–84; *wen/wu* dyad of, 92–93. *See also* female masculinity
Mango TV, 16n3
Manoban, Lalisa (a.k.a. Lisa), 44, 45, 47, 181
Masked Singer (TV show), 155
masqueraded bromance, 115–18
May Fourth New Culture period, 11
media queerness, 73, 74
MingEr family, 177, 187–88, 190
Mingming. *See* Saintsup
"minoritizing" approach, 8–9, 17
Mix Xiao, 161, 169–70
mom fans: conditional love of, 194–95; vs. elder-sis fans, 184–85; motherly feelings to their idol, 186–87, 188; phenomenon of, 22, 178, 179. *See also* Chinese moms

Moxiangtongxiu (Chinese writer), 115
multimedia broadcasting, 12
My Hero (talent show), 108
My Mischievous Fiancée (TV series), 192

National Radio and Television Administration (NRTA), 15n2, 71, 112, 131
Na Ying, 147, 154
neo-Confucianism, 12
neutrosexuality, 17, 54
New Age of Girl Power, A (film), 43
niang (娘) and *niangpao* (娘炮): concepts of, 147–48
nonheterosexuality, 13, 45, 47, 52n4, 54
nonnormative gender, 42, 45, 145
nonnormative sexualities: representations of, 175–76

Ossan's Love (TV drama), 21; characters of, 135–36; HIV theme, 126; plot of, 135–36; queer presentism in, 126, 134, 135–37, 142; scene of kissing in a queer presentist mode, *136*; transnational success, 135

Palace of Desire (TV drama), 16–17
pan-rotten culture: on Chinese television, 108; consumerism and, 111; cultivation of audience for, 107–11; definition of, 108; emergence of, 114
People's Daily (newspaper), 16, 49, 73
Person of Interest (TV series), 54
phallicity, 71
phallic potency, 78
physique magazines, 72–73
popular culture: gender presentation in, 56, 59, 63, 65, 159; ideal masculinity in, 148; media and, 70–71
popular feminism, 19, 41, 45, 50, 54, 55–56, 66
Portland Street Blues (film), 132
postliberal temporality, 126, 127, 137, 138–39, 140, 141
Priest (Chinese writer), 114
Produce 101 (music-group manufacturing show), 29, 30, 30n1

Qiao Wenyi, 75, 76

"Qinglang Rectification on the 'Fan-Circle' Chaos," 14n1
Qiu Haiyang, 74
Qiu Yiwei, 74, 78; Weibo videos, *79*
queer: Chinese-language terms for, 7; commodification of, 154, 155; definitions of, 4–5, 8, 23; in entertainment industry, 123; identity formation, 23–24, 38, 94; in mainland China, 103–4, 146; media representations of, 26, 32, 175; minoritizing and universalizing approaches to, 8–9; in premodern culture, 10; Sinophone visuality of, 124; theory of, 5–6
queerbaiting, 108
Queer Eye for the Straight Guy (reality show), 170
queer fandom, 2, 4, 8, 19, 22, 53n5, 54, 55, 57, 59
queer gossip, 25, 54–55
queer/ing: notion of, 4–5, 18, 21, 23
queerness, 3–4, 5–6, 7, 146; Chineseness and, 7; on Chinese TV, 14, 16, 17; cinematic, 128–29; media, 73, 74; unhistorical, 2, 21, 126, 127, 128, 131, 141; vocal, 9, 145, 147, 150–56, 157, 159; Western conception of, 8
queer presentism, 21, 126, 127, 132, 134, 135, 136, 137, 141
queer regionalism, 134, 135
queer temporalities, 126–27, 137, 138–39, 140, 141–42
queer TV China: analytical framework of, 3, 5, 8, 9, 17, 23–24; evolution of, 1–2, 11, 17–18; future of, 23–26; genres, 53, 125; globalization of, 2; political-economic system and, 10; regulatory policies, 2, 14–16; scholarship on, 2–3, 4, 24–26
queer TV studies, 5, 6–7, 9, 19–20
queer utopia, 20, 88
queer utopianism, 88, 90, 103–4
queer women: visibility of, 25

Rap of China, The (rap competition), 29
reality talent shows: mentorship in, 44–45; modern trend of, 42; nonnormative expressions of, 53, 175–76; popularity of, 16, 29–30
reality TV, 9, 18, 32
rebellious humor, 169, 170
Rocket Girls (pop group), 30
Romance of the Three Kingdoms, 92
rotten culture, 108, 110, 111, 114, 117, 121n14
"rotten girls," 105
RPS (real person slash), 107

Saintsup (Suppapong Udomkaewkanjana): acting career of, 181, 183, 191–92, 195; appearance of, 185–86; celebrity ranking of, 177–78, 181; Chinese given name, 182; ethnic background of, 189–90, 191; fandom names of, 187, 189; *ke'ai* (cuteness) of, 185–87, 189, 193; language skills of, 188; live sessions of, 177, 181–82; material support of, 190; personality of, 190; relations with fans, 188, 189; social media followers, 177
Saintsup's fandom: age groups, 184; amateur translators, 190; girlfriend fans, 183; from mainland China, 189; mom fans engagement with, 22–23, 178, 179, 182–83, 186–88, 194; Sinophone base of, 180–82; span of, 178; sub-fandoms of, 187–88; survey of, 183–84, 185; transnational nature of, 191
same-sex love: Chinese-language terms for, 10
SARFT (State Administration of Radio, Film and Television), 111
Secret Life of Pets, The (animation film), 186
sects, 127, 128
Sedgwick, Eve Kosofsky, 76, 96; *Tendencies*, 5
self-censorship, 15–16, 16n3, 96, 157
sexual minorities: media representations of, 24, 161–62; social status of, 37
S.H.E. (Taiwanese girl group), 45
Shih, Shu-mei, 7, 124, 179
shipper stans, 183n5, 194
shou (受), 81
Singer (TV program), 150

"Sinophone": concept of, 124n2, 178, 179
Sinophone fans, 180–83, 187–91, 194–95
Sissies Coming (talk show), 169
sissiness, 161, 162, 167–69
sissyphobia, 13, 22, 149
Sisters Who Make Waves (*SWMW*) (reality show), 19; big sister personas in, 54, 56, 66; contestants of, 52, 52n4, 56, 63–65; display of intimate relationship, 64, 65; *jiquan* fans' reading of, 52–53, 54, 55, 61; popular feminist rhetoric of, 65–66; popularity of, 52, 61; queering stars of, 60–61
Sisters Who Make Waves Group, 54, 61, 61n24, 63
socialist androgyny, 35–36
socialist brotherhood, 77
socialist feminism, 35, 36
socialist modernization, 35
social media, 79, 117
Sodagreen band, 152, 156, 157
soft masculinity, 22, 124, 145, 148–49, 151
solo stans, 183n5, 194
SOTUS (TV series), 180
spornosexuality, 19, 68, 71, 79
Spring Festival Gala, 16
S-style Show (food talk show), 165
State Administration of Press, Publication, Radio, Film and Television (SAPPRFT), 15n2, 111–12, 113, 131
Stewart, Kristen, 58
Sunny Face, 172–73
"sunshine middle-class good gay" (阳光中产好 gay), 56
Super Voice Girls (talent TV show), 17, 29, 57, 59, 108, 127
symbolic order, 88n2

Taifu fans, 180–81, 190, 193–94
Taiwan: BL culture in, 8, 21; educational reforms, 153; entertainment industry, 146, 167; gender discrimination, 149; gym culture, 173; vs. Hong Kong, 136–37; LBTQ rights movements in, 132, 166; legalization of same-sex marriage in, 21, 126, 132, 137, 140, 157; queer cinema, 125; school violence, 152–53; status of queer in, 136, 137
Taoism, 120

teen idol drama, 140–41
television industry. *See* Chinese TV
Tencent, 105, 113, 114, 121, 154
TharnType (TV series), 180
THE9 (Chinese girl band), 29
Tianfu Taiju, 180
Tianyi (BL novelist), 125
2gether: The Series (TV series), 125, 180
tomboyism: in Chinese-language media, representation of, 50–51; circulation of term, 34–35; definition of, 32, 34; in Mainland China, 33–38; manifestation of "girl power" and, 41–42, 47–48; in pop culture, 37–38; public tolerance to, 37; on reality TV, 18, 38–43; studies of, 18–19; visual-cultural narratives of, 50
top: euphemism for sexual disposition of, 81
traffic data (流量), 109
Truth of the Prismatic Universe, The (lifestyle talk show), 165
Tsai, Jolin, 47, 157; "Womxnly" song of, 153
Tsai, Kevin: awards of, 164; blog of, 167–68; career of, 164–65; criticism of, 168; as host of reality shows, 13, 166, 172; humor of, 166, 169; on male effeminacy, 167–68
Tse, Nicholas, 42
T-style, 59–60
T-style celebrities, 59–61, 59n14, 60n18
Tudou.com, 163
2Moons (TV series), 180
227 Incident, 107–8, 110, 112

U Can U Bibi (talk show): hosts of, 165; representation of gay men, 22, 161, 162, 174, 175; sissy performances, 169–70
Uncontrolled Love (TV drama), 98
unhistorical queerness, 2, 21, 126, 127, 128, 131, 141
universalizing approaches, 9, 12, 17
Untamed, The (TV drama): cast of, 107; censorship of, 130; characters of, 110, 115, 116–17, 127–28, 130; commercial success of, 121, 122; dark desires in, 114; depiction of romantic relationships, 116–17; ending of, 121;

fight under the moon scene, *129*; final episode of, 130–31; influence of, 107; marketing of, 110; plot of, 105, 115–16, 127–29; pursuit of freedom and justice in, 120–21; real person slash (RPS), 118–21; release of, 105; resemblance of original fiction, 114–15, 116, 121; reviews of, 121–22; same-sex romance in, 2, 20, 128–30; social media comments about, 117; sublimated themes, 120–22; unhistorical queerness in, 126, 127, 130; version aired in Japan and Thailand, 121n14; world of *jianghu*, 127–28, 130, 141

Until We Meet Again (TV series), 180

Up Young! (TV show): dancing competition, 40–41; embodiment of tomboyism, 39–40; guests in, 39; launch of, 38; participants, 39; themes of, 38–39

utopian mode of critique, 88

Voice of China, The (reality singing competition), 29, 70, 154

Wang Yibo, 107, 122

Wan Qian, 55, 61, 64–65

Water Margins, The, 92

Weibo (online platform), 16n3, 44

Weibo Super Topic, 115

Wei Wuxian, 110, 115

wen/wu (文/武) dyad of masculine traits, 69–70, 92–93, 148

Western-centric perspective on masculinity, 24, 34

Why R U? (TV series), 180, 181, 192

women in China: discrimination of, 36; socialist subjectivization of, 35–36; social status of, 11

Words of Honor (BL-adapted drama), 114

Wu, Nicky, 42

Wu, Patty, 172

Wu Tsing-Fong: awards of, 157; on "Beyond the Wall" song, 157; career of, 146; education of, 148; gendered social stigma, 156; interview with, 150; participation in TV shows, 22, 150, 153; "Peter and the Wolf" song, 152; public criticism of, 151; social media followers, 156; Sodagreen band and, 152, 156–57; soft masculinity of, 151; as target of verbal abuse, 145, 153–54; vocal queerness of, 145, 147, 151, 159

X-Fire (talent show), 110n3

Xiao Zhan, 107, 122

Xi Jinping, 111, 112, 113n4

xianxia (仙侠), 2, 106, 115, 116

Xinhua.net, 73

Xuese Canyang (TV drama), 17

Xu Fei, 63

Xu Zhibin, 75, 76, 78

Yang, Tony, 137

Yang Kun, 154

Yang Tianzhen, 46

Yeh Yung-chih, 152

yin/yang (阴/阳): philosophical concepts of, 92–93, 147

Your Name Engraved Herein (film), 125

Youth With You 2 (reality show): backstage interview, 48; final episode, 48, 49; "For Every Girl" song, 48–49, 50; format of, 44, 47; pilot episode, 44; popularity of, 29, 44; rounds of rating and elimination, 45–46; stars of, 18, 34; tomboyism in, 33, 43–50, 59–60; trainees and mentors in, 44–45; "Yes! OK!" theme song, 48

YouTube, 89, 101, 102

Y-series, 179–80, 181, 192

ZaintSee CP fans, 182, 182n4, 192, 192n8, 193

Zhang, Charlie Yi, 126

Zhang, Hans, 141

Zhang Jike, 77

Zhang Xindong: personality of, 79–80; social media presence, 80–81; Weibo photos, 80, *81*

Zhao Liying, 141

Zhihu (social media platform), 89

zhongxing (中性; neutral gender or sex), 37, 41, 45, 54

Zhou Shen: career of, 146, 158; "Dalabengba" song, 158; education of, 148; gendered social stigma, 154, 156;

influence of, 158–59; interviews with, 150–51, 154; popularity of, 156; public criticism of, 151, 155–56; queerness of, 22, 145, 147, 151, 154–55, 157, 159; soft masculinity of, 151; as target of verbal abuse, 145; traumatic experiences of, 154; TV singing competitions, 147, 150, 154, 155, 158

Zhu Jingxi, 55, 61, 63–64, 63n27, 65

Zhu Yilong, 122